PREACHER

ALAMO

PREACHER
ALAMO

GARTH ENNIS
WRITER

STEVE DILLON
ARTIST

PAMELA RAMBO
COLORIST

CLEM ROBINS
LETTERER

GLENN FABRY
ORIGINAL COVERS

PREACHER created by Garth Ennis and Steve Dillon

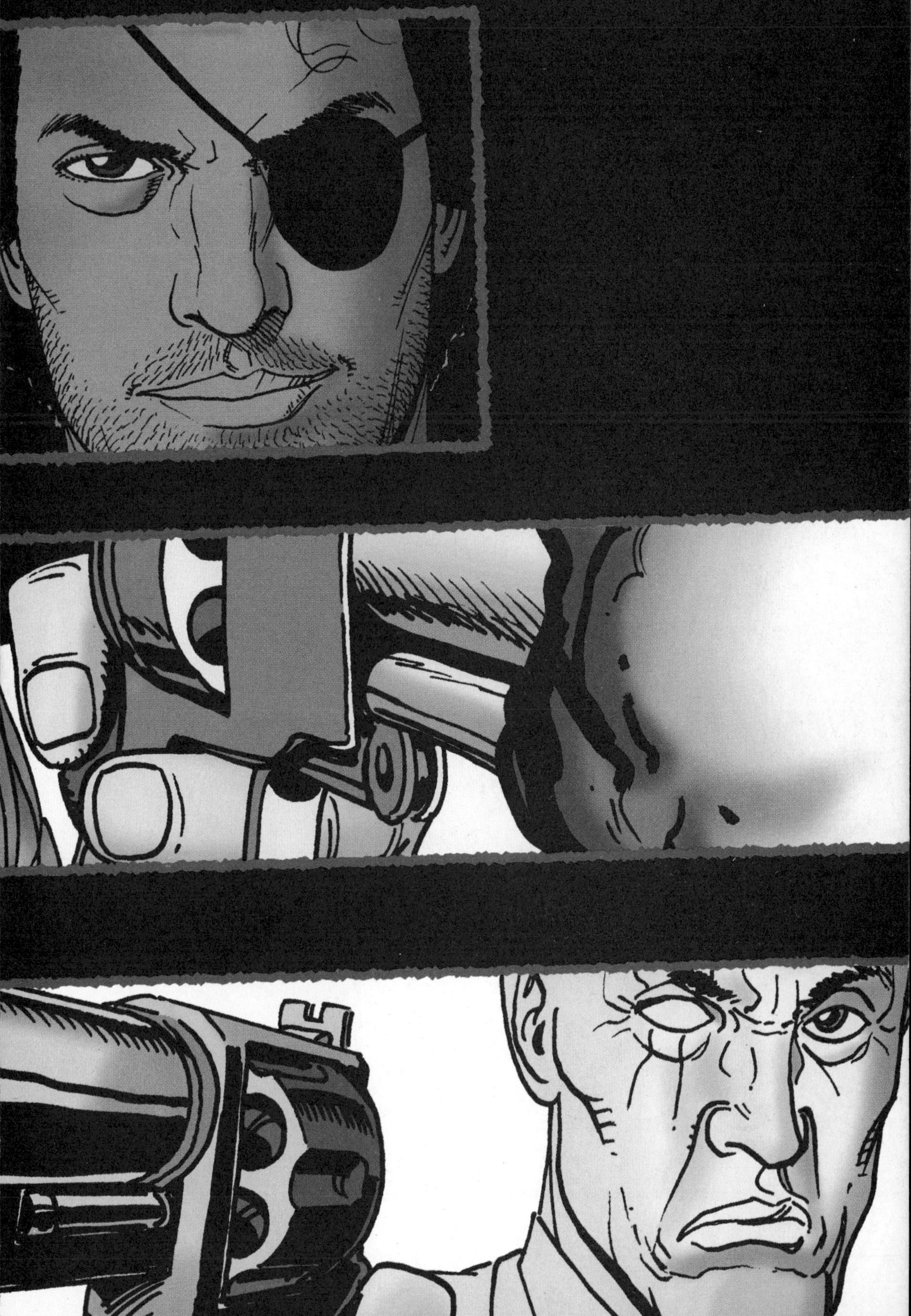

Karen Berger VP-Executive Editor Axel Alonso Editor-original series Scott Nybakken Editor-collected edition

Robbin Brosterman Art Director Paul Levitz President & Publisher

Georg Brewer VP-Design & Retail Product Development Richard Bruning Senior VP-Creative Director

Patrick Caldon Senior VP-Finance & Operations Chris Caramalis VP-Finance Terri Cunningham VP-Managing Editor

Dan Didio-VP Editorial Alison Gill VP-Manufacturing Rich Johnson VP-Book Trade Sales

Hank Kanalz VP-General Manager, WildStorm Lillian Laserson Senior VP & General Counsel

Jim Lee Editorial Director-WildStorm David McKillips VP-Advertising & Custom Publishing

John Nee VP-Business Development Gregory Noveck Senior VP-Creative Affairs

Cheryl Rubin Senior VP-Brand Management Bob Wayne VP-Sales & Marketing

REVEREND JESSE CUSTER

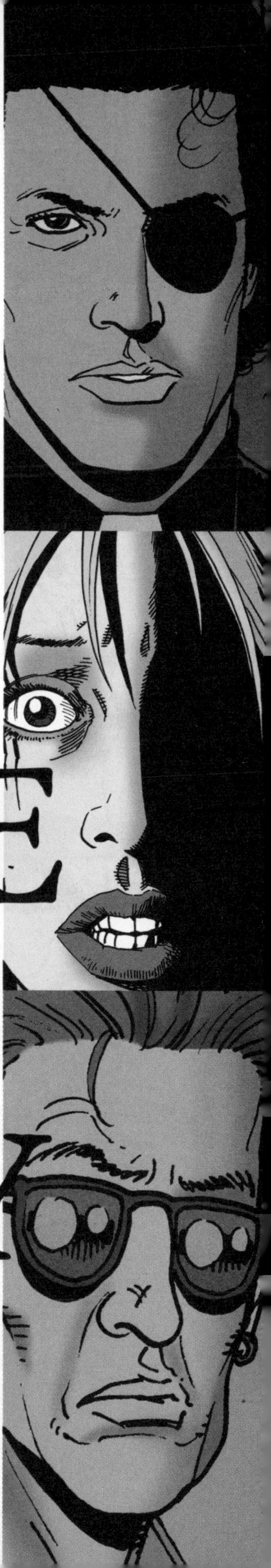

Jesse Custer isn't averse to smoking and cussing, and he might drink a little more than seems proper for a minister, but he's a decent man who tries his best to live honorably. When he was possessed by the all-powerful entity Genesis, though, his church and congregation went up in flames, and so did his patience with God's mysterious ways. Using Genesis' power to speak the Word of God — a Word that must be obeyed by all who hear it — Jesse and the love of his life, Tulip, set out with the Irish vampire Cassidy to find God and get an explanation from Him. What awaits him at the end of his search isn't certain, but one thing is: he's come too far and lost too much to be denied.

TULIP O'HARE

When she met Jesse Custer, Tulip knew that she had found what she had been looking for all her life. After he disappeared the first time, she barely survived an ill-advised stint as a paid hit woman. The second time, when she thought he was dead, she fled the pain in a sea of alcohol and pills, supplied by Jesse's vampire buddy Cassidy. Now, after hauling herself out of Cassidy's nest of vice, she's reunited with her true love and told him the truth about what happened to her. Tulip's already lost Jesse twice, and she'll go to Hell and back to make sure it doesn't happen again.

CASSIDY

God named him Beast, and he's lived up to the name. After a hundred years of hard-drinkin' vampire living, Proinsias Cassidy has burned pretty much every bridge he's ever made, including those with his best mate, Jesse Custer. After he came crawling back looking for one more chance, Jesse gave Cassidy a time and place to say his piece — the Alamo. When he's done, Jesse will say his — and chances are it will be the final word.

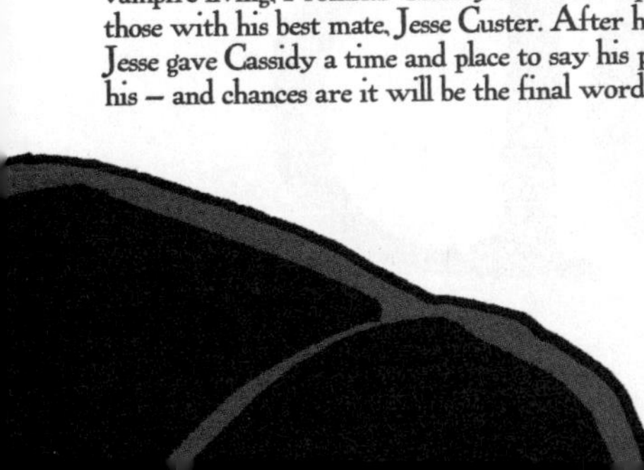

HERR STARR

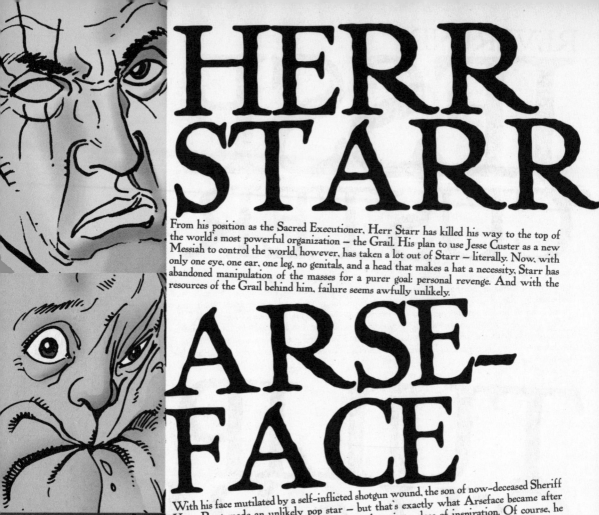

From his position as the Sacred Executioner, Herr Starr has killed his way to the top of the world's most powerful organization – the Grail. His plan to use Jesse Custer as a new Messiah to control the world, however, has taken a lot out of Starr – literally. Now, with only one eye, one ear, one leg, no genitals, and a head that makes a hat a necessity, Starr has abandoned manipulation of the masses for a purer goal: personal revenge. And with the resources of the Grail behind him, failure seems awfully unlikely.

ARSE-FACE

With his face mutilated by a self-inflicted shotgun wound, the son of now-deceased Sheriff Hugo Root made an unlikely pop star – but that's exactly what Arseface became after meeting up with Jesse, Tulip and Cassidy and getting a dose of inspiration. Of course, he eventually became prey for an opportunistic manager who bled him for all his money and hung him out to dry, but that didn't break his spirit. On the road again, Arseface may finally catch an even break from cruel, cruel Fate.

SAINT OF KILLERS

Unstoppable and unkillable, empowered by God Himself, the Saint is Death in a duster and hat, with two six-guns ready to deal out annihilation to anyone or anything that gets in his way. The Saint was a man once, but that was a long time ago, and you wouldn't have wanted to cross him even then. Now, after meeting Jesse Custer one last time, he's got one final score to settle.

GOD

The alpha and the omega.

God hasn't made it easy on the Reverend Jesse Custer.

First, He allowed an unholy union between an angel and a devil to occur, and then He allowed the fruit of that union, unformed and all-powerful, to escape from Heaven. And after the entity, called Genesis, fell to Earth and melded with the spirit of a small-town preacher – killing everyone else in the town – God just up and left.

Jesse Custer was left with the ability to speak with the Word of God – making all who hear him obey his every command – and a lot of questions. The only thing to do was to track God down to his hiding place and hold Him accountable for His sins, and once he had reunited with his a long-lost love, Tulip O'Hare, and teamed up with a vampire named Cassidy, that's just what Jesse set out to do. Along the way, however, there turned out to be a few sidetracks.

For one, it turned out there was a massive worldwide conspiracy called the Grail that was aiming to bring the supposed direct blood descendant of Jesus Christ to power and rule the world. One member of the Grail, Herr Starr, decided to use Jesse Custer and his miraculous abilities as a puppet messiah. Things turned out badly for just about everyone involved in that, and a mutilated Starr, still in command of what's left of the Grail, has turned his attention to killing Jesse at all costs.

And then, with Jesse seemingly dead after Starr's last-ditch nuclear strike in Monument Valley, Tulip fell into a drink-and-drug-fueled haze that wound up in the too-comforting arms of Cassidy. By the time she'd crawled her way out and left Cassidy cowering from the sun with a few new holes in him, Jesse — back from the dead and missing an eye — had left to get some serious thinking done in a little town named Salvation.

Becoming Salvation's sheriff and cleaning up the human garbage that had settled there — as well as discovering his long-lost mother — did Jesse a world of good, and finally convinced him to go back and find Tulip again.

With the two of them reunited, Jesse discovered the sordid details of Cassidy's long, blood-soaked existence and the people who had paid the price for knowing him, not realizing that Herr Starr was still hunting him.

And so, with the remaining forces of the Grail gathering around him, Jesse has planned a final meeting with Cassidy to settle things between them once and for all. A final meeting at the Alamo.

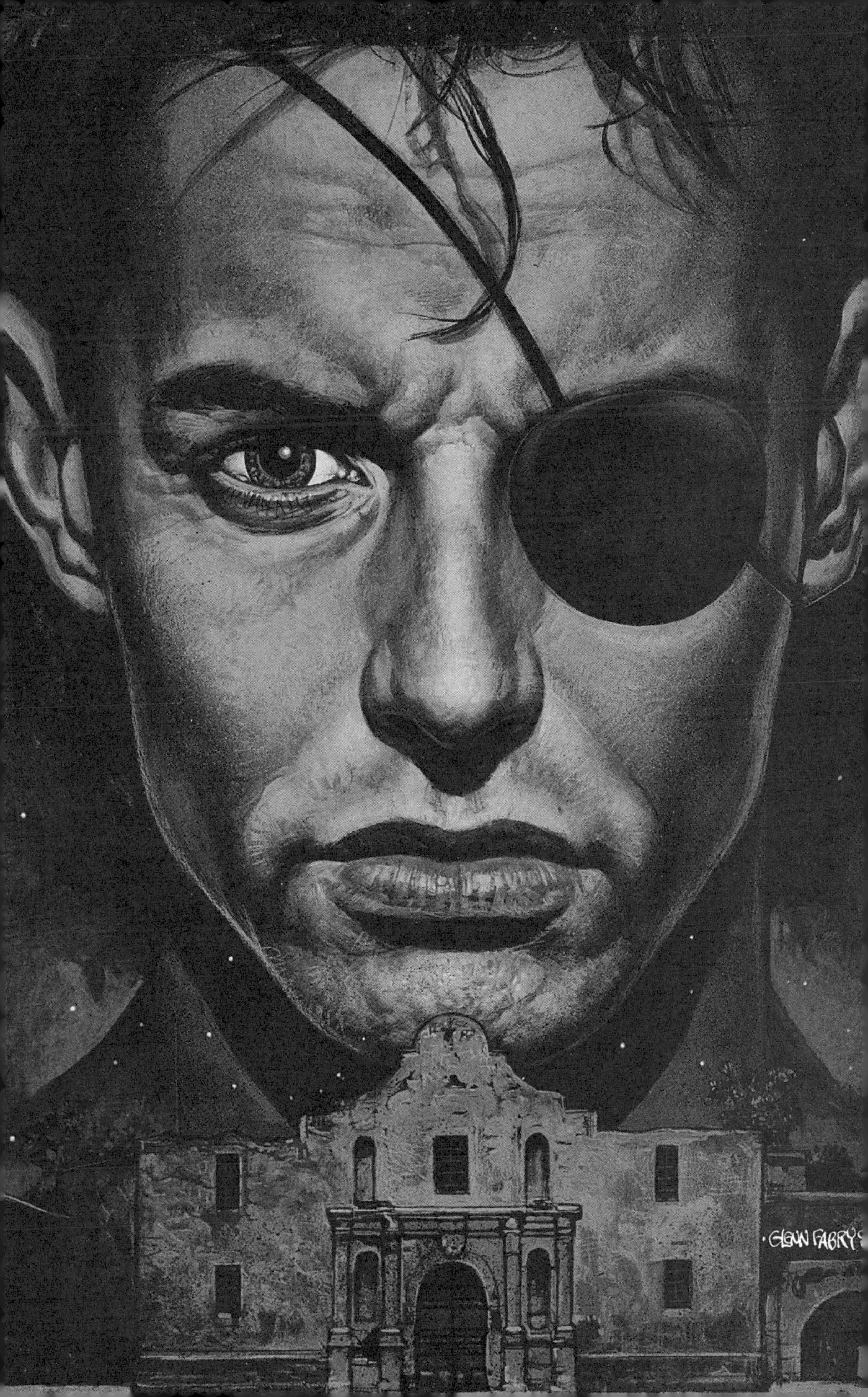
GLENN FABRY

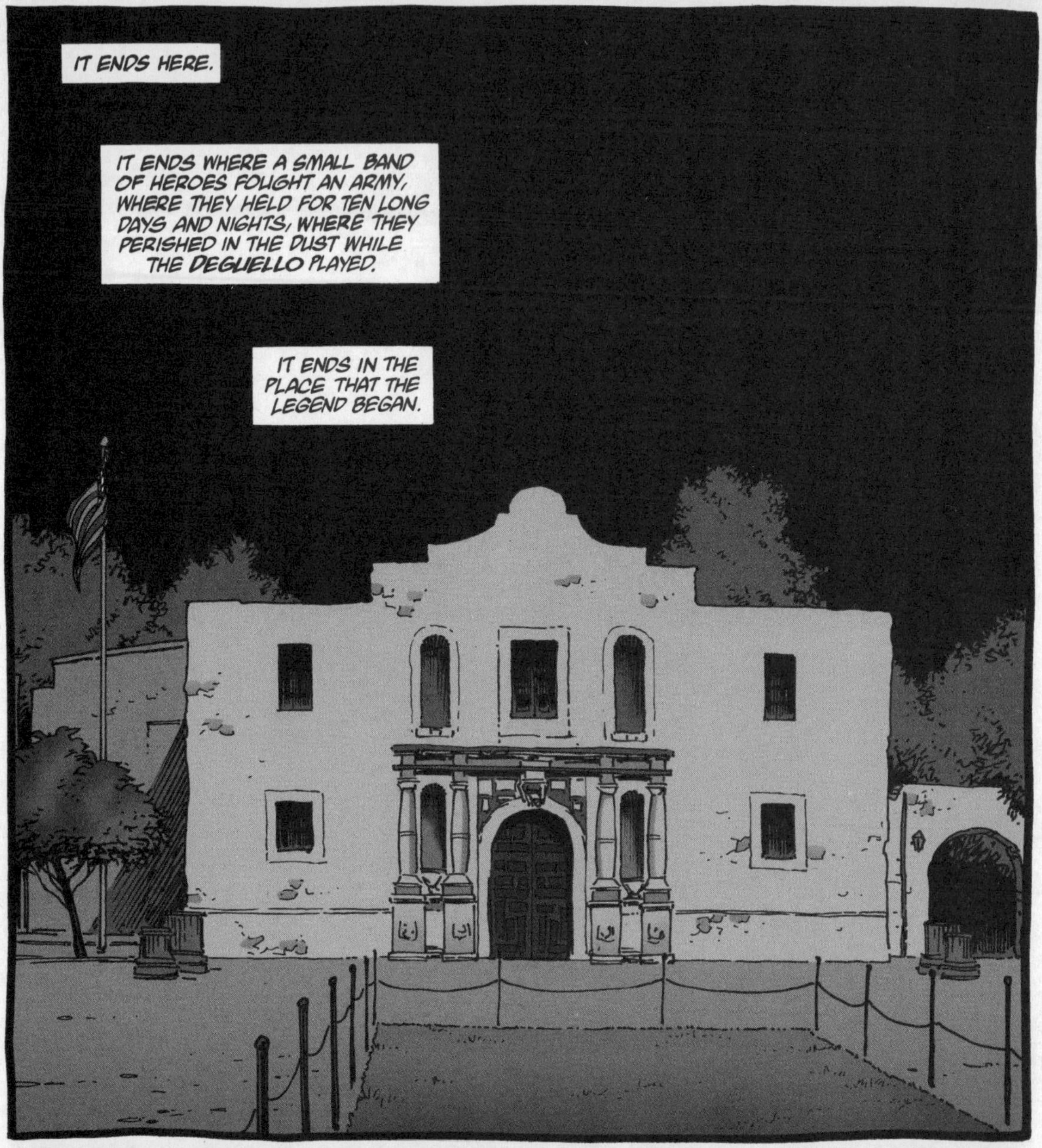
IT ENDS HERE.
IT ENDS WHERE A SMALL BAND OF HEROES FOUGHT AN ARMY, WHERE THEY HELD FOR TEN LONG DAYS AND NIGHTS, WHERE THEY PERISHED IN THE DUST WHILE THE DEGUELLO PLAYED.
IT ENDS IN THE PLACE THAT THE LEGEND BEGAN.

TEXAS, BY GOD

GARTH ENNIS - Writer STEVE DILLON - Artist

PAMELA RAMBO - Colorist CLEM ROBINS - Letterer AXEL ALONSO - Editor

PREACHER created by GARTH ENNIS and STEVE DILLON

LOOK TOO CLOSE AND THE LEGEND CRACKS; BUT THEN, THAT'S LEGENDS FOR YOU.

WAS BOWIE A SLAVER, A DRUNK, A PSYCHOTIC? DID CROCKETT BEG FOR HIS LIFE BEFORE SANTA ANNA, FOR MERCY THAT COULD NEVER COME? ARE HEROES NOTHING MORE THAN DESPERATE MEN?

NO. TO DWELL ON SUCH THINGS IS TO MISS THE POINT.

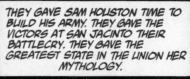

THEY GAVE SAM HOUSTON TIME TO BUILD HIS ARMY. THEY GAVE THE VICTORS AT SAN JACINTO THEIR BATTLECRY. THEY GAVE THE GREATEST STATE IN THE UNION HER MYTHOLOGY.

FOR TEXAS, IT WAS THE BEGINNING.

BUT FOR BOWIE AND CROCKETT AND TRAVIS, AND A HUNDRED AND EIGHTY MEN...

IT WAS THE END.

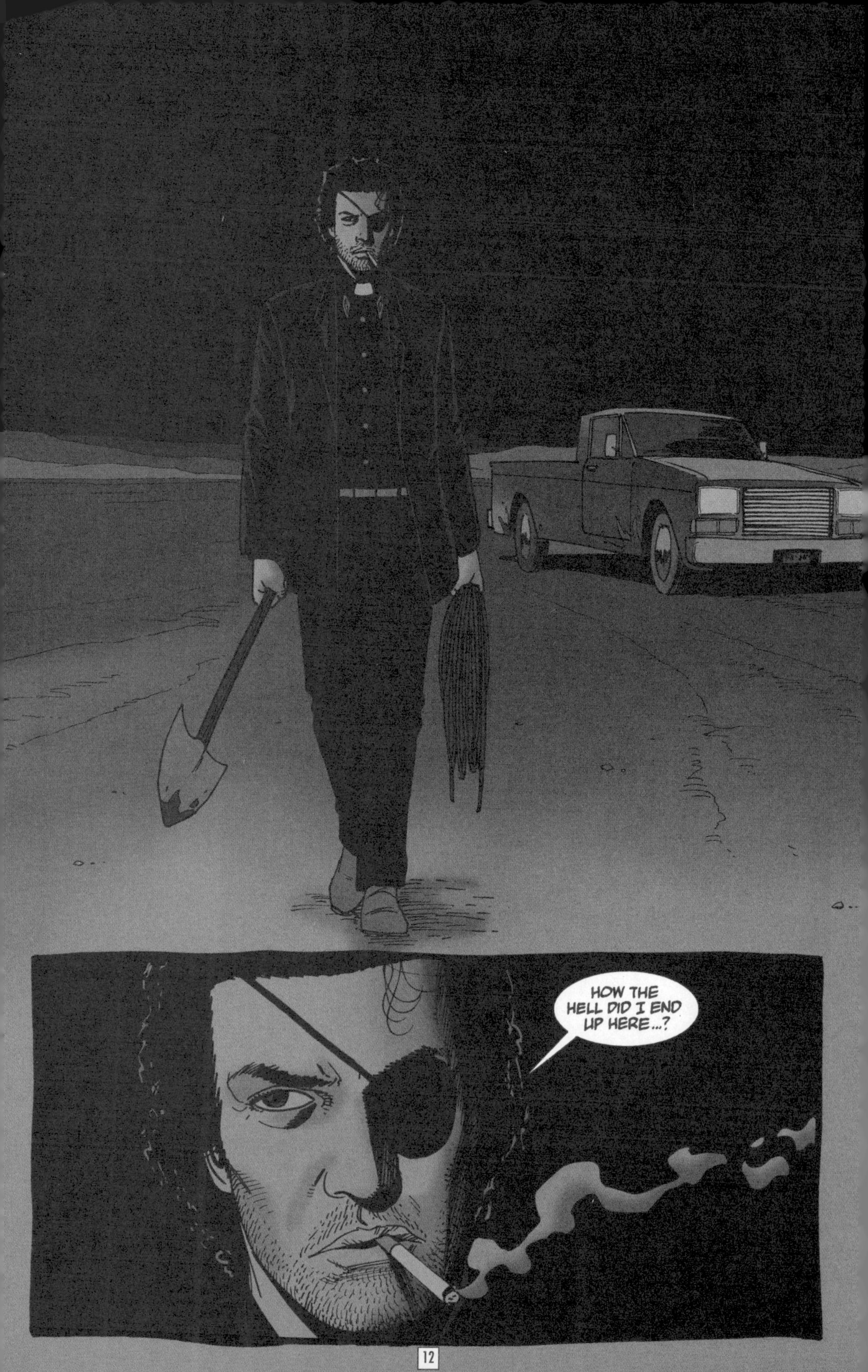
HOW THE HELL DID I END UP HERE...?

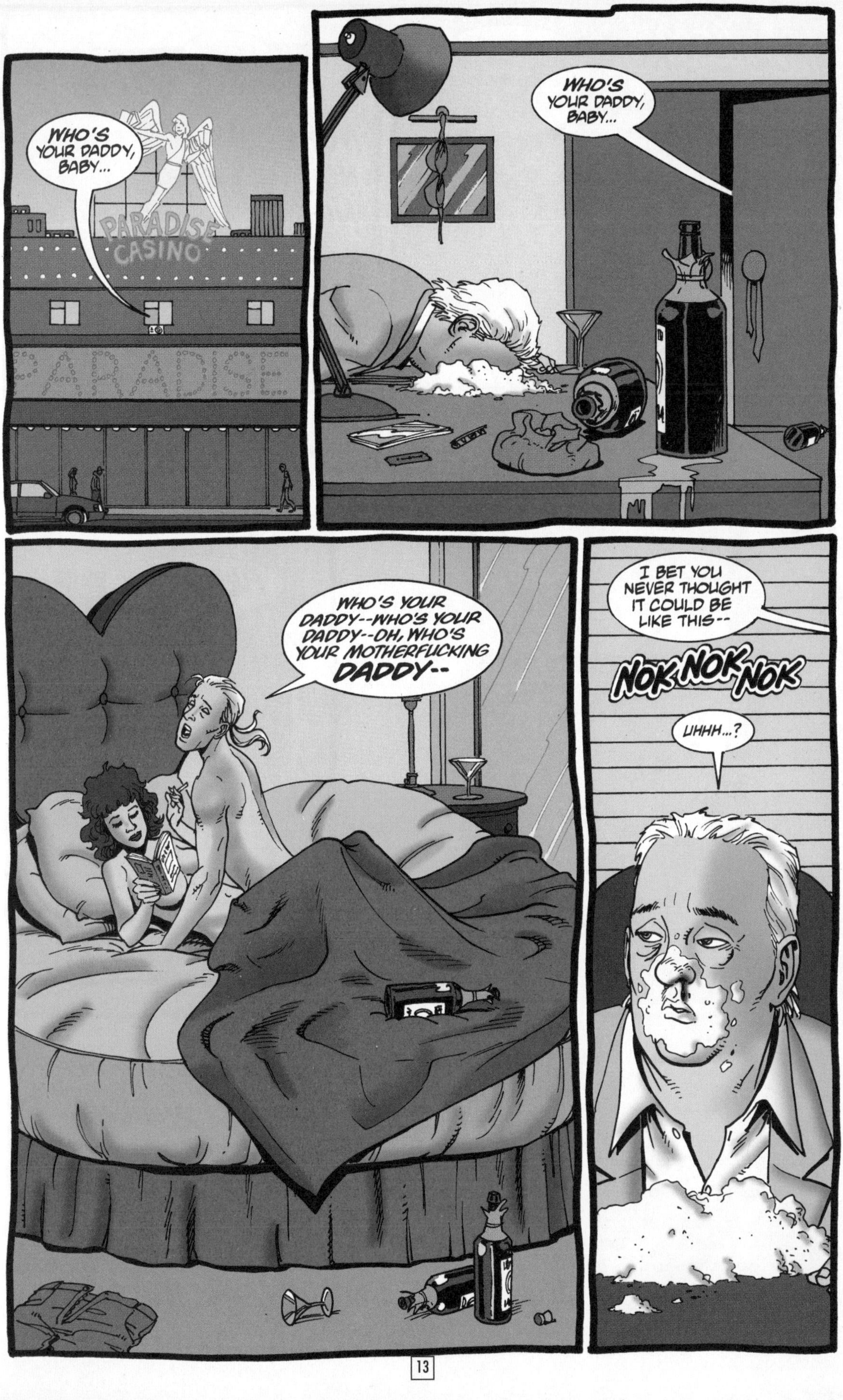
WHO'S YOUR DADDY, BABY...
PARADISE CASINO
PARADISE
WHO'S YOUR DADDY, BABY...
WHO'S YOUR DADDY--WHO'S YOUR DADDY--OH, WHO'S YOUR MOTHERFUCKING DADDY--
I BET YOU NEVER THOUGHT IT COULD BE LIKE THIS--
NOK NOK NOK
UHHH...?

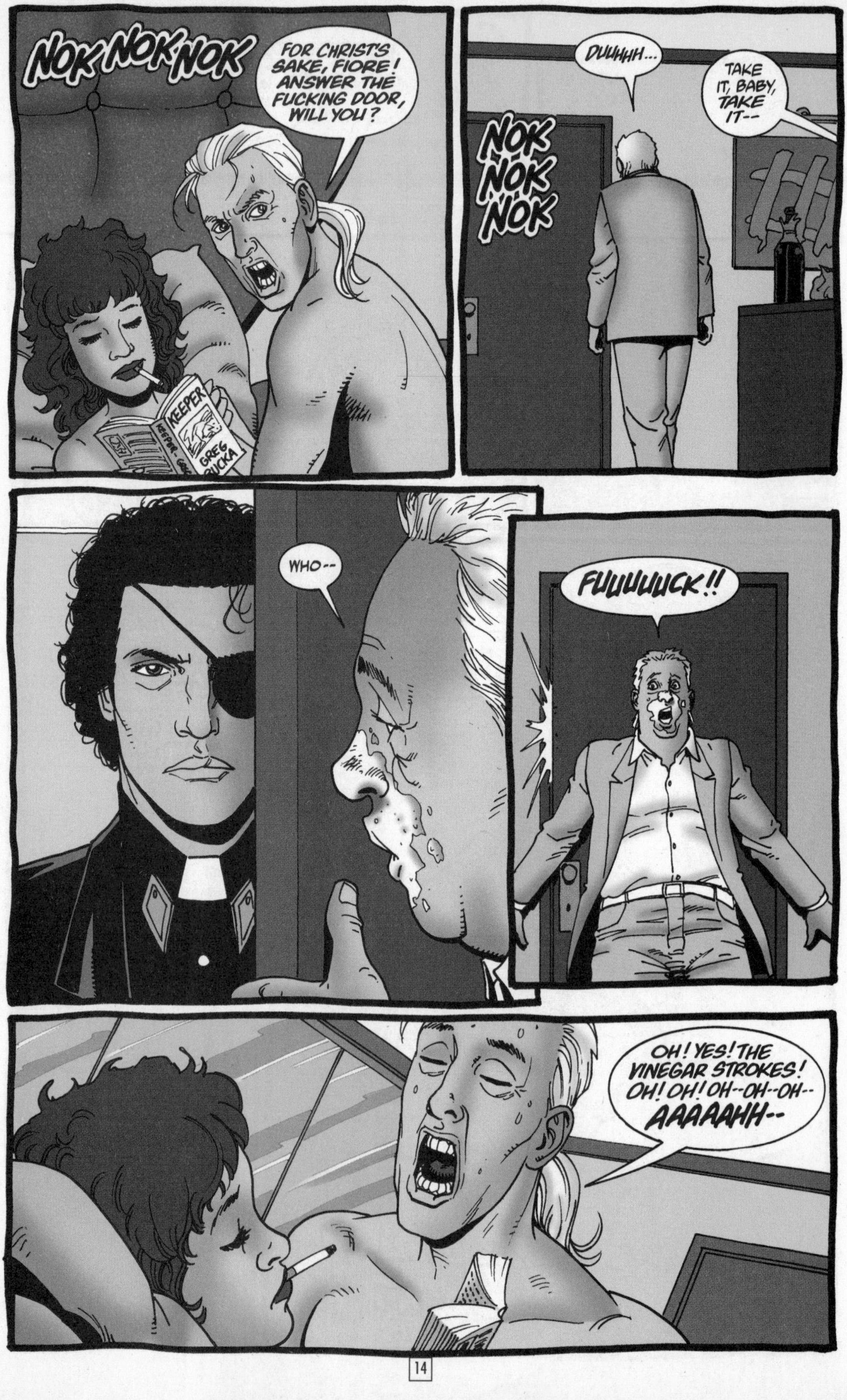
NOK NOK NOK
FOR CHRIST'S SAKE, FIORE! ANSWER THE FUCKING DOOR, WILL YOU?
KEEPER
GREG RUCKA
DUUHHH...
TAKE IT, BABY, TAKE IT--
NOK NOK NOK
WHO--
FUUUUUCK!!
OH! YES! THE VINEGAR STROKES! OH! OH! OH--OH--OH-- AAAAAHH--

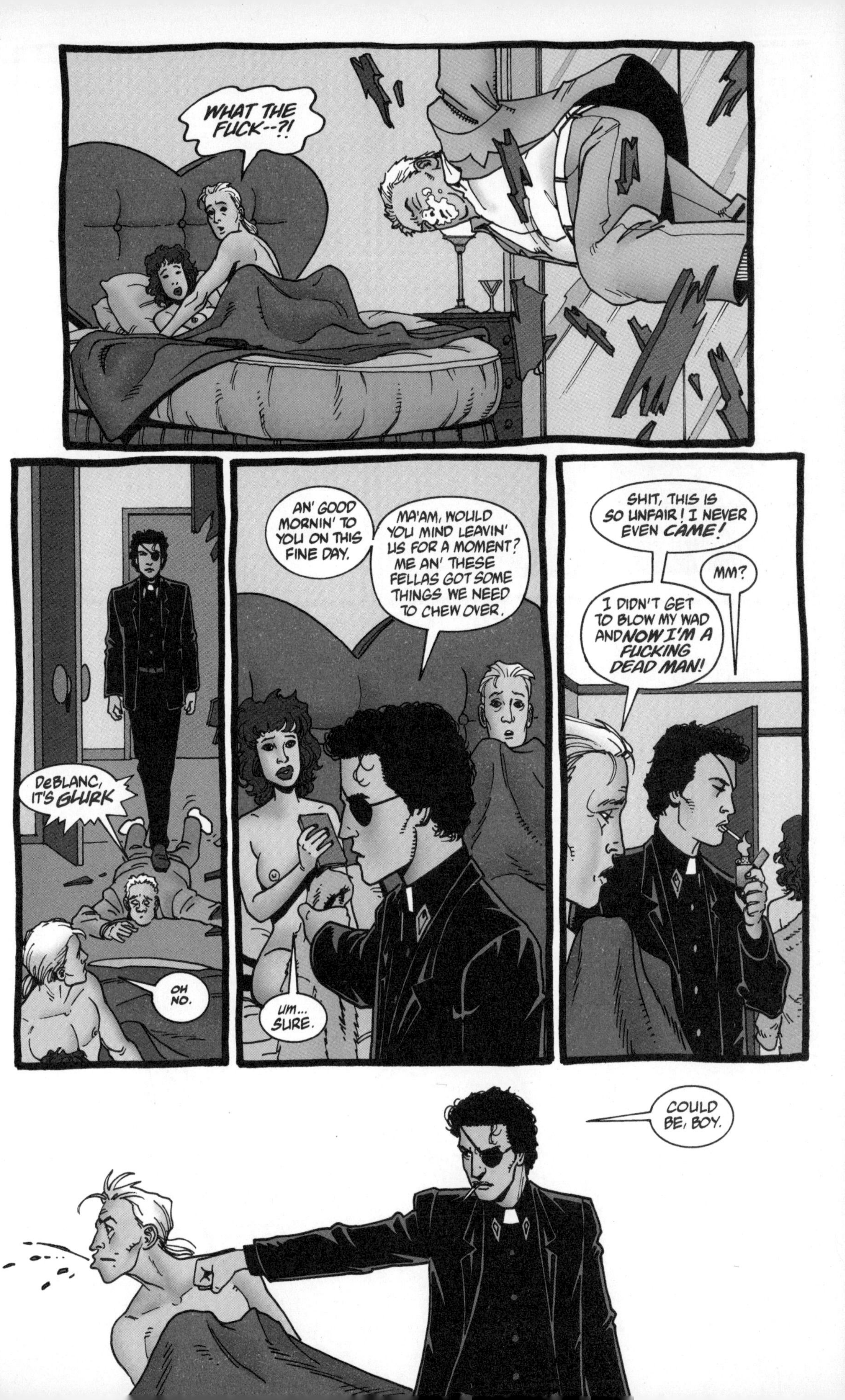
WHAT THE FUCK--?!
DeBLANC, IT'S GLURK
OH NO.
AN' GOOD MORNIN' TO YOU ON THIS FINE DAY.
MA'AM, WOULD YOU MIND LEAVIN' US FOR A MOMENT? ME AN' THESE FELLAS GOT SOME THINGS WE NEED TO CHEW OVER.
UM... SURE.
SHIT, THIS IS SO UNFAIR! I NEVER EVEN CAME!
MM?
I DIDN'T GET TO BLOW MY WAD AND NOW I'M A FUCKING DEAD MAN!
COULD BE, BOY.

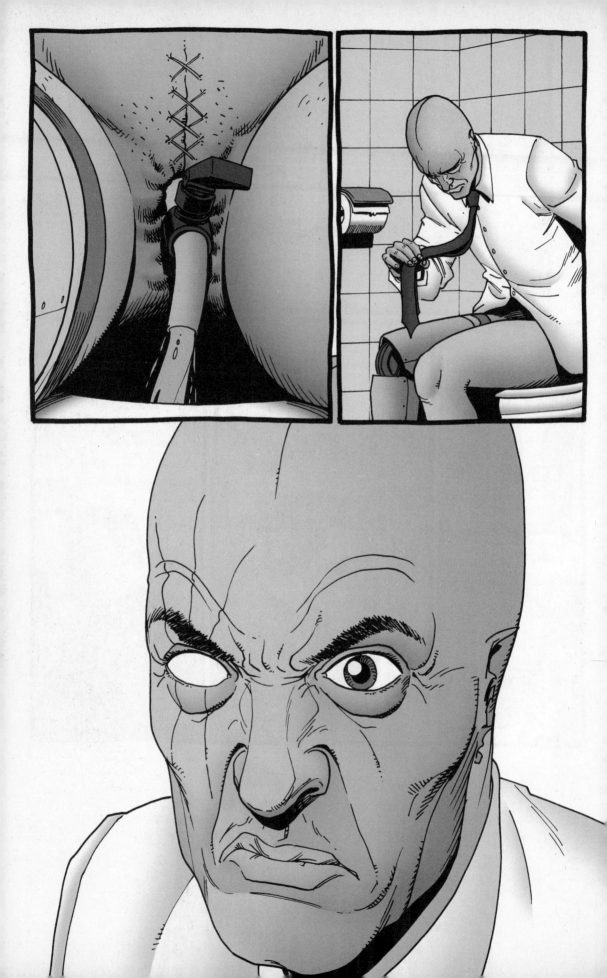

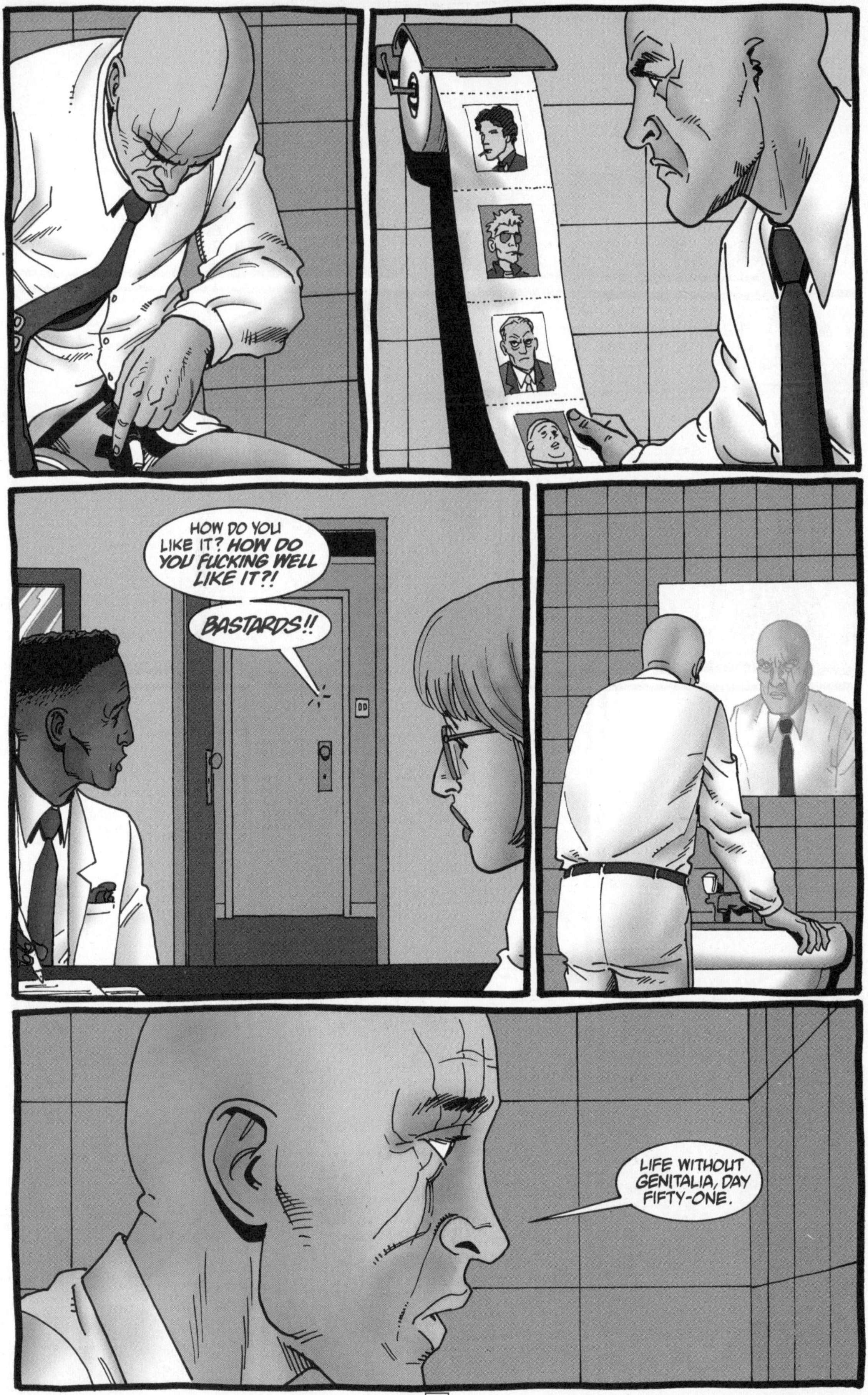
HOW DO YOU LIKE IT? HOW DO YOU FUCKING WELL LIKE IT?!
BASTARDS!!
LIFE WITHOUT GENITALIA, DAY FIFTY-ONE.

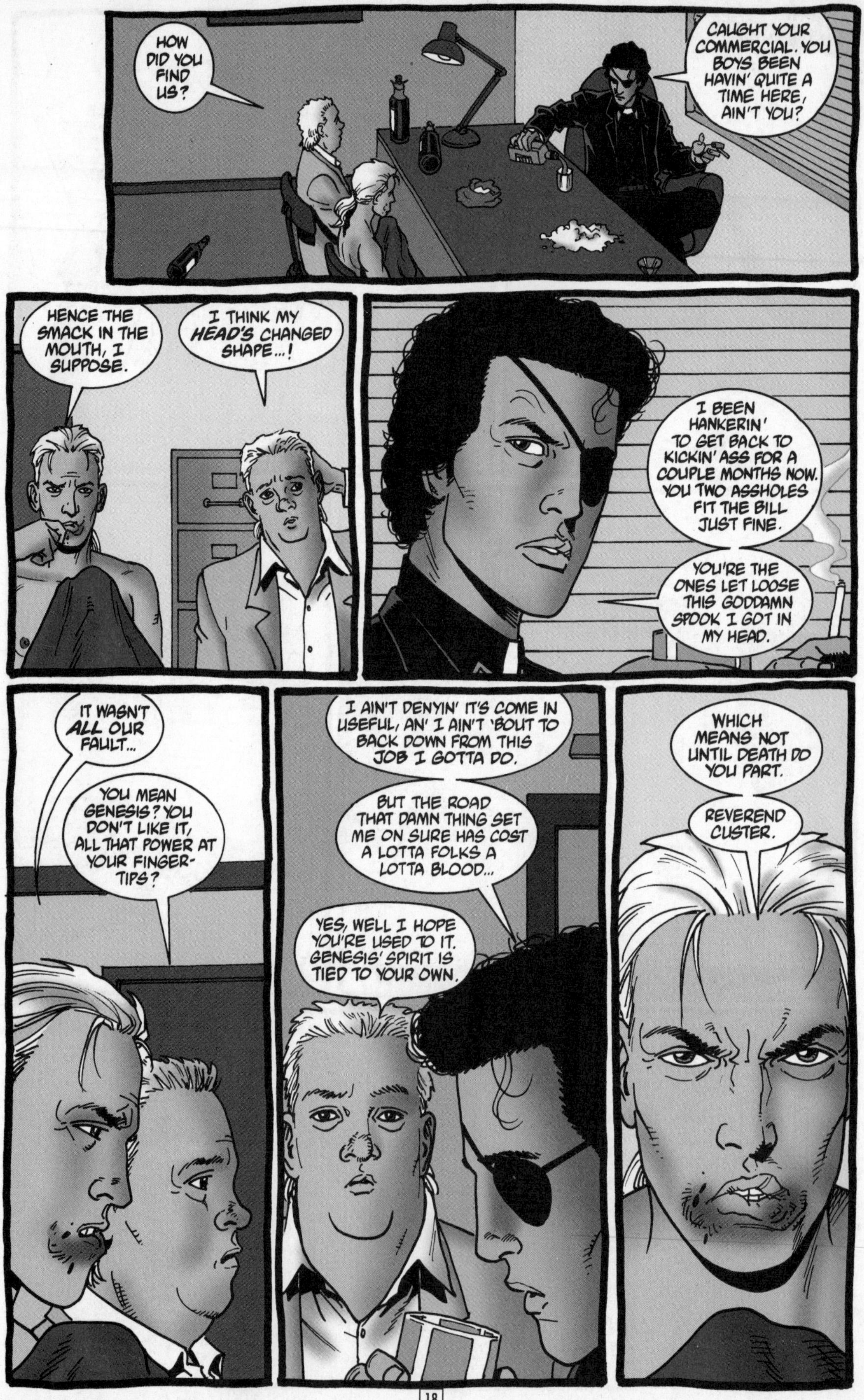
HOW DID YOU FIND US?
CAUGHT YOUR COMMERCIAL. YOU BOYS BEEN HAVIN' QUITE A TIME HERE, AIN'T YOU?
HENCE THE SMACK IN THE MOUTH, I SUPPOSE.
I THINK MY HEAD'S CHANGED SHAPE...!
I BEEN HANKERIN' TO GET BACK TO KICKIN' ASS FOR A COUPLE MONTHS NOW. YOU TWO ASSHOLES FIT THE BILL JUST FINE.
YOU'RE THE ONES LET LOOSE THIS GODDAMN SPOOK I GOT IN MY HEAD.
IT WASN'T ALL OUR FAULT...
YOU MEAN GENESIS? YOU DON'T LIKE IT, ALL THAT POWER AT YOUR FINGER-TIPS?
I AIN'T DENYIN' IT'S COME IN USEFUL, AN' I AIN'T 'BOUT TO BACK DOWN FROM THIS JOB I GOTTA DO.
BUT THE ROAD THAT DAMN THING SET ME ON SURE HAS COST A LOTTA FOLKS A LOTTA BLOOD...
YES, WELL I HOPE YOU'RE USED TO IT. GENESIS' SPIRIT IS TIED TO YOUR OWN.
WHICH MEANS NOT UNTIL DEATH DO YOU PART.
REVEREND CUSTER.

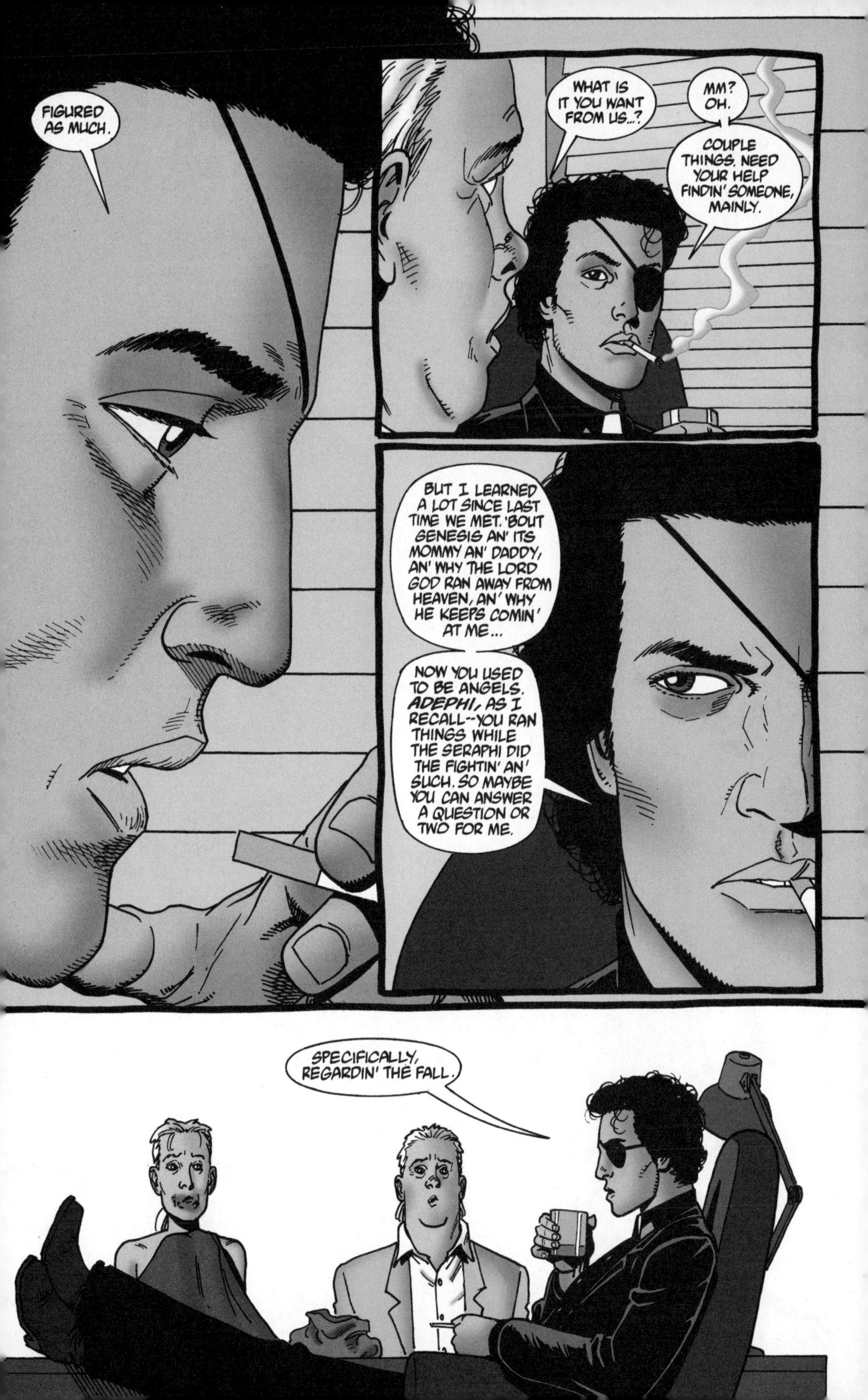
FIGURED AS MUCH.
WHAT IS IT YOU WANT FROM US...?
MM? OH.
COUPLE THINGS. NEED YOUR HELP FINDIN' SOMEONE, MAINLY.
BUT I LEARNED A LOT SINCE LAST TIME WE MET. 'BOUT GENESIS AN' ITS MOMMY AN' DADDY, AN' WHY THE LORD GOD RAN AWAY FROM HEAVEN, AN' WHY HE KEEPS COMIN' AT ME...
NOW YOU USED TO BE ANGELS. ADEPHI, AS I RECALL--YOU RAN THINGS WHILE THE SERAPHI DID THE FIGHTIN' AN' SUCH. SO MAYBE YOU CAN ANSWER A QUESTION OR TWO FOR ME.
SPECIFICALLY, REGARDIN' THE FALL.

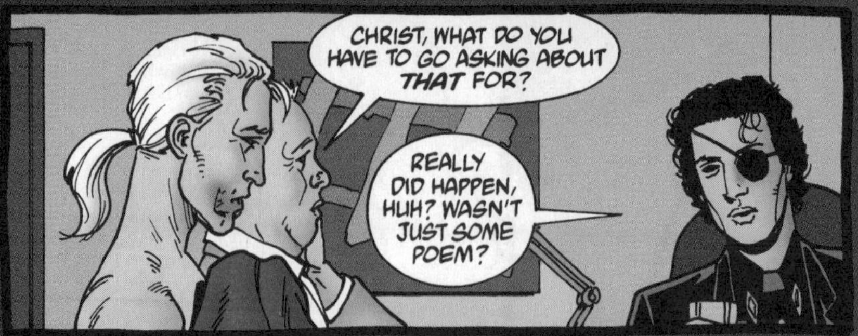
CHRIST, WHAT DO YOU HAVE TO GO ASKING ABOUT *THAT* FOR?
REALLY DID HAPPEN, HUH? WASN'T JUST SOME POEM?

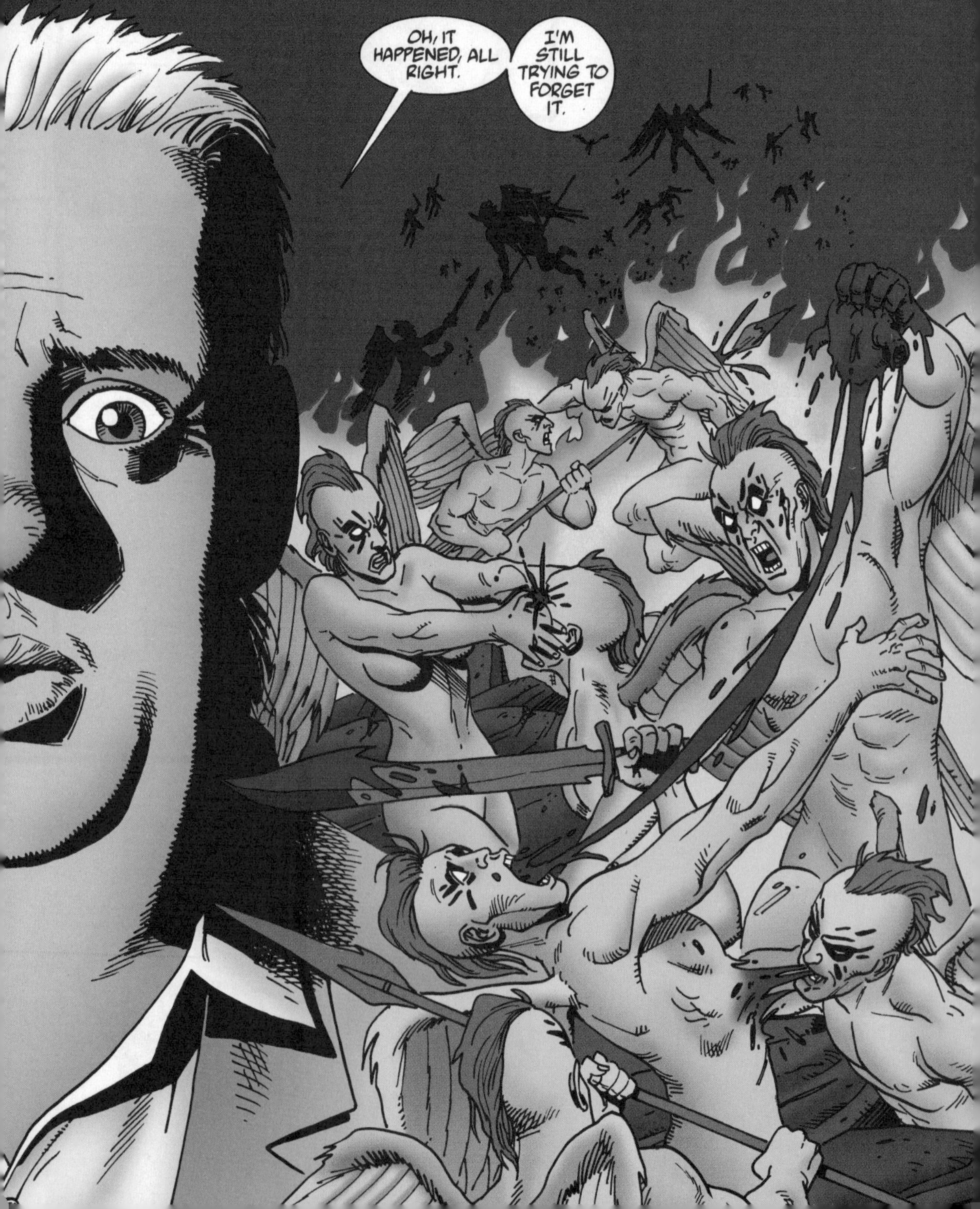
OH, IT HAPPENED, ALL RIGHT.
I'M STILL TRYING TO FORGET IT.

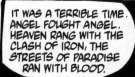

IT WAS A TERRIBLE TIME. ANGEL FOUGHT ANGEL. HEAVEN RANG WITH THE CLASH OF IRON, THE STREETS OF PARADISE RAN WITH BLOOD.

EVERYONE FOUGHT ON THAT AWFUL DAY. EVEN WE ADEPHI STOOD READY FOR BATTLE...

SPEAK FOR YOURSELF, CHUM. I FUCKED OFF DOWN TO THE CELLARS AND HID IN A BARREL OF BRANDY.

BUT THE LOYALIST SERAPHI TRIUMPHED WITHOUT US.

THE TRANSGRESSORS-- THE FEW SURVIVORS, ANYWAY WERE ROUNDED UP. AND JUDGED. AND CAST DOWN.

THAT WAS THE LONGEST FALL OF ALL.

SO...WHY?

BECAUSE OF YOU.

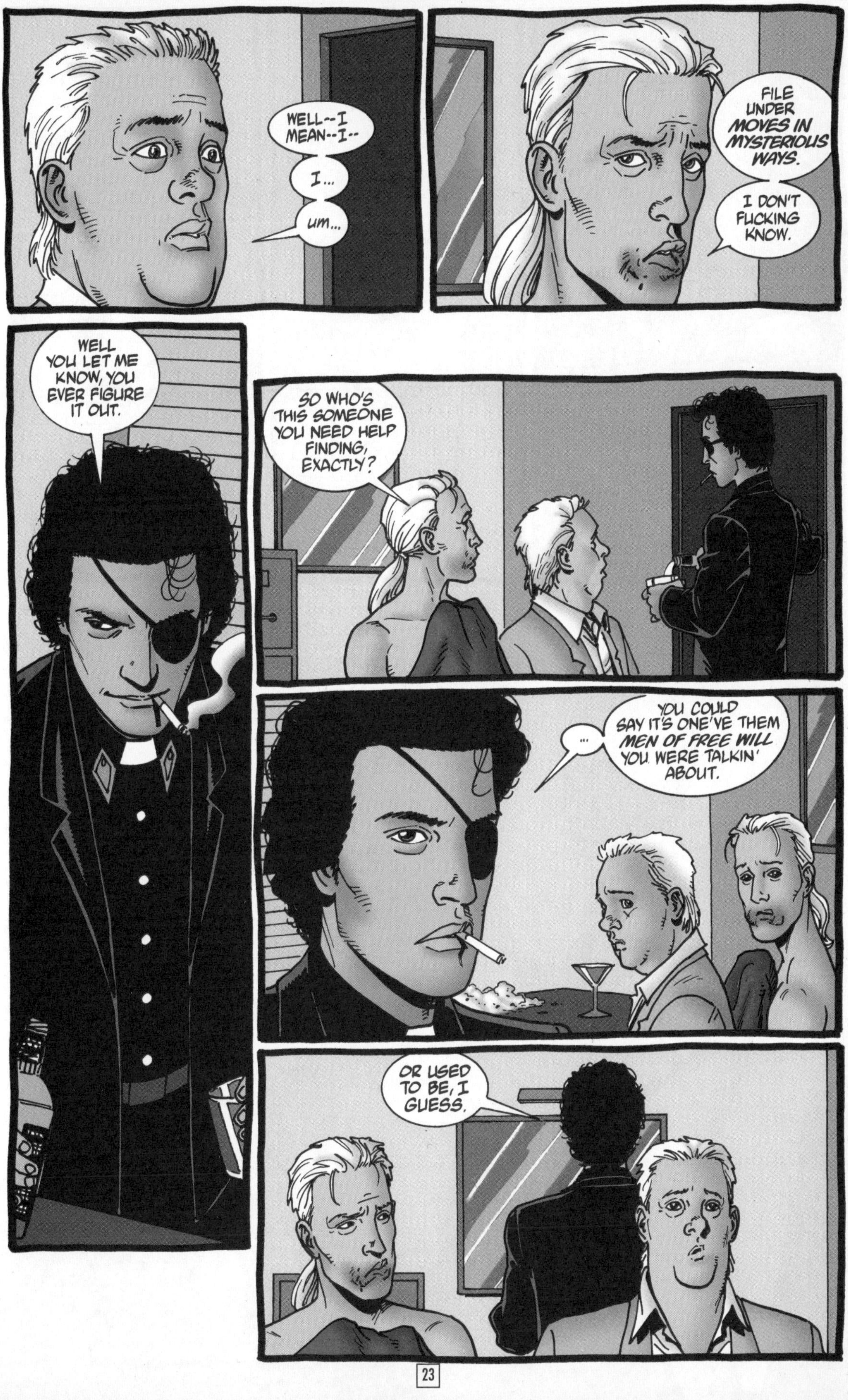
WELL--I MEAN--I--
I...
um...
FILE UNDER MOVES IN MYSTERIOUS WAYS.
I DON'T FUCKING KNOW.
WELL YOU LET ME KNOW, YOU EVER FIGURE IT OUT.
SO WHO'S THIS SOMEONE YOU NEED HELP FINDING, EXACTLY?
...
YOU COULD SAY IT'S ONE'VE THEM MEN OF FREE WILL YOU WERE TALKIN' ABOUT.
OR USED TO BE, I GUESS.

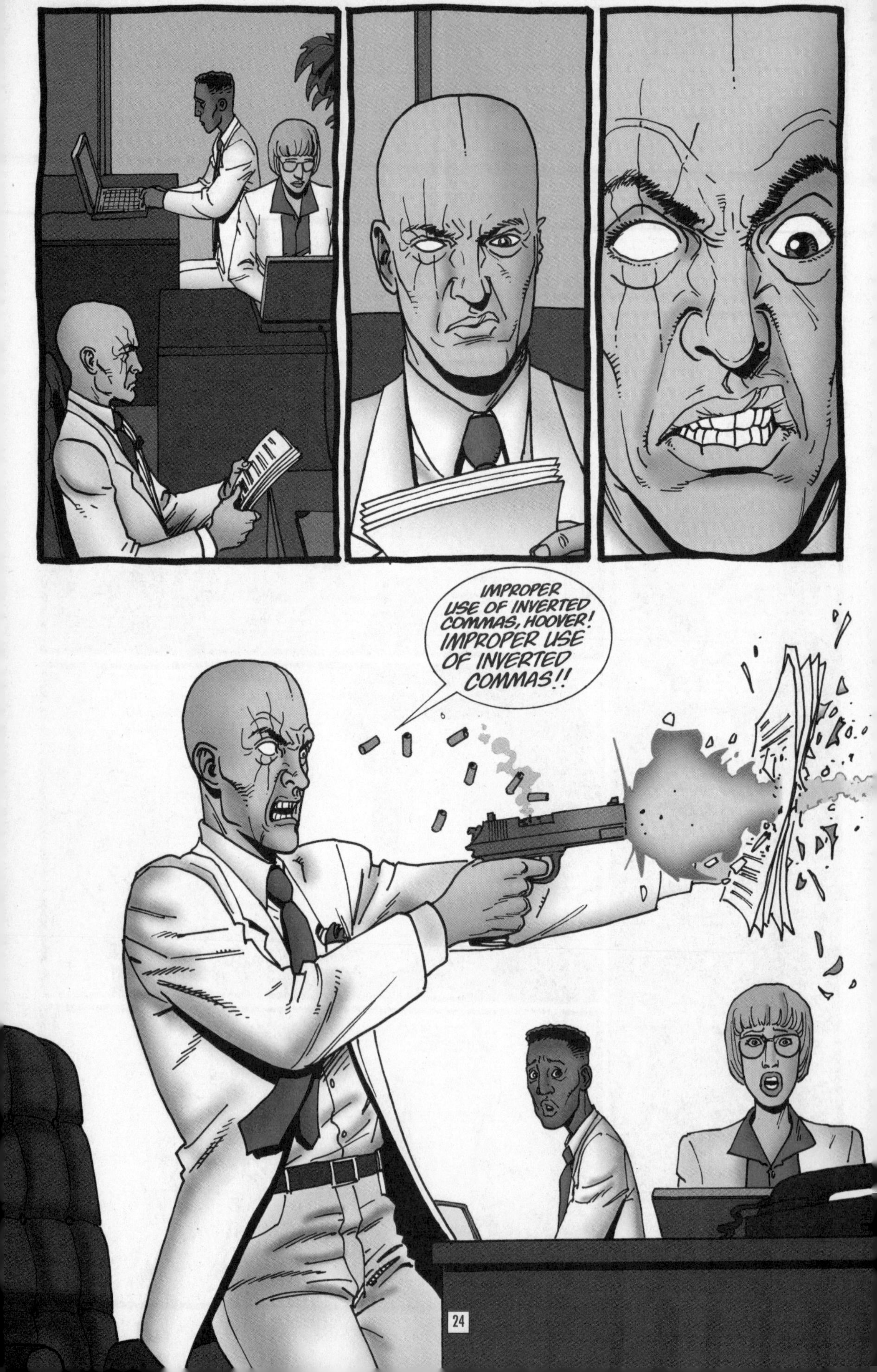
IMPROPER USE OF INVERTED COMMAS, HOOVER! IMPROPER USE OF INVERTED COMMAS!!

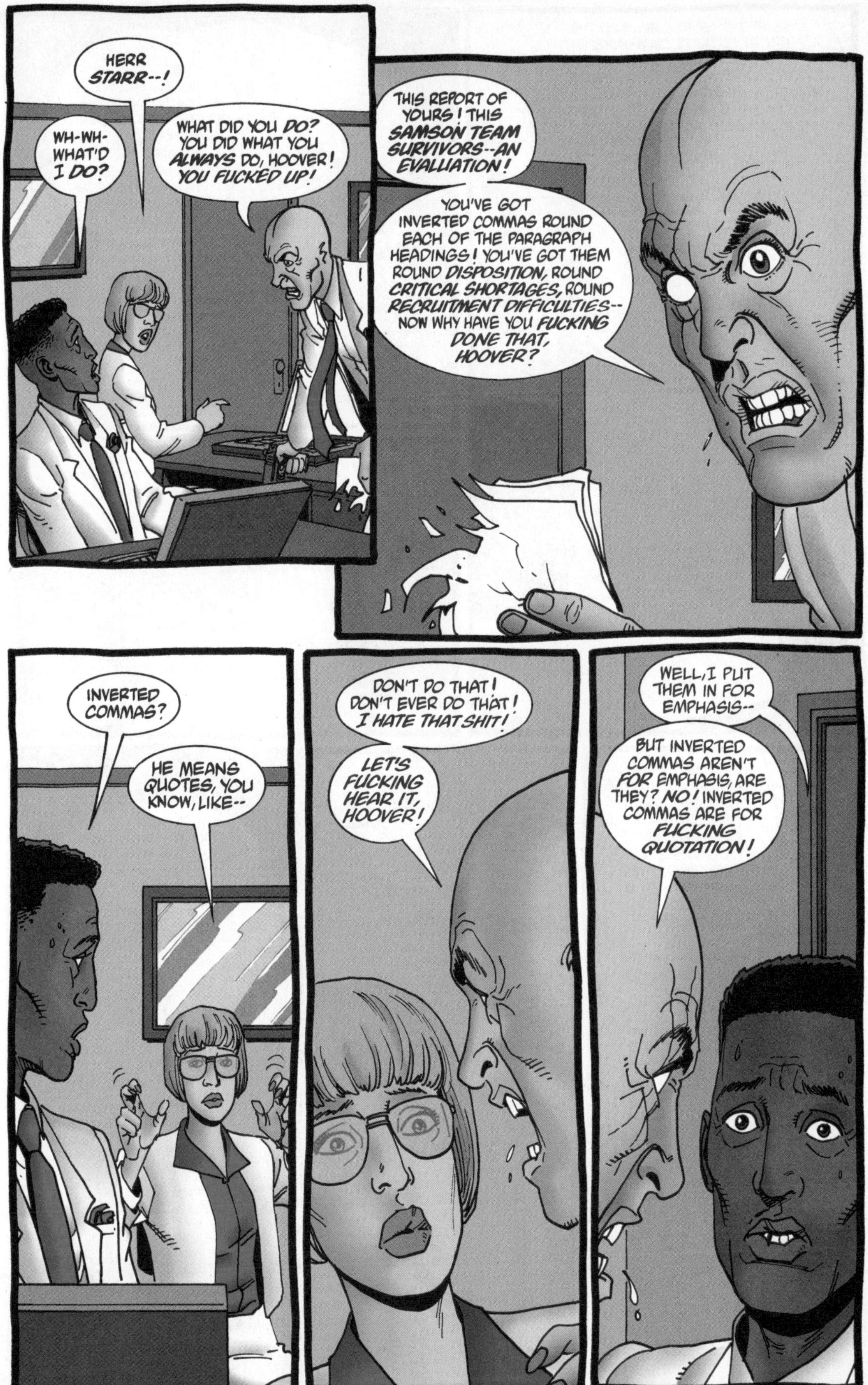
HERR STARR--!
WH-WH-WHAT'D I DO?
WHAT DID YOU DO? YOU DID WHAT YOU ALWAYS DO, HOOVER! YOU FUCKED UP!
THIS REPORT OF YOURS! THIS SAMSON TEAM SURVIVORS--AN EVALUATION!
YOU'VE GOT INVERTED COMMAS ROUND EACH OF THE PARAGRAPH HEADINGS! YOU'VE GOT THEM ROUND DISPOSITION, ROUND CRITICAL SHORTAGES, ROUND RECRUITMENT DIFFICULTIES--NOW WHY HAVE YOU FUCKING DONE THAT, HOOVER?
INVERTED COMMAS?
HE MEANS QUOTES, YOU KNOW, LIKE--
DON'T DO THAT! DON'T EVER DO THAT! I HATE THAT SHIT!
LET'S FUCKING HEAR IT, HOOVER!
WELL, I PUT THEM IN FOR EMPHASIS--
BUT INVERTED COMMAS AREN'T FOR EMPHASIS, ARE THEY? NO! INVERTED COMMAS ARE FOR FUCKING QUOTATION!

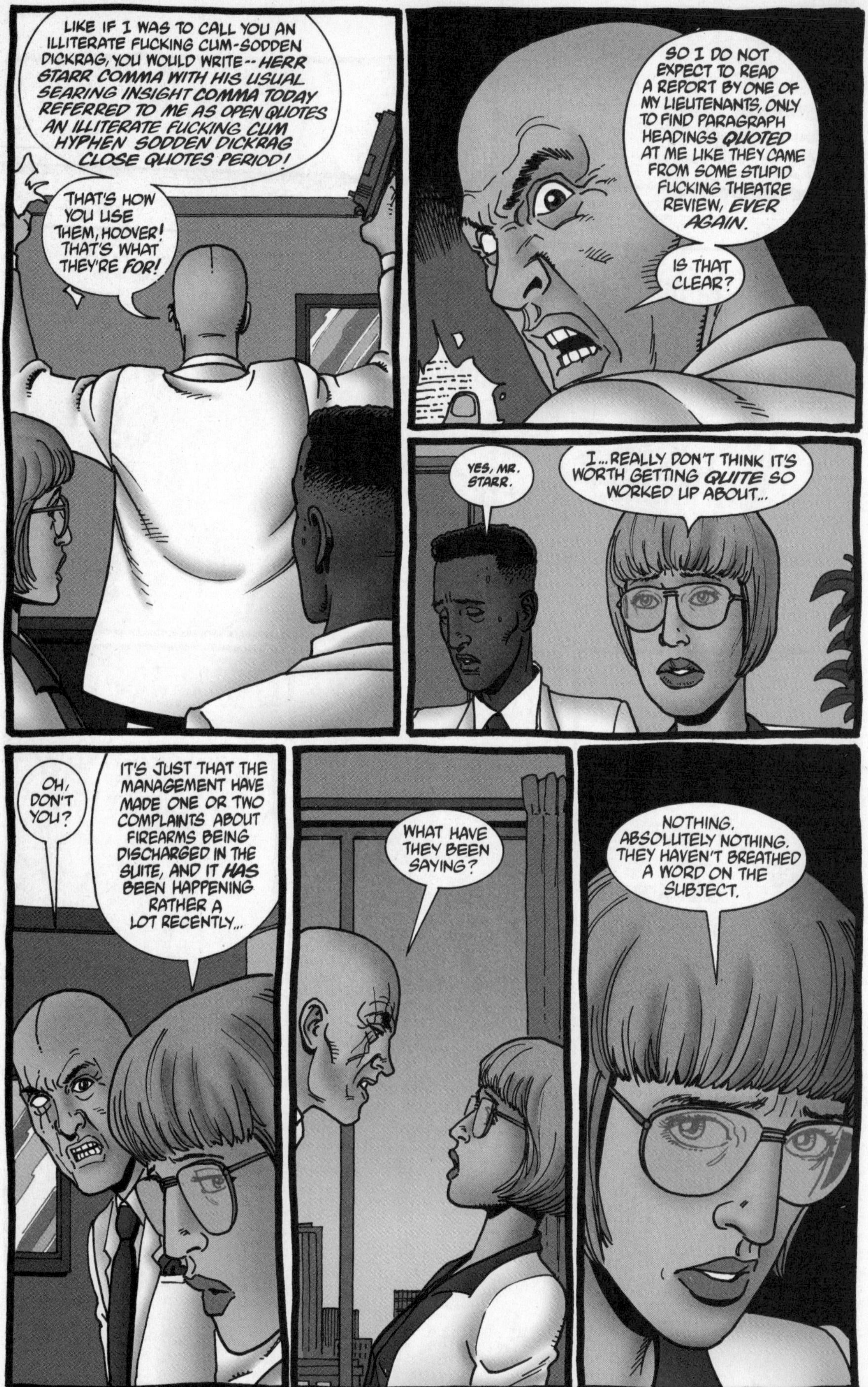
LIKE IF I WAS TO CALL YOU AN ILLITERATE FUCKING CUM-SODDEN DICKRAG, YOU WOULD WRITE-- HERR STARR COMMA WITH HIS USUAL SEARING INSIGHT COMMA TODAY REFERRED TO ME AS OPEN QUOTES AN ILLITERATE FUCKING CUM HYPHEN SODDEN DICKRAG CLOSE QUOTES PERIOD!
THAT'S HOW YOU USE THEM, HOOVER! THAT'S WHAT THEY'RE FOR!
SO I DO NOT EXPECT TO READ A REPORT BY ONE OF MY LIEUTENANTS, ONLY TO FIND PARAGRAPH HEADINGS QUOTED AT ME LIKE THEY CAME FROM SOME STUPID FUCKING THEATRE REVIEW, EVER AGAIN.
IS THAT CLEAR?
YES, MR. STARR.
I...REALLY DON'T THINK IT'S WORTH GETTING QUITE SO WORKED UP ABOUT...
OH, DON'T YOU?
IT'S JUST THAT THE MANAGEMENT HAVE MADE ONE OR TWO COMPLAINTS ABOUT FIREARMS BEING DISCHARGED IN THE SUITE, AND IT HAS BEEN HAPPENING RATHER A LOT RECENTLY...
WHAT HAVE THEY BEEN SAYING?
NOTHING. ABSOLUTELY NOTHING. THEY HAVEN'T BREATHED A WORD ON THE SUBJECT.

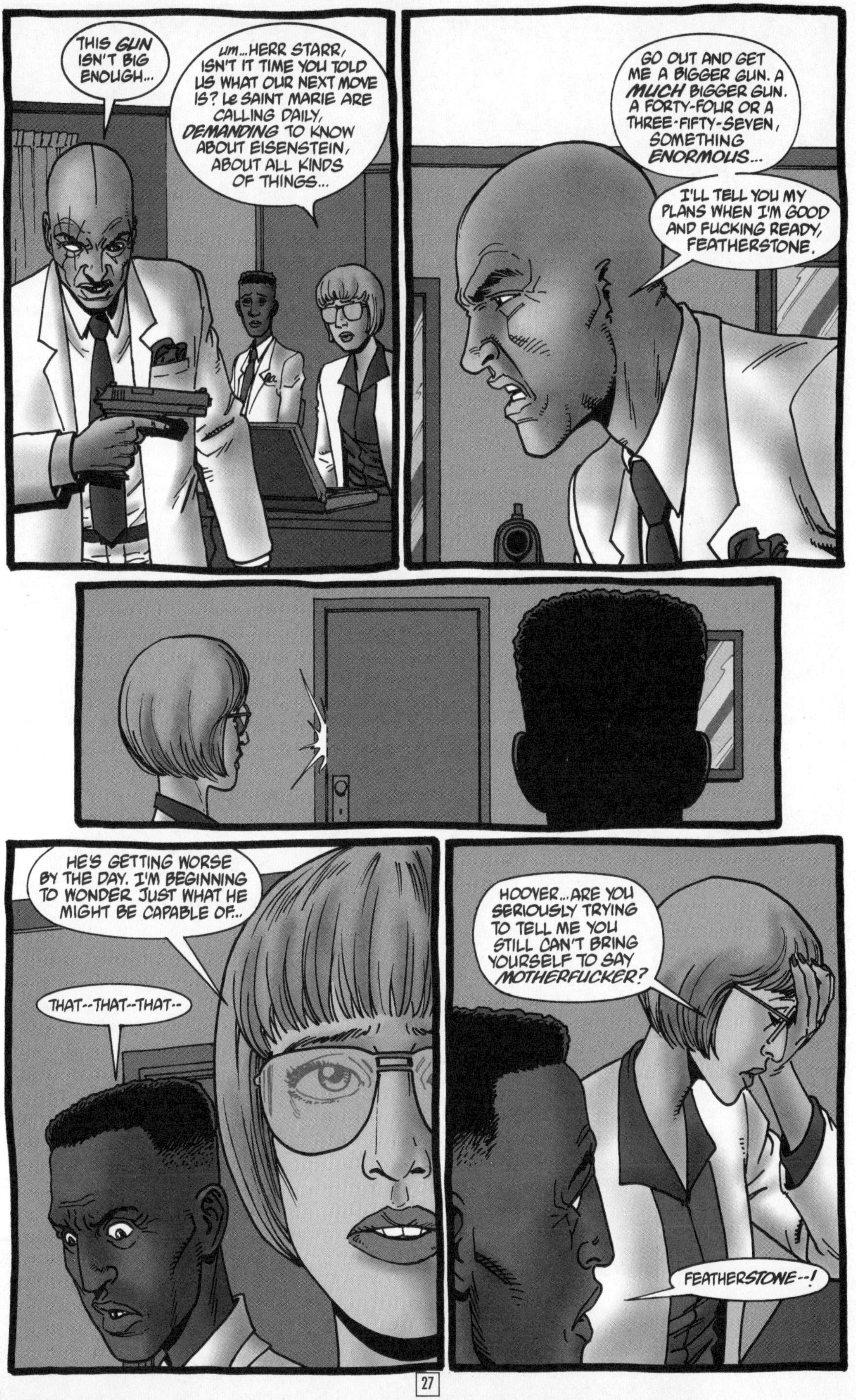
THIS GUN ISN'T BIG ENOUGH...
UM...HERR STARR, ISN'T IT TIME YOU TOLD US WHAT OUR NEXT MOVE IS? Le SAINT MARIE ARE CALLING DAILY, DEMANDING TO KNOW ABOUT EISENSTEIN, ABOUT ALL KINDS OF THINGS...
GO OUT AND GET ME A BIGGER GUN. A MUCH BIGGER GUN. A FORTY-FOUR OR A THREE-FIFTY-SEVEN, SOMETHING ENORMOUS...
I'LL TELL YOU MY PLANS WHEN I'M GOOD AND FUCKING READY, FEATHERSTONE.
HE'S GETTING WORSE BY THE DAY. I'M BEGINNING TO WONDER JUST WHAT HE MIGHT BE CAPABLE OF...
THAT--THAT--THAT--
HOOVER...ARE YOU SERIOUSLY TRYING TO TELL ME YOU STILL CAN'T BRING YOURSELF TO SAY MOTHERFUCKER?
FEATHERSTONE--!

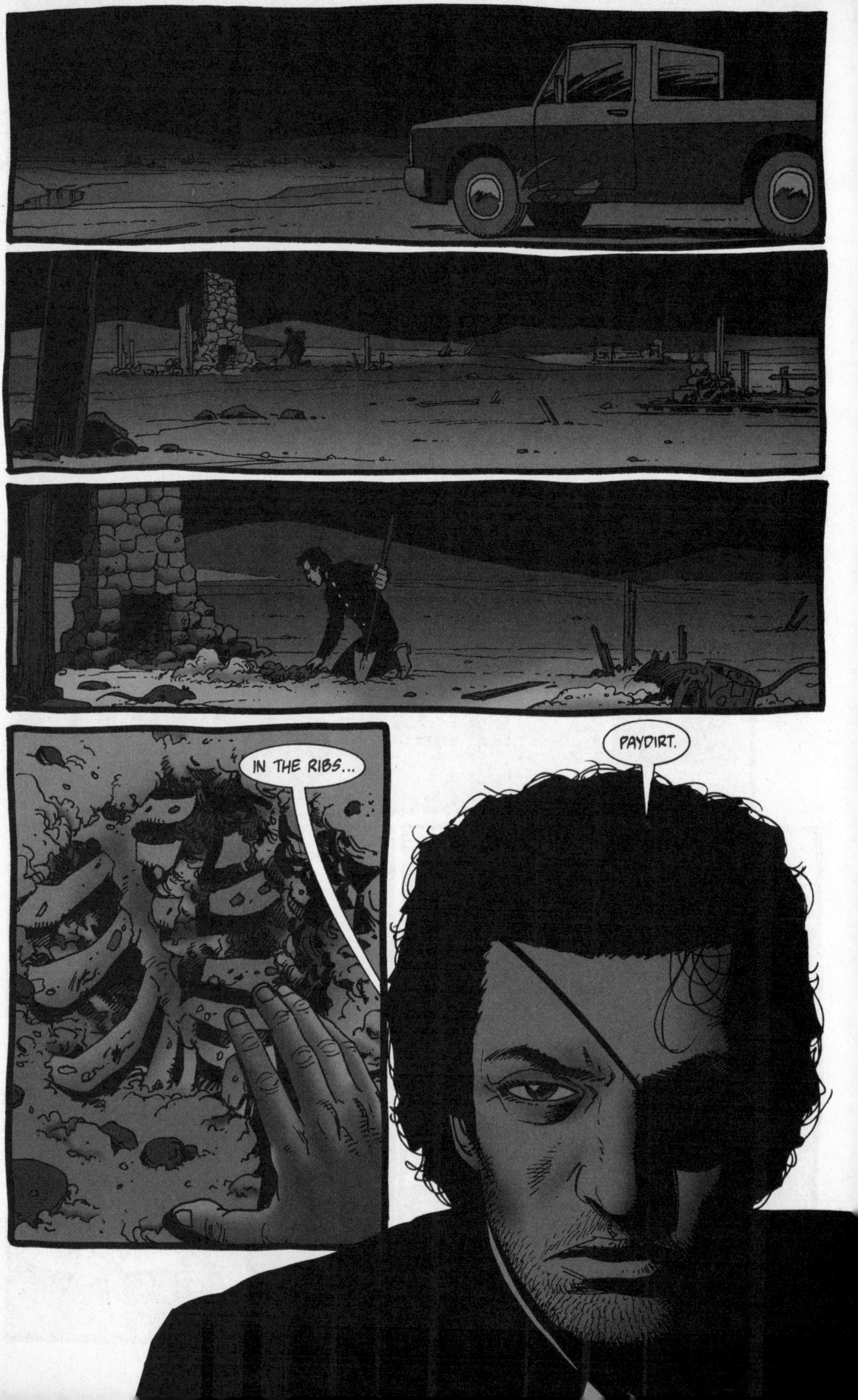
IN THE RIBS...
PAYDIRT.

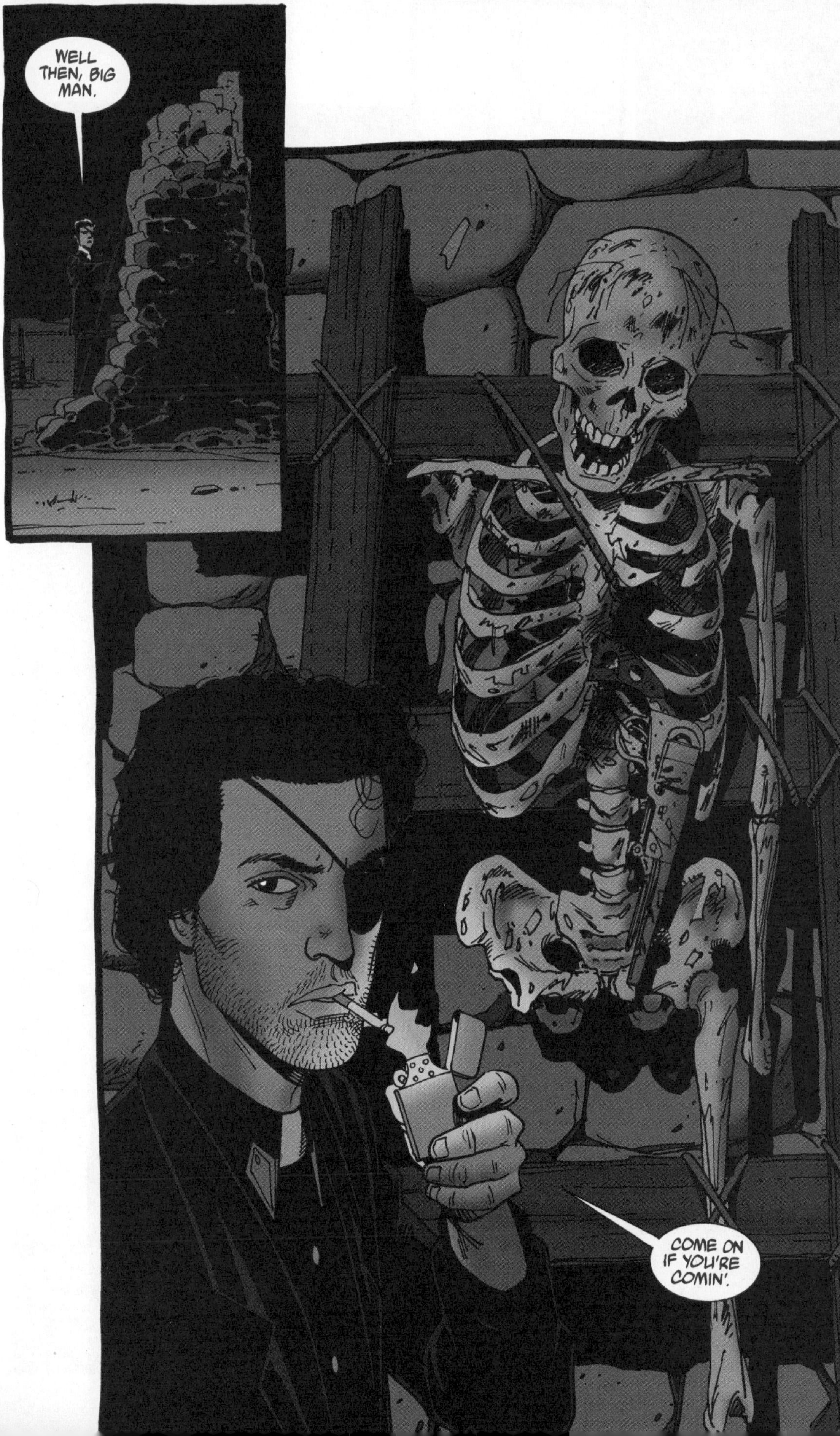
WELL THEN, BIG MAN.
COME ON IF YOU'RE COMIN'.

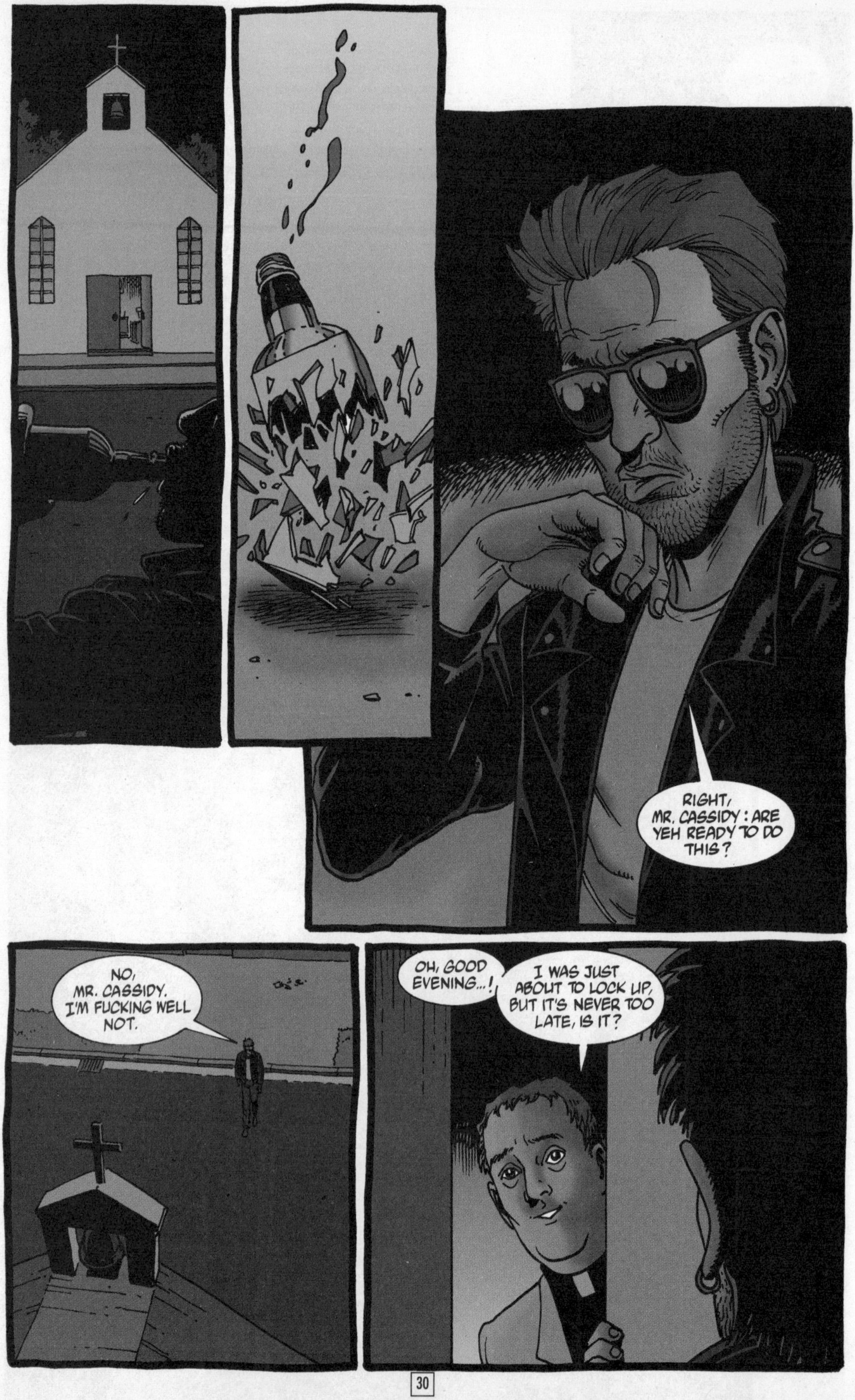
RIGHT, MR. CASSIDY : ARE YEH READY TO DO THIS?
NO, MR. CASSIDY. I'M FUCKING WELL NOT.
OH, GOOD EVENING...!
I WAS JUST ABOUT TO LOCK UP, BUT IT'S NEVER TOO LATE, IS IT?

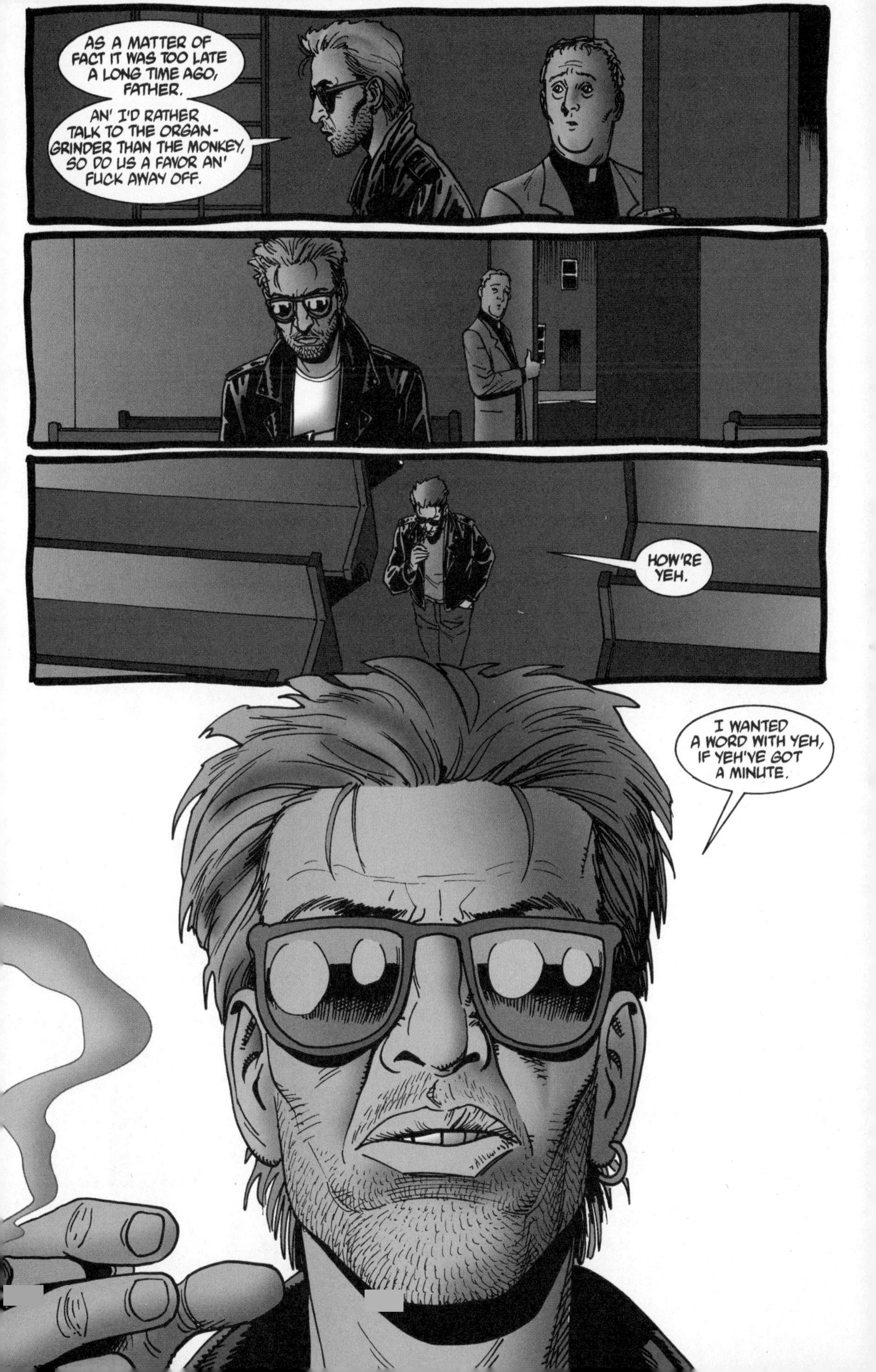
AS A MATTER OF FACT IT WAS TOO LATE A LONG TIME AGO, FATHER.
AN' I'D RATHER TALK TO THE ORGAN-GRINDER THAN THE MONKEY, SO DO US A FAVOR AN' FUCK AWAY OFF.
HOW'RE YEH.
I WANTED A WORD WITH YEH, IF YEH'VE GOT A MINUTE.

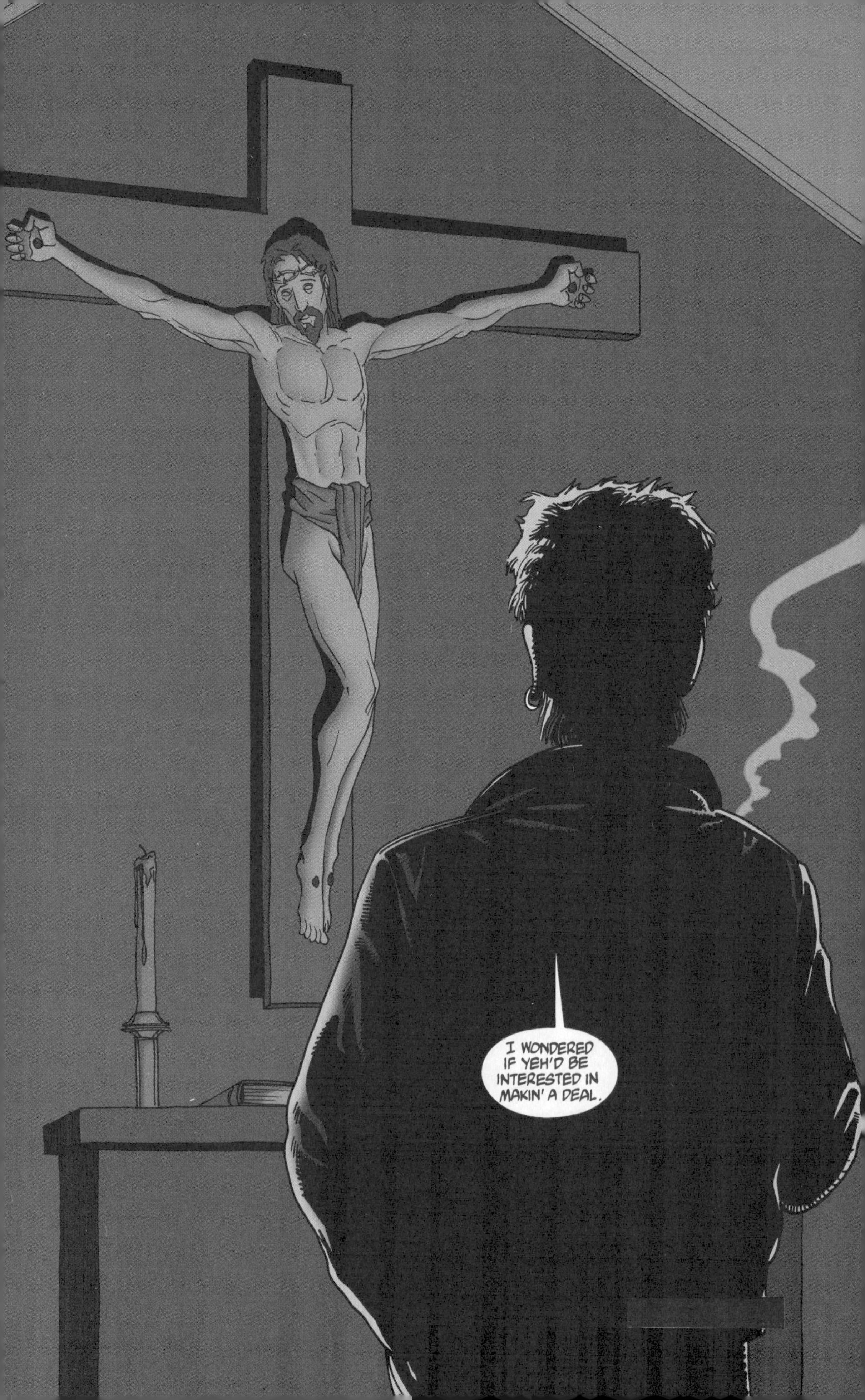
I WONDERED IF YEH'D BE INTERESTED IN MAKIN' A DEAL.

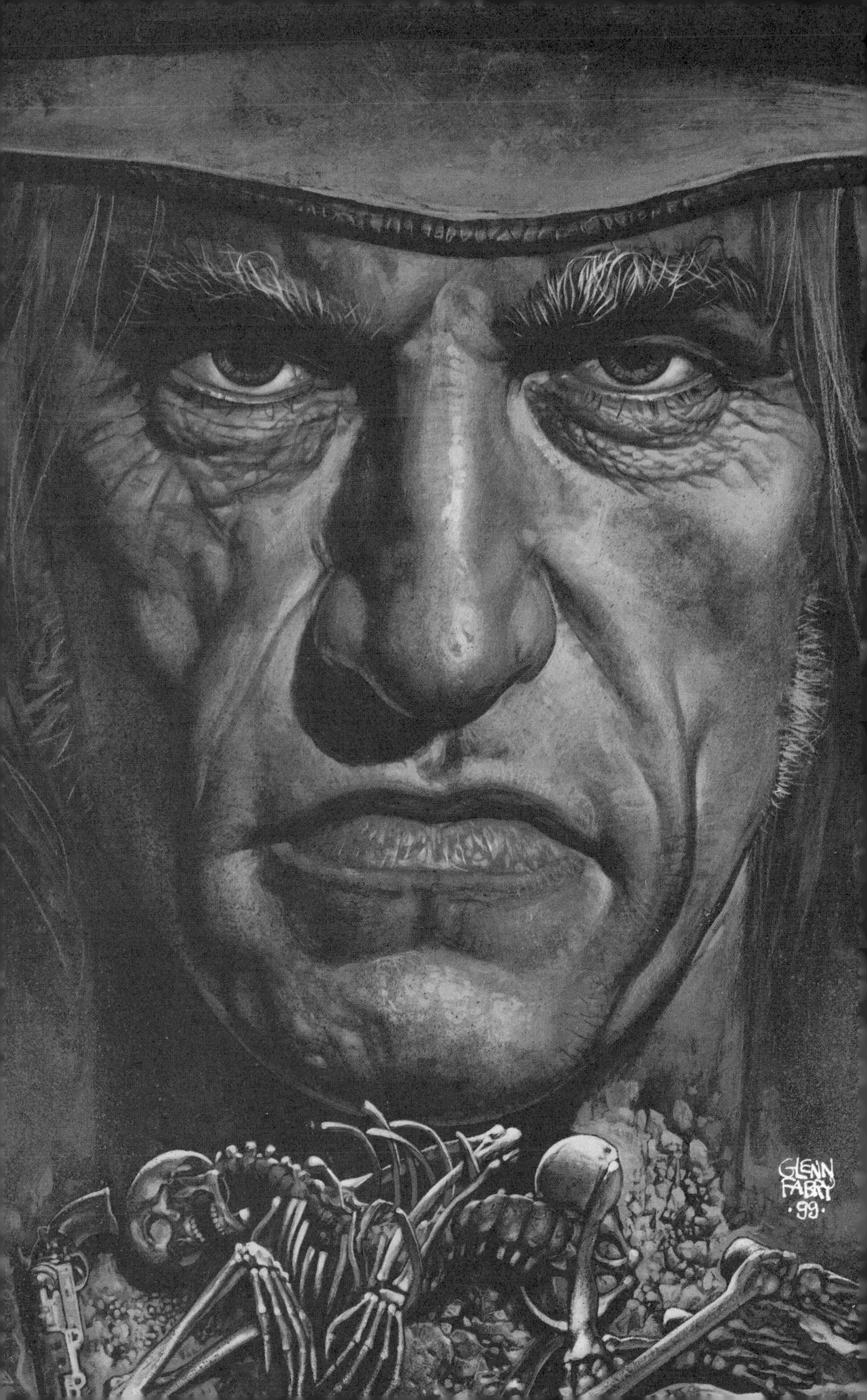
GLENN FABRY ·99·

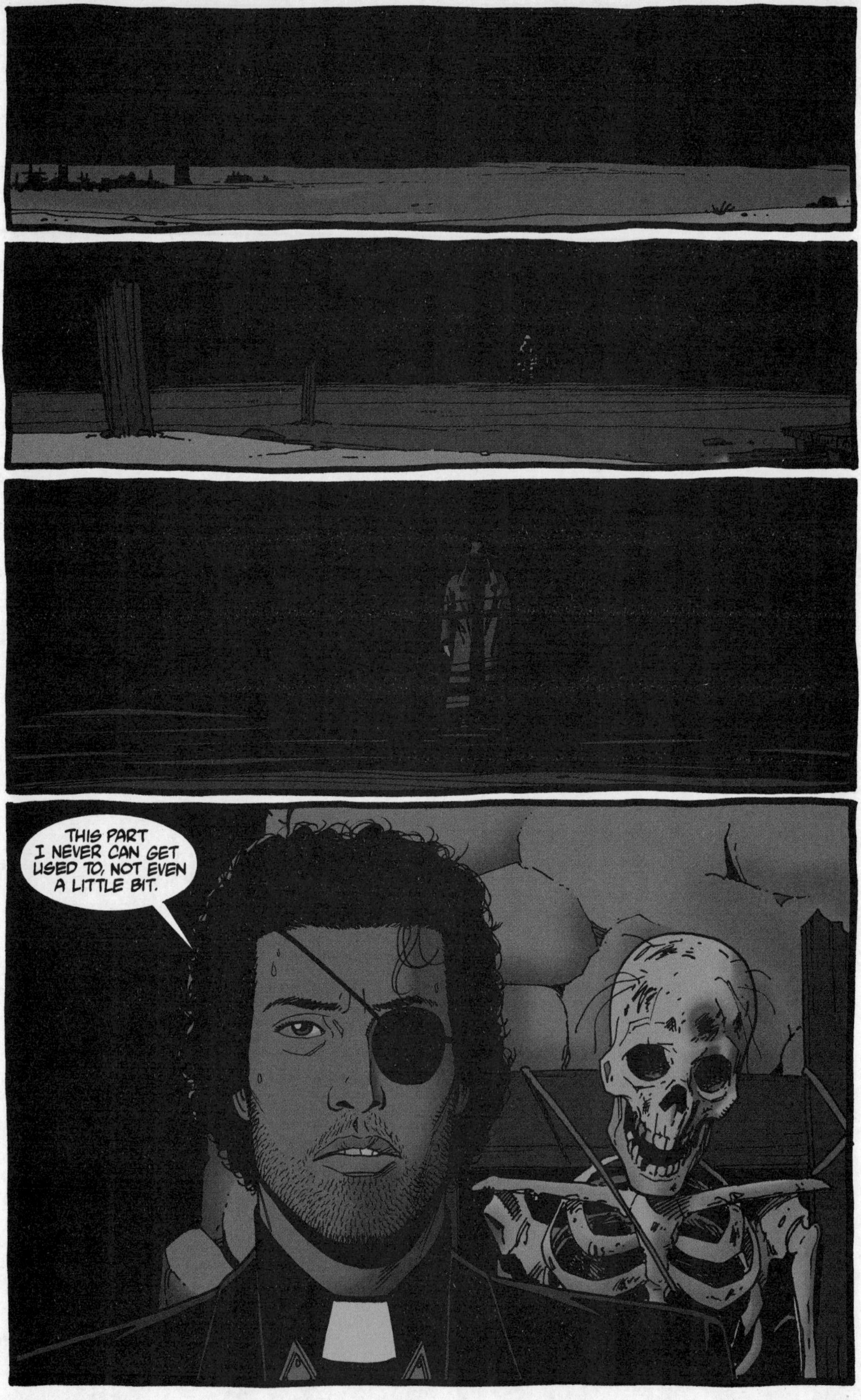
THIS PART I NEVER CAN GET USED TO, NOT EVEN A LITTLE BIT.

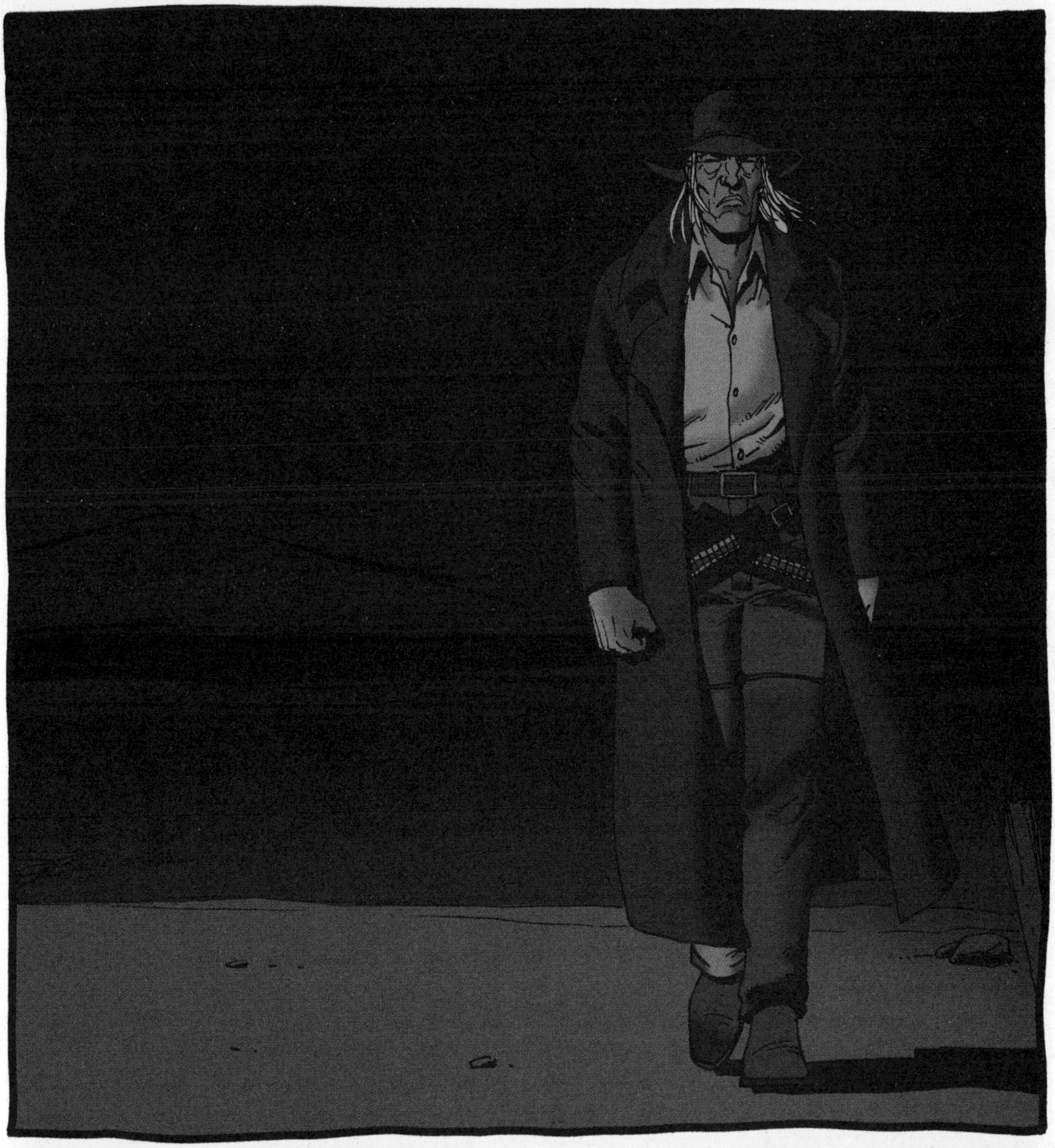

THE THUNDER OF HIS GUNS

GARTH ENNIS - Writer   STEVE DILLON - Artist

PAMELA RAMBO - Colorist   CLEM ROBINS - Letterer   AXEL ALONSO - Editor

PREACHER created by GARTH ENNIS and STEVE DILLON

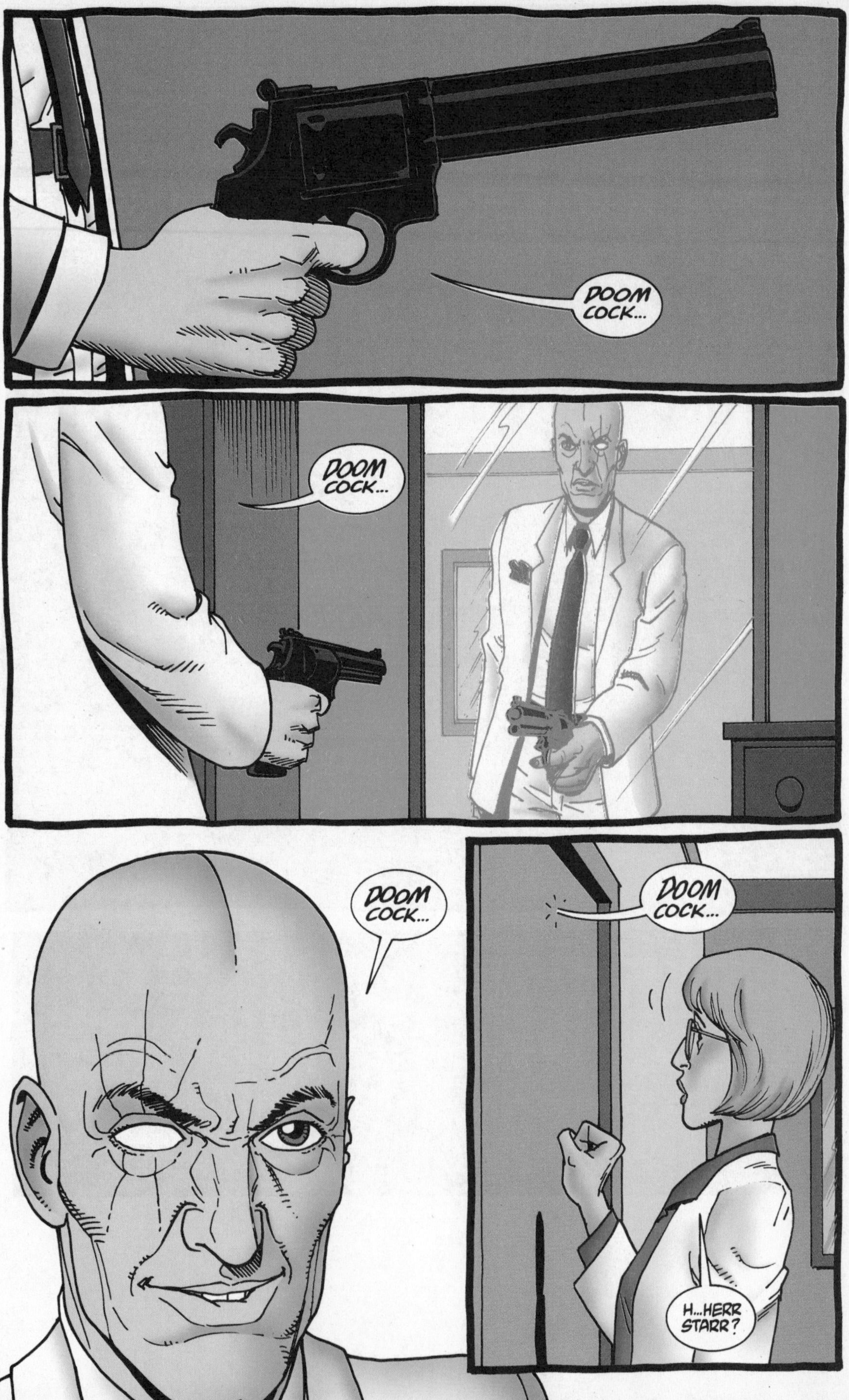
DOOM COCK...
DOOM COCK...
DOOM COCK...
DOOM COCK...
H...HERR STARR?

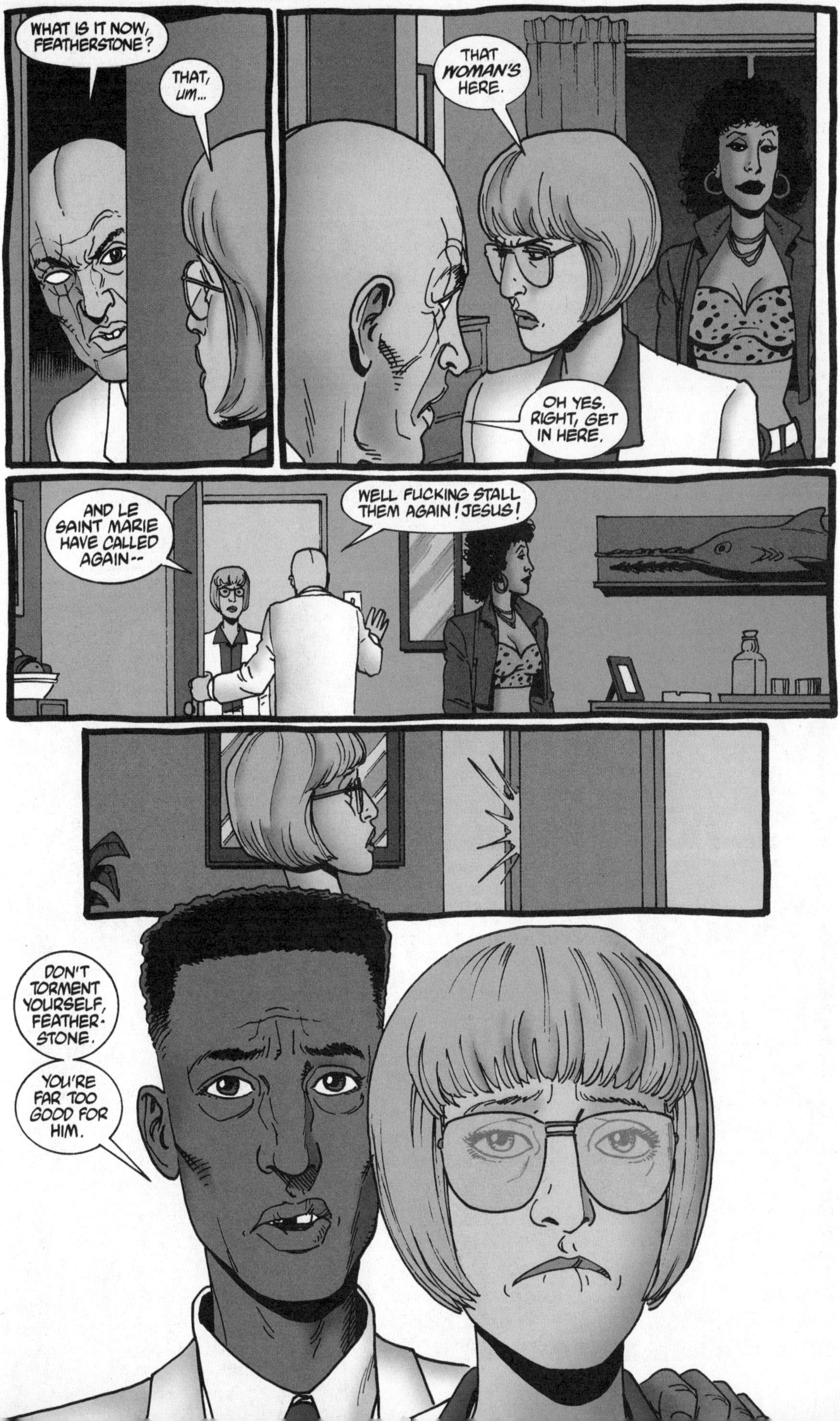
WHAT IS IT NOW, FEATHERSTONE?
THAT, UM...
THAT WOMAN'S HERE.
OH YES. RIGHT, GET IN HERE.
AND LE SAINT MARIE HAVE CALLED AGAIN--
WELL FUCKING STALL THEM AGAIN! JESUS!
DON'T TORMENT YOURSELF, FEATHER-STONE.
YOU'RE FAR TOO GOOD FOR HIM.

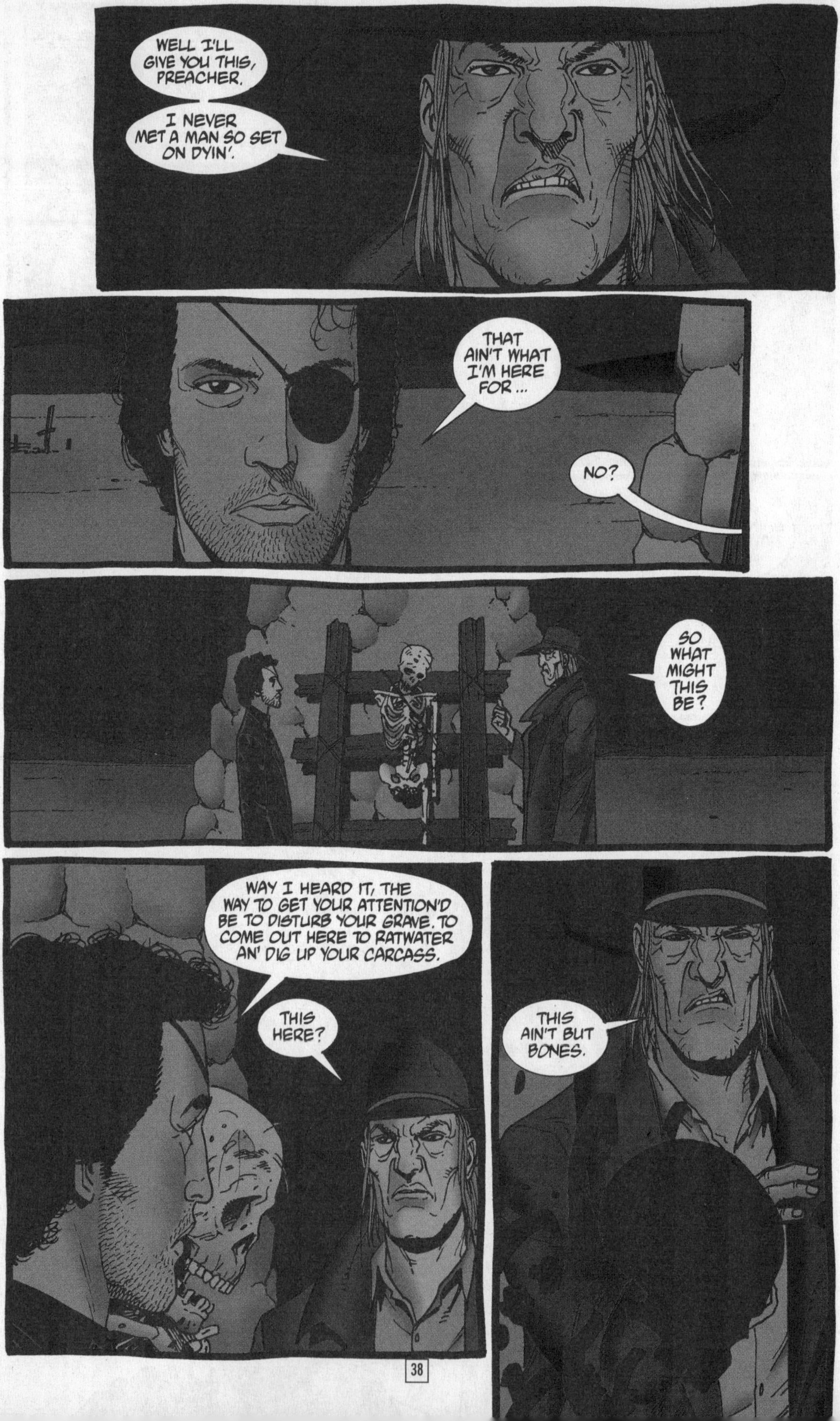

WELL I'LL GIVE YOU THIS, PREACHER.
I NEVER MET A MAN SO SET ON DYIN'.
THAT AIN'T WHAT I'M HERE FOR...
NO?
SO WHAT MIGHT THIS BE?
WAY I HEARD IT, THE WAY TO GET YOUR ATTENTION'D BE TO DISTURB YOUR GRAVE. TO COME OUT HERE TO RATWATER AN' DIG UP YOUR CARCASS.
THIS HERE?
THIS AIN'T BUT BONES.

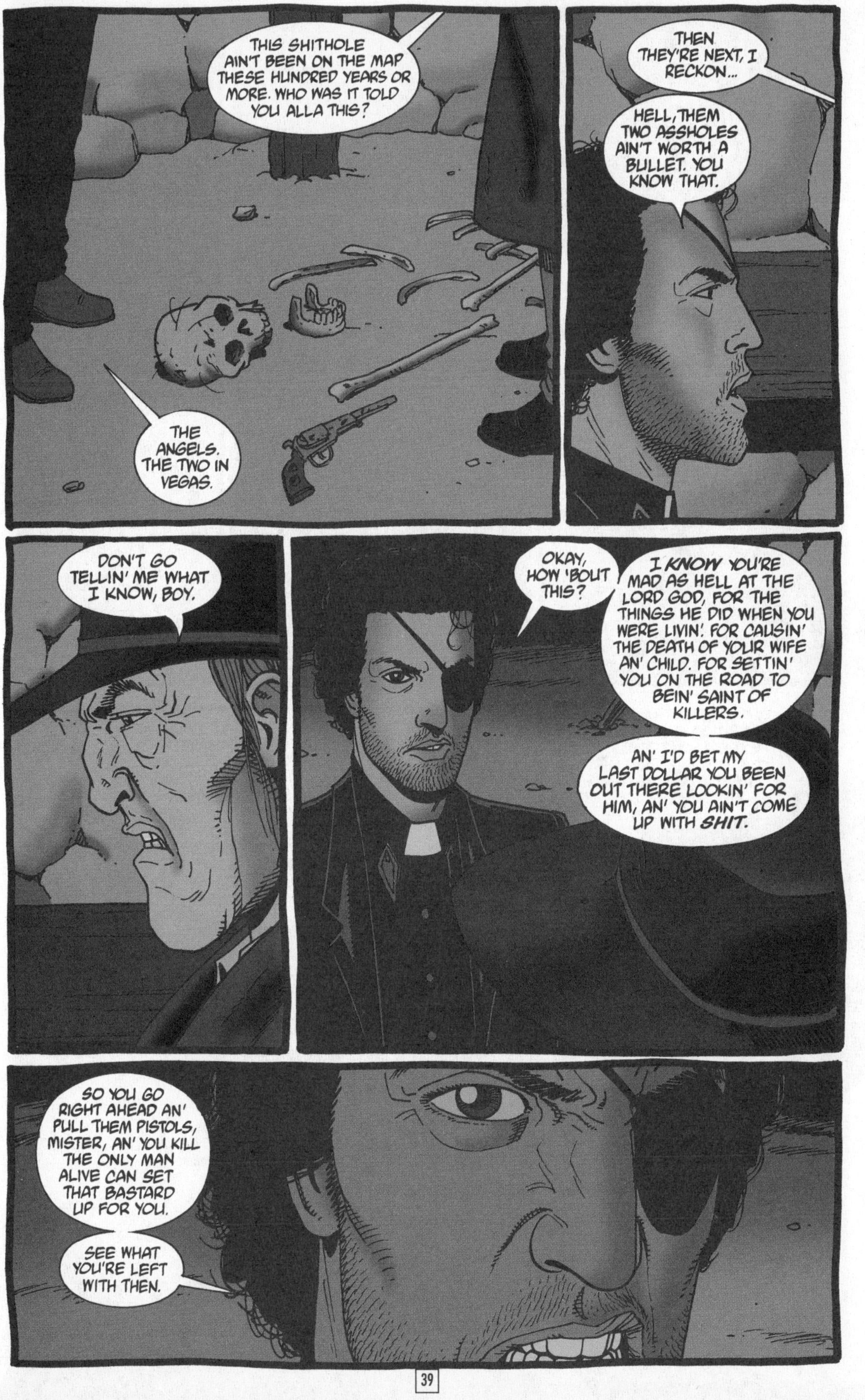
THIS SHITHOLE AIN'T BEEN ON THE MAP THESE HUNDRED YEARS OR MORE. WHO WAS IT TOLD YOU ALLA THIS?
THE ANGELS. THE TWO IN VEGAS.
THEN THEY'RE NEXT, I RECKON...
HELL, THEM TWO ASSHOLES AIN'T WORTH A BULLET. YOU KNOW THAT.
DON'T GO TELLIN' ME WHAT I KNOW, BOY.
OKAY, HOW 'BOUT THIS?
I KNOW YOU'RE MAD AS HELL AT THE LORD GOD, FOR THE THINGS HE DID WHEN YOU WERE LIVIN'. FOR CAUSIN' THE DEATH OF YOUR WIFE AN' CHILD. FOR SETTIN' YOU ON THE ROAD TO BEIN' SAINT OF KILLERS.
AN' I'D BET MY LAST DOLLAR YOU BEEN OUT THERE LOOKIN' FOR HIM, AN' YOU AIN'T COME UP WITH SHIT.
SO YOU GO RIGHT AHEAD AN' PULL THEM PISTOLS, MISTER, AN' YOU KILL THE ONLY MAN ALIVE CAN SET THAT BASTARD UP FOR YOU.
SEE WHAT YOU'RE LEFT WITH THEN.

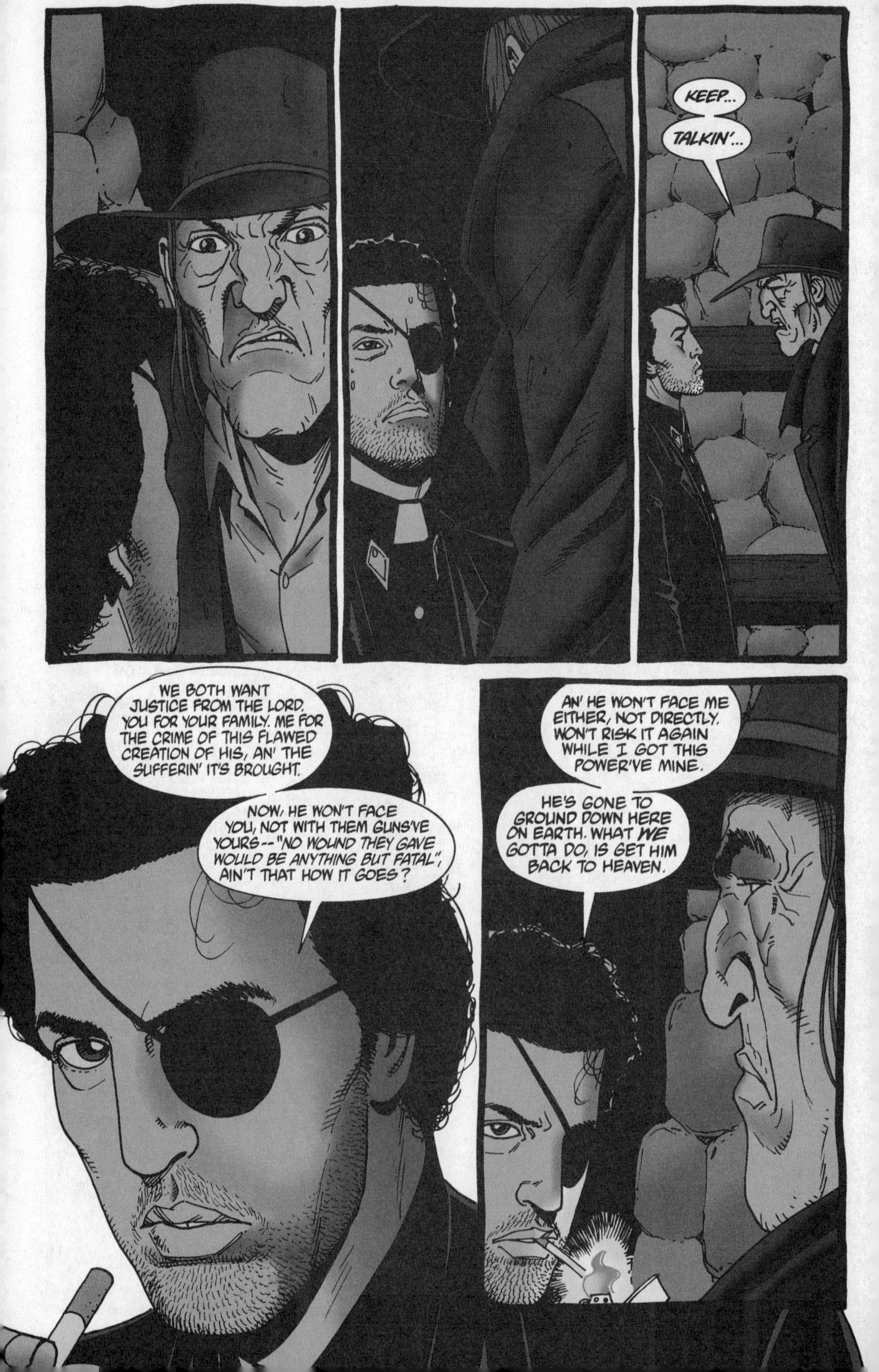
KEEP...
TALKIN'...
WE BOTH WANT JUSTICE FROM THE LORD. YOU FOR YOUR FAMILY. ME FOR THE CRIME OF THIS FLAWED CREATION OF HIS, AN' THE SUFFERIN' IT'S BROUGHT.
NOW, HE WON'T FACE YOU, NOT WITH THEM GUNS'VE YOURS--"NO WOUND THEY GAVE WOULD BE ANYTHING BUT FATAL", AIN'T THAT HOW IT GOES?
AN' HE WON'T FACE ME EITHER, NOT DIRECTLY. WON'T RISK IT AGAIN WHILE I GOT THIS POWER'VE MINE.
HE'S GONE TO GROUND DOWN HERE ON EARTH. WHAT WE GOTTA DO, IS GET HIM BACK TO HEAVEN.

HE WON'T BREAK COVER TO GET BACK THERE. NOT WHILE HE KNOWS I'M WATCHIN' OUT FOR HIM. I'D SEE HIM THE SECOND HE MADE HIS MOVE.

HOW YOU FIGURE THAT?

GENESIS. PART DEMON, PART ANGEL. A POWER LIKE THE ALMIGHTY GETS *NEAR* THE PEARLY GATES, THIS DAMN SPOOK'LL KNOW.

AN' SO WILL I.

BUT SAY GENESIS WAS GONE, AN' HE FELT SAFE ENOUGH TO TRY A RUN FOR HOME...

WON'T WORK.

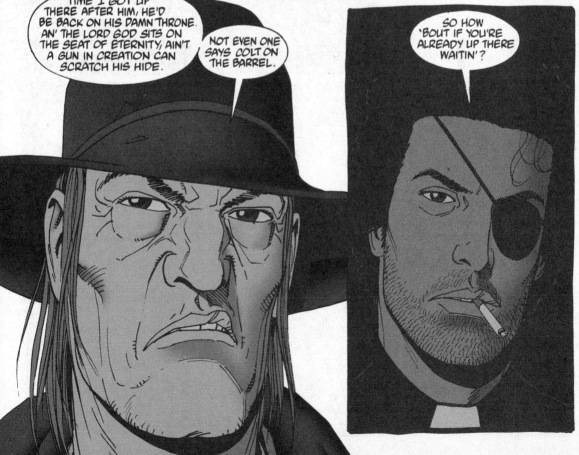

TIME I GOT UP THERE AFTER HIM, HE'D BE BACK ON HIS DAMN THRONE. AN' THE LORD GOD SITS ON THE SEAT OF ETERNITY, AIN'T A GUN IN CREATION CAN SCRATCH HIS HIDE.

NOT EVEN ONE SAYS COLT ON THE BARREL.

SO HOW 'BOUT IF YOU'RE ALREADY UP THERE WAITIN'?

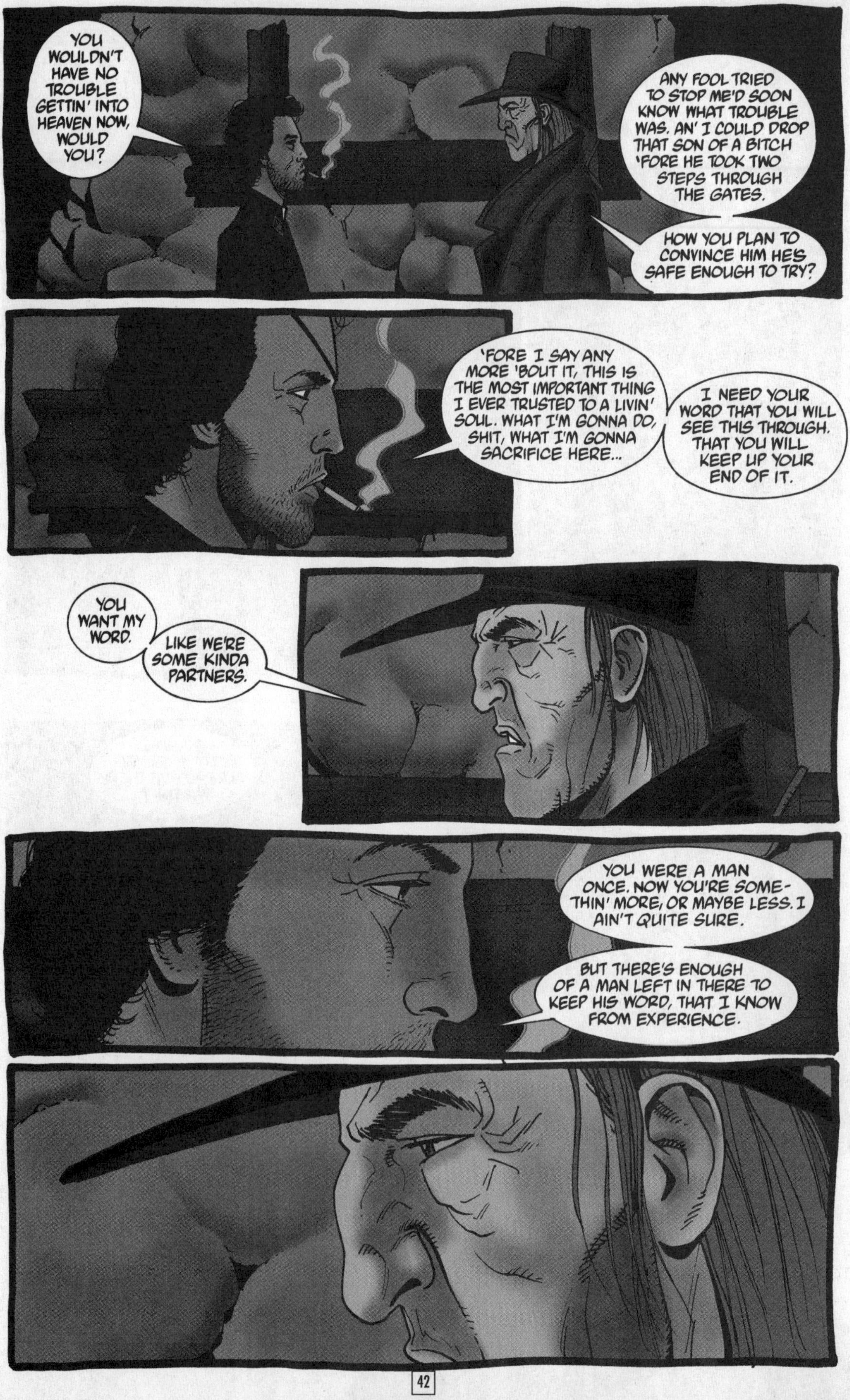
YOU WOULDN'T HAVE NO TROUBLE GETTIN' INTO HEAVEN NOW, WOULD YOU?
ANY FOOL TRIED TO STOP ME'D SOON KNOW WHAT TROUBLE WAS. AN' I COULD DROP THAT SON OF A BITCH 'FORE HE TOOK TWO STEPS THROUGH THE GATES.
HOW YOU PLAN TO CONVINCE HIM HE'S SAFE ENOUGH TO TRY?
'FORE I SAY ANY MORE 'BOUT IT, THIS IS THE MOST IMPORTANT THING I EVER TRUSTED TO A LIVIN' SOUL. WHAT I'M GONNA DO, SHIT, WHAT I'M GONNA SACRIFICE HERE...
I NEED YOUR WORD THAT YOU WILL SEE THIS THROUGH. THAT YOU WILL KEEP UP YOUR END OF IT.
YOU WANT MY WORD.
LIKE WE'RE SOME KINDA PARTNERS.
YOU WERE A MAN ONCE. NOW YOU'RE SOME-THIN' MORE, OR MAYBE LESS. I AIN'T QUITE SURE.
BUT THERE'S ENOUGH OF A MAN LEFT IN THERE TO KEEP HIS WORD, THAT I KNOW FROM EXPERIENCE.

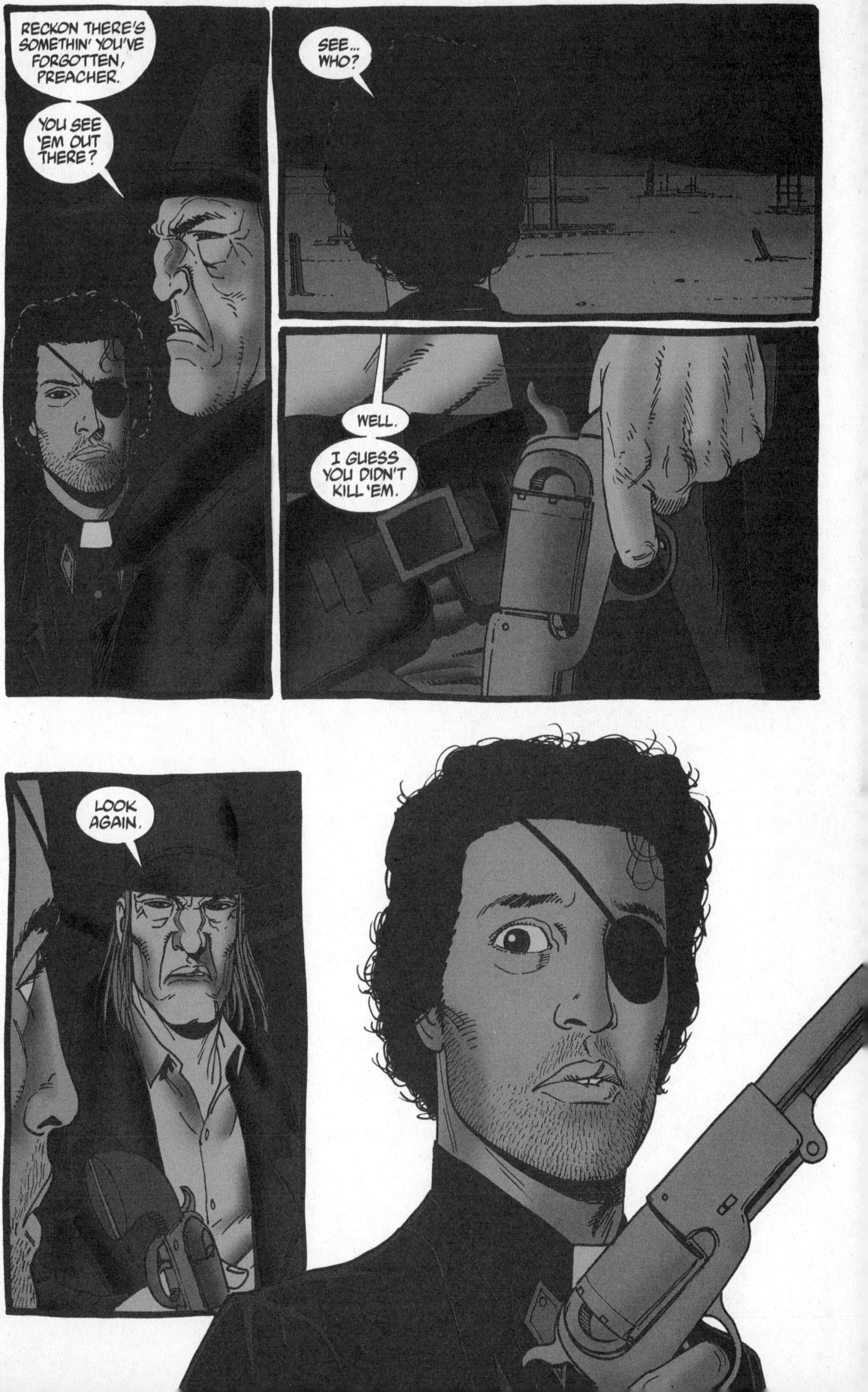

RECKON THERE'S SOMETHIN' YOU'VE FORGOTTEN, PREACHER.
YOU SEE 'EM OUT THERE?
SEE... WHO?
WELL.
I GUESS YOU DIDN'T KILL 'EM.
LOOK AGAIN.

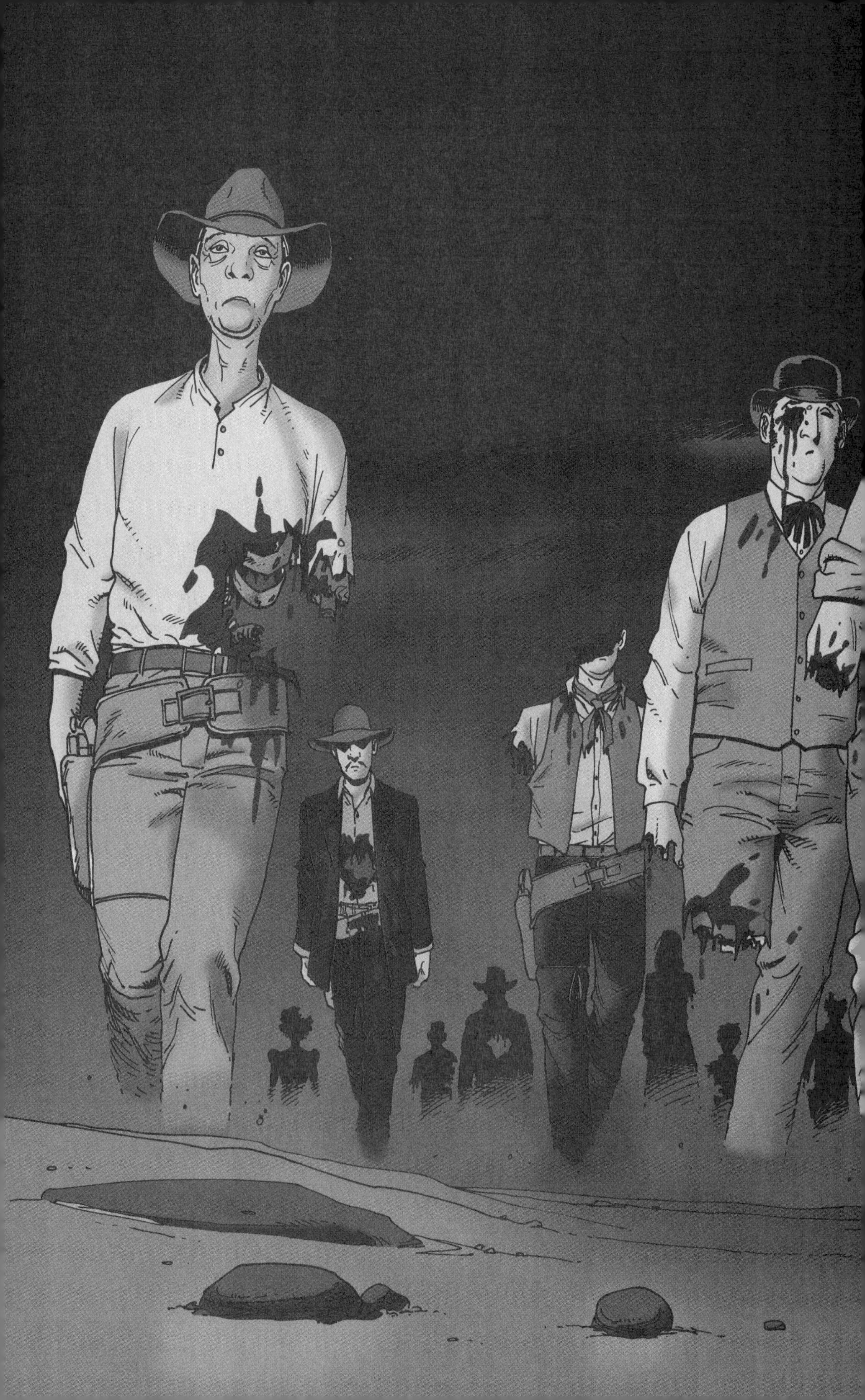

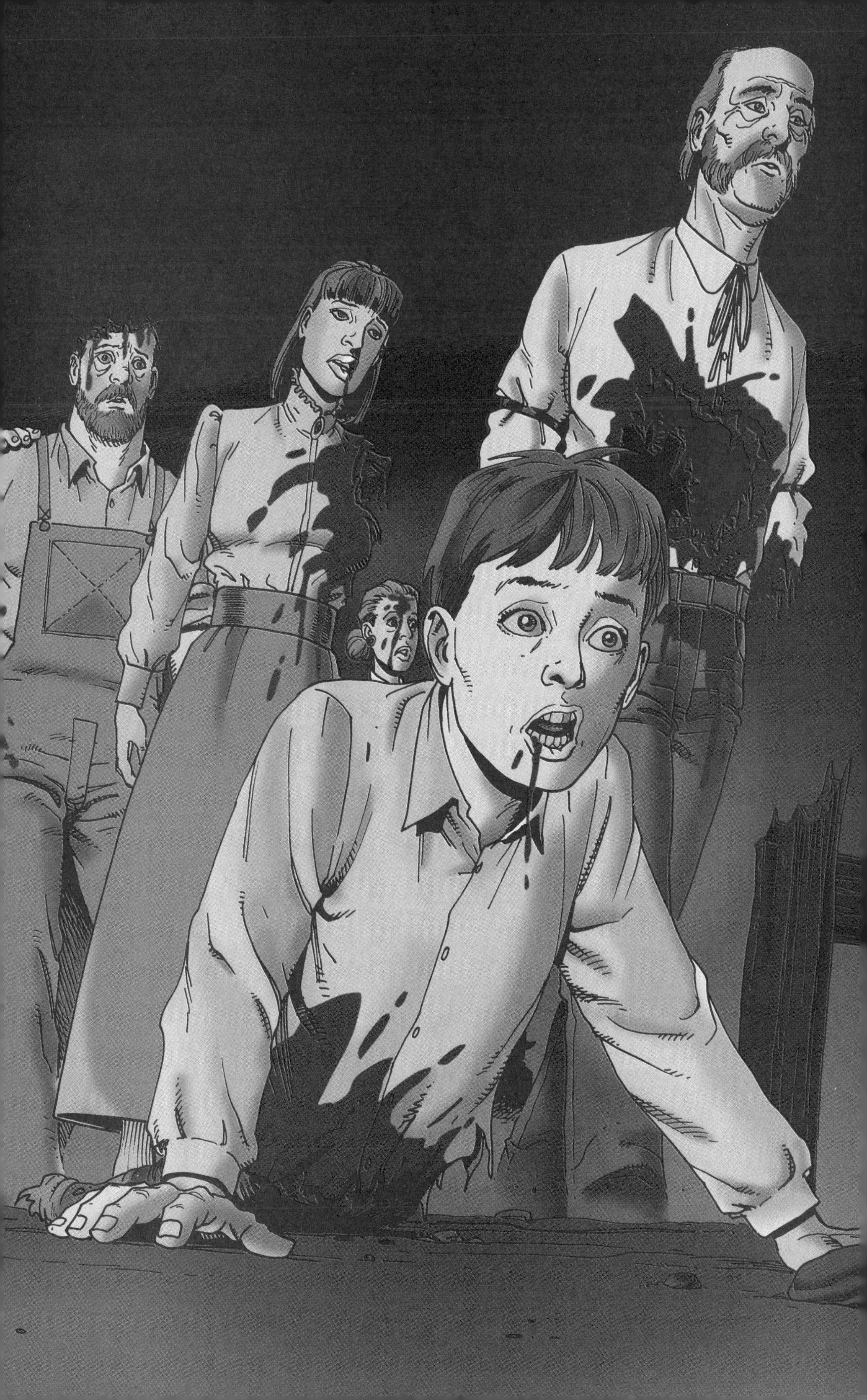

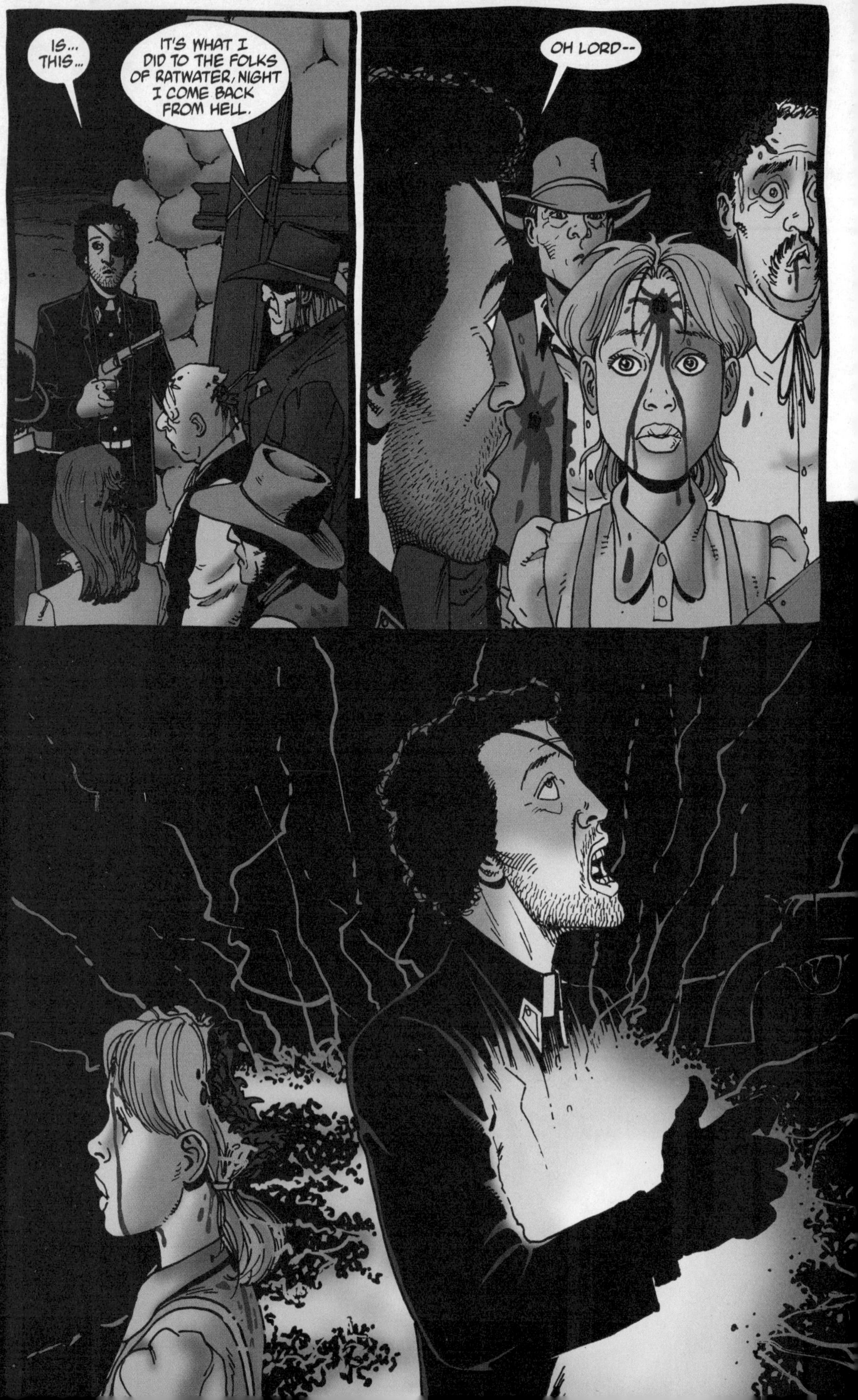
IS... THIS...
IT'S WHAT I DID TO THE FOLKS OF RATWATER, NIGHT I COME BACK FROM HELL.
OH LORD--

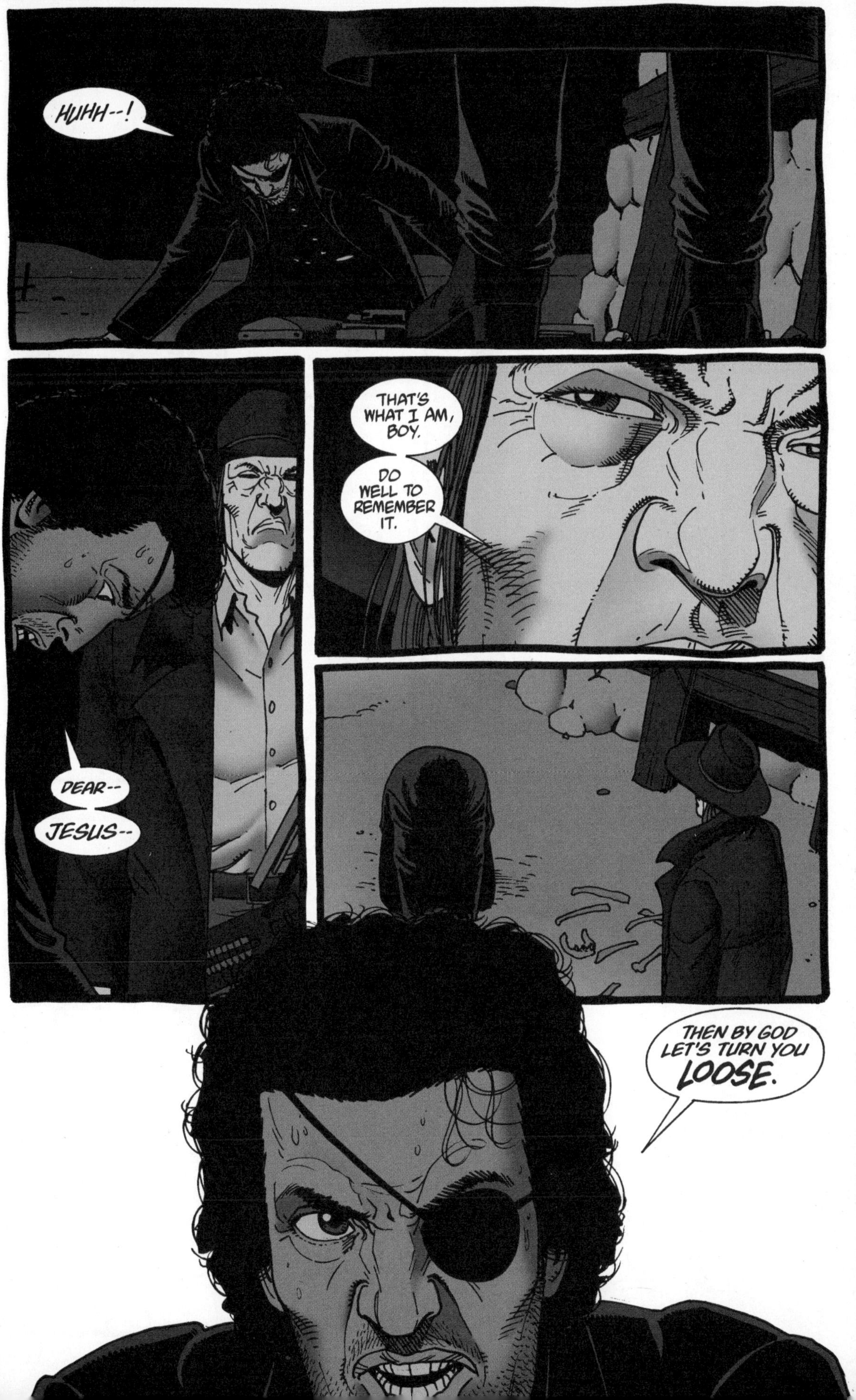
HUHH--!
DEAR--
JESUS--
THAT'S WHAT I AM, BOY.
DO WELL TO REMEMBER IT.
THEN BY GOD LET'S TURN YOU LOOSE.

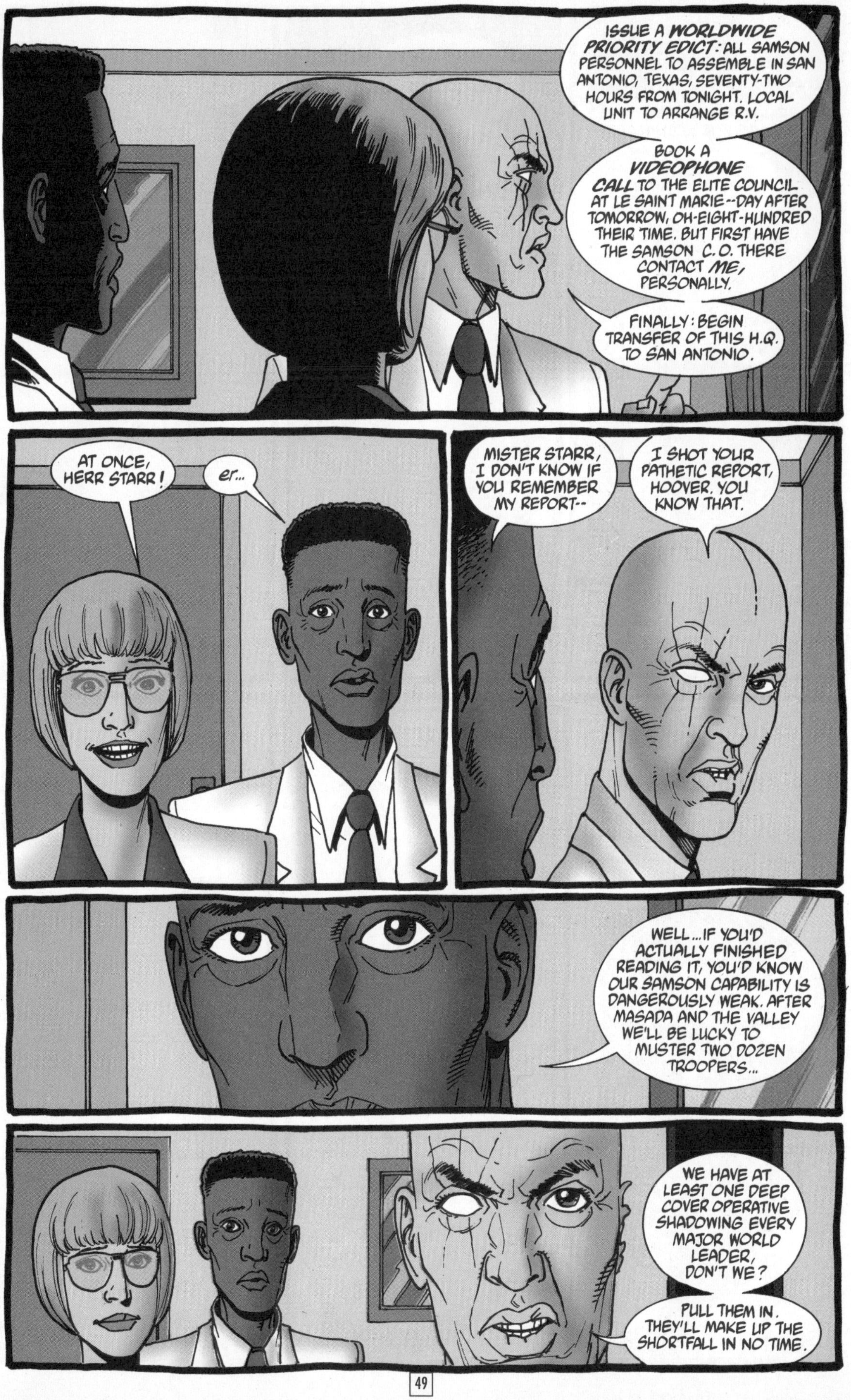
ISSUE A WORLDWIDE PRIORITY EDICT: ALL SAMSON PERSONNEL TO ASSEMBLE IN SAN ANTONIO, TEXAS, SEVENTY-TWO HOURS FROM TONIGHT. LOCAL UNIT TO ARRANGE R.V.
BOOK A VIDEOPHONE CALL TO THE ELITE COUNCIL AT LE SAINT MARIE--DAY AFTER TOMORROW, OH-EIGHT-HUNDRED THEIR TIME. BUT FIRST HAVE THE SAMSON C.O. THERE CONTACT ME, PERSONALLY.
FINALLY: BEGIN TRANSFER OF THIS H.Q. TO SAN ANTONIO.
AT ONCE, HERR STARR!
er...
MISTER STARR, I DON'T KNOW IF YOU REMEMBER MY REPORT--
I SHOT YOUR PATHETIC REPORT, HOOVER. YOU KNOW THAT.
WELL...IF YOU'D ACTUALLY FINISHED READING IT, YOU'D KNOW OUR SAMSON CAPABILITY IS DANGEROUSLY WEAK. AFTER MASADA AND THE VALLEY WE'LL BE LUCKY TO MUSTER TWO DOZEN TROOPERS...
WE HAVE AT LEAST ONE DEEP COVER OPERATIVE SHADOWING EVERY MAJOR WORLD LEADER, DON'T WE?
PULL THEM IN. THEY'LL MAKE UP THE SHORTFALL IN NO TIME.

BUT THEY'VE SPENT YEARS, *DECADES*, GAINING THE CONFIDENCE OF THEIR TARGETS! IF WE BRING THEM IN NOW IT'LL ALL BE FOR NOTHING!

WHAT ABOUT THE PLAN? WHAT ABOUT ARMAGEDDON?

WHAT ABOUT *SHUTTING UP AND DOING AS YOU'RE TOLD?*

ARMAGEDDON CAN *WAIT*, HOOVER.

NOW GET TO IT.

DID YOU...HEAR THAT...?

YES.

THAT VOICE.

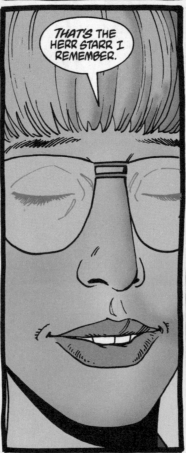

THAT'S THE HERR STARR I REMEMBER.

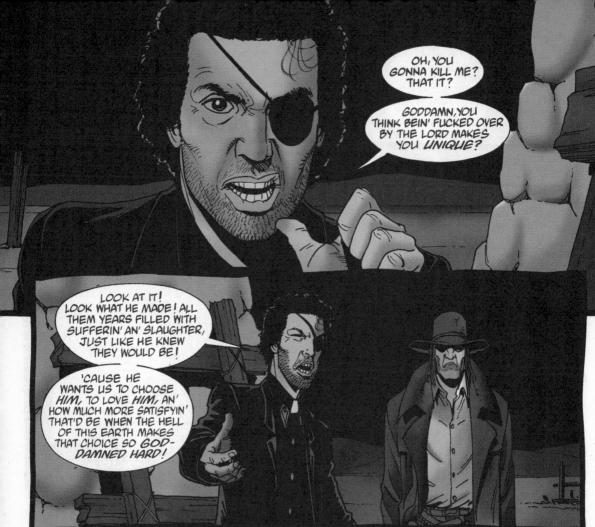

OH, YOU GONNA KILL ME? THAT IT?

GODDAMN, YOU THINK BEIN' FUCKED OVER BY THE LORD MAKES YOU *UNIQUE*?

LOOK AT IT! LOOK WHAT HE MADE! ALL THEM YEARS FILLED WITH SUFFERIN' AN' SLAUGHTER, JUST LIKE HE KNEW THEY WOULD BE!

'CAUSE HE WANTS US TO CHOOSE *HIM*, TO LOVE *HIM*, AN' HOW MUCH MORE SATISFYIN' THAT'D BE WHEN THE HELL OF THIS EARTH MAKES THAT CHOICE SO GOD-DAMNED HARD!

HE WANTS OUR LOVE. IT *FEEDS* HIM.

AN' HE CAME AFTER ME AN' GAVE ME ALL THEM CHANCES TO QUIT, HE TOOK THE RISK OF FACIN' GENESIS, AN' ALL FOR THAT EXACT SAME REASON.

HE WANTS THE LOVE OF THE GREATEST THREAT TO HIS POWER THAT EVER WAS.

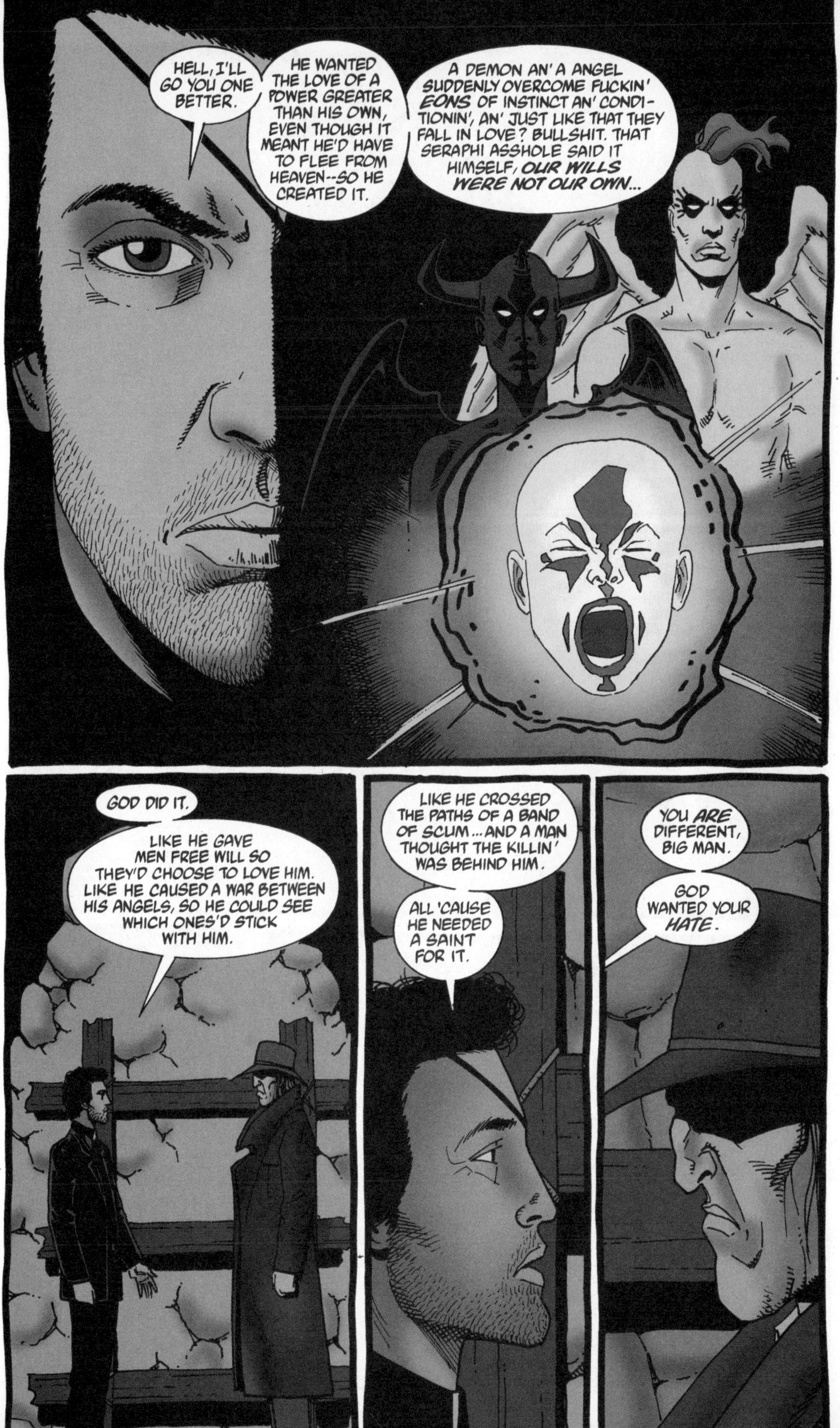
HELL, I'LL GO YOU ONE BETTER.
HE WANTED THE LOVE OF A POWER GREATER THAN HIS OWN, EVEN THOUGH IT MEANT HE'D HAVE TO FLEE FROM HEAVEN--SO HE CREATED IT.
A DEMON AN' A ANGEL SUDDENLY OVERCOME FUCKIN' EONS OF INSTINCT AN' CONDITIONIN', AN' JUST LIKE THAT THEY FALL IN LOVE? BULLSHIT. THAT SERAPHI ASSHOLE SAID IT HIMSELF, OUR WILLS WERE NOT OUR OWN...
GOD DID IT.
LIKE HE GAVE MEN FREE WILL SO THEY'D CHOOSE TO LOVE HIM. LIKE HE CAUSED A WAR BETWEEN HIS ANGELS, SO HE COULD SEE WHICH ONES'D STICK WITH HIM.
LIKE HE CROSSED THE PATHS OF A BAND OF SCUM... AND A MAN THOUGHT THE KILLIN' WAS BEHIND HIM.
ALL 'CAUSE HE NEEDED A SAINT FOR IT.
YOU ARE DIFFERENT, BIG MAN.
GOD WANTED YOUR HATE.

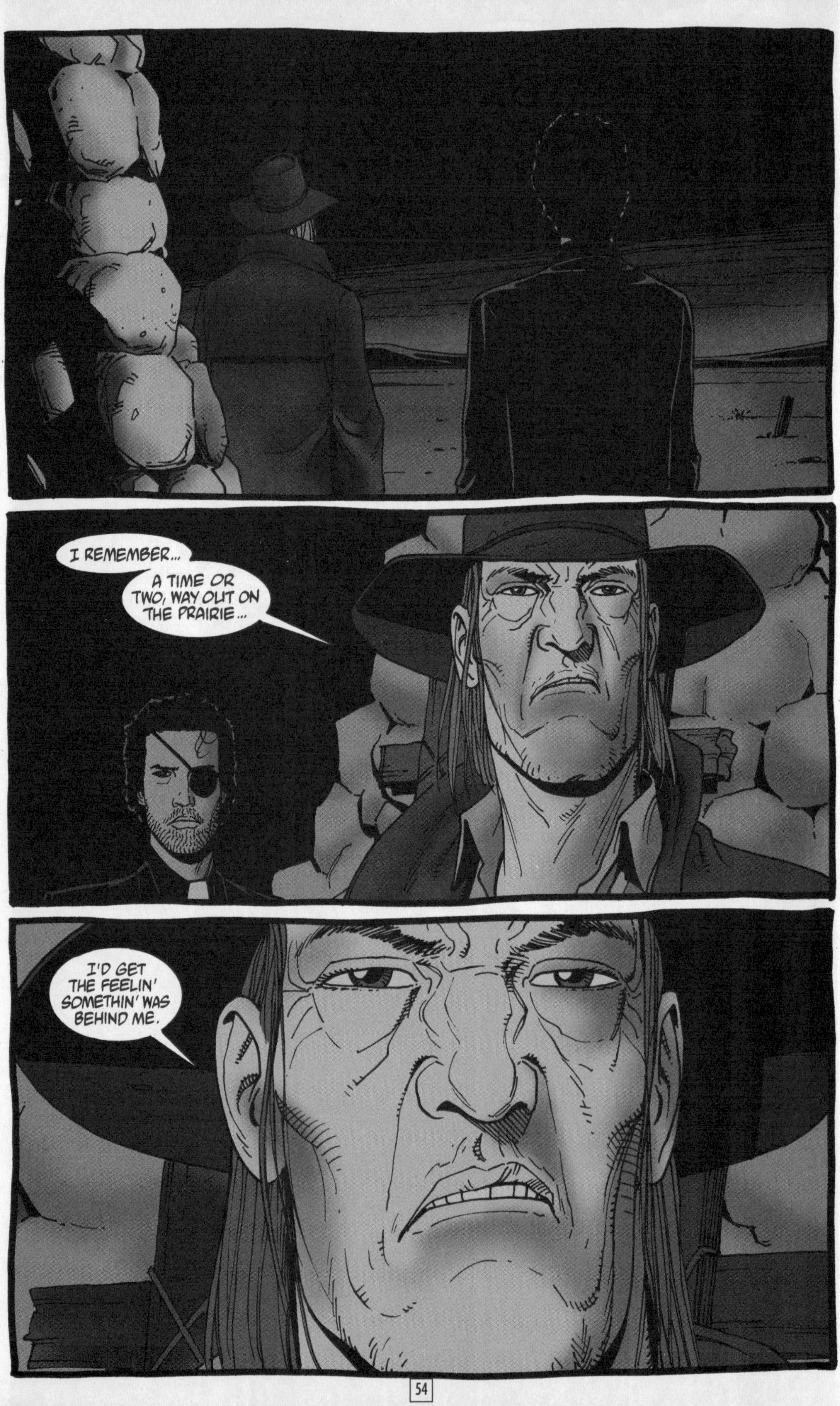
I REMEMBER...
A TIME OR TWO, WAY OUT ON THE PRAIRIE...
I'D GET THE FEELIN' SOMETHIN' WAS BEHIND ME.

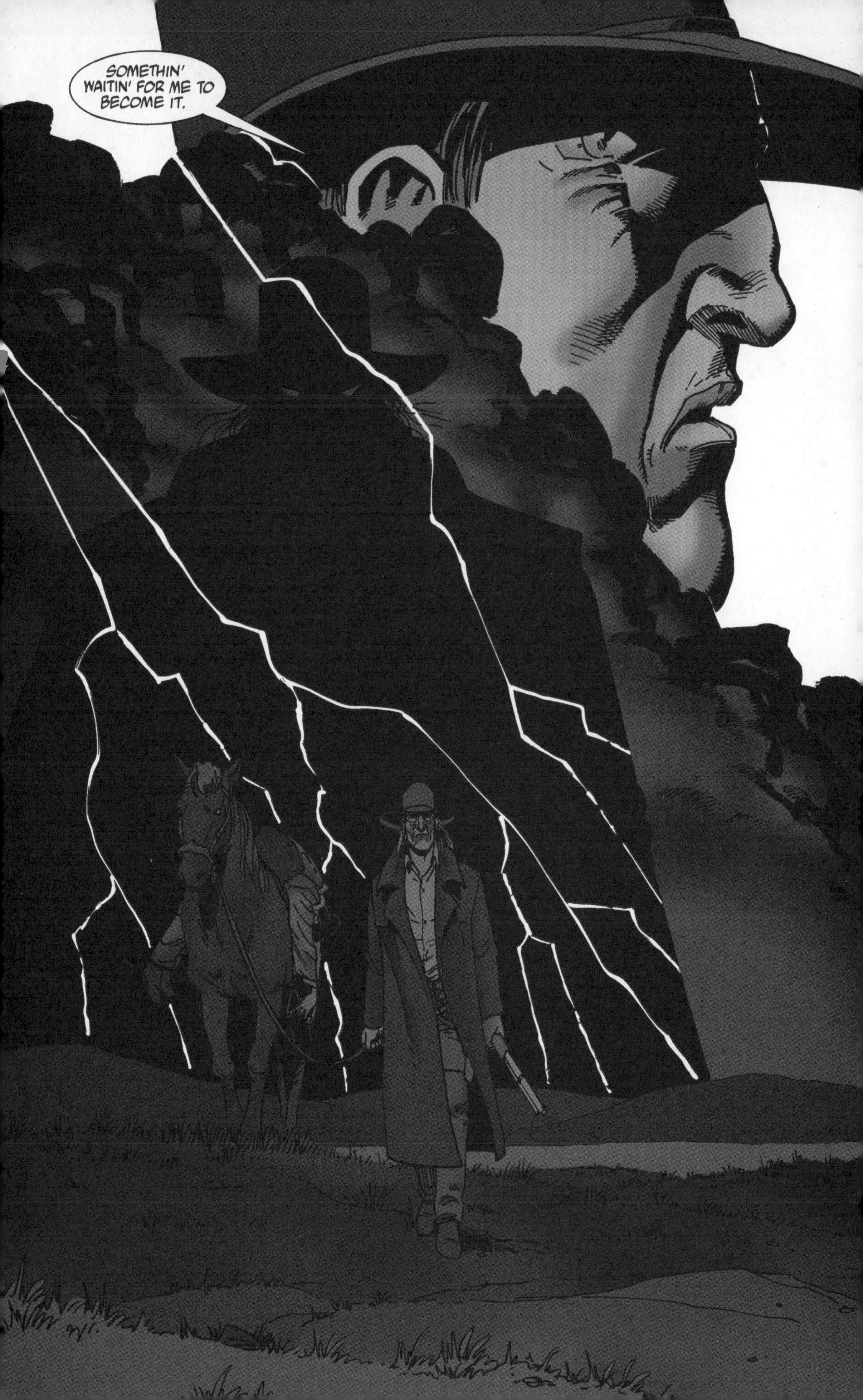
SOMETHIN' WAITIN' FOR ME TO BECOME IT.

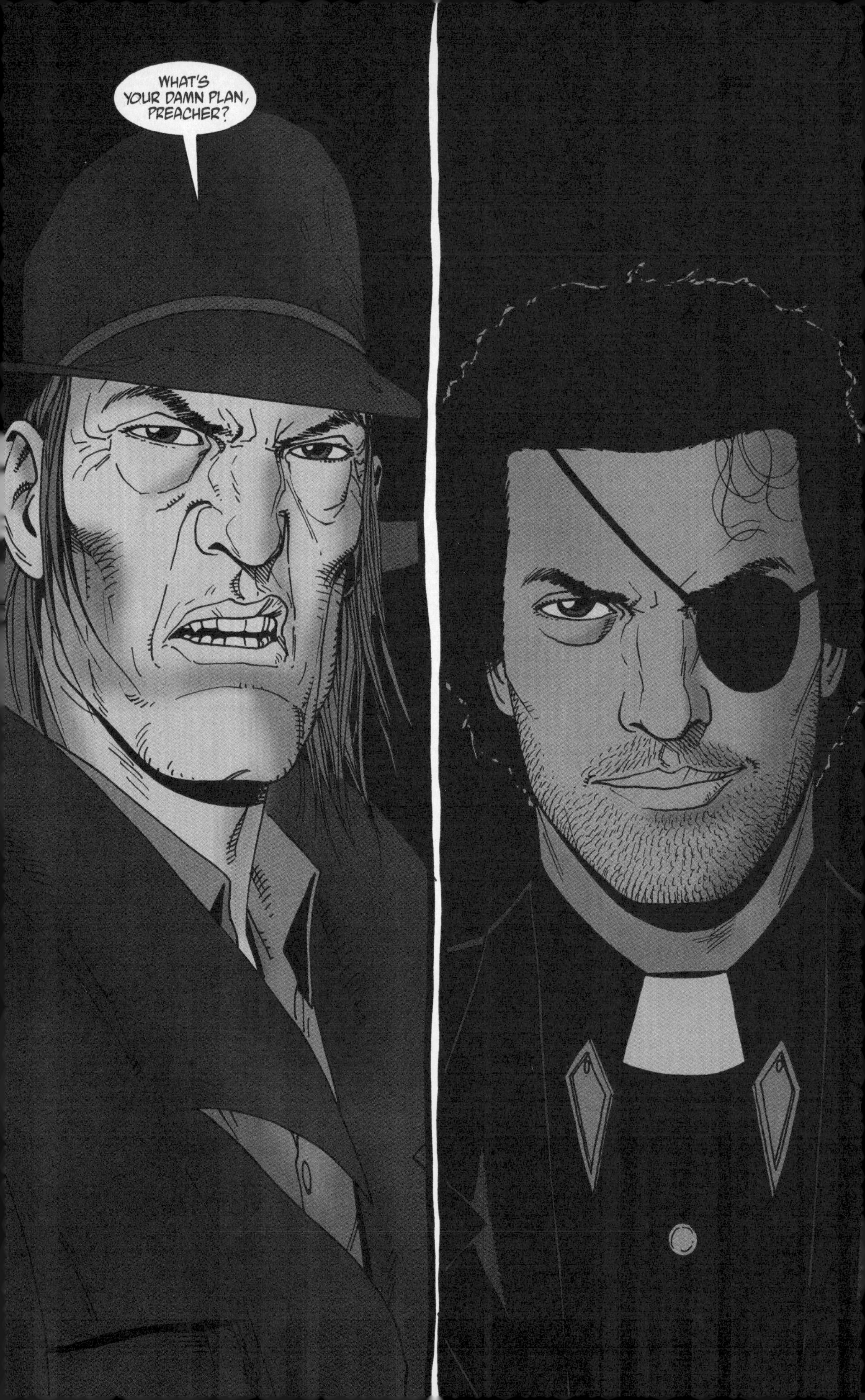
WHAT'S YOUR DAMN PLAN, PREACHER?

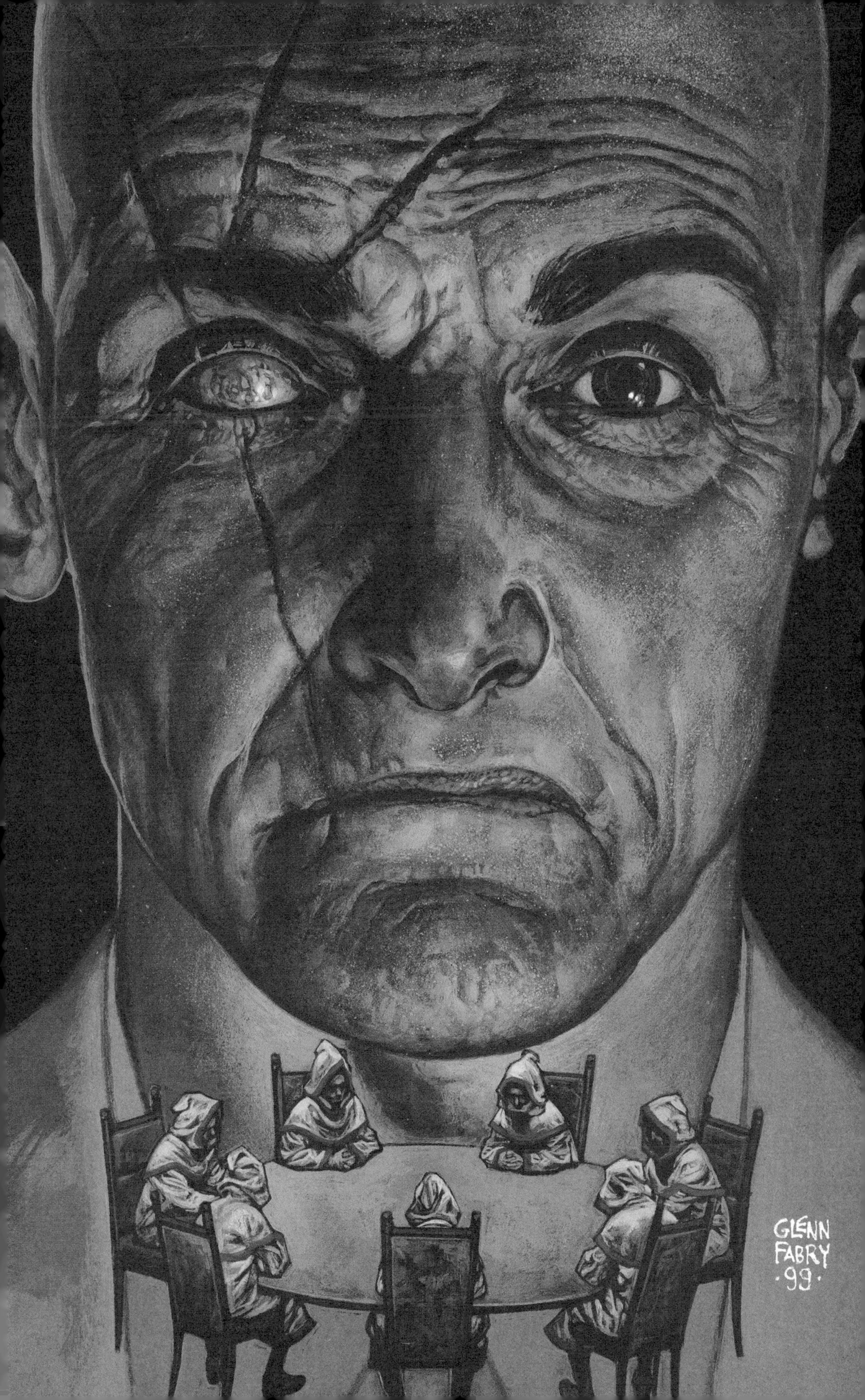
GLENN
FABRY
·99·

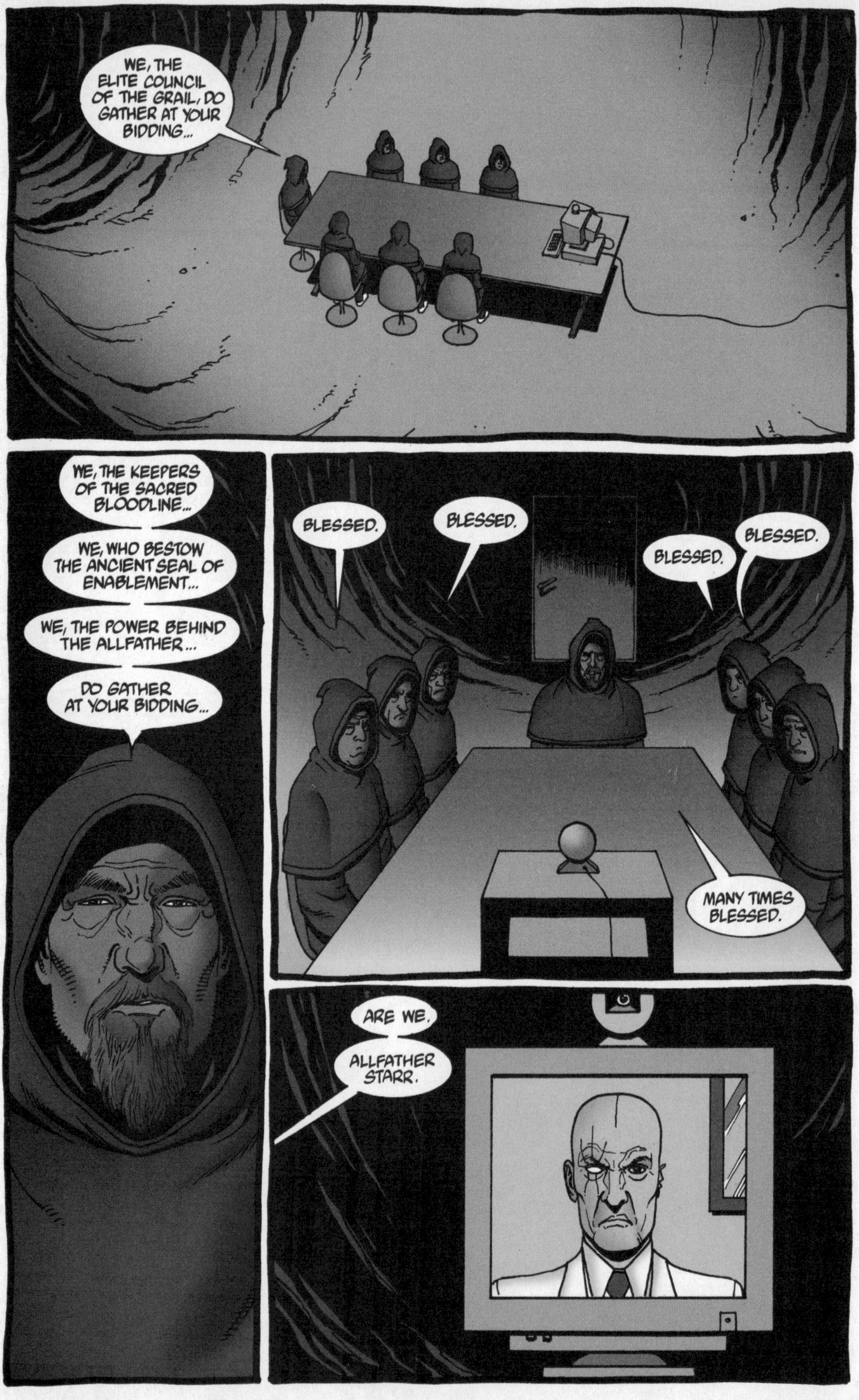
WE, THE ELITE COUNCIL OF THE GRAIL, DO GATHER AT YOUR BIDDING...
WE, THE KEEPERS OF THE SACRED BLOODLINE...
WE, WHO BESTOW THE ANCIENT SEAL OF ENABLEMENT...
WE, THE POWER BEHIND THE ALLFATHER...
DO GATHER AT YOUR BIDDING...
BLESSED.
BLESSED.
BLESSED.
BLESSED.
MANY TIMES BLESSED.
ARE WE.
ALLFATHER STARR.

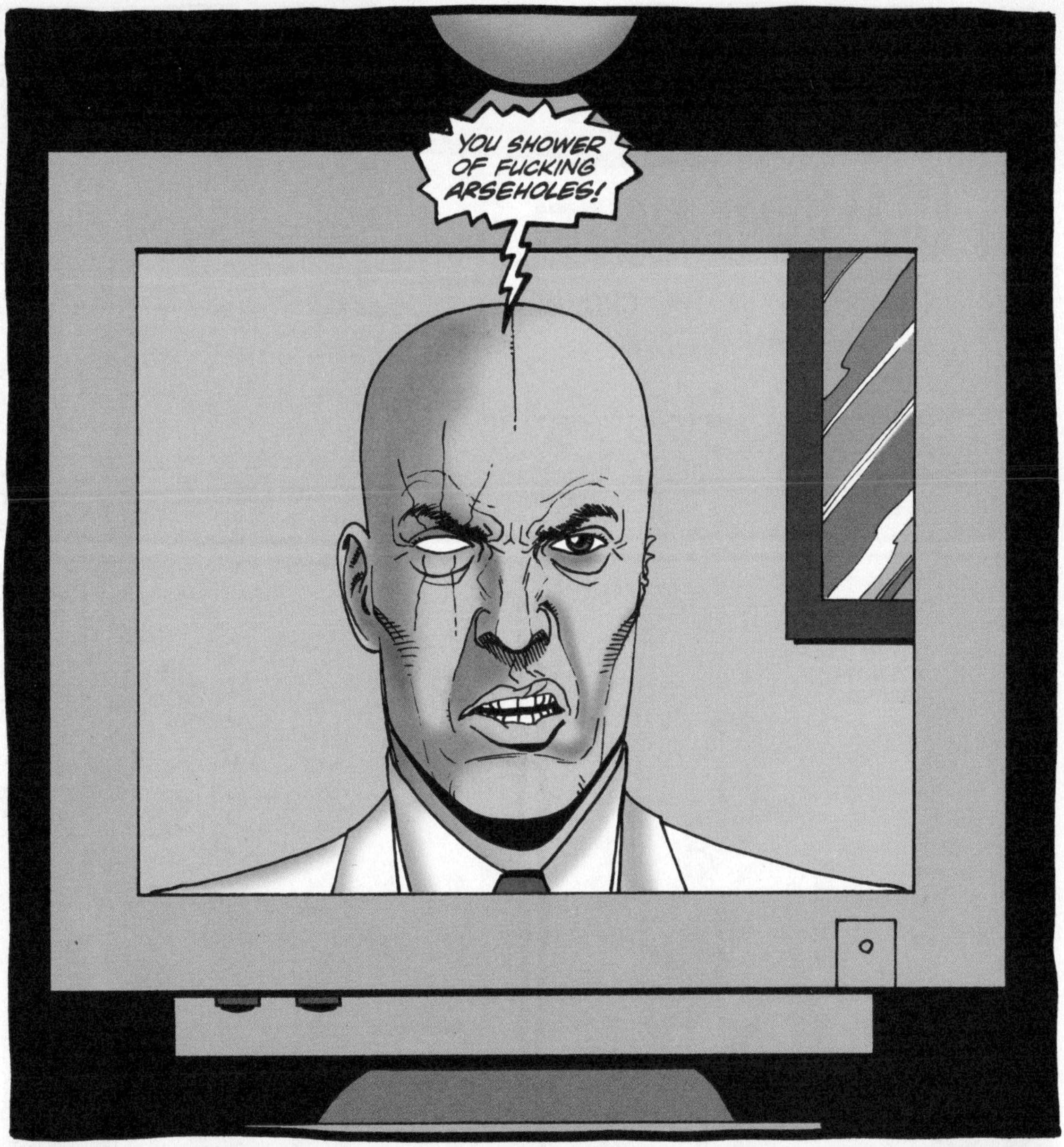
YOU SHOWER OF FUCKING ARSEHOLES!

THE WONDER OF YOU

GARTH ENNIS - Writer STEVE DILLON - Artist

PAMELA RAMBO - Colorist CLEM ROBINS - Letterer AXEL ALONSO - Editor

PREACHER created by GARTH ENNIS and STEVE DILLON

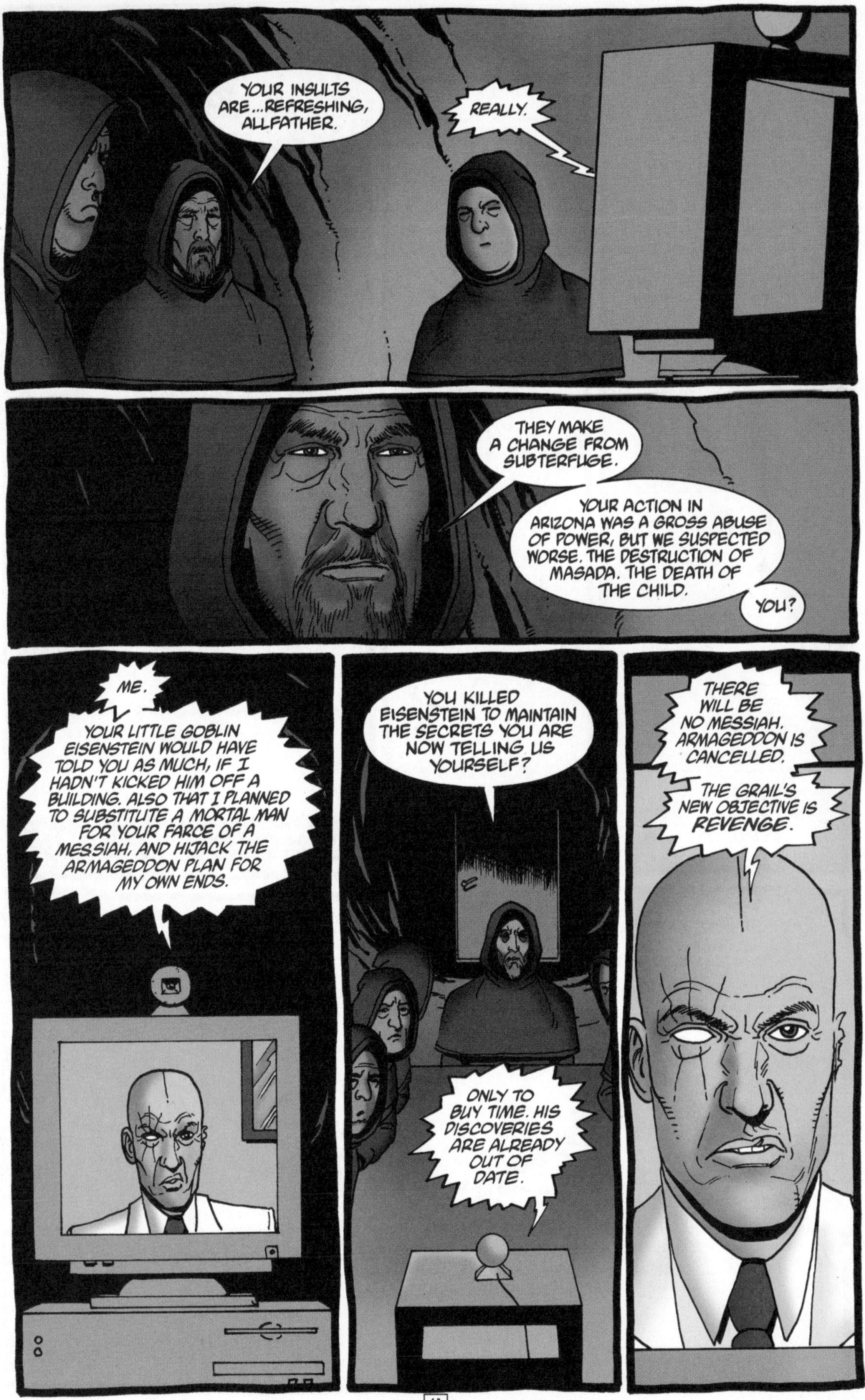
YOUR INSULTS ARE...REFRESHING, ALLFATHER.
REALLY.
THEY MAKE A CHANGE FROM SUBTERFUGE.
YOUR ACTION IN ARIZONA WAS A GROSS ABUSE OF POWER, BUT WE SUSPECTED WORSE. THE DESTRUCTION OF MASADA. THE DEATH OF THE CHILD.
YOU?
ME.
YOUR LITTLE GOBLIN EISENSTEIN WOULD HAVE TOLD YOU AS MUCH, IF I HADN'T KICKED HIM OFF A BUILDING. ALSO THAT I PLANNED TO SUBSTITUTE A MORTAL MAN FOR YOUR FARCE OF A MESSIAH, AND HIJACK THE ARMAGEDDON PLAN FOR MY OWN ENDS.
YOU KILLED EISENSTEIN TO MAINTAIN THE SECRETS YOU ARE NOW TELLING US YOURSELF?
ONLY TO BUY TIME. HIS DISCOVERIES ARE ALREADY OUT OF DATE.
THERE WILL BE NO MESSIAH. ARMAGEDDON IS CANCELLED.
THE GRAIL'S NEW OBJECTIVE IS REVENGE.

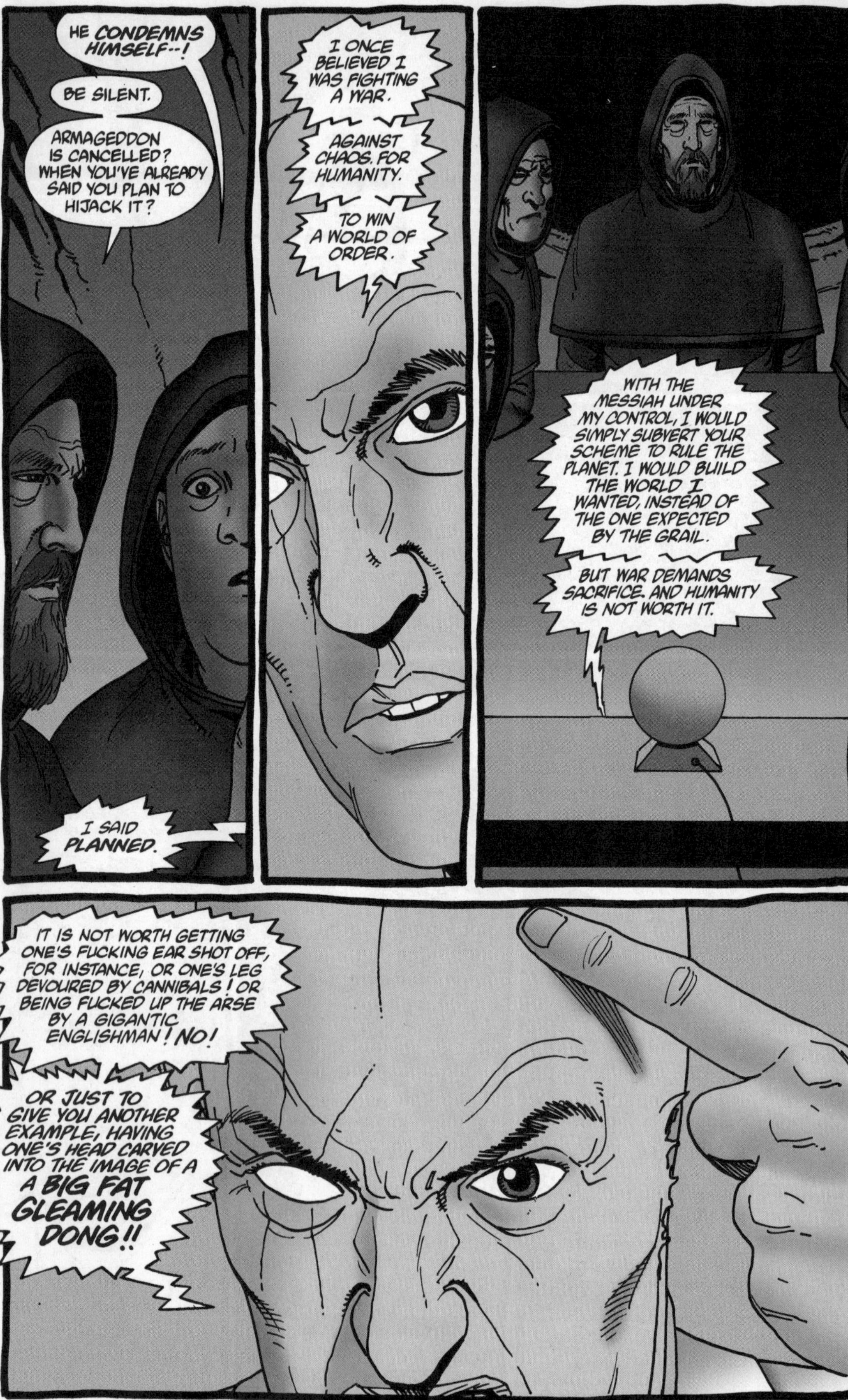
HE CONDEMNS HIMSELF--!
BE SILENT.
ARMAGEDDON IS CANCELLED? WHEN YOU'VE ALREADY SAID YOU PLAN TO HIJACK IT?
I SAID PLANNED.
I ONCE BELIEVED I WAS FIGHTING A WAR.
AGAINST CHAOS. FOR HUMANITY.
TO WIN A WORLD OF ORDER.
WITH THE MESSIAH UNDER MY CONTROL, I WOULD SIMPLY SUBVERT YOUR SCHEME TO RULE THE PLANET. I WOULD BUILD THE WORLD I WANTED, INSTEAD OF THE ONE EXPECTED BY THE GRAIL.
BUT WAR DEMANDS SACRIFICE. AND HUMANITY IS NOT WORTH IT.
IT IS NOT WORTH GETTING ONE'S FUCKING EAR SHOT OFF, FOR INSTANCE, OR ONE'S LEG DEVOURED BY CANNIBALS! OR BEING FUCKED UP THE ARSE BY A GIGANTIC ENGLISHMAN! NO!
OR JUST TO GIVE YOU ANOTHER EXAMPLE, HAVING ONE'S HEAD CARVED INTO THE IMAGE OF A A BIG FAT GLEAMING DONG!!

BUT ALL OF THAT PALES INTO INSIGNIFICANCE BESIDE *THIS* LITTLE ATROCITY! YES! LOOK AT IT! LOOK AT MY *GREATEST* SACRIFICE!

GAZE ON THE FACE OF WAR!!

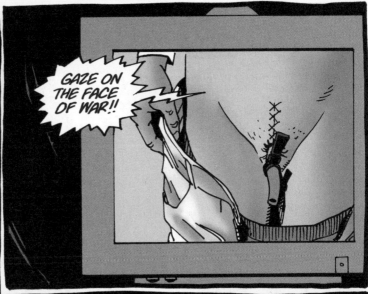

SO FUCK HUMANITY. FUCK ARMAGEDDON. FUCK THE GRAIL. AND FUCK YOU.

ALL THAT MATTERS NOW IS ONE SINGLE MAN...

JESSE CUSTER.

A NAME THAT LIVES IN INFAMY. THAT SET ME DOWN THE ROAD TO THE RUIN YOU SEE BEFORE YOU. THAT *BURNS* IN MY BRAIN.

THE RESOURCES AND MATERIEL YOU WOULD HAVE PISSED AWAY WILL BRING ABOUT HIS DOOM.

STARR...

YOU ARE THE ONE WHO IS DOOMED.

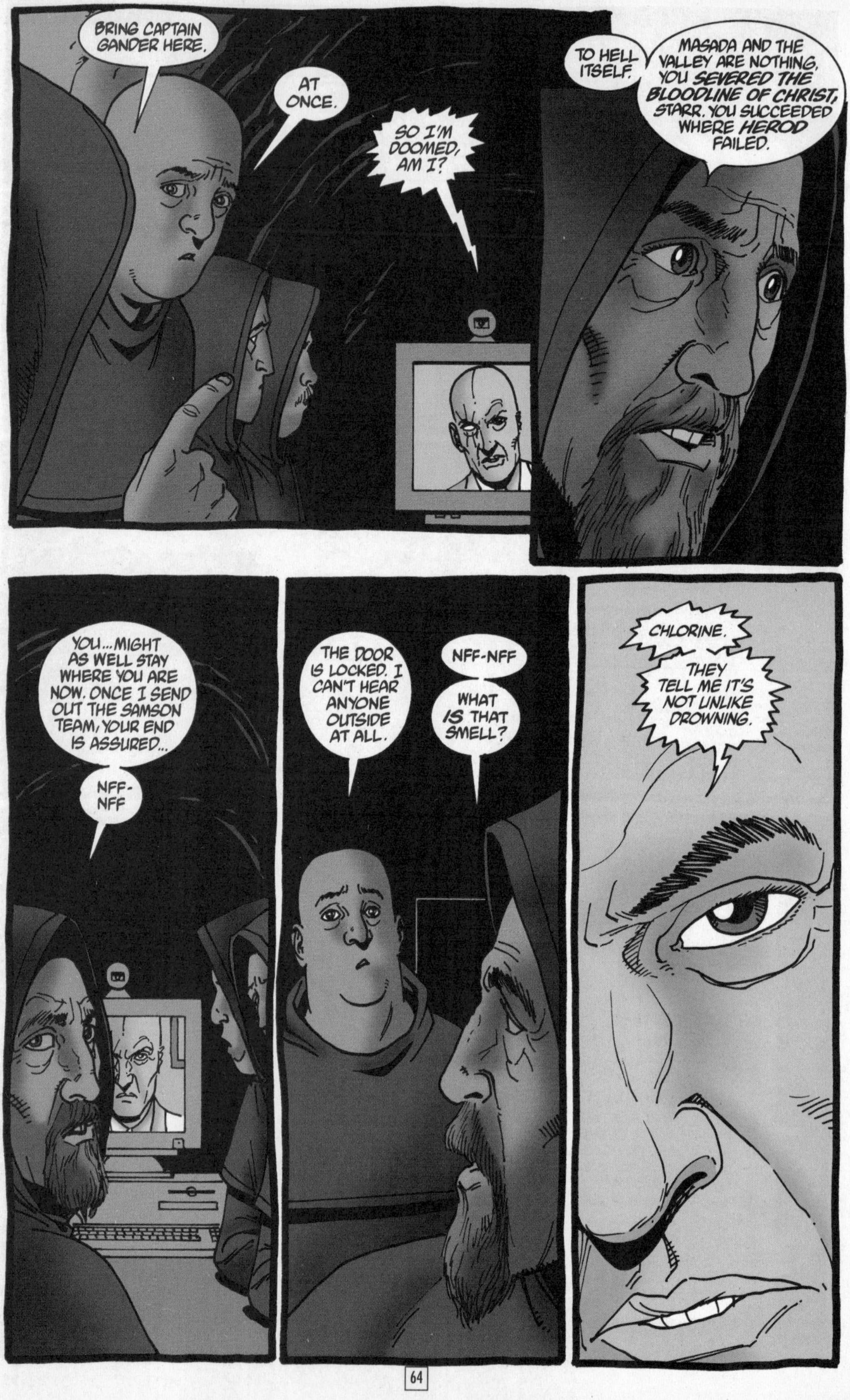

BRING CAPTAIN GANDER HERE.
AT ONCE.
SO I'M DOOMED, AM I?
TO HELL ITSELF.
MASADA AND THE VALLEY ARE NOTHING. YOU SEVERED THE BLOODLINE OF CHRIST, STARR. YOU SUCCEEDED WHERE HEROD FAILED.
YOU...MIGHT AS WELL STAY WHERE YOU ARE NOW. ONCE I SEND OUT THE SAMSON TEAM, YOUR END IS ASSURED...
NFF-NFF
THE DOOR IS LOCKED. I CAN'T HEAR ANYONE OUTSIDE AT ALL.
NFF-NFF
WHAT IS THAT SMELL?
CHLORINE.
THEY TELL ME IT'S NOT UNLIKE DROWNING.

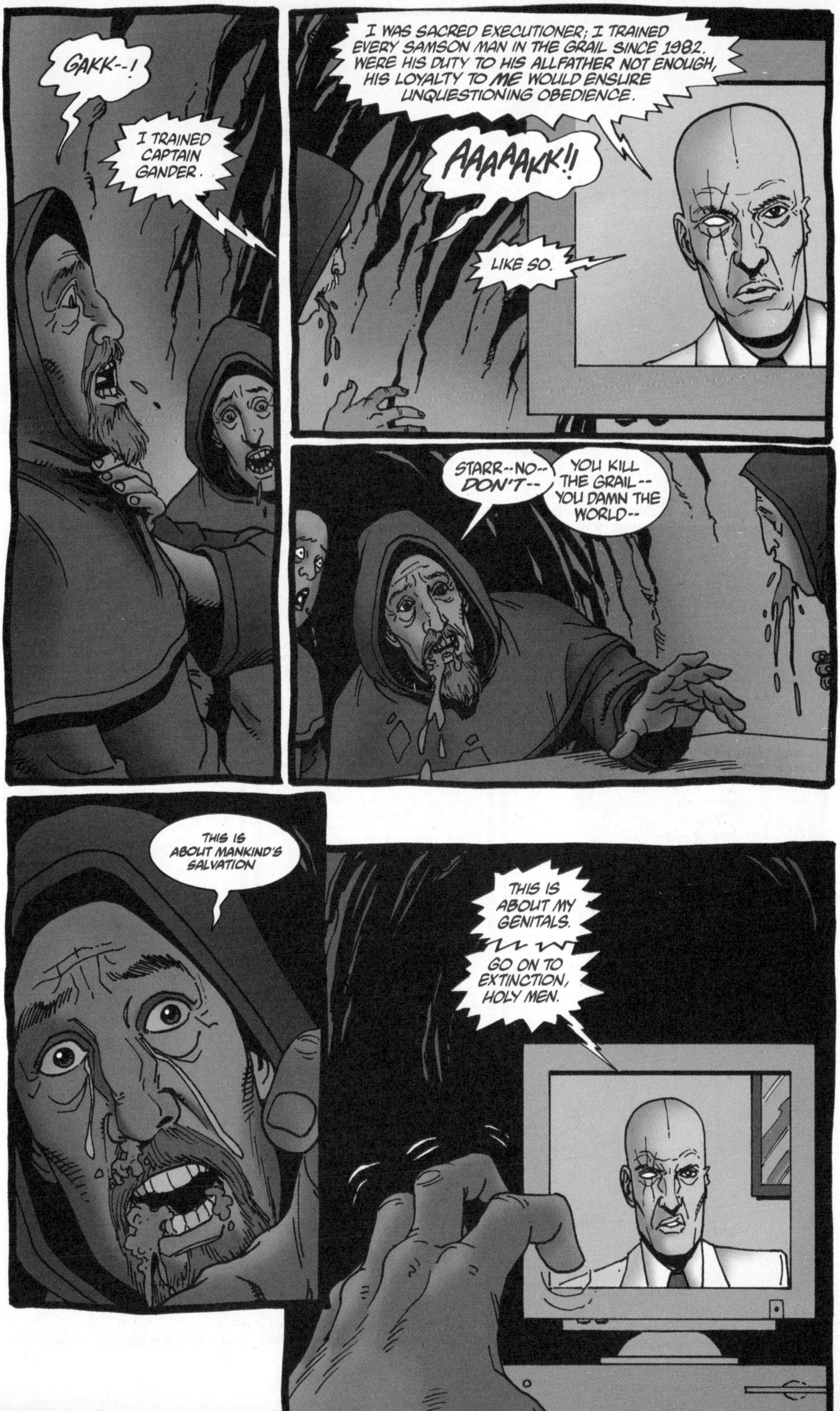
GAKK--!
I TRAINED CAPTAIN GANDER.
I WAS SACRED EXECUTIONER; I TRAINED EVERY SAMSON MAN IN THE GRAIL SINCE 1982. WERE HIS DUTY TO HIS ALLFATHER NOT ENOUGH, HIS LOYALTY TO *ME* WOULD ENSURE UNQUESTIONING OBEDIENCE.
AAAAAKK!!
LIKE SO.
STARR--NO-- *DON'T*--
YOU KILL THE GRAIL-- YOU DAMN THE WORLD--
THIS IS ABOUT MANKIND'S SALVATION
THIS IS ABOUT MY GENITALS.
GO ON TO EXTINCTION, HOLY MEN.

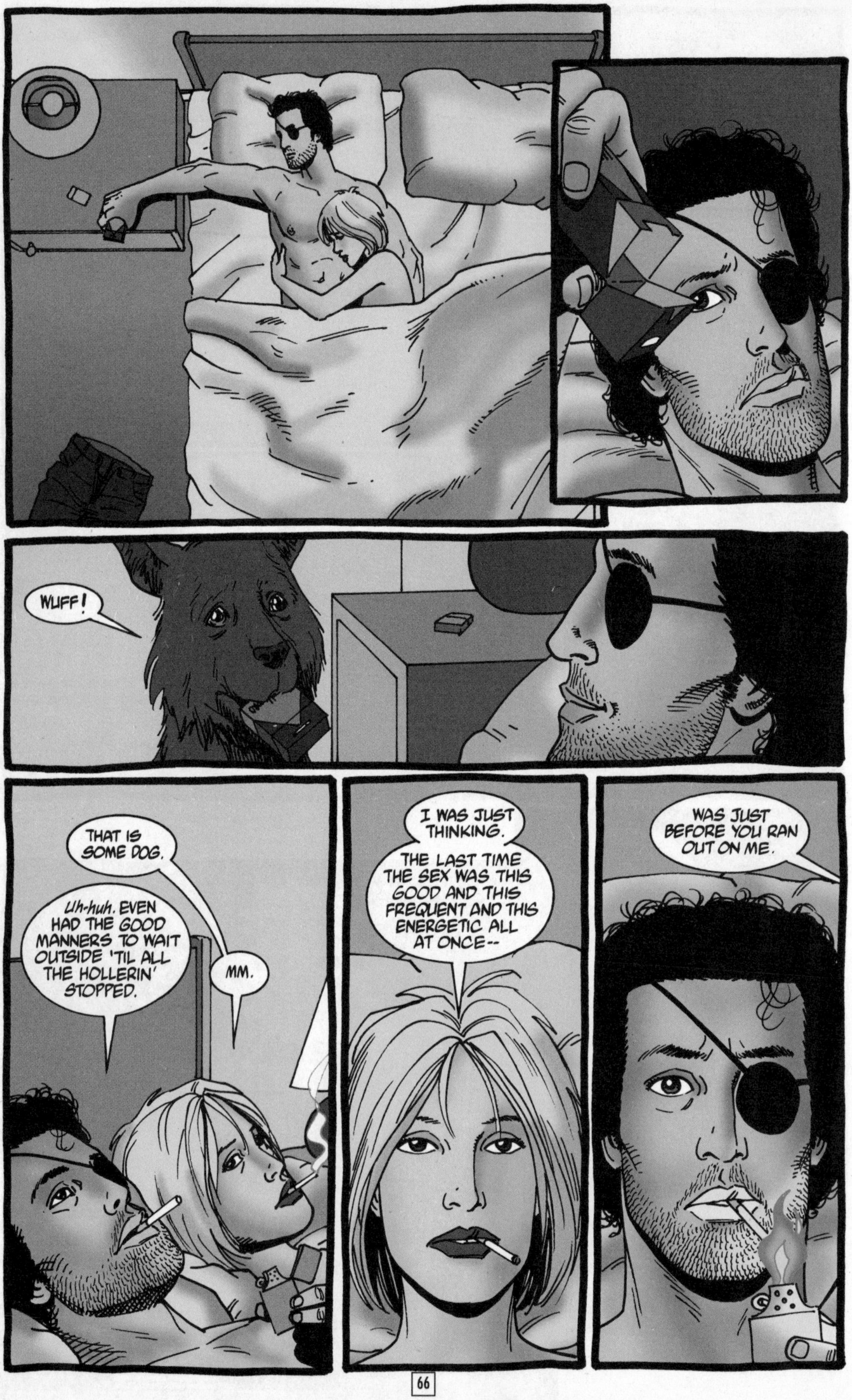
WUFF!
THAT IS SOME DOG.
Uh-huh. EVEN HAD THE GOOD MANNERS TO WAIT OUTSIDE 'TIL ALL THE HOLLERIN' STOPPED.
MM.
I WAS JUST THINKING.
THE LAST TIME THE SEX WAS THIS GOOD AND THIS FREQUENT AND THIS ENERGETIC ALL AT ONCE--
WAS JUST BEFORE YOU RAN OUT ON ME.

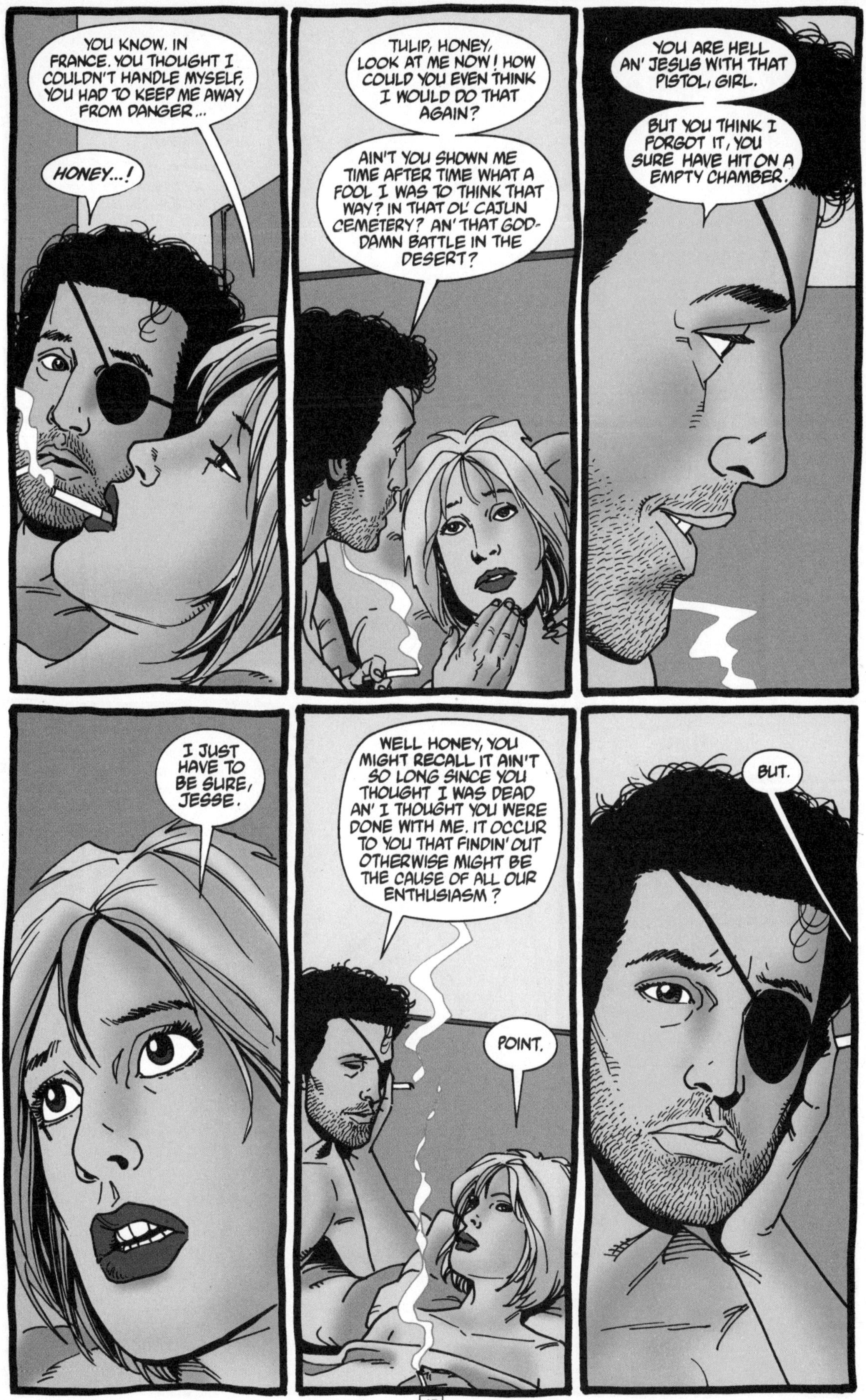
YOU KNOW. IN FRANCE. YOU THOUGHT I COULDN'T HANDLE MYSELF, YOU HAD TO KEEP ME AWAY FROM DANGER...
HONEY...!
TULIP, HONEY, LOOK AT ME NOW! HOW COULD YOU EVEN THINK I WOULD DO THAT AGAIN?
AIN'T YOU SHOWN ME TIME AFTER TIME WHAT A FOOL I WAS TO THINK THAT WAY? IN THAT OL' CAJUN CEMETERY? AN' THAT GOD-DAMN BATTLE IN THE DESERT?
YOU ARE HELL AN' JESUS WITH THAT PISTOL, GIRL.
BUT YOU THINK I FORGOT IT, YOU SURE HAVE HIT ON A EMPTY CHAMBER.
I JUST HAVE TO BE SURE, JESSE.
WELL HONEY, YOU MIGHT RECALL IT AIN'T SO LONG SINCE YOU THOUGHT I WAS DEAD AN' I THOUGHT YOU WERE DONE WITH ME. IT OCCUR TO YOU THAT FINDIN' OUT OTHERWISE MIGHT BE THE CAUSE OF ALL OUR ENTHUSIASM?
POINT.
BUT.

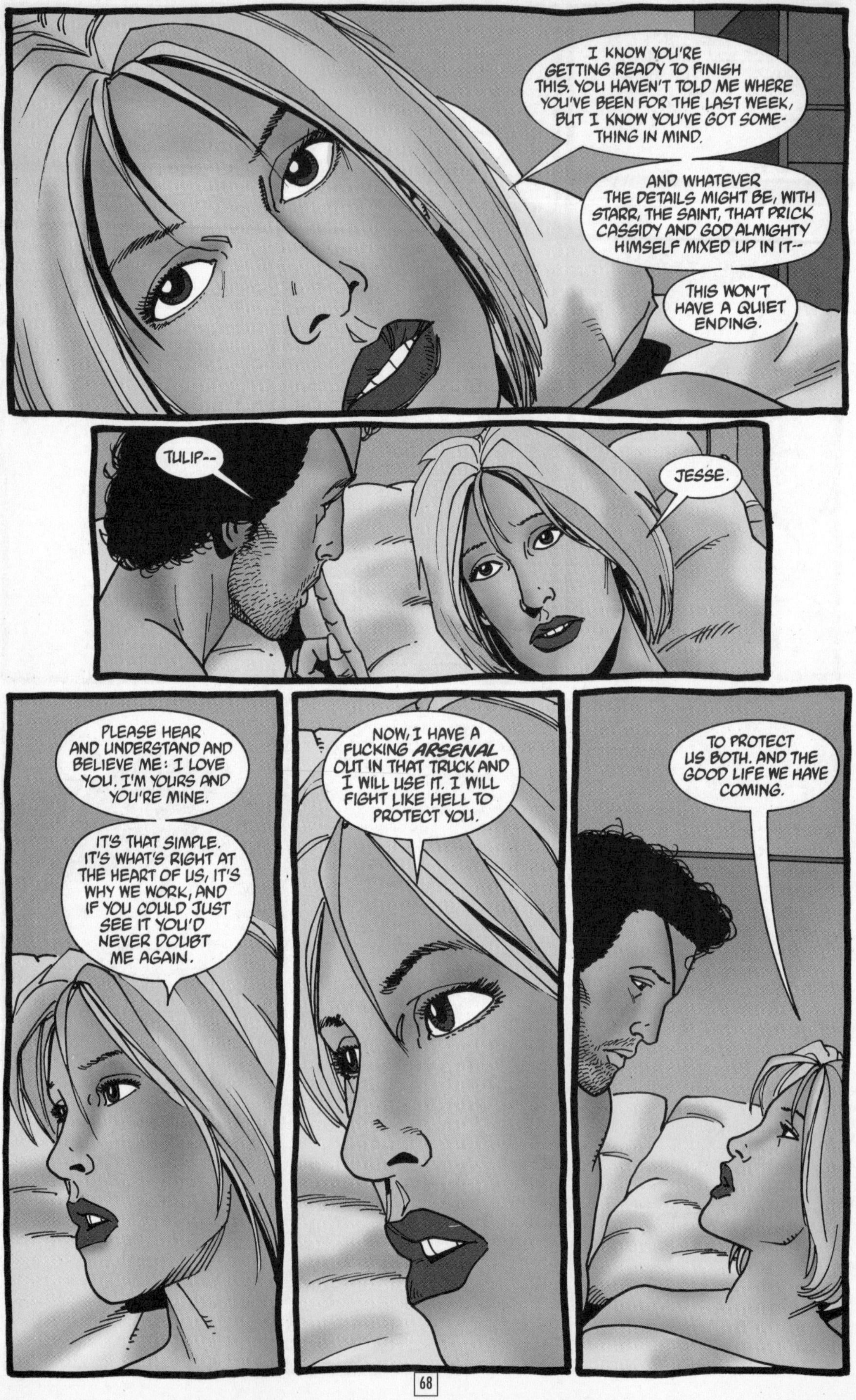
I KNOW YOU'RE GETTING READY TO FINISH THIS. YOU HAVEN'T TOLD ME WHERE YOU'VE BEEN FOR THE LAST WEEK, BUT I KNOW YOU'VE GOT SOMETHING IN MIND.
AND WHATEVER THE DETAILS MIGHT BE, WITH STARR, THE SAINT, THAT PRICK CASSIDY AND GOD ALMIGHTY HIMSELF MIXED UP IN IT--
THIS WON'T HAVE A QUIET ENDING.
TULIP--
JESSE.
PLEASE HEAR AND UNDERSTAND AND BELIEVE ME: I LOVE YOU. I'M YOURS AND YOU'RE MINE.
IT'S THAT SIMPLE. IT'S WHAT'S RIGHT AT THE HEART OF US, IT'S WHY WE WORK, AND IF YOU COULD JUST SEE IT YOU'D NEVER DOUBT ME AGAIN.
NOW, I HAVE A FUCKING *ARSENAL* OUT IN THAT TRUCK AND I WILL USE IT. I WILL FIGHT LIKE HELL TO PROTECT YOU.
TO PROTECT US BOTH. AND THE GOOD LIFE WE HAVE COMING.

YOU FOUND IT? GOOD.

WEAPONS AND AMMUNITION CRATED UNDER THE FLOOR, FOOD IN STORAGE AT THE REAR. NO, NO ONE MENTIONED EXPLOSIVES TO ME.

I DON'T KNOW, CAN'T YOU JUST IMPROVISE? ISN'T THAT WHAT YOU PEOPLE DO? OH, THERE'S NO CALL FOR THAT KIND OF LANGUAGE...!

LOOK, THERE'LL BE MORE UNITS ARRIVING IN THE NEXT DAY OR TWO. MAKE SURE THEY'RE FED AND EQUIPPED, OKAY?

YES, HE'S COMING...

HE'LL BRIEF YOU IN PERSON WHEN HE--

WHAT... WHAT WAS MY SIN...?

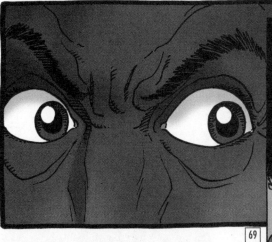

FUCKIN' WITH ME AN' MINE.

GET TO IT.

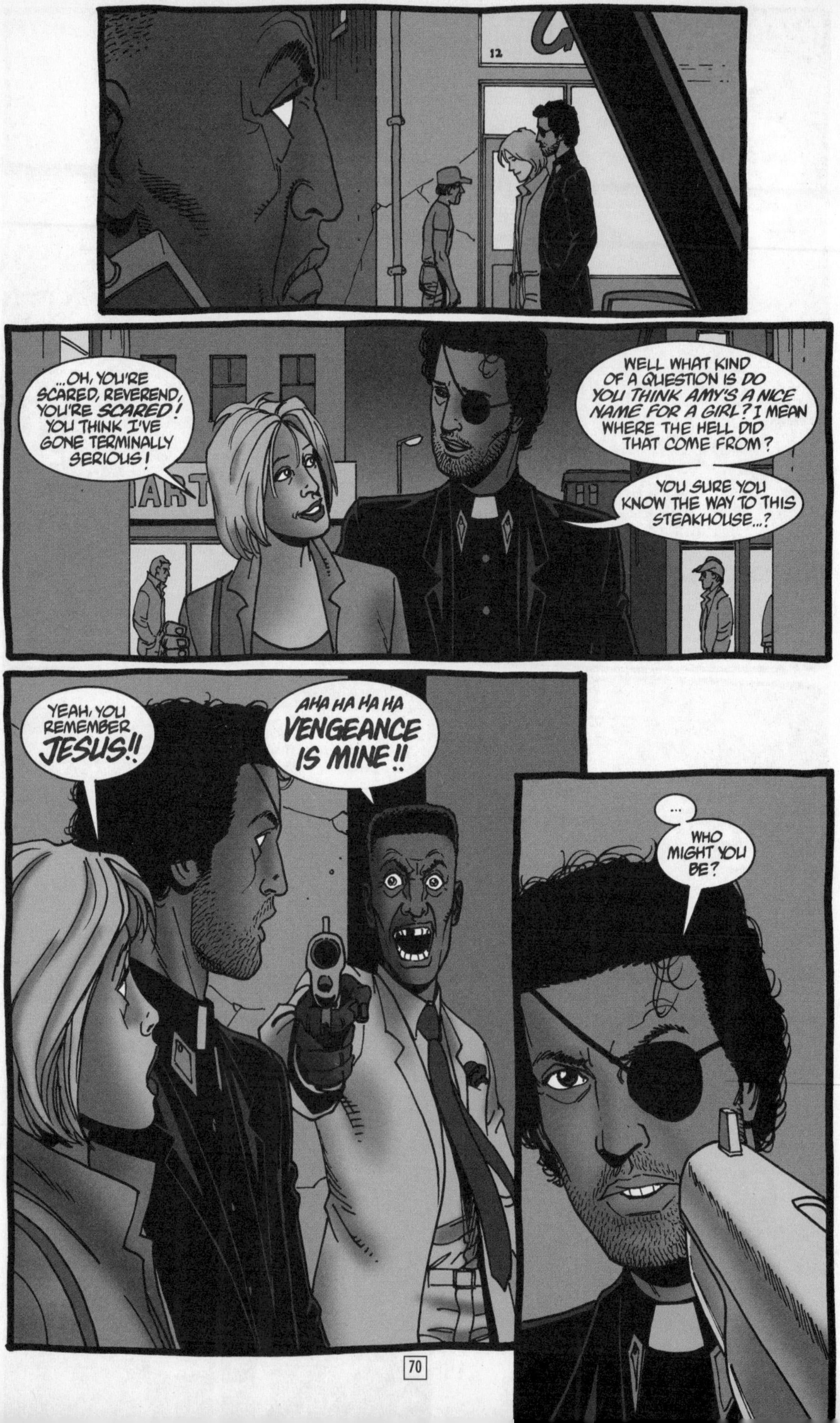
12
...OH, YOU'RE SCARED, REVEREND, YOU'RE SCARED! YOU THINK I'VE GONE TERMINALLY SERIOUS!
WELL WHAT KIND OF A QUESTION IS DO YOU THINK AMY'S A NICE NAME FOR A GIRL? I MEAN WHERE THE HELL DID THAT COME FROM?
YOU SURE YOU KNOW THE WAY TO THIS STEAKHOUSE...?
YEAH, YOU REMEMBER JESUS!!
AHA HA HA HA VENGEANCE IS MINE!!
...
WHO MIGHT YOU BE?

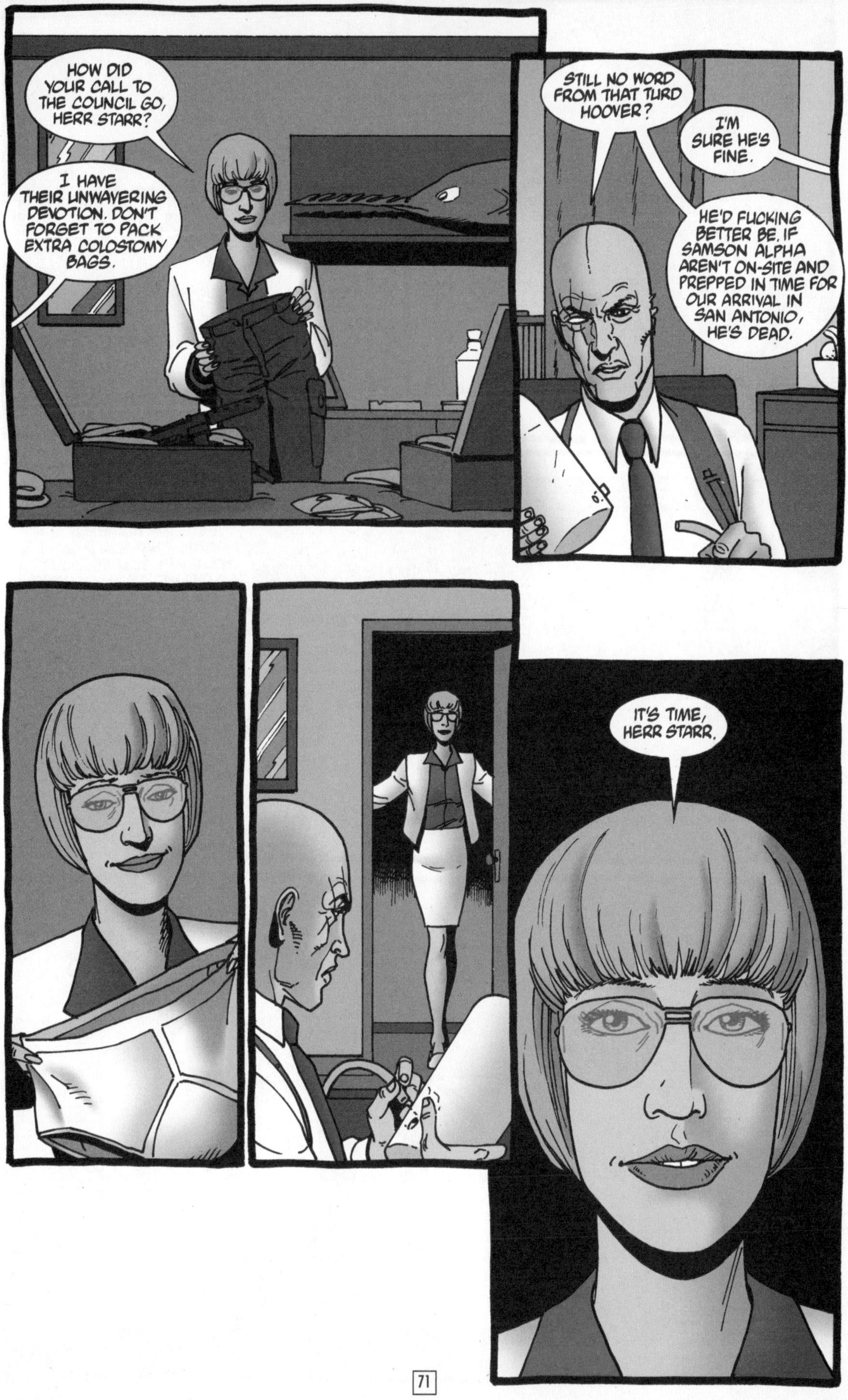
HOW DID YOUR CALL TO THE COUNCIL GO, HERR STARR?
I HAVE THEIR UNWAVERING DEVOTION. DON'T FORGET TO PACK EXTRA COLOSTOMY BAGS.
STILL NO WORD FROM THAT TURD HOOVER?
I'M SURE HE'S FINE.
HE'D FUCKING BETTER BE. IF SAMSON ALPHA AREN'T ON-SITE AND PREPPED IN TIME FOR OUR ARRIVAL IN SAN ANTONIO, HE'S DEAD.
IT'S TIME, HERR STARR.

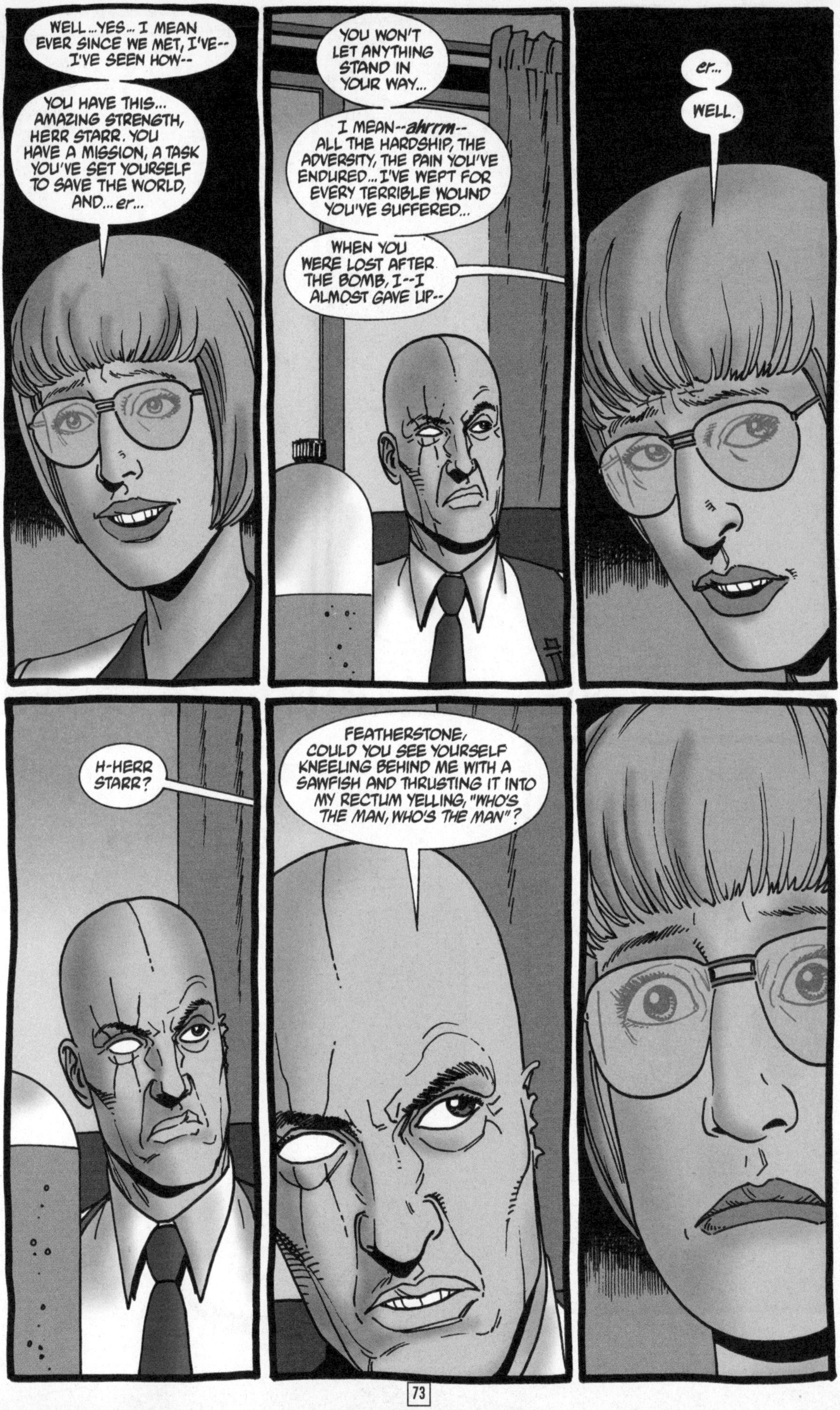
WELL...YES... I MEAN EVER SINCE WE MET, I'VE-- I'VE SEEN HOW--
YOU HAVE THIS... AMAZING STRENGTH, HERR STARR. YOU HAVE A MISSION, A TASK YOU'VE SET YOURSELF TO SAVE THE WORLD, AND... er...
YOU WON'T LET ANYTHING STAND IN YOUR WAY...
I MEAN--ahrrm-- ALL THE HARDSHIP, THE ADVERSITY, THE PAIN YOU'VE ENDURED... I'VE WEPT FOR EVERY TERRIBLE WOUND YOU'VE SUFFERED...
WHEN YOU WERE LOST AFTER THE BOMB, I--I ALMOST GAVE UP--
er...
WELL.
H-HERR STARR?
FEATHERSTONE, COULD YOU SEE YOURSELF KNEELING BEHIND ME WITH A SAWFISH AND THRUSTING IT INTO MY RECTUM YELLING, "WHO'S THE MAN, WHO'S THE MAN"?

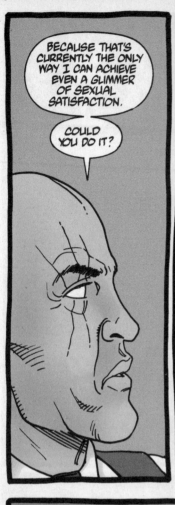

BECAUSE THAT'S CURRENTLY THE ONLY WAY I CAN ACHIEVE EVEN A GLIMMER OF SEXUAL SATISFACTION.

COULD YOU DO IT?

NO, OF COURSE YOU COULDN'T.

YOU MAKE A MUCH BETTER ADJUTANT THAN YOU EVER WOULD A LOVER, FEATHERSTONE.

FINISH PACKING. LET ME KNOW WHEN THE LIMO ARRIVES.

YES... HERR STARR...

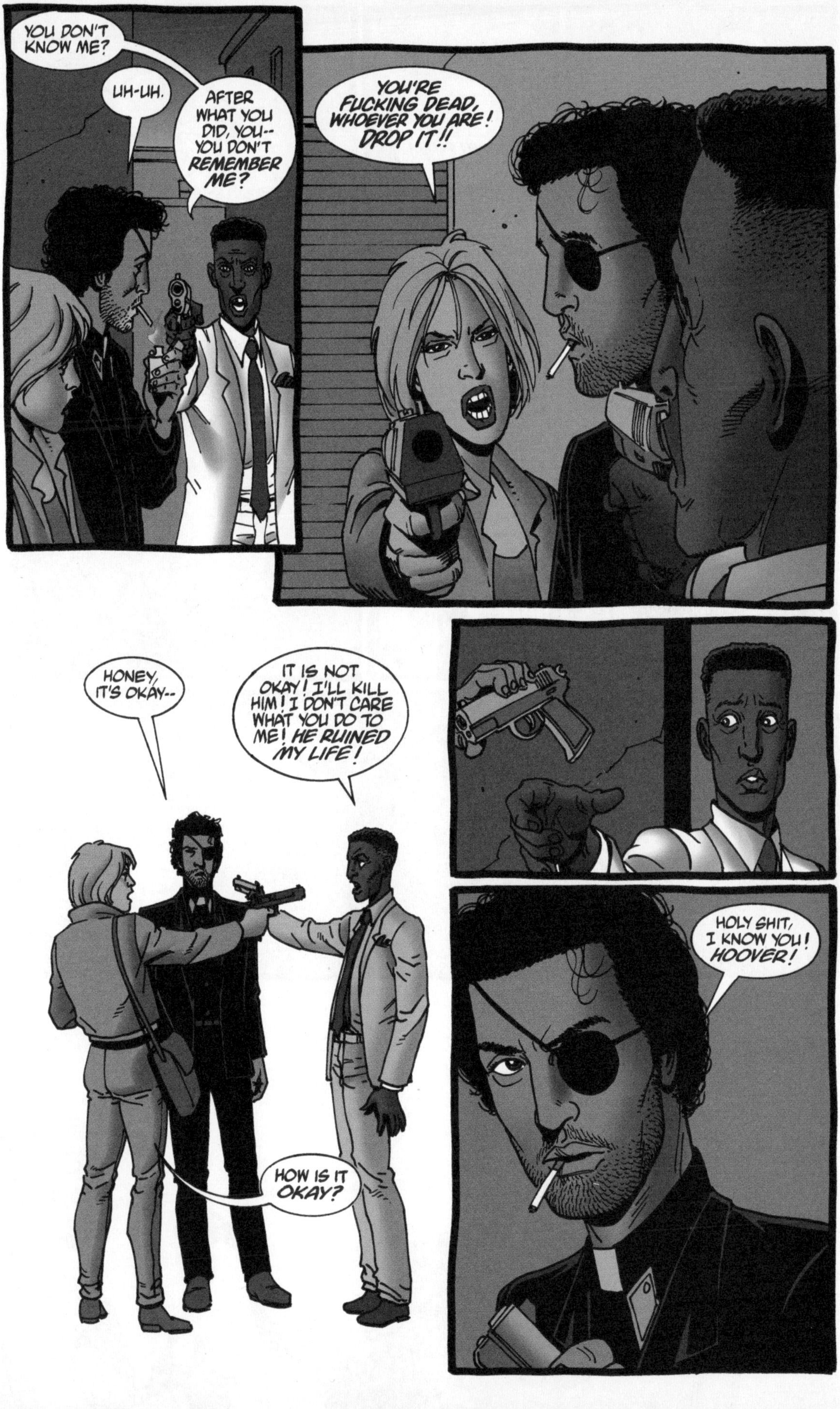
YOU DON'T KNOW ME?
UH-UH.
AFTER WHAT YOU DID, YOU-- YOU DON'T REMEMBER ME?
YOU'RE FUCKING DEAD, WHOEVER YOU ARE! DROP IT!!
HONEY, IT'S OKAY--
IT IS NOT OKAY! I'LL KILL HIM! I DON'T CARE WHAT YOU DO TO ME! HE RUINED MY LIFE!
HOW IS IT OKAY?
HOLY SHIT, I KNOW YOU! HOOVER!

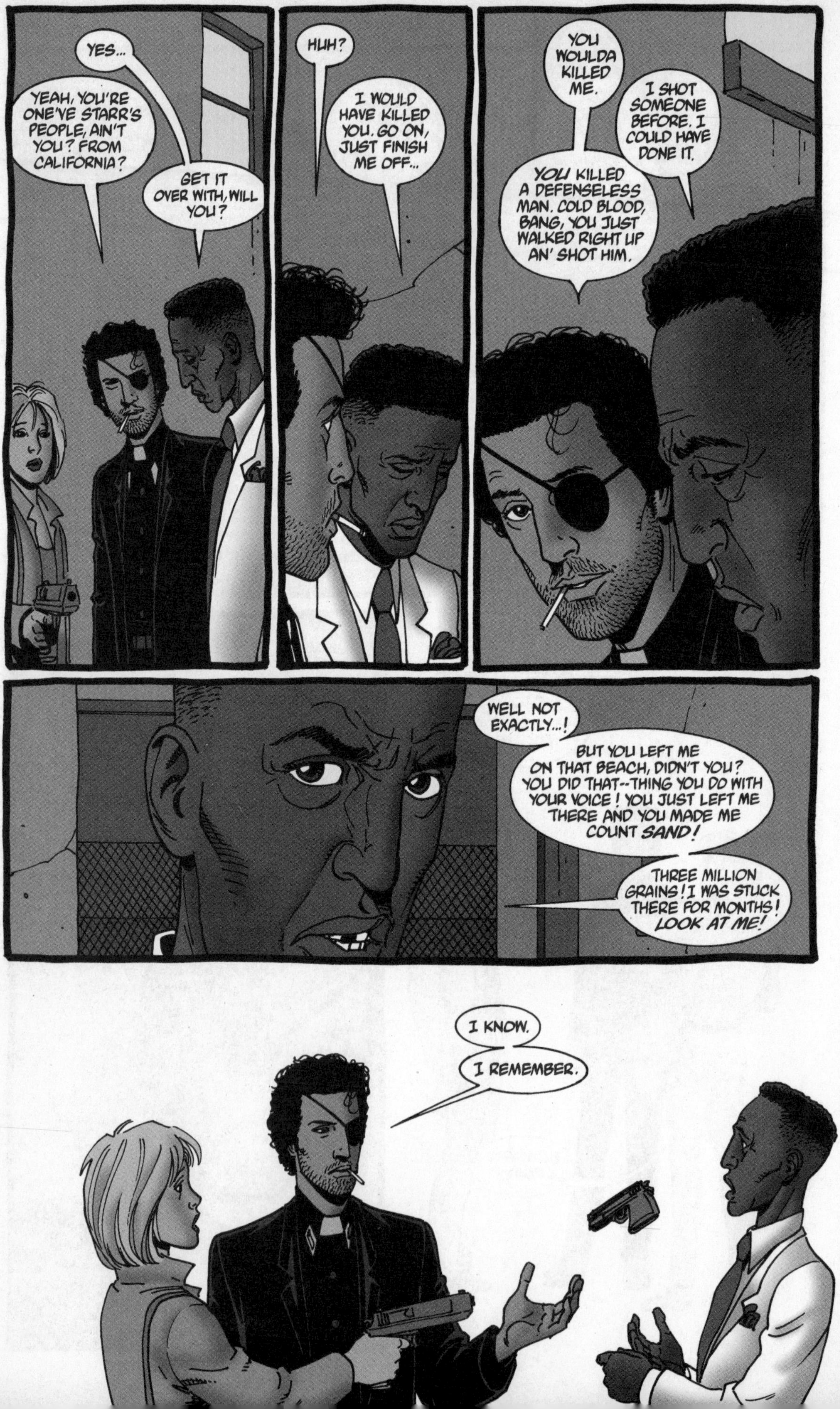
YES...
YEAH, YOU'RE ONE'VE STARR'S PEOPLE, AIN'T YOU? FROM CALIFORNIA?
GET IT OVER WITH, WILL YOU?
HUH?
I WOULD HAVE KILLED YOU. GO ON, JUST FINISH ME OFF...
YOU WOULDA KILLED ME.
I SHOT SOMEONE BEFORE. I COULD HAVE DONE IT.
YOU KILLED A DEFENSELESS MAN. COLD BLOOD, BANG, YOU JUST WALKED RIGHT UP AN' SHOT HIM.
WELL NOT EXACTLY...!
BUT YOU LEFT ME ON THAT BEACH, DIDN'T YOU? YOU DID THAT--THING YOU DO WITH YOUR VOICE! YOU JUST LEFT ME THERE AND YOU MADE ME COUNT SAND!
THREE MILLION GRAINS! I WAS STUCK THERE FOR MONTHS! LOOK AT ME!
I KNOW.
I REMEMBER.

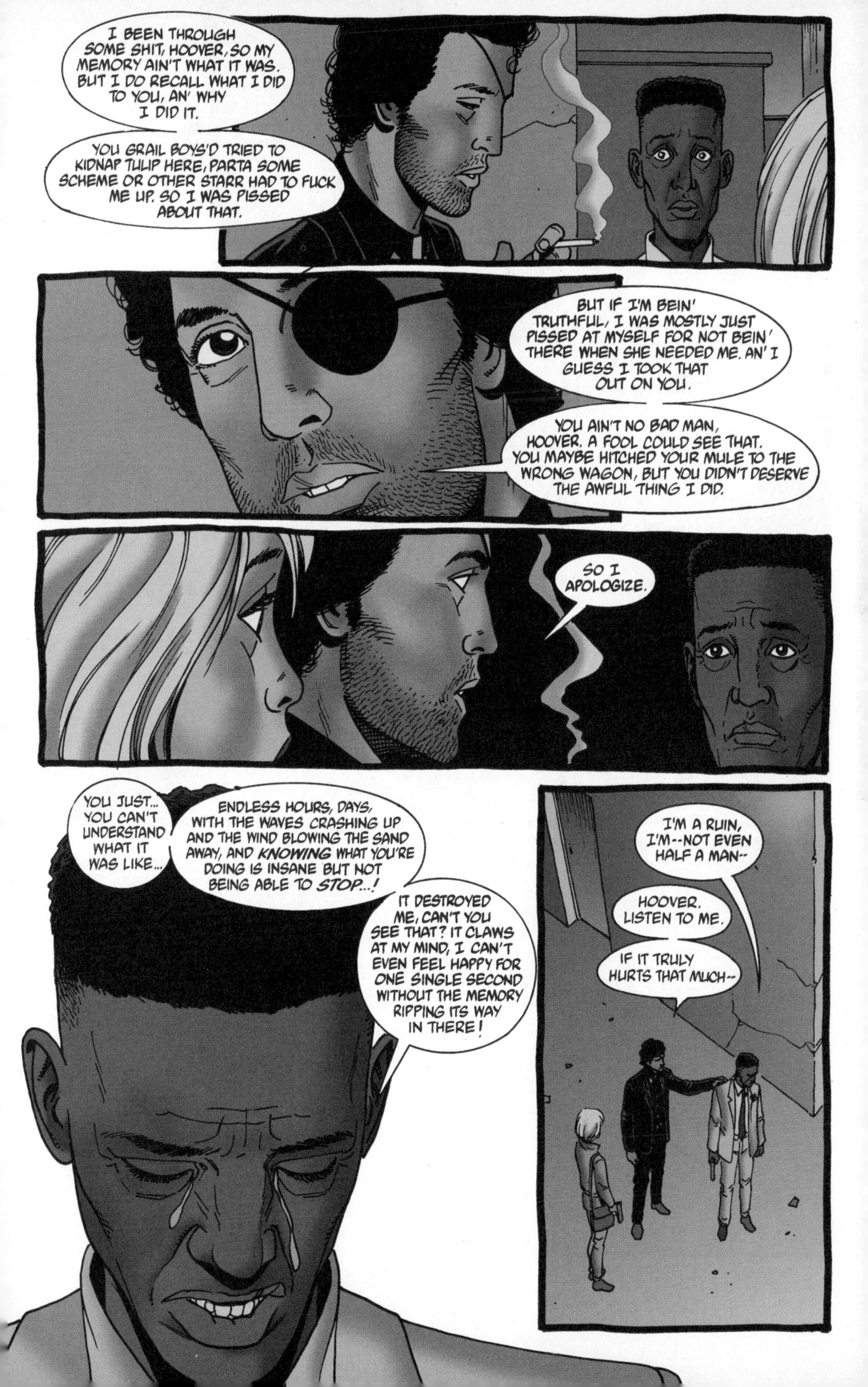
I BEEN THROUGH SOME SHIT, HOOVER, SO MY MEMORY AIN'T WHAT IT WAS. BUT I DO RECALL WHAT I DID TO YOU, AN' WHY I DID IT.
YOU GRAIL BOYS'D TRIED TO KIDNAP TULIP HERE, PARTA SOME SCHEME OR OTHER STARR HAD TO FUCK ME UP. SO I WAS PISSED ABOUT THAT.
BUT IF I'M BEIN' TRUTHFUL, I WAS MOSTLY JUST PISSED AT MYSELF FOR NOT BEIN' THERE WHEN SHE NEEDED ME. AN' I GUESS I TOOK THAT OUT ON YOU.
YOU AIN'T NO BAD MAN, HOOVER. A FOOL COULD SEE THAT. YOU MAYBE HITCHED YOUR MULE TO THE WRONG WAGON, BUT YOU DIDN'T DESERVE THE AWFUL THING I DID.
SO I APOLOGIZE.
YOU JUST... YOU CAN'T UNDERSTAND WHAT IT WAS LIKE...
ENDLESS HOURS, DAYS, WITH THE WAVES CRASHING UP AND THE WIND BLOWING THE SAND AWAY, AND *KNOWING* WHAT YOU'RE DOING IS INSANE BUT NOT BEING ABLE TO *STOP*...!
IT DESTROYED ME, CAN'T YOU SEE THAT? IT CLAWS AT MY MIND, I CAN'T EVEN FEEL HAPPY FOR ONE SINGLE SECOND WITHOUT THE MEMORY RIPPING ITS WAY IN THERE!
I'M A RUIN, I'M--NOT EVEN HALF A MAN--
HOOVER. LISTEN TO ME.
IF IT TRULY HURTS THAT MUCH--

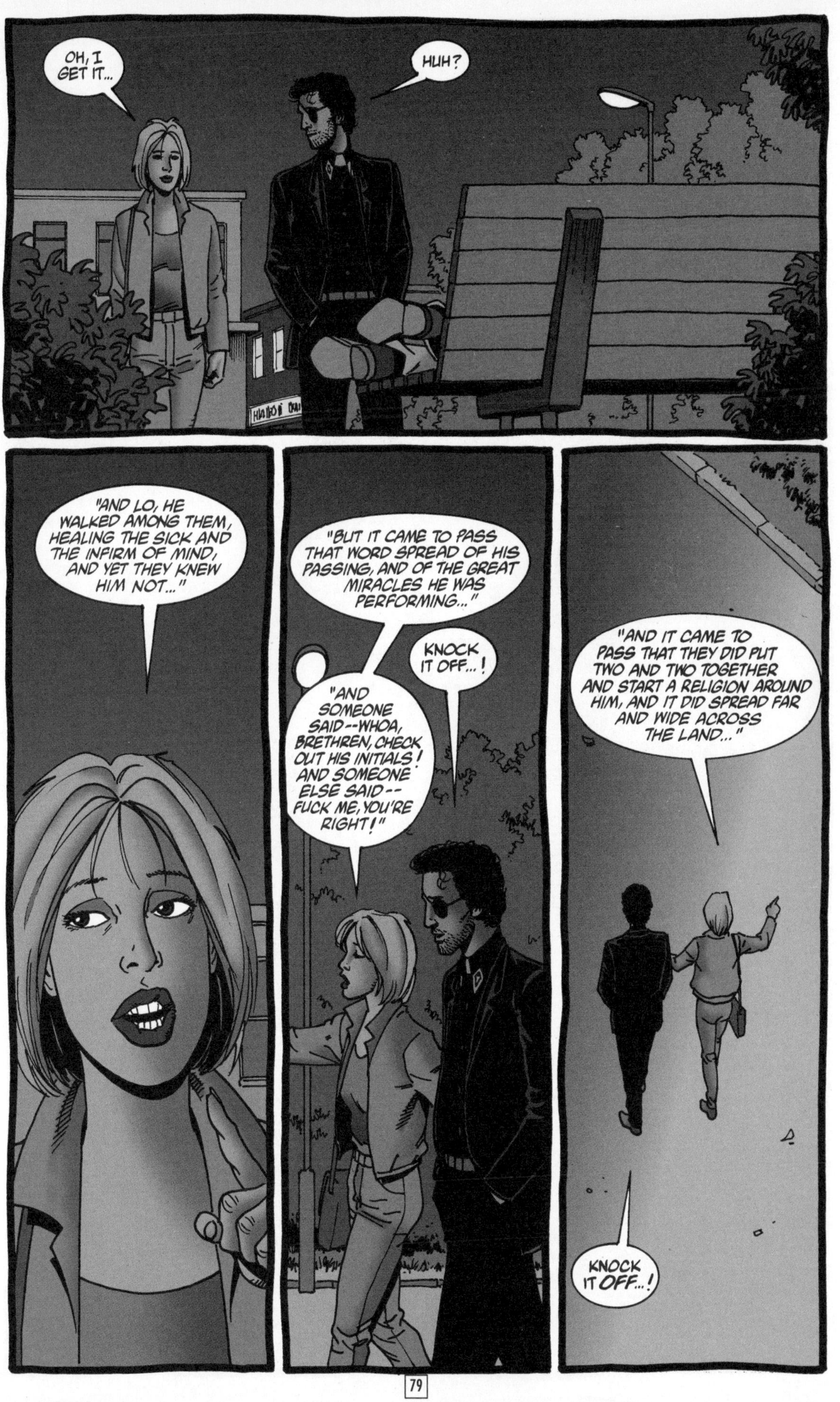
OH, I GET IT...
HUH?
"AND LO, HE WALKED AMONG THEM, HEALING THE SICK AND THE INFIRM OF MIND, AND YET THEY KNEW HIM NOT..."
"BUT IT CAME TO PASS THAT WORD SPREAD OF HIS PASSING, AND OF THE GREAT MIRACLES HE WAS PERFORMING..."
KNOCK IT OFF...!
"AND SOMEONE SAID--WHOA, BRETHREN, CHECK OUT HIS INITIALS! AND SOMEONE ELSE SAID--FUCK ME, YOU'RE RIGHT!"
"AND IT CAME TO PASS THAT THEY DID PUT TWO AND TWO TOGETHER AND START A RELIGION AROUND HIM, AND IT DID SPREAD FAR AND WIDE ACROSS THE LAND..."
KNOCK IT OFF...!

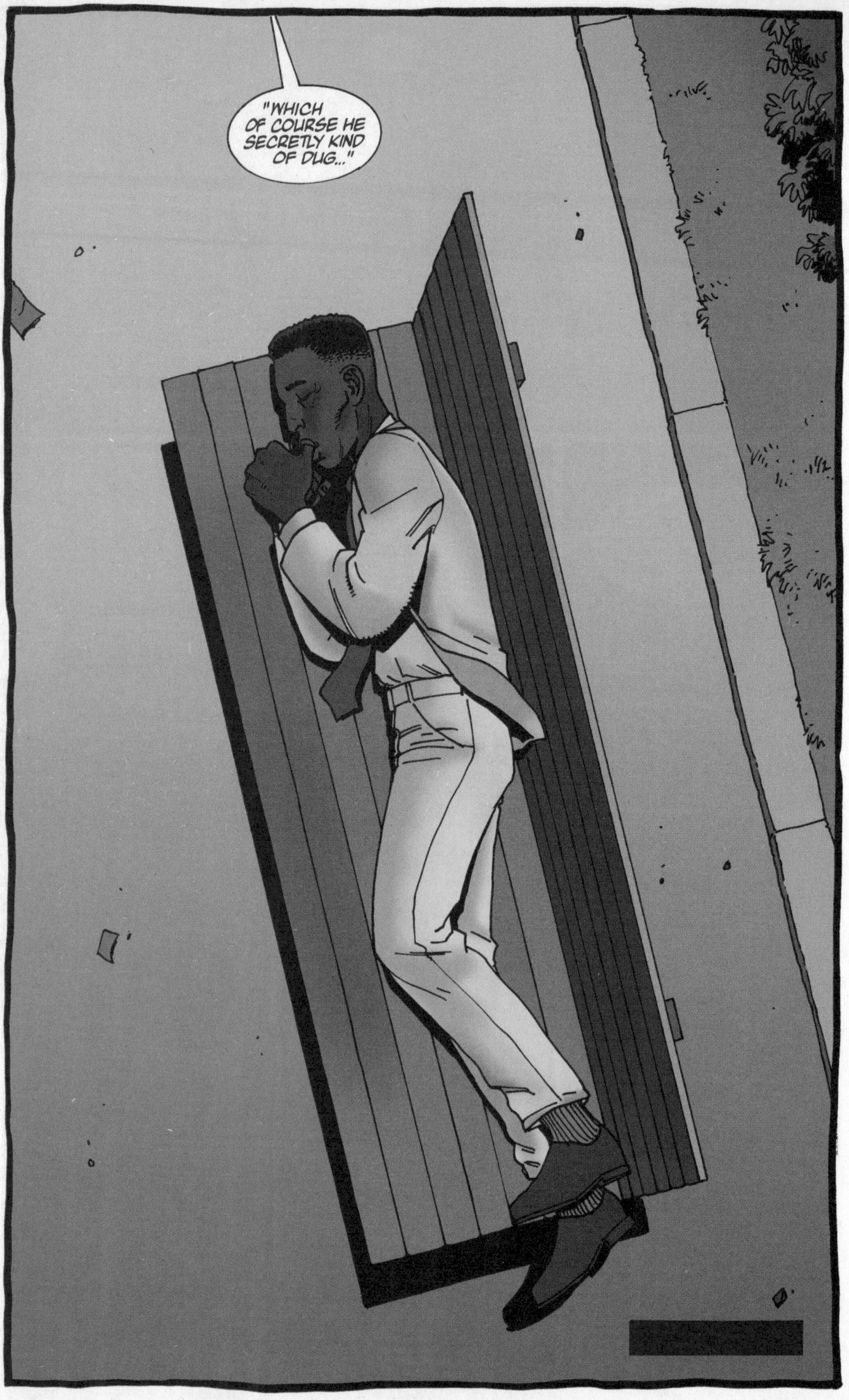
"WHICH OF COURSE HE SECRETLY KIND OF DUG..."

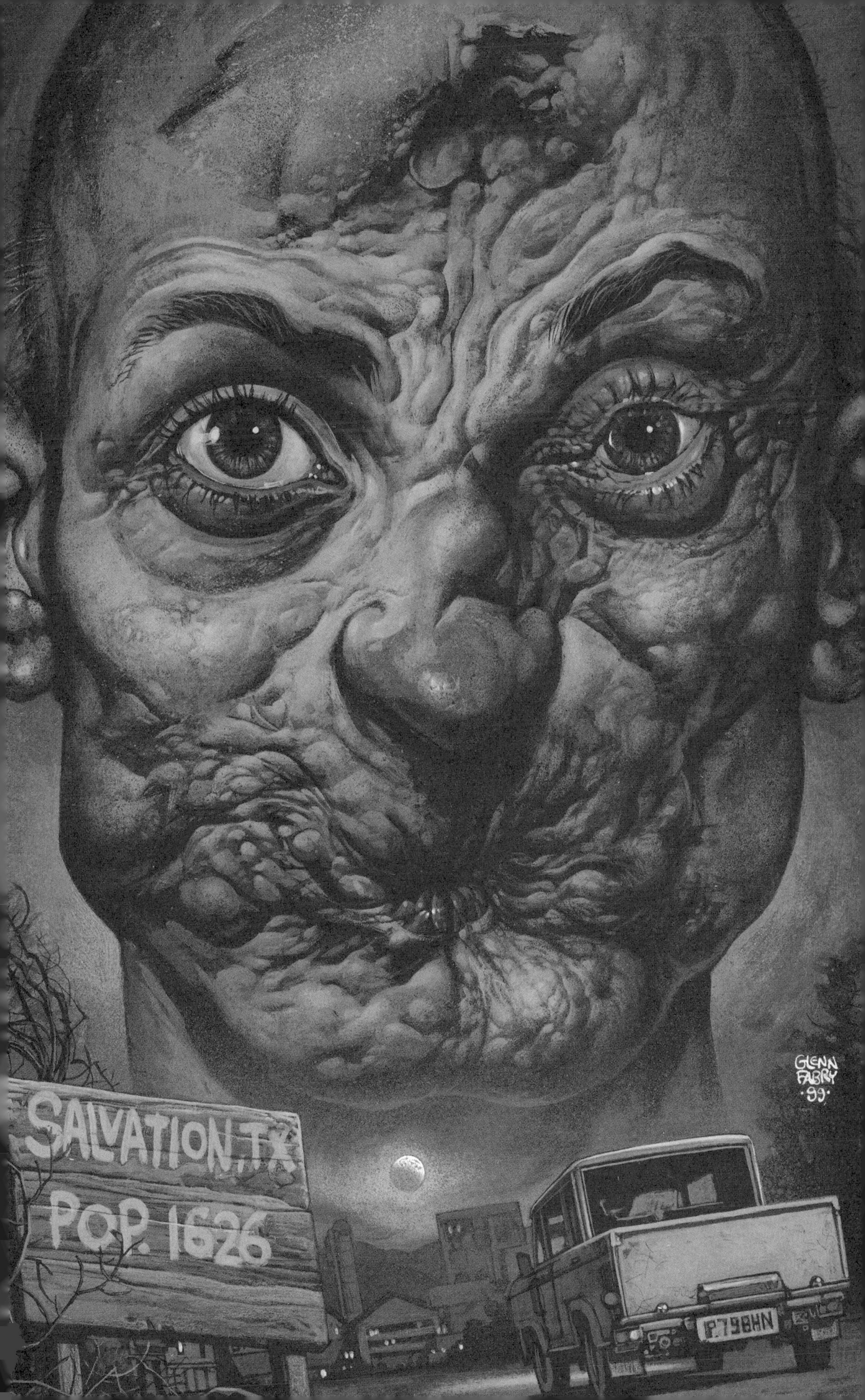
GLENN FABRY ·99·
SALVATION, TX
POP. 1626
P 798 HN

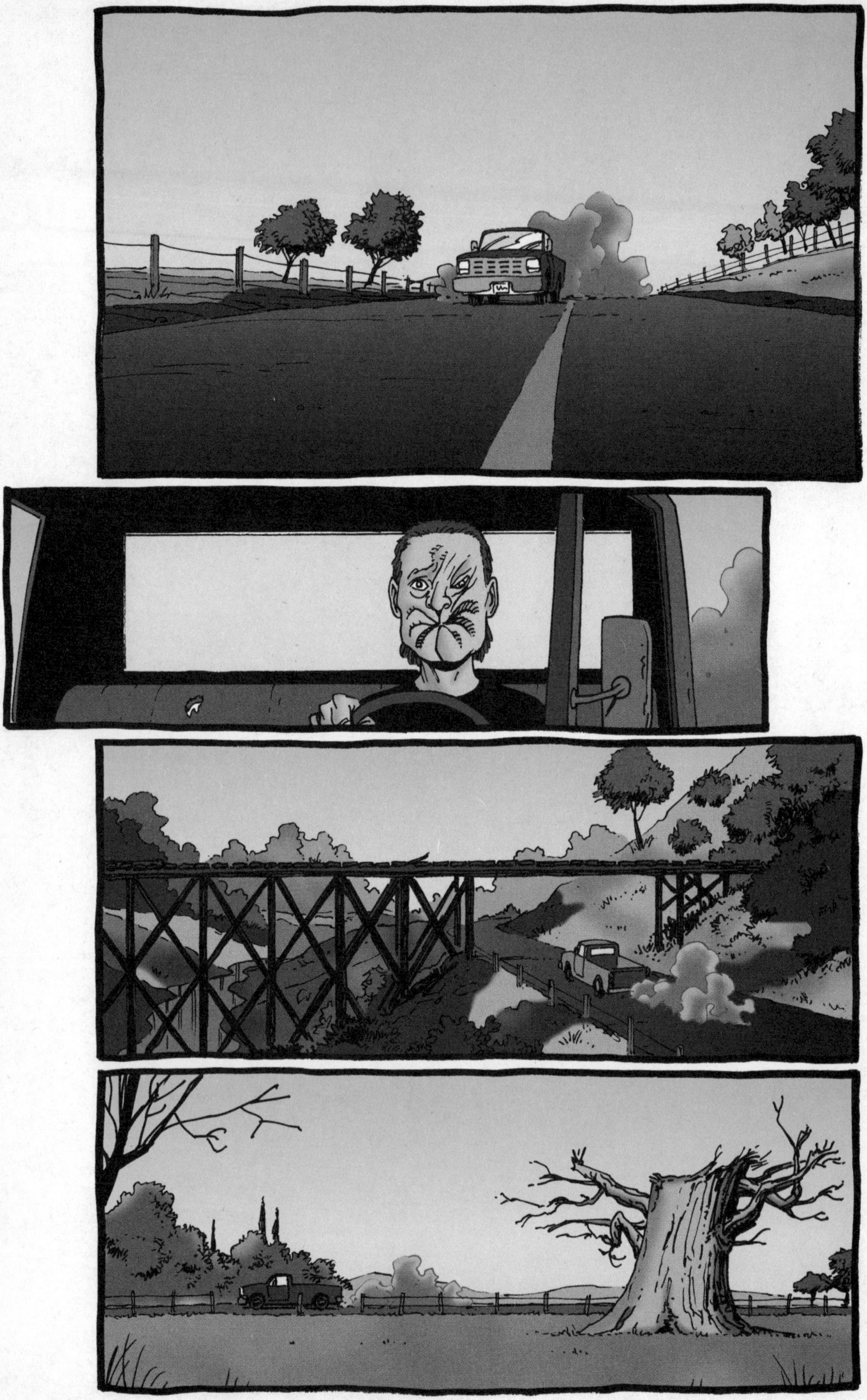

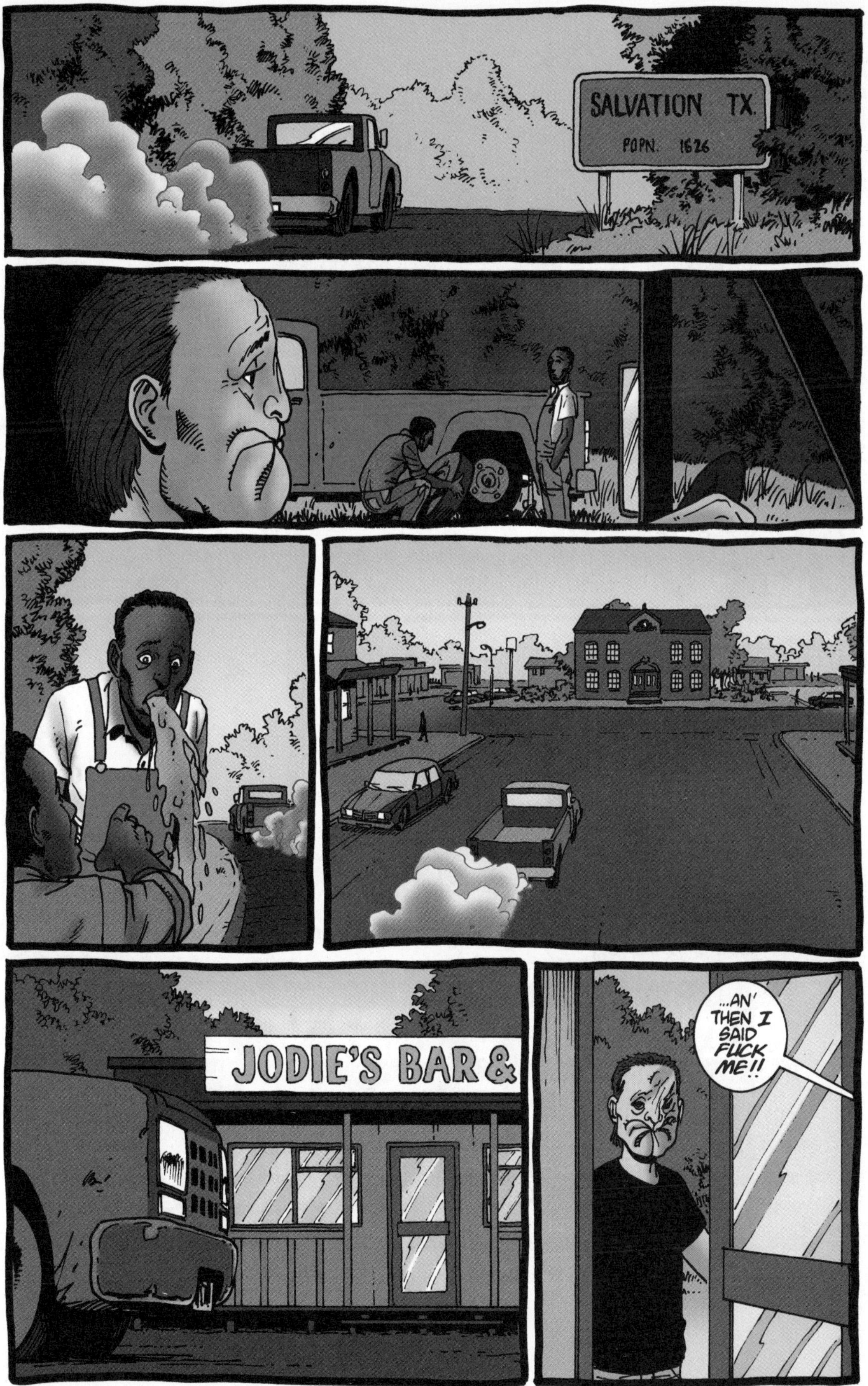
SALVATION TX.
POPN. 1626
JODIE'S BAR &
...AN' THEN I SAID FUCK ME!!

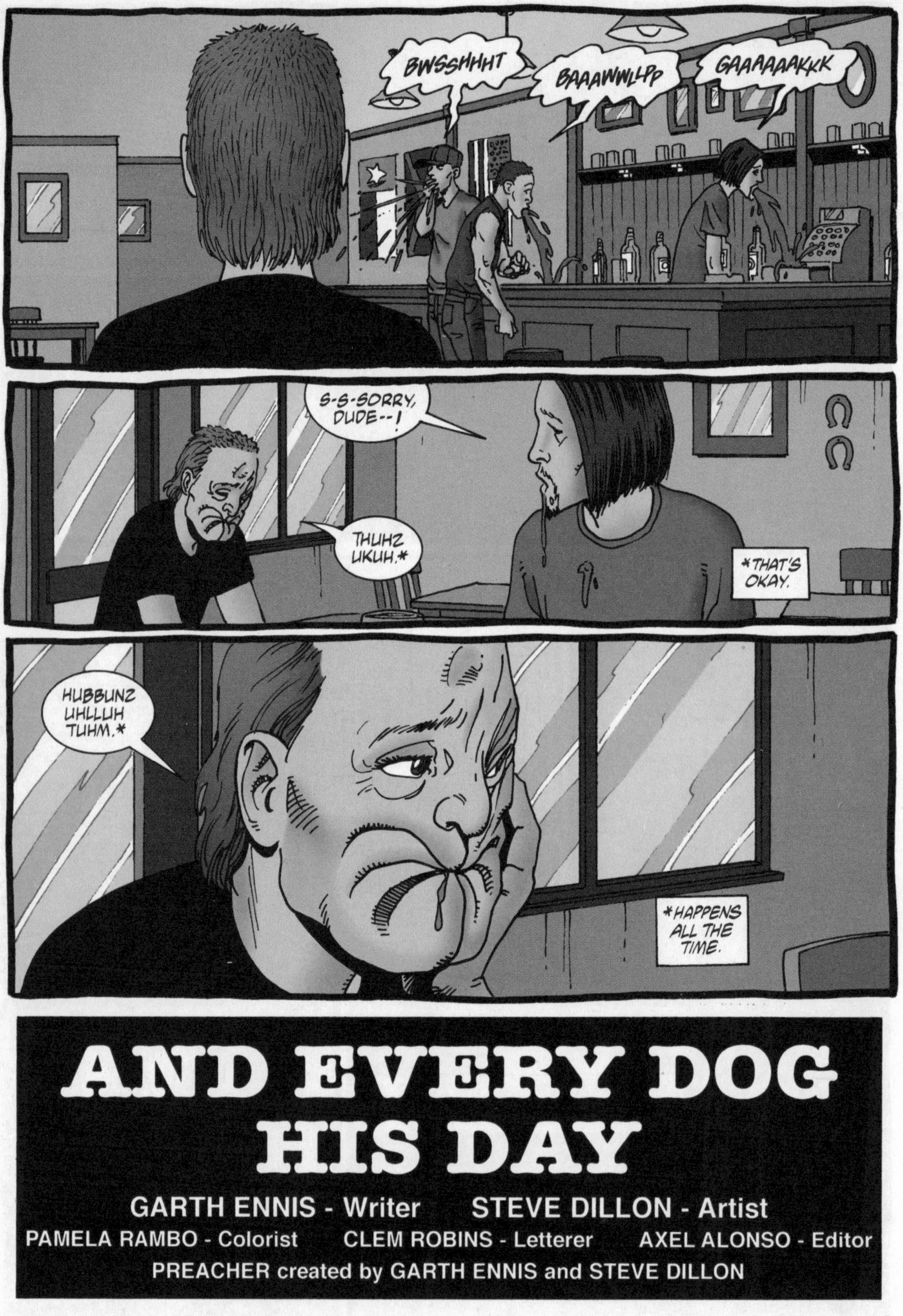
BWSSHHHT
BAAAWWLLPP
GAAAAAAKKK
S-S-SORRY, DUDE--!
THUHZ UKUH.*
*THAT'S OKAY.
HUBBUNZ UHLLUH TUHM.*
*HAPPENS ALL THE TIME.

AND EVERY DOG HIS DAY

GARTH ENNIS - Writer   STEVE DILLON - Artist

PAMELA RAMBO - Colorist   CLEM ROBINS - Letterer   AXEL ALONSO - Editor

PREACHER created by GARTH ENNIS and STEVE DILLON

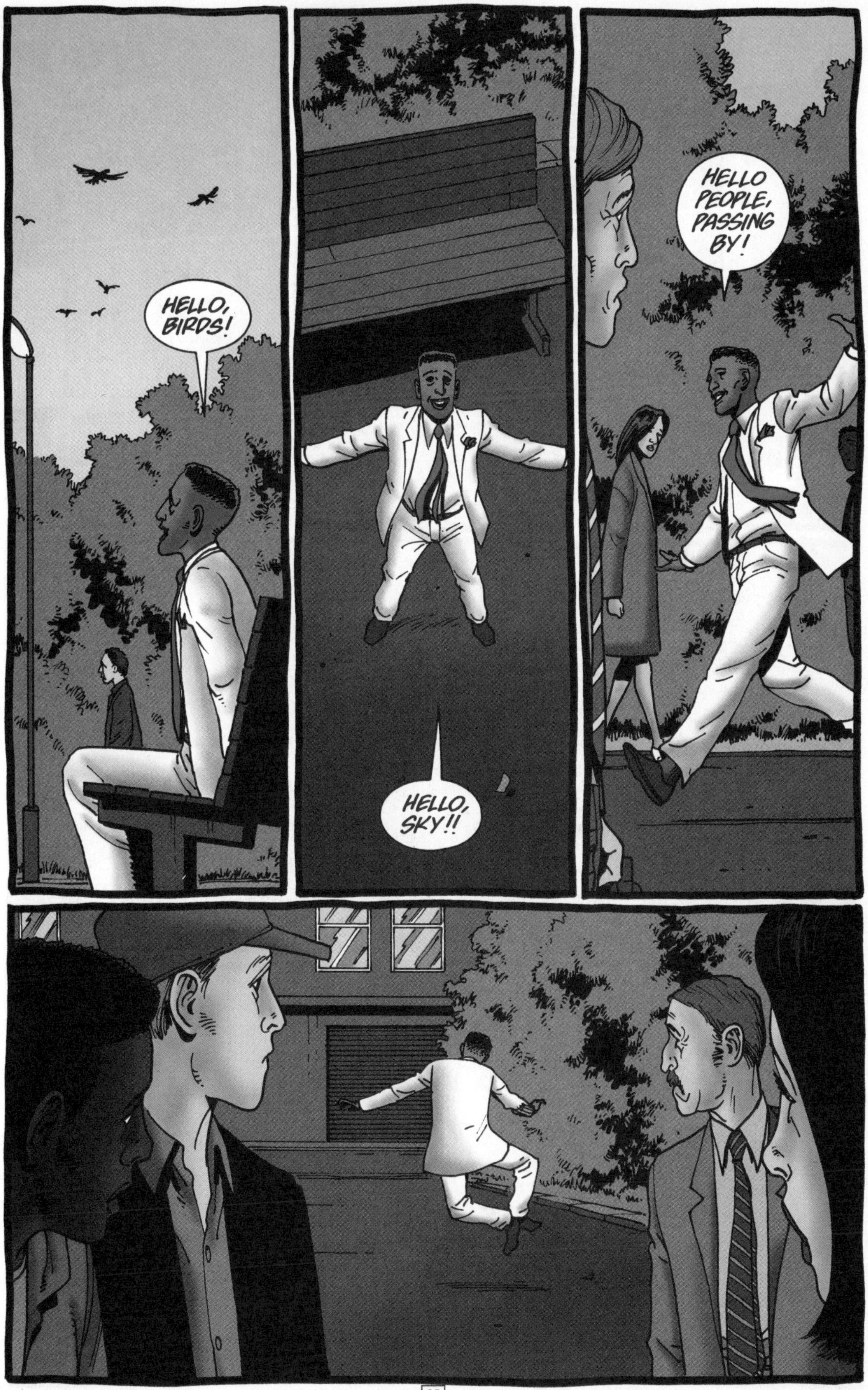
HELLO, BIRDS!
HELLO, SKY!!
HELLO PEOPLE, PASSING BY!

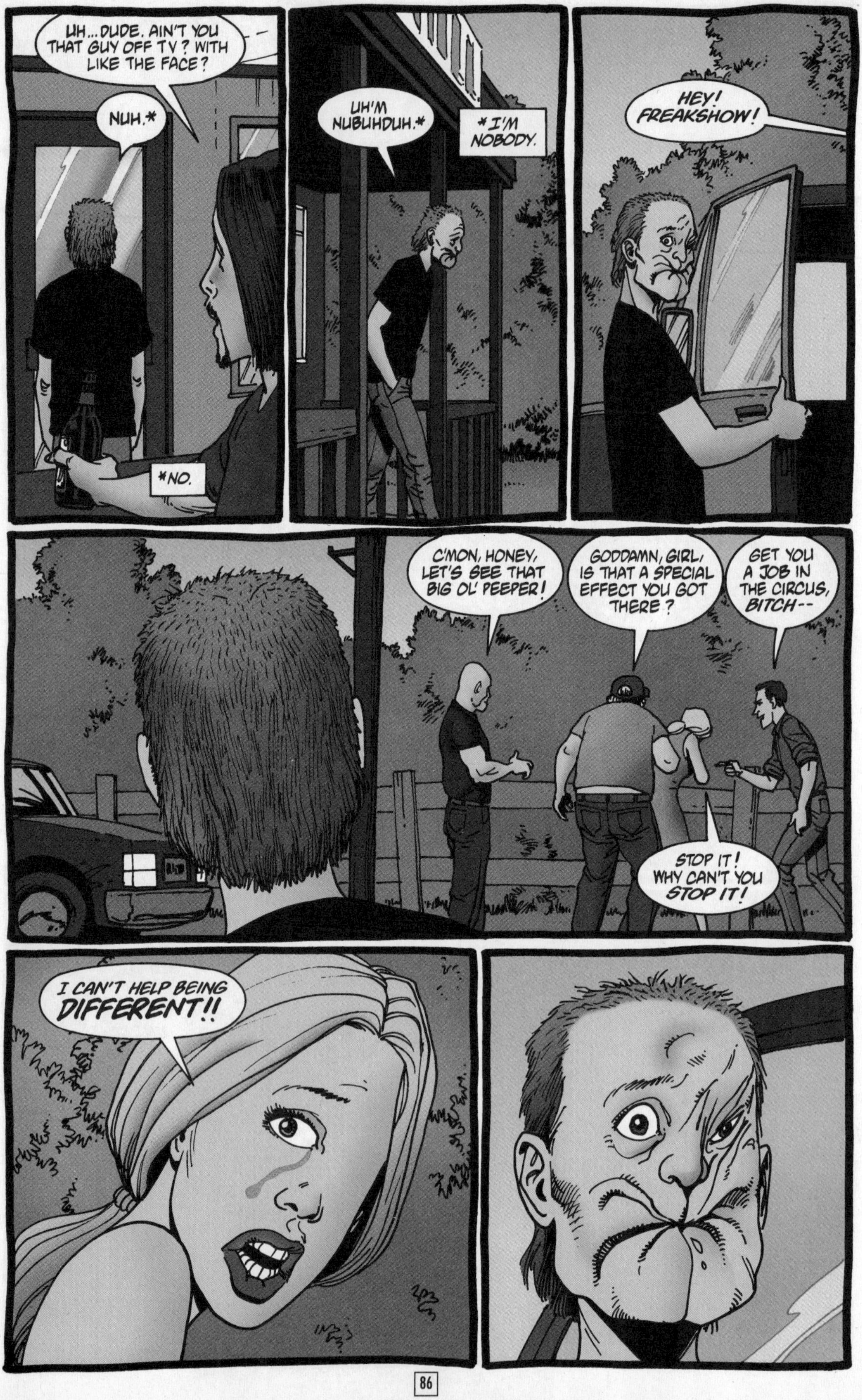

UH... DUDE. AIN'T YOU THAT GUY OFF TV? WITH LIKE THE FACE?
NUH.*
*NO.
UH'M NUBUHDUH.*
*I'M NOBODY.
HEY! FREAKSHOW!
C'MON, HONEY, LET'S SEE THAT BIG OL' PEEPER!
GODDAMN, GIRL, IS THAT A SPECIAL EFFECT YOU GOT THERE?
GET YOU A JOB IN THE CIRCUS, BITCH--
STOP IT! WHY CAN'T YOU STOP IT!
I CAN'T HELP BEING DIFFERENT!!

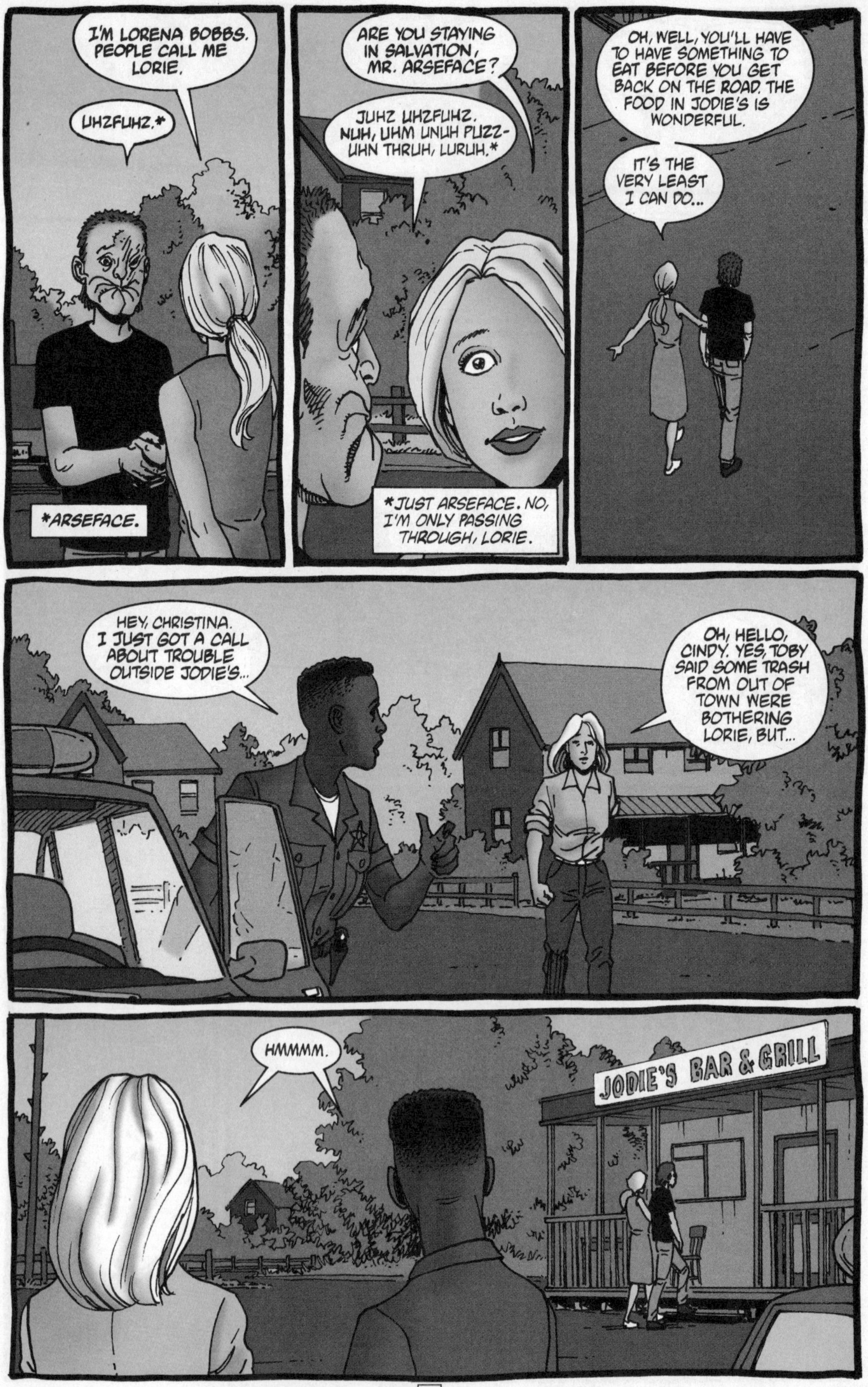
I'M LORENA BOBBS. PEOPLE CALL ME LORIE.
UHZFUHZ.*
*ARSEFACE.
ARE YOU STAYING IN SALVATION, MR. ARSEFACE?
JUHZ UHZFUHZ. NUH, UHM UNUH PUZZ-UHN THRUH, LURUH.*
*JUST ARSEFACE. NO, I'M ONLY PASSING THROUGH, LORIE.
OH, WELL, YOU'LL HAVE TO HAVE SOMETHING TO EAT BEFORE YOU GET BACK ON THE ROAD. THE FOOD IN JODIE'S IS WONDERFUL.
IT'S THE VERY LEAST I CAN DO...
HEY, CHRISTINA. I JUST GOT A CALL ABOUT TROUBLE OUTSIDE JODIE'S...
OH, HELLO, CINDY. YES, TOBY SAID SOME TRASH FROM OUT OF TOWN WERE BOTHERING LORIE, BUT...
HMMMM.
JODIE'S BAR & GRILL

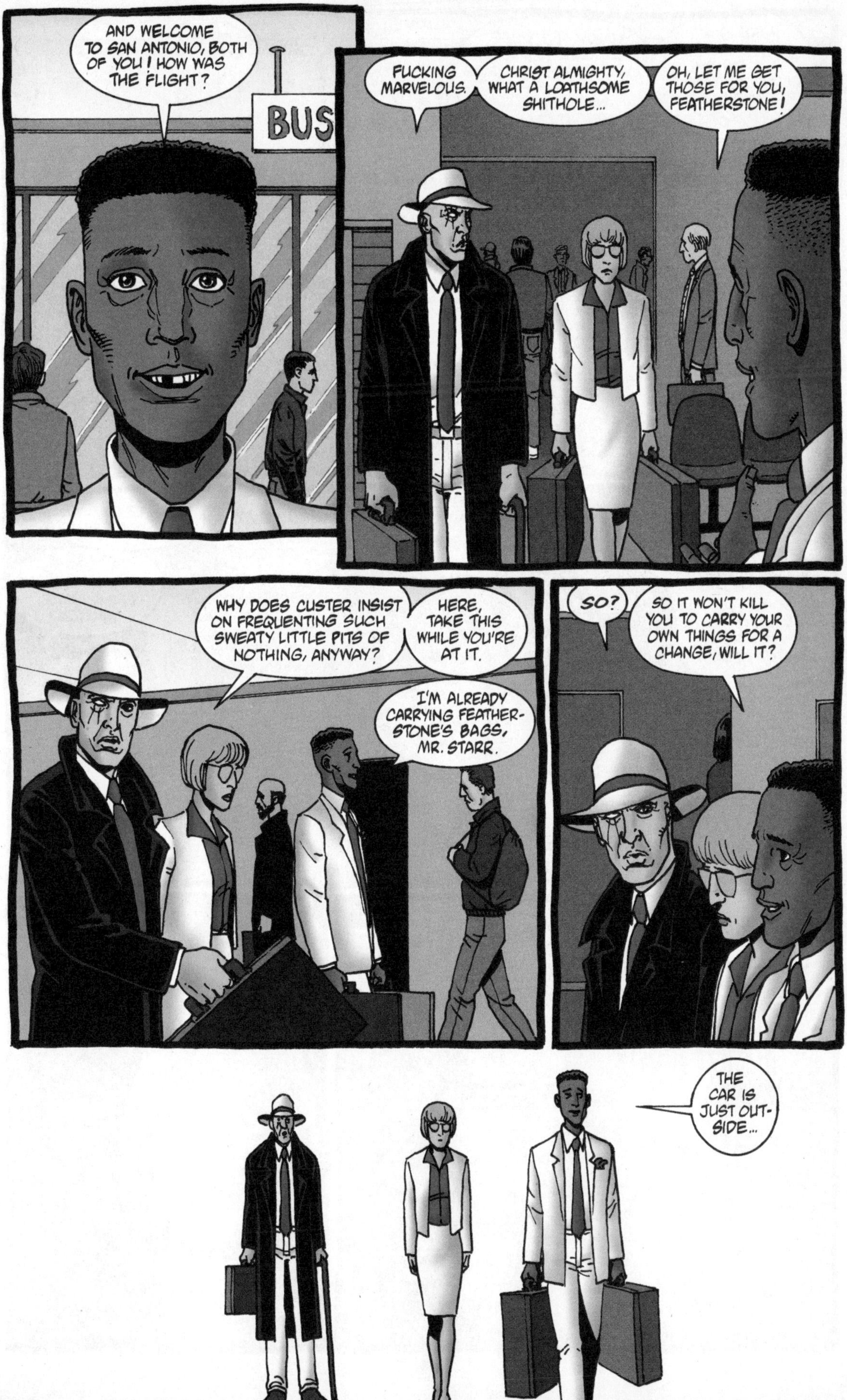
AND WELCOME TO SAN ANTONIO, BOTH OF YOU! HOW WAS THE FLIGHT?
BUS
FUCKING MARVELOUS.
CHRIST ALMIGHTY, WHAT A LOATHSOME SHITHOLE...
OH, LET ME GET THOSE FOR YOU, FEATHERSTONE!
WHY DOES CUSTER INSIST ON FREQUENTING SUCH SWEATY LITTLE PITS OF NOTHING, ANYWAY?
HERE, TAKE THIS WHILE YOU'RE AT IT.
I'M ALREADY CARRYING FEATHER-STONE'S BAGS, MR. STARR.
SO?
SO IT WON'T KILL YOU TO CARRY YOUR OWN THINGS FOR A CHANGE, WILL IT?
THE CAR IS JUST OUT-SIDE...

HERE IS A GOOD ONE! WHY DID THE REDNECKS END UP WORKING FOR THE MEXICAN?

EASY! BECAUSE THEY WERE TOO BUSY MAKING WETBACK JOKES TO ASK IF HE HAD ANY FORMAL EDUCATION--

AND TOO BUSY FUCKING THE BIG FAT CRACKER SOW WHO QUITE OFTEN TOOK THEM ON TWO OR THREE AT A TIME TO NOTICE HIM GOING FOR THE FOREMAN'S JOB AT THE NEW PLANT! *AHA HA HA HA!*

AAAW-HAAAW!

AHA HA HA, THAT IS A GOOD ONE!

SURE IS ONE'VE MY FAVORITES!

SAY, LEMME GET YOU ANOTHER DRINK THERE, HECTOR!

...SO THINGS HAVE REALLY CHANGED IN THE LAST FEW MONTHS. THERE'S HARDLY ANY TROUBLE, NOW THAT CINDY'S THE SHERIFF...

RULUH?*

*REALLY?

YES, SHE'S WONDERFUL--OH, HELLO, MR. QUINCANNON!

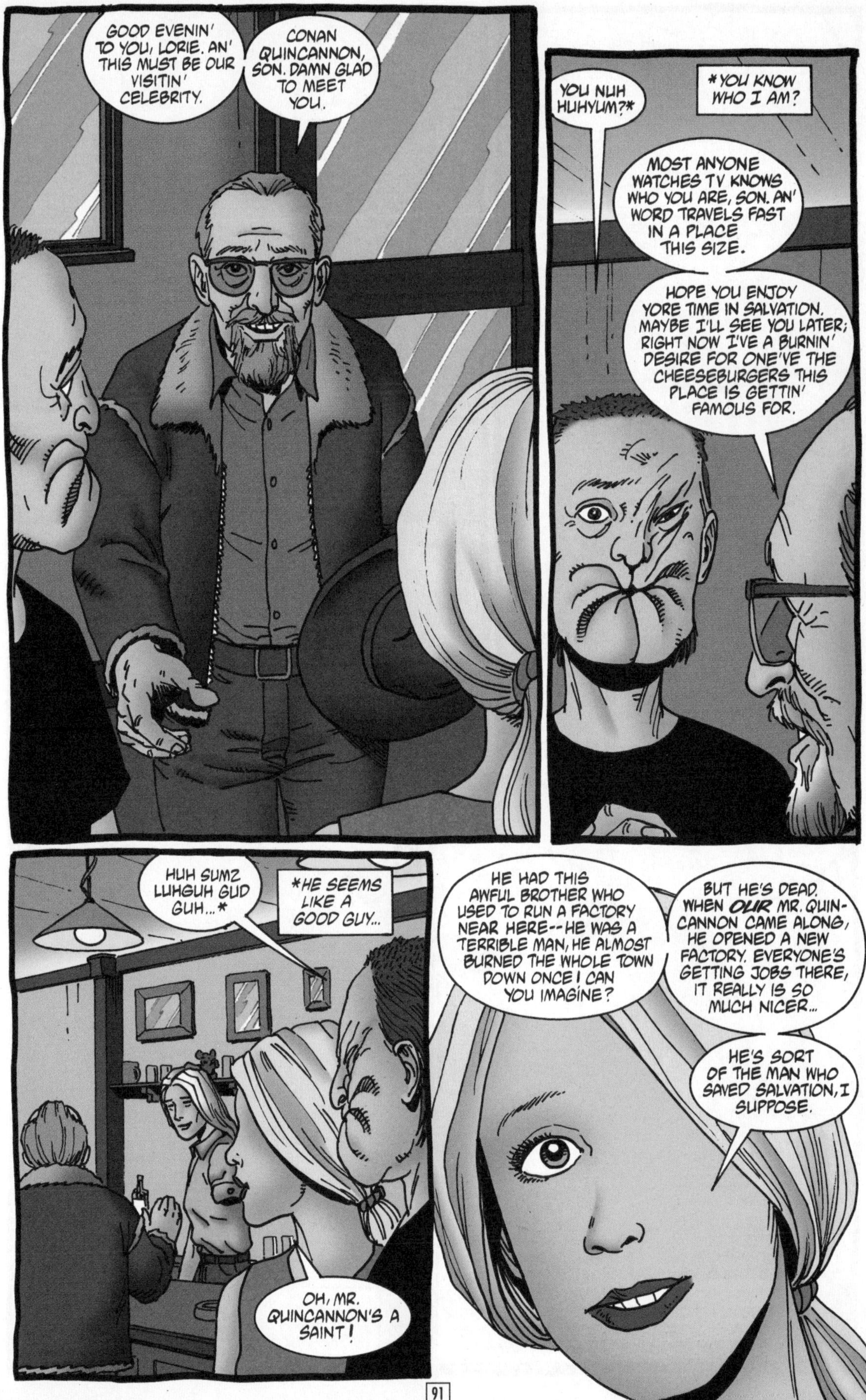
GOOD EVENIN' TO YOU, LORIE. AN' THIS MUST BE OUR VISITIN' CELEBRITY.
CONAN QUINCANNON, SON. DAMN GLAD TO MEET YOU.
YOU NUH HUHYUM?*
*YOU KNOW WHO I AM?
MOST ANYONE WATCHES TV KNOWS WHO YOU ARE, SON. AN' WORD TRAVELS FAST IN A PLACE THIS SIZE.
HOPE YOU ENJOY YORE TIME IN SALVATION. MAYBE I'LL SEE YOU LATER; RIGHT NOW I'VE A BURNIN' DESIRE FOR ONE'VE THE CHEESEBURGERS THIS PLACE IS GETTIN' FAMOUS FOR.
HUH SUMZ LUHGUH GUD GUH...*
*HE SEEMS LIKE A GOOD GUY...
OH, MR. QUINCANNON'S A SAINT!
HE HAD THIS AWFUL BROTHER WHO USED TO RUN A FACTORY NEAR HERE--HE WAS A TERRIBLE MAN, HE ALMOST BURNED THE WHOLE TOWN DOWN ONCE! CAN YOU IMAGINE?
BUT HE'S DEAD. WHEN OUR MR. QUINCANNON CAME ALONG, HE OPENED A NEW FACTORY. EVERYONE'S GETTING JOBS THERE, IT REALLY IS SO MUCH NICER...
HE'S SORT OF THE MAN WHO SAVED SALVATION, I SUPPOSE.

SO YOU WERE ON TV? I DON'T WATCH IT MUCH, IT KIND OF CONFUSES ME...

UH WUZ SUHD UV UH RUG STUH, UH SPUZ. BUHD THUHZ ULL UVUH NUH.

DUHD UN BURUD, YUZ SUH...*

A ROCK STAR.

I THOUGHT IT WOULD BE SOMETHING LIKE THAT.

*I WAS SORT OF A ROCK STAR, I SUPPOSE. BUT THAT'S ALL OVER NOW.

DEAD AND BURIED, YES SIR.

WHAT ARE YOUR PLANS NOW?

WUHL, UH... UH DUNNUH, RULUH. UHV GUHD NUH MUNUH, NUH JUHB...UH DUNNUH HUHDA *DUH* UNUHTHUNG...

UH DUNN WUHNA BUH UH RUG STUH UNUNMUH, UHNYWUH.*

UH UHM *THRUH* WUTH FUHM.*

*WELL, I...I DON'T KNOW, REALLY. I'VE GOT NO MONEY, NO JOB...I DON'T KNOW HOW TO *DO* ANYTHING...

I DON'T WANT TO BE A ROCK STAR ANYMORE, ANYWAY.

*I AM *THROUGH* WITH FAME.

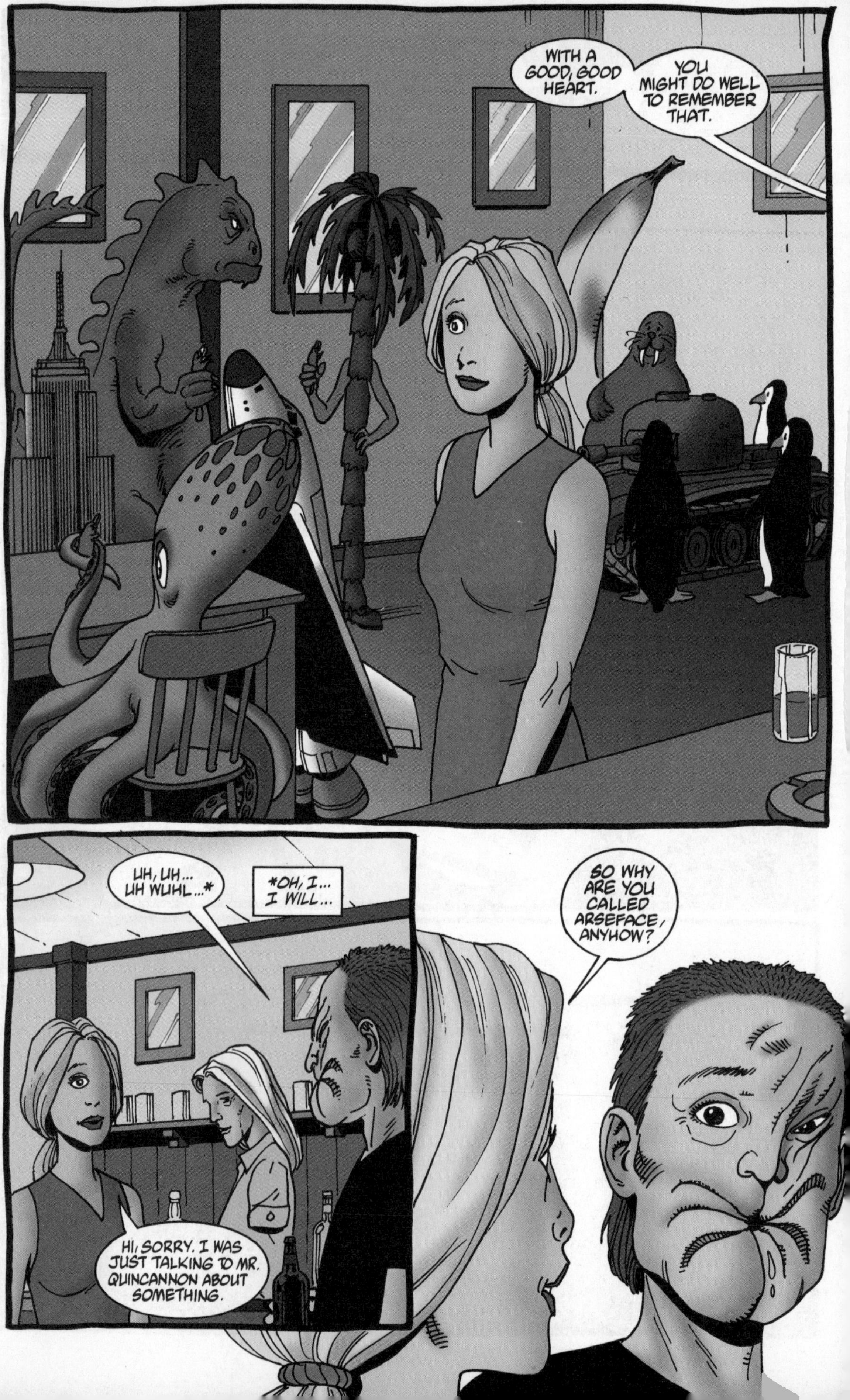
WITH A GOOD, GOOD HEART.
YOU MIGHT DO WELL TO REMEMBER THAT.
UH, UH... UH WUHL...*
*OH, I... I WILL...
HI; SORRY. I WAS JUST TALKING TO MR. QUINCANNON ABOUT SOMETHING.
SO WHY ARE YOU CALLED ARSEFACE, ANYHOW?

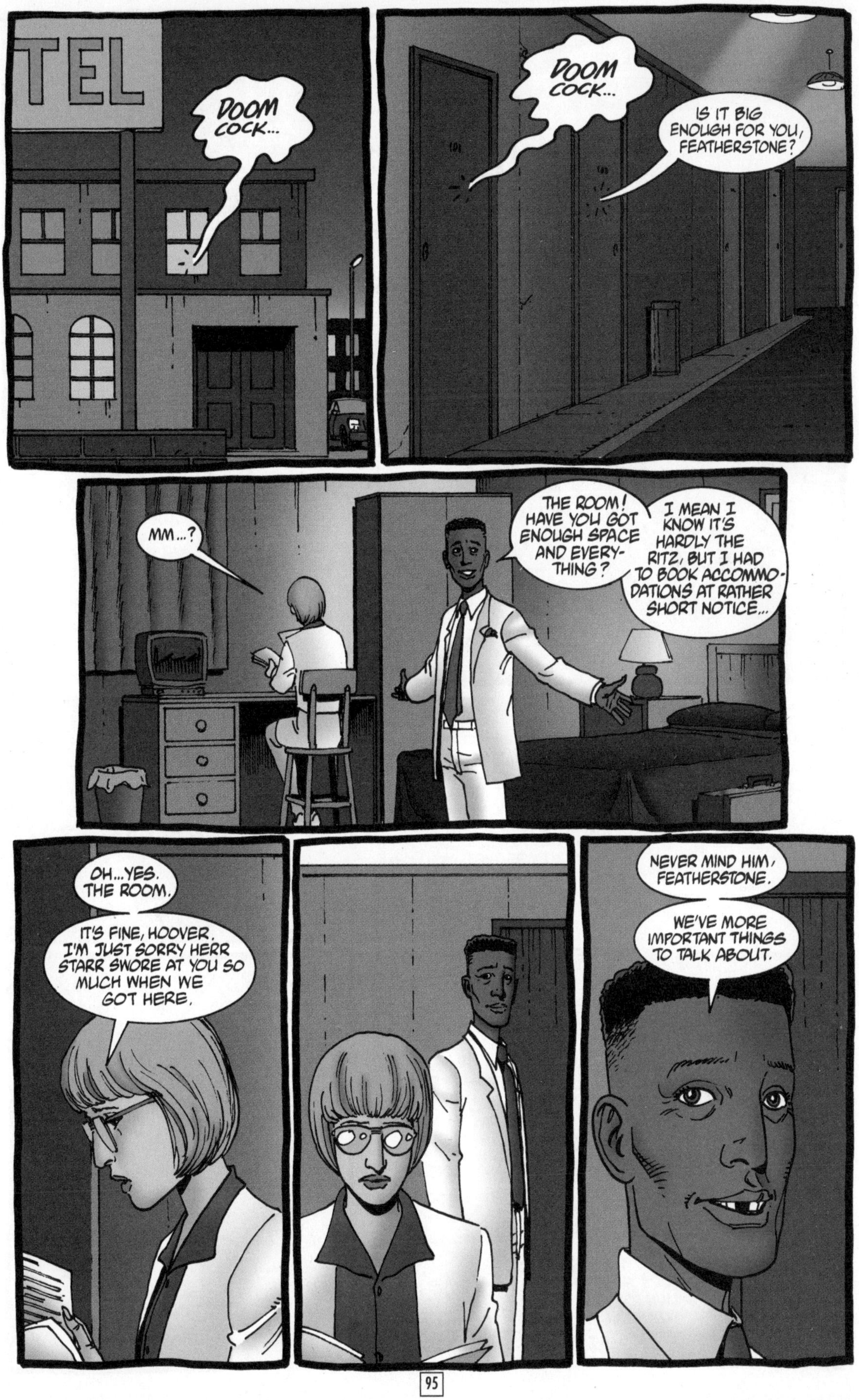
TEL
DOOM COCK...
DOOM COCK...
IS IT BIG ENOUGH FOR YOU, FEATHERSTONE?
MM...?
THE ROOM! HAVE YOU GOT ENOUGH SPACE AND EVERYTHING?
I MEAN I KNOW IT'S HARDLY THE RITZ, BUT I HAD TO BOOK ACCOMMODATIONS AT RATHER SHORT NOTICE...
OH...YES. THE ROOM.
IT'S FINE, HOOVER. I'M JUST SORRY HERR STARR SWORE AT YOU SO MUCH WHEN WE GOT HERE.
NEVER MIND HIM, FEATHERSTONE.
WE'VE MORE IMPORTANT THINGS TO TALK ABOUT.

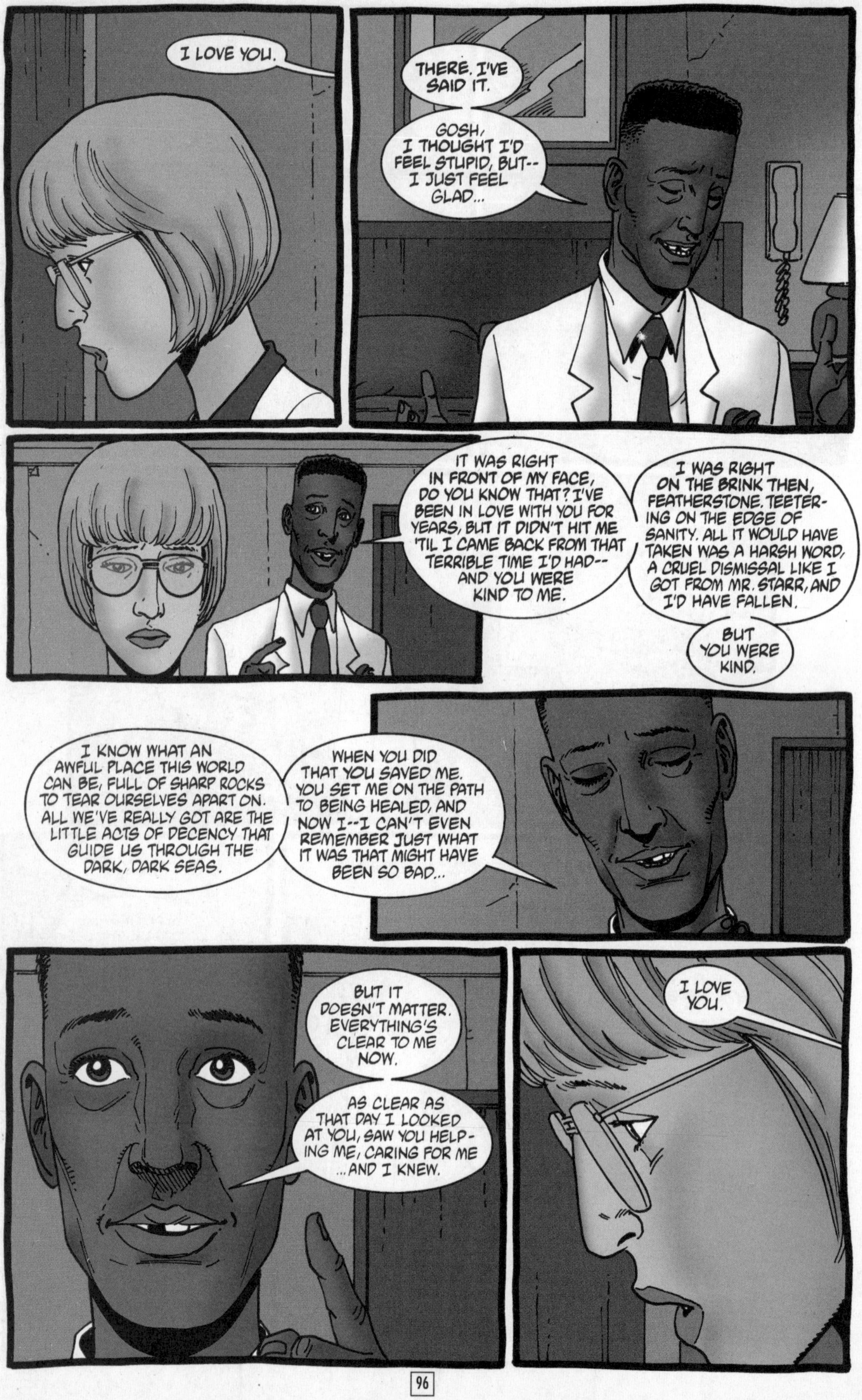
I LOVE YOU.
THERE. I'VE SAID IT.
GOSH, I THOUGHT I'D FEEL STUPID, BUT-- I JUST FEEL GLAD...
IT WAS RIGHT IN FRONT OF MY FACE, DO YOU KNOW THAT? I'VE BEEN IN LOVE WITH YOU FOR YEARS, BUT IT DIDN'T HIT ME 'TIL I CAME BACK FROM THAT TERRIBLE TIME I'D HAD-- AND YOU WERE KIND TO ME.
I WAS RIGHT ON THE BRINK THEN, FEATHERSTONE, TEETERING ON THE EDGE OF SANITY. ALL IT WOULD HAVE TAKEN WAS A HARSH WORD, A CRUEL DISMISSAL LIKE I GOT FROM MR. STARR, AND I'D HAVE FALLEN.
BUT YOU WERE KIND.
I KNOW WHAT AN AWFUL PLACE THIS WORLD CAN BE, FULL OF SHARP ROCKS TO TEAR OURSELVES APART ON. ALL WE'VE REALLY GOT ARE THE LITTLE ACTS OF DECENCY THAT GUIDE US THROUGH THE DARK, DARK SEAS.
WHEN YOU DID THAT YOU SAVED ME. YOU SET ME ON THE PATH TO BEING HEALED, AND NOW I--I CAN'T EVEN REMEMBER JUST WHAT IT WAS THAT MIGHT HAVE BEEN SO BAD...
BUT IT DOESN'T MATTER. EVERYTHING'S CLEAR TO ME NOW.
AS CLEAR AS THAT DAY I LOOKED AT YOU, SAW YOU HELPING ME, CARING FOR ME ...AND I KNEW.
I LOVE YOU.

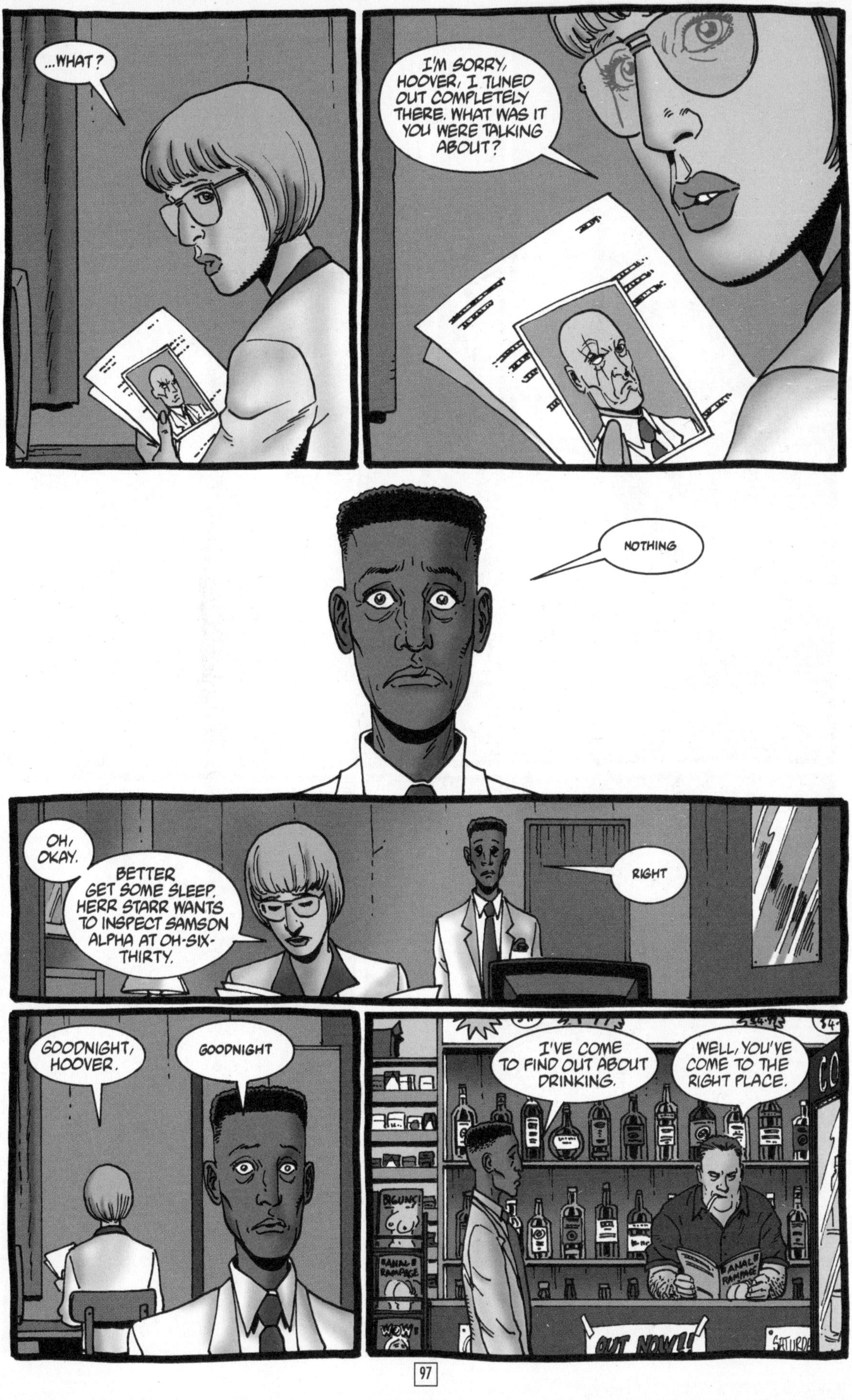
...WHAT?
I'M SORRY, HOOVER, I TUNED OUT COMPLETELY THERE. WHAT WAS IT YOU WERE TALKING ABOUT?
NOTHING
OH, OKAY.
BETTER GET SOME SLEEP. HERR STARR WANTS TO INSPECT SAMSON ALPHA AT OH-SIX-THIRTY.
RIGHT
GOODNIGHT, HOOVER.
GOODNIGHT
I'VE COME TO FIND OUT ABOUT DRINKING.
WELL, YOU'VE COME TO THE RIGHT PLACE.
BIGUNS!
ANAL RAMPAGE
ANAL RAMPAGE
OUT NOW!!

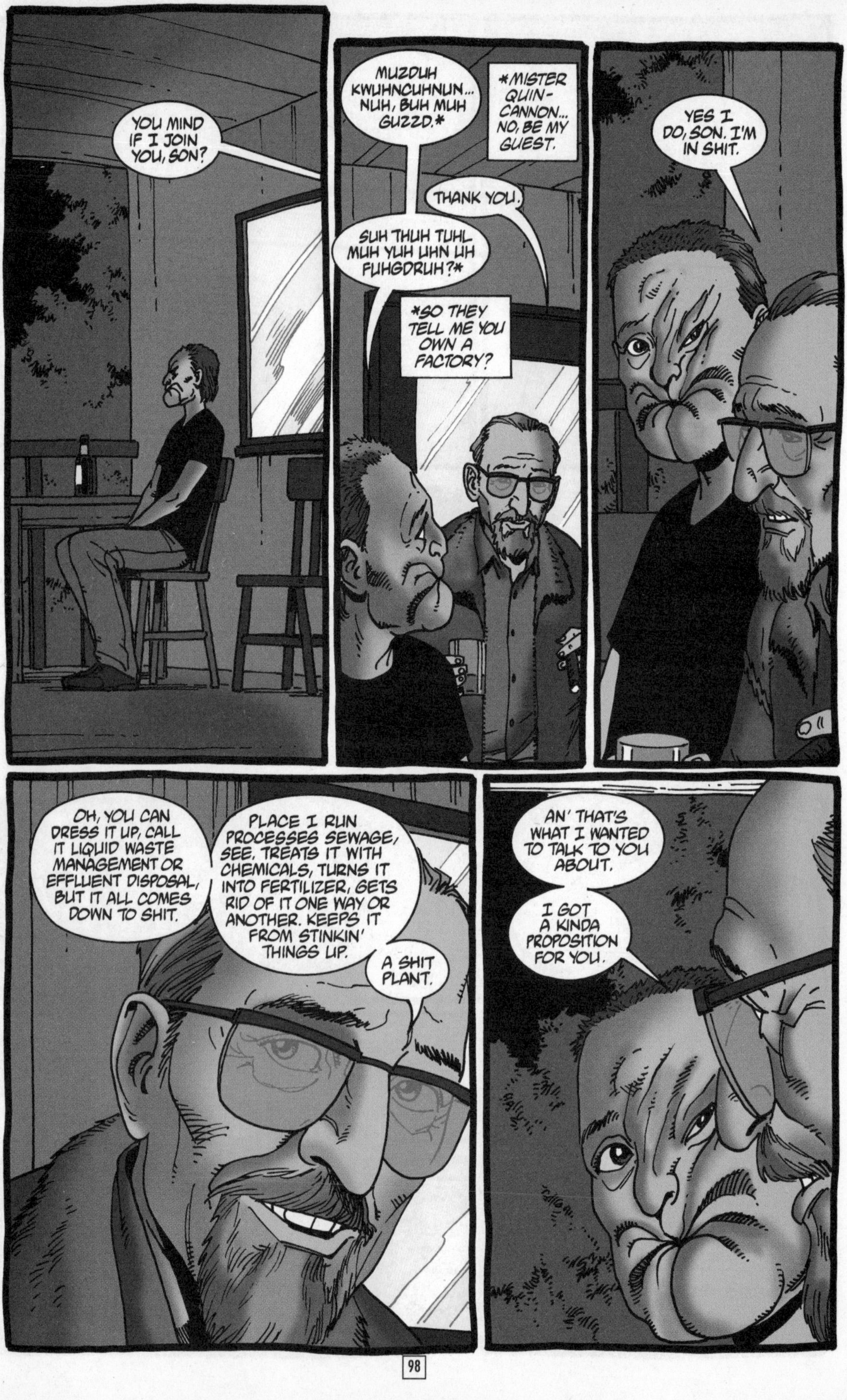

YOU MIND IF I JOIN YOU, SON?
MUZDUH KWUHNCUHNUN... NUH, BUH MUH GUZZD.*
*MISTER QUIN-CANNON... NO, BE MY GUEST.
THANK YOU.
SUH THUH TUHL MUH YUH UHN UH FUHGDRUH?*
*SO THEY TELL ME YOU OWN A FACTORY?
YES I DO, SON. I'M IN SHIT.
OH, YOU CAN DRESS IT UP, CALL IT LIQUID WASTE MANAGEMENT OR EFFLUENT DISPOSAL, BUT IT ALL COMES DOWN TO SHIT.
PLACE I RUN PROCESSES SEWAGE, SEE. TREATS IT WITH CHEMICALS, TURNS IT INTO FERTILIZER, GETS RID OF IT ONE WAY OR ANOTHER. KEEPS IT FROM STINKIN' THINGS UP.
A SHIT PLANT.
AN' THAT'S WHAT I WANTED TO TALK TO YOU ABOUT.
I GOT A KINDA PROPOSITION FOR YOU.

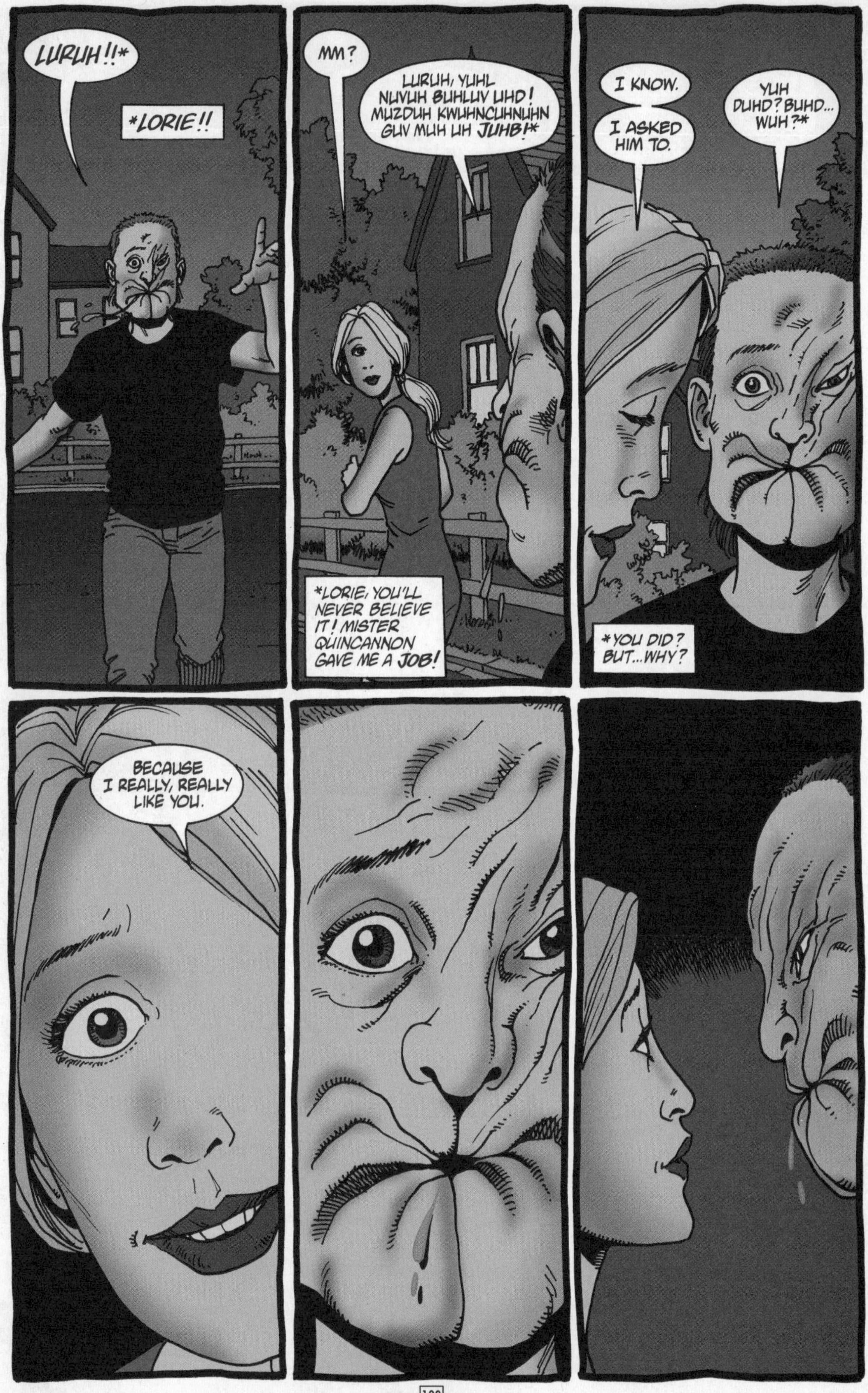
LURUH!!*
*LORIE!!
MM?
LURUH, YUHL NUVUH BUHLUV UHD! MUZDUH KWUHNCUHNUHN GUV MUH UH JUHB!*
*LORIE, YOU'LL NEVER BELIEVE IT! MISTER QUINCANNON GAVE ME A JOB!
I KNOW.
I ASKED HIM TO.
YUH DUHD? BUHD... WUH?*
*YOU DID? BUT...WHY?
BECAUSE I REALLY, REALLY LIKE YOU.

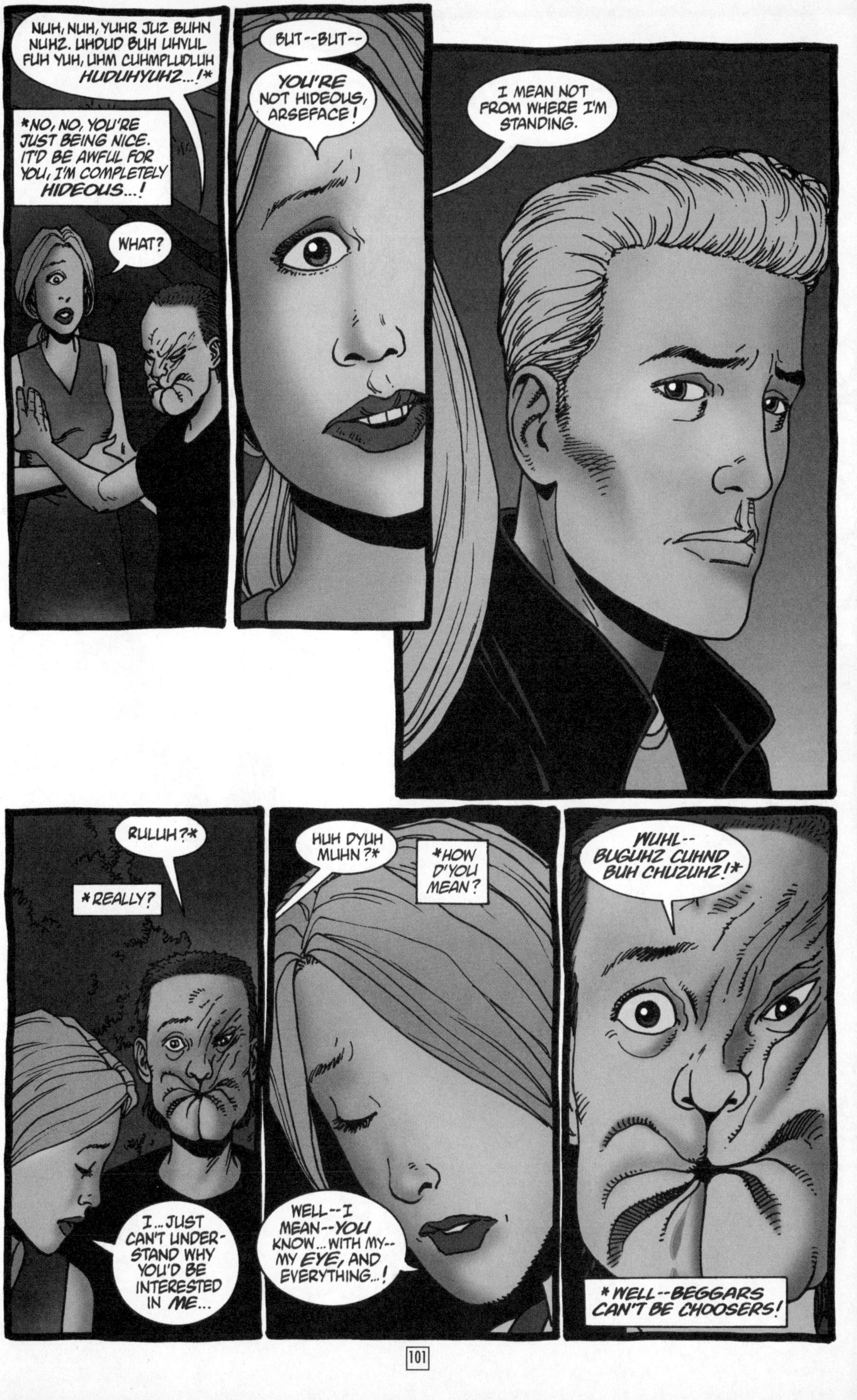
NUH, NUH, YUHR JUZ BUHN NUHZ. UHDUD BUH UHYUL FUH YUH, UHM CUHMPLUDLUH HUDUHYUHZ...!*
*NO, NO, YOU'RE JUST BEING NICE. IT'D BE AWFUL FOR YOU, I'M COMPLETELY HIDEOUS...!
WHAT?
BUT--BUT--
YOU'RE NOT HIDEOUS, ARSEFACE!
I MEAN NOT FROM WHERE I'M STANDING.
RULUH?*
*REALLY?
I...JUST CAN'T UNDERSTAND WHY YOU'D BE INTERESTED IN ME...
HUH DYUH MUHN?*
*HOW D'YOU MEAN?
WELL--I MEAN--YOU KNOW...WITH MY--MY EYE, AND EVERYTHING...!
WUHL--BUGUHZ CUHND BUH CHUZUHZ!*
*WELL--BEGGARS CAN'T BE CHOOSERS!

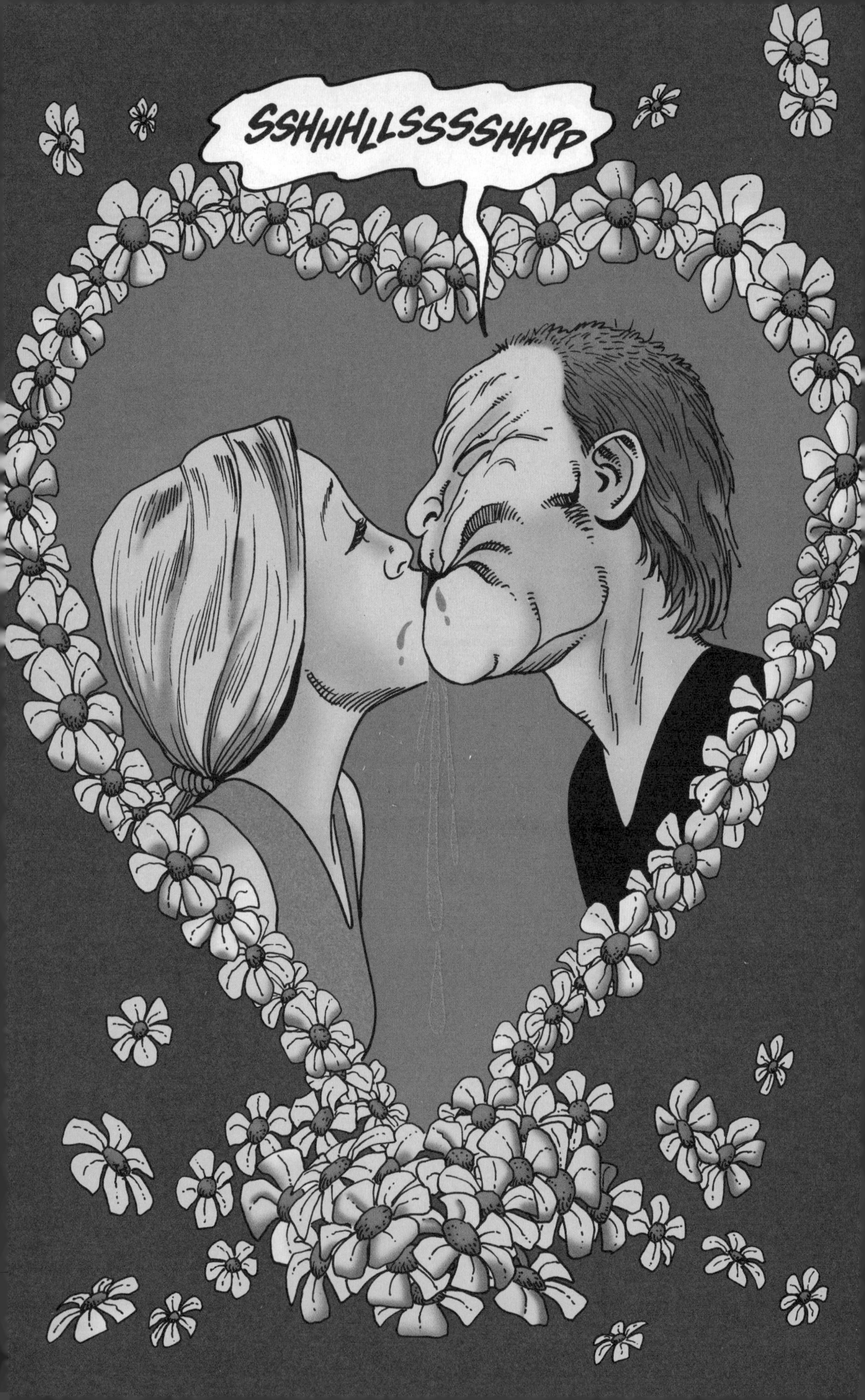
SSHHHLLSSSSSHHPP

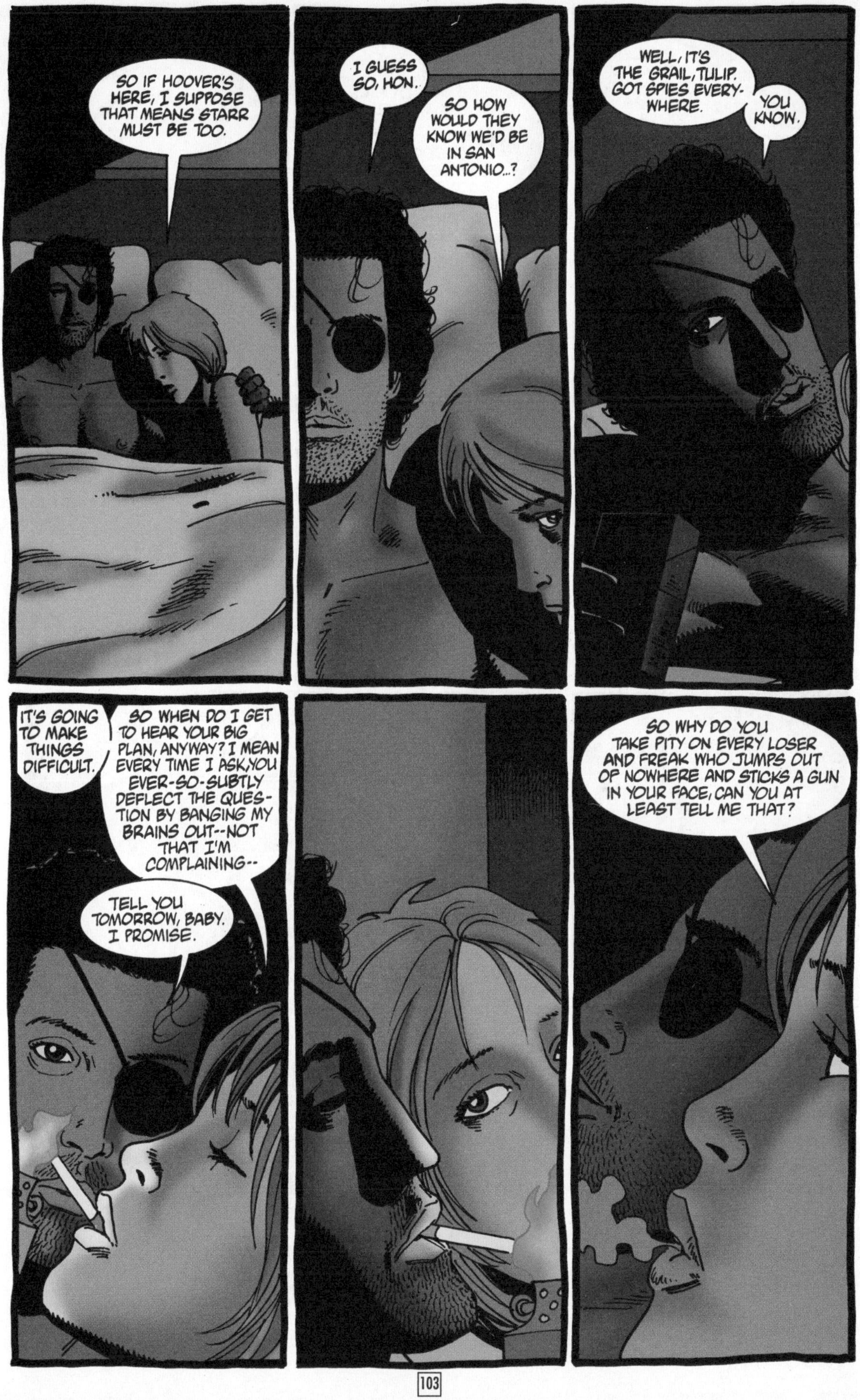
SO IF HOOVER'S HERE, I SUPPOSE THAT MEANS STARR MUST BE TOO.
I GUESS SO, HON.
SO HOW WOULD THEY KNOW WE'D BE IN SAN ANTONIO...?
WELL, IT'S THE GRAIL, TULIP. GOT SPIES EVERYWHERE.
YOU KNOW.
IT'S GOING TO MAKE THINGS DIFFICULT.
SO WHEN DO I GET TO HEAR YOUR BIG PLAN, ANYWAY? I MEAN EVERY TIME I ASK, YOU EVER-SO-SUBTLY DEFLECT THE QUESTION BY BANGING MY BRAINS OUT--NOT THAT I'M COMPLAINING--
TELL YOU TOMORROW, BABY. I PROMISE.
SO WHY DO YOU TAKE PITY ON EVERY LOSER AND FREAK WHO JUMPS OUT OF NOWHERE AND STICKS A GUN IN YOUR FACE, CAN YOU AT LEAST TELL ME THAT?

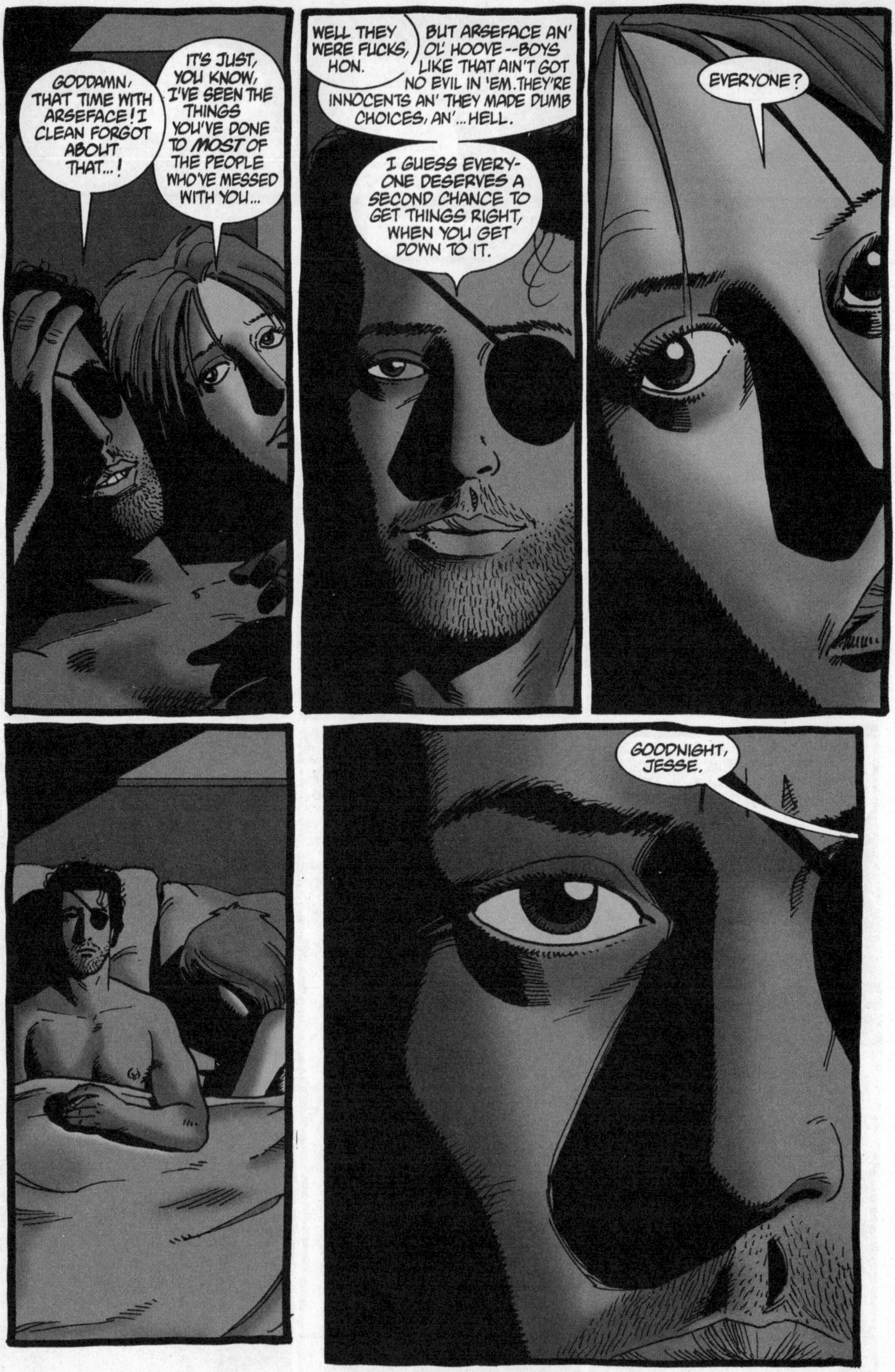
GODDAMN, THAT TIME WITH ARSEFACE! I CLEAN FORGOT ABOUT THAT...!
IT'S JUST, YOU KNOW, I'VE SEEN THE THINGS YOU'VE DONE TO MOST OF THE PEOPLE WHO'VE MESSED WITH YOU...
WELL THEY WERE FUCKS, HON.
BUT ARSEFACE AN' OL' HOOVE --BOYS LIKE THAT AIN'T GOT NO EVIL IN 'EM. THEY'RE INNOCENTS AN' THEY MADE DUMB CHOICES, AN'... HELL.
I GUESS EVERY-ONE DESERVES A SECOND CHANCE TO GET THINGS RIGHT, WHEN YOU GET DOWN TO IT.
EVERYONE?
GOODNIGHT, JESSE.

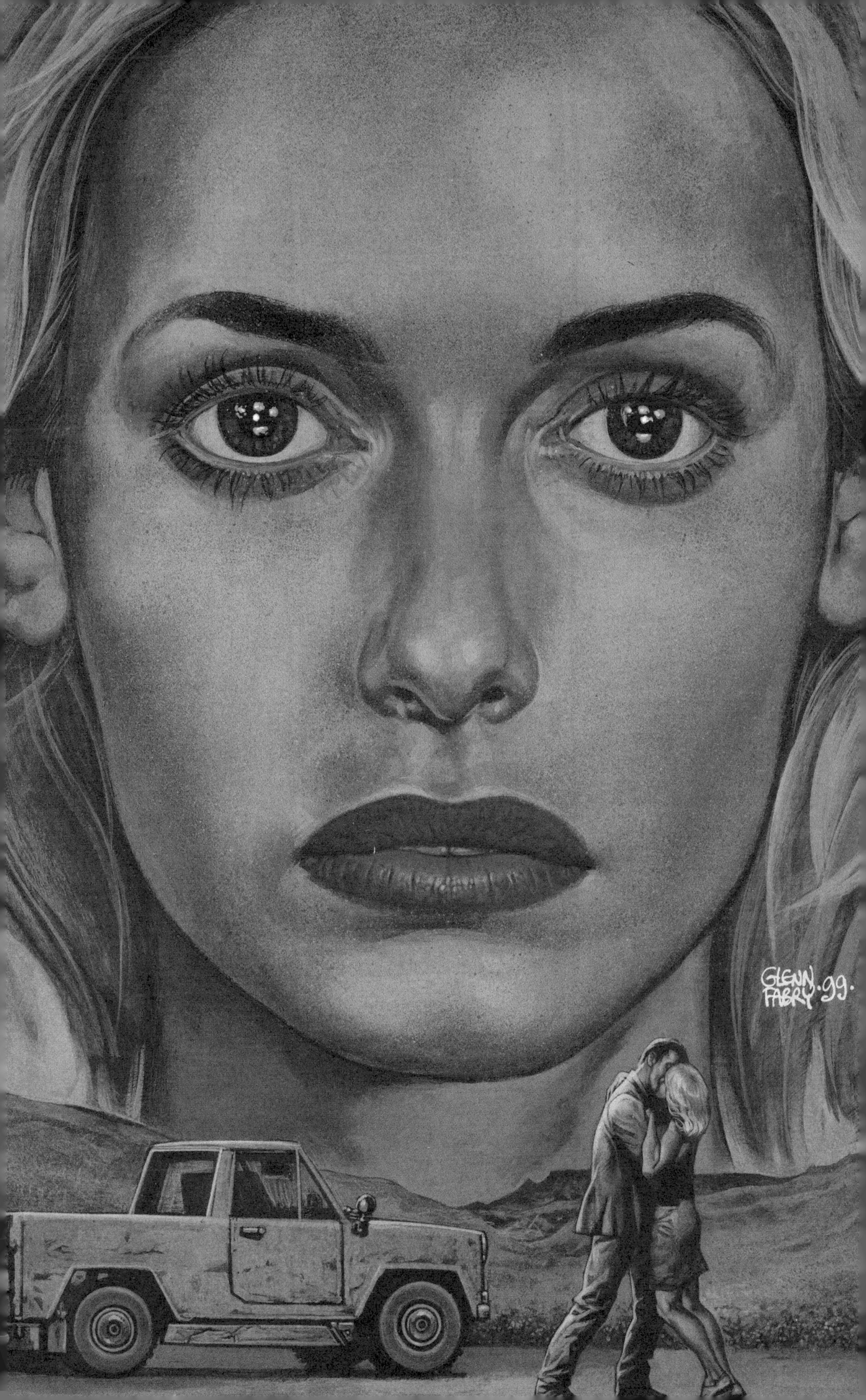
GLENN FABRY ·99·

HUH?

I DIDN'T MAKE IT.

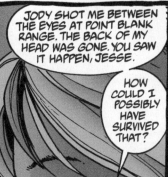

JODY SHOT ME BETWEEN THE EYES AT POINT BLANK RANGE. THE BACK OF MY HEAD WAS GONE. YOU SAW IT HAPPEN, JESSE.

HOW COULD I POSSIBLY HAVE SURVIVED THAT?

TULIP... HONEY, WHAT'RE YOU TALKIN' 'BOUT?

YOU KNOW WHAT HAPPENED. GOD BROUGHT YOU BACK. IT WAS A WARNIN'; HE SAVED YOU SO I'D LEAVE HIM BE...

BUT WHY WOULD GOD SAVE ME, JESSE?

YOU KNOW AS WELL AS I DO:

GOD'S A BASTARD.

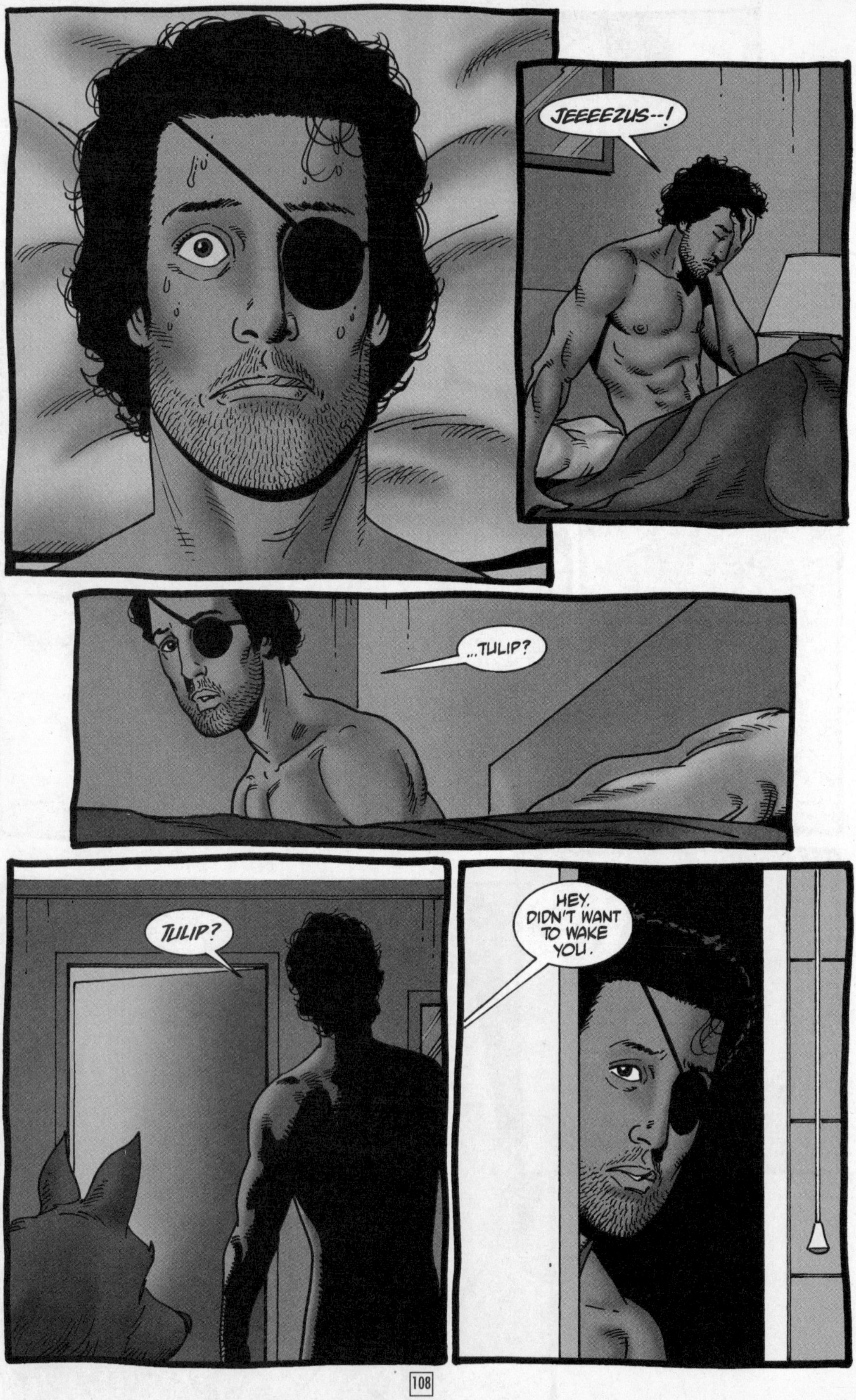
JEEEEZUS--!
...TULIP?
TULIP?
HEY. DIDN'T WANT TO WAKE YOU.

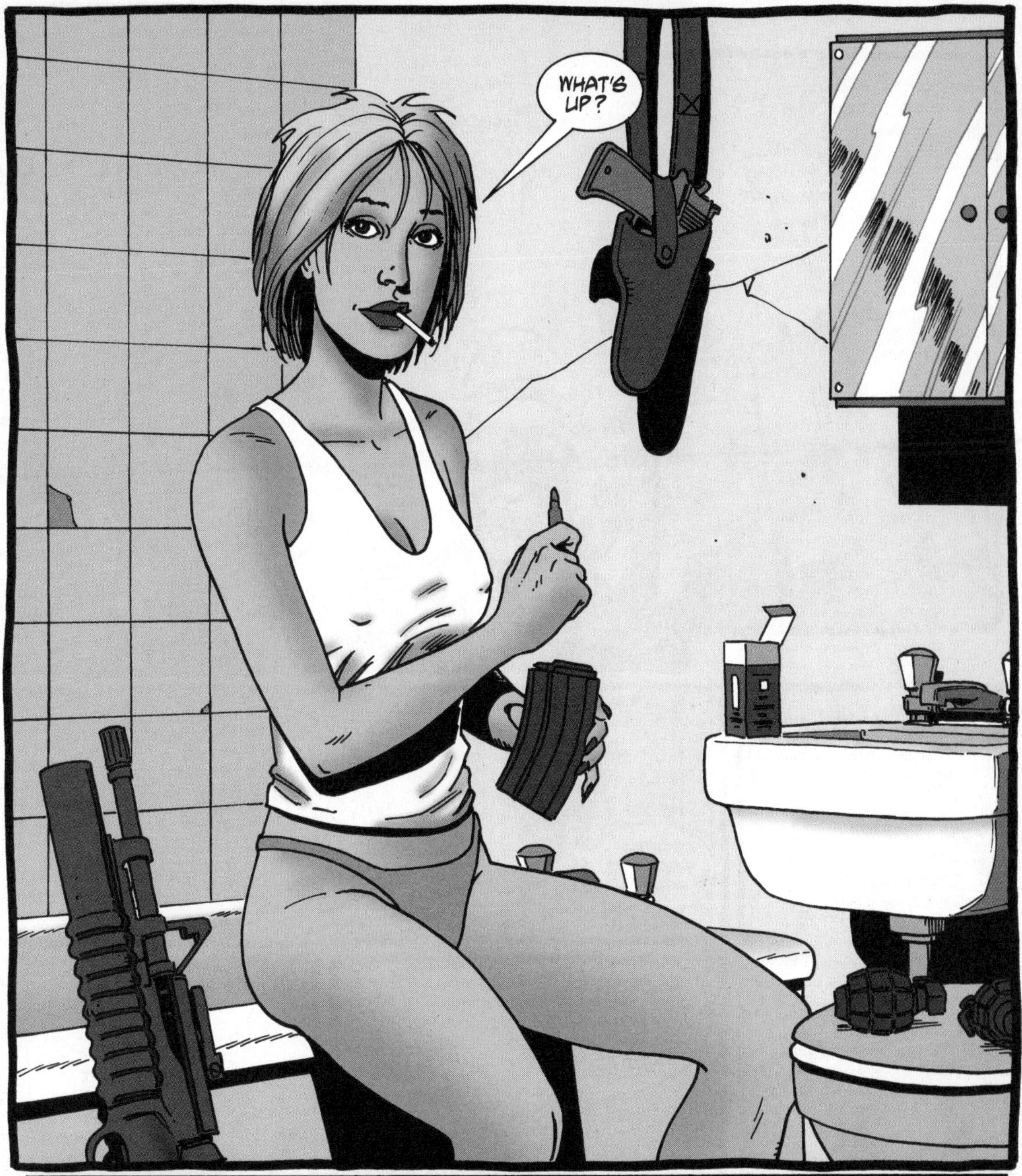
WHAT'S UP?

JESSE'S GIRL

GARTH ENNIS - Writer STEVE DILLON - Artist
PAMELA RAMBO - Colorist CLEM ROBINS - Letterer AXEL ALONSO - Editor
PREACHER created by GARTH ENNIS and STEVE DILLON

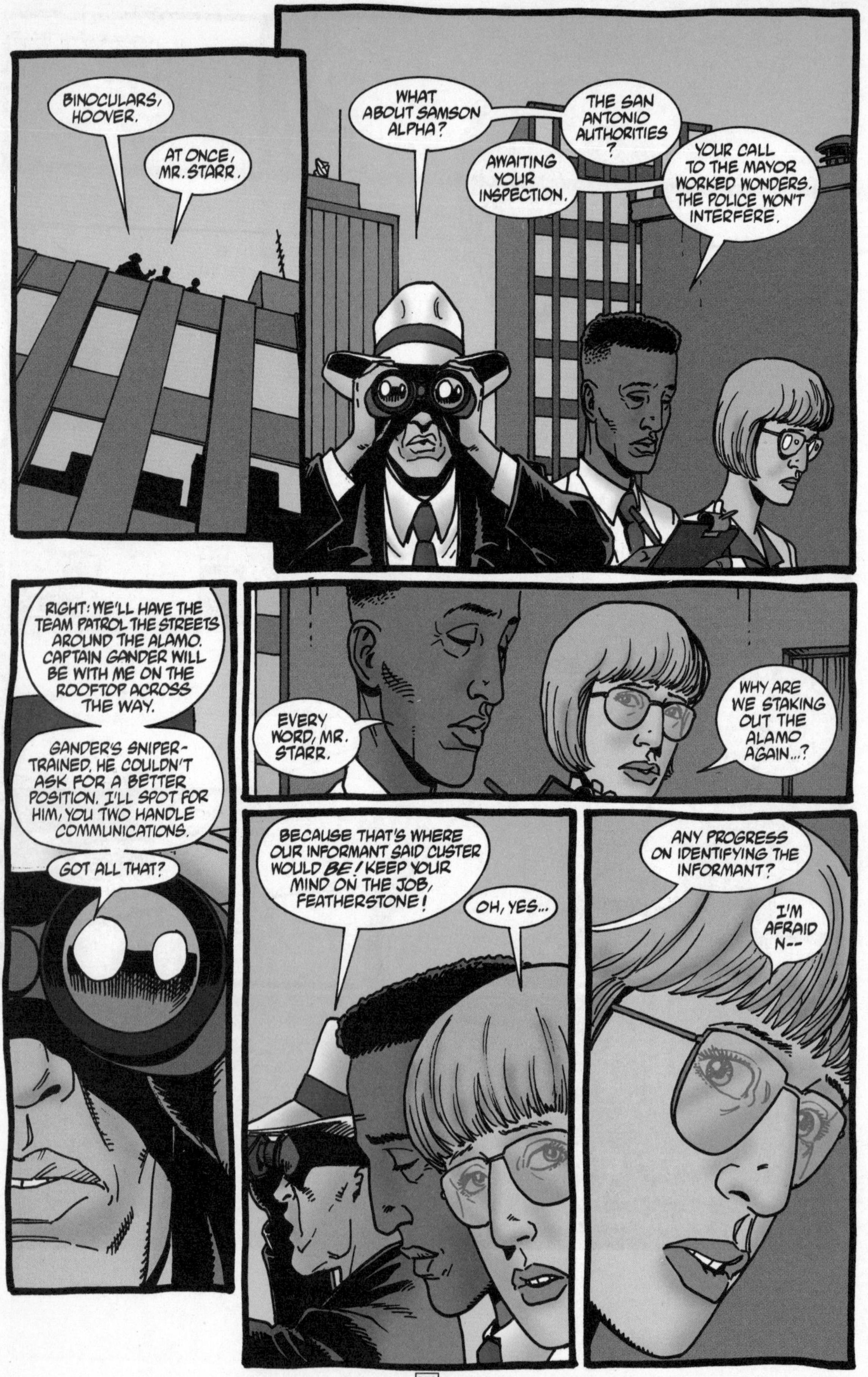

BINOCULARS, HOOVER.
AT ONCE, MR. STARR.
WHAT ABOUT SAMSON ALPHA?
THE SAN ANTONIO AUTHORITIES?
AWAITING YOUR INSPECTION.
YOUR CALL TO THE MAYOR WORKED WONDERS. THE POLICE WON'T INTERFERE.
RIGHT: WE'LL HAVE THE TEAM PATROL THE STREETS AROUND THE ALAMO. CAPTAIN GANDER WILL BE WITH ME ON THE ROOFTOP ACROSS THE WAY.
GANDER'S SNIPER-TRAINED. HE COULDN'T ASK FOR A BETTER POSITION. I'LL SPOT FOR HIM, YOU TWO HANDLE COMMUNICATIONS.
GOT ALL THAT?
EVERY WORD, MR. STARR.
WHY ARE WE STAKING OUT THE ALAMO AGAIN...?
BECAUSE THAT'S WHERE OUR INFORMANT SAID CUSTER WOULD *BE*! KEEP YOUR MIND ON THE JOB, FEATHERSTONE!
OH, YES...
ANY PROGRESS ON IDENTIFYING THE INFORMANT?
I'M AFRAID N--

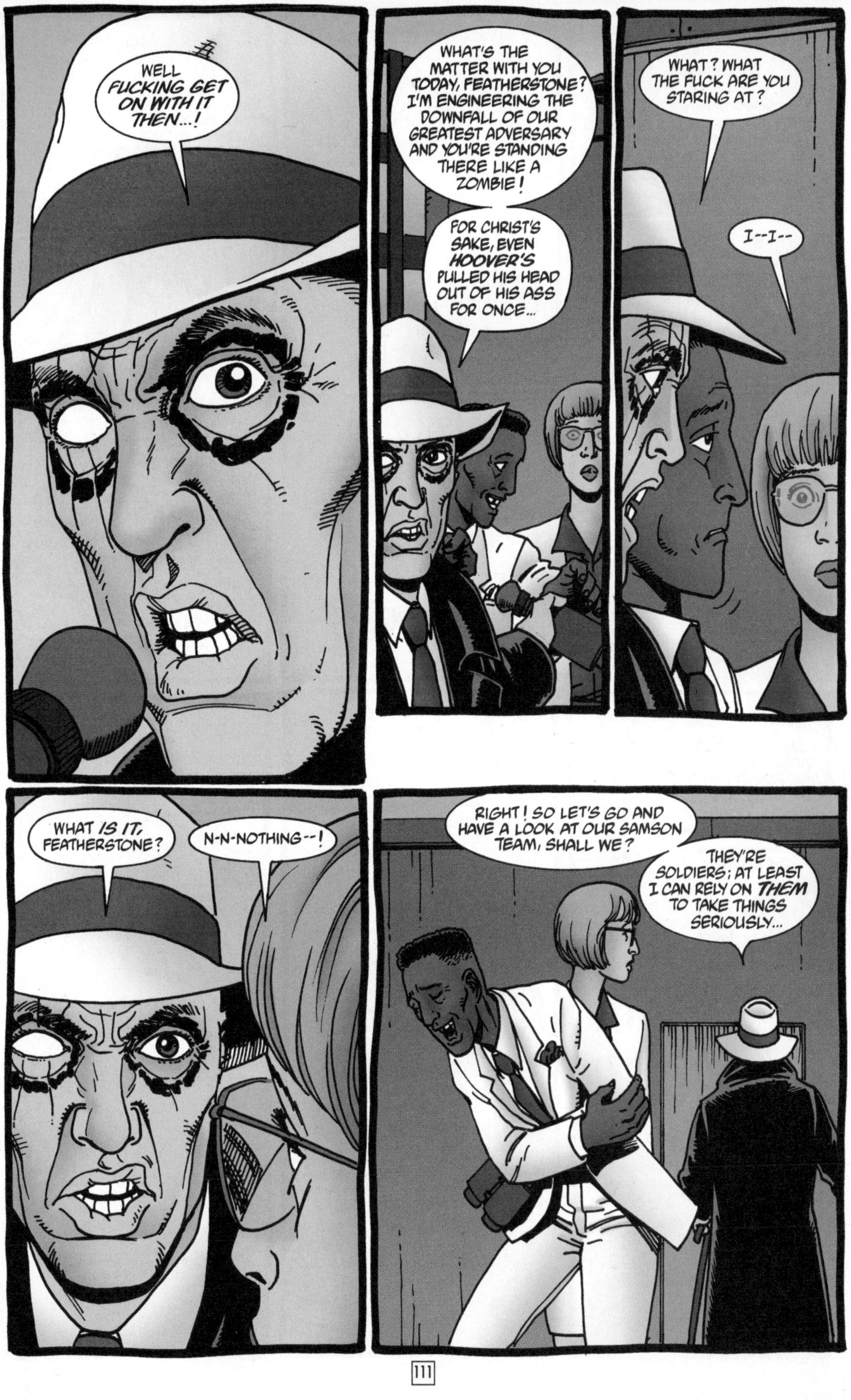
WELL FUCKING GET ON WITH IT THEN...!
WHAT'S THE MATTER WITH YOU TODAY, FEATHERSTONE? I'M ENGINEERING THE DOWNFALL OF OUR GREATEST ADVERSARY AND YOU'RE STANDING THERE LIKE A ZOMBIE!
FOR CHRIST'S SAKE, EVEN HOOVER'S PULLED HIS HEAD OUT OF HIS ASS FOR ONCE...
WHAT? WHAT THE FUCK ARE YOU STARING AT?
I--I--
WHAT IS IT, FEATHERSTONE?
N-N-NOTHING--!
RIGHT! SO LET'S GO AND HAVE A LOOK AT OUR SAMSON TEAM, SHALL WE?
THEY'RE SOLDIERS; AT LEAST I CAN RELY ON THEM TO TAKE THINGS SERIOUSLY...

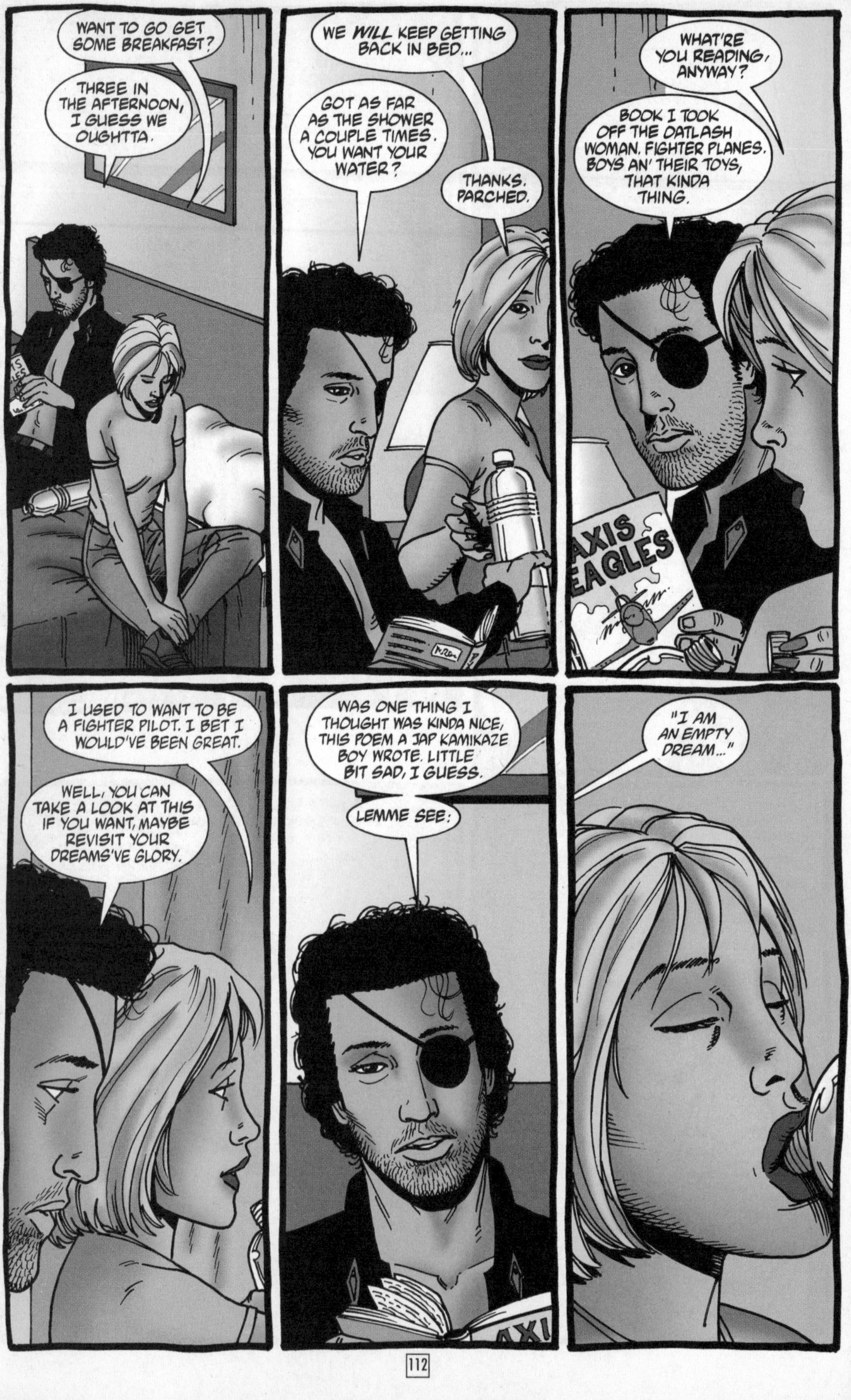
WANT TO GO GET SOME BREAKFAST?
THREE IN THE AFTERNOON, I GUESS WE OUGHTTA.
WE WILL KEEP GETTING BACK IN BED...
GOT AS FAR AS THE SHOWER A COUPLE TIMES. YOU WANT YOUR WATER?
THANKS. PARCHED.
WHAT'RE YOU READING, ANYWAY?
BOOK I TOOK OFF THE DATLASH WOMAN. FIGHTER PLANES. BOYS AN' THEIR TOYS, THAT KINDA THING.
AXIS EAGLES
I USED TO WANT TO BE A FIGHTER PILOT. I BET I WOULD'VE BEEN GREAT.
WELL, YOU CAN TAKE A LOOK AT THIS IF YOU WANT, MAYBE REVISIT YOUR DREAMS'VE GLORY.
WAS ONE THING I THOUGHT WAS KINDA NICE, THIS POEM A JAP KAMIKAZE BOY WROTE. LITTLE BIT SAD, I GUESS.
LEMME SEE:
"I AM AN EMPTY DREAM..."

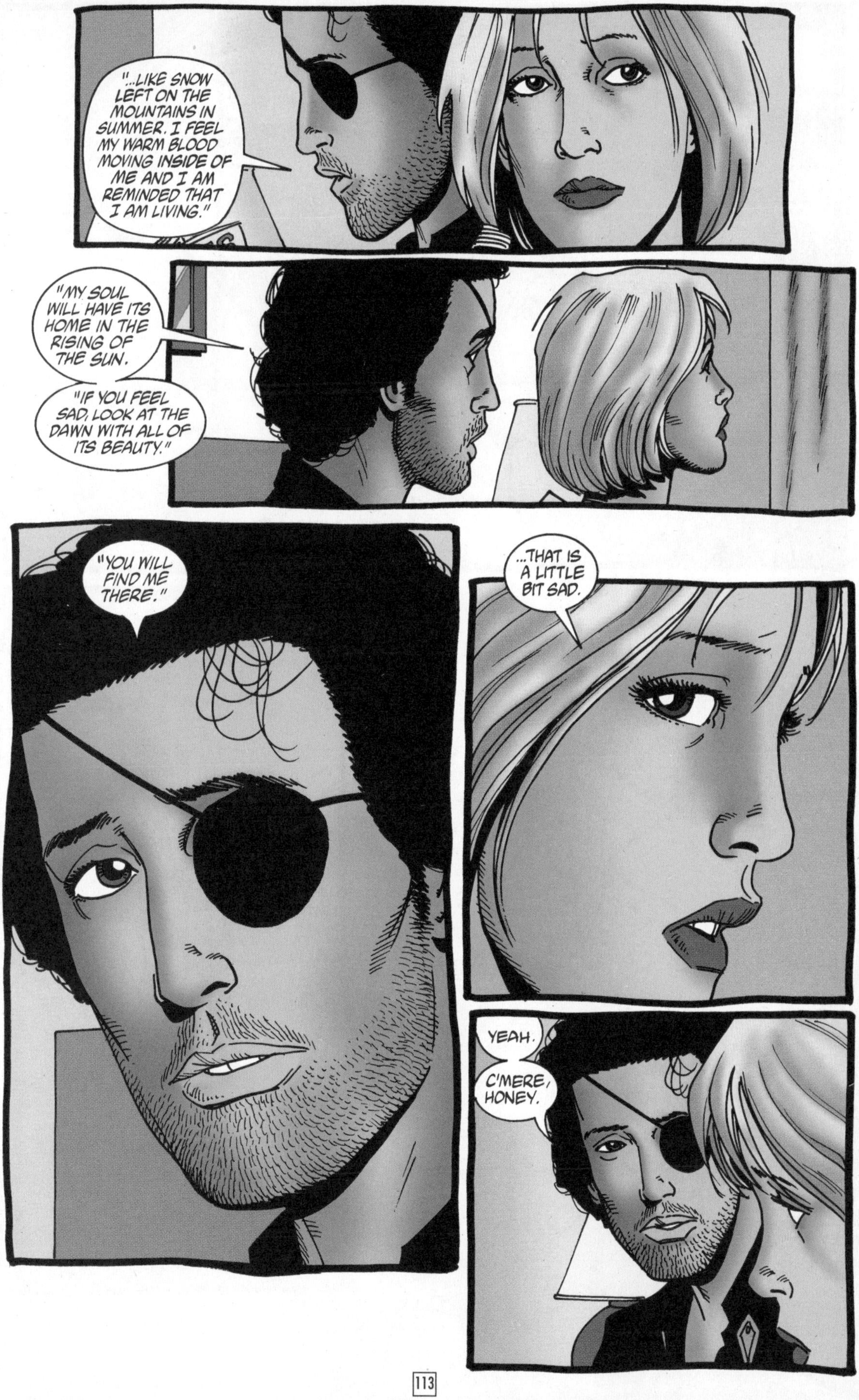
"...LIKE SNOW LEFT ON THE MOUNTAINS IN SUMMER. I FEEL MY WARM BLOOD MOVING INSIDE OF ME AND I AM REMINDED THAT I AM LIVING."
"MY SOUL WILL HAVE ITS HOME IN THE RISING OF THE SUN.
"IF YOU FEEL SAD, LOOK AT THE DAWN WITH ALL OF ITS BEAUTY."
"YOU WILL FIND ME THERE."
...THAT IS A LITTLE BIT SAD.
YEAH.
C'MERE, HONEY.

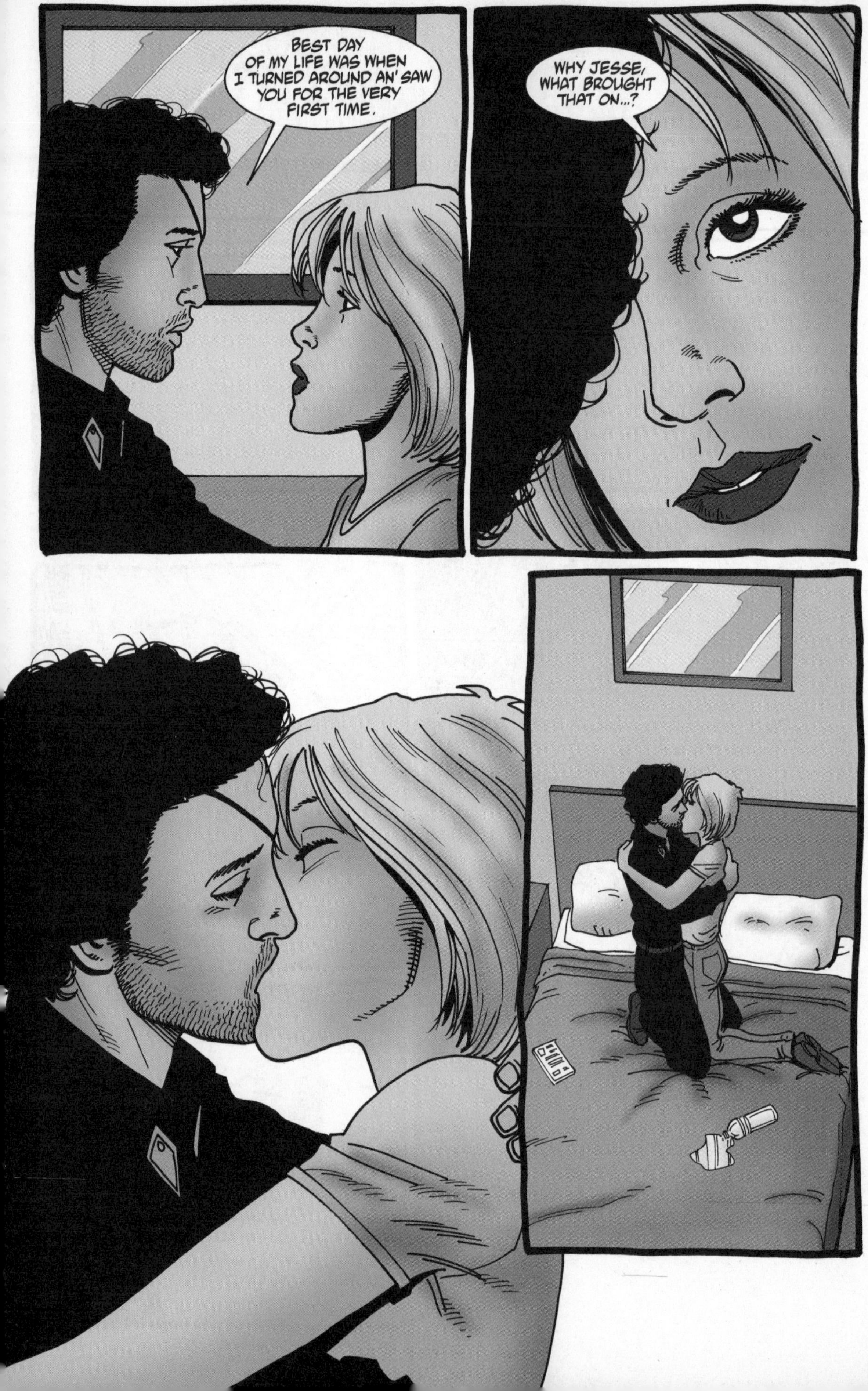
BEST DAY OF MY LIFE WAS WHEN I TURNED AROUND AN' SAW YOU FOR THE VERY FIRST TIME.
WHY JESSE, WHAT BROUGHT THAT ON...?

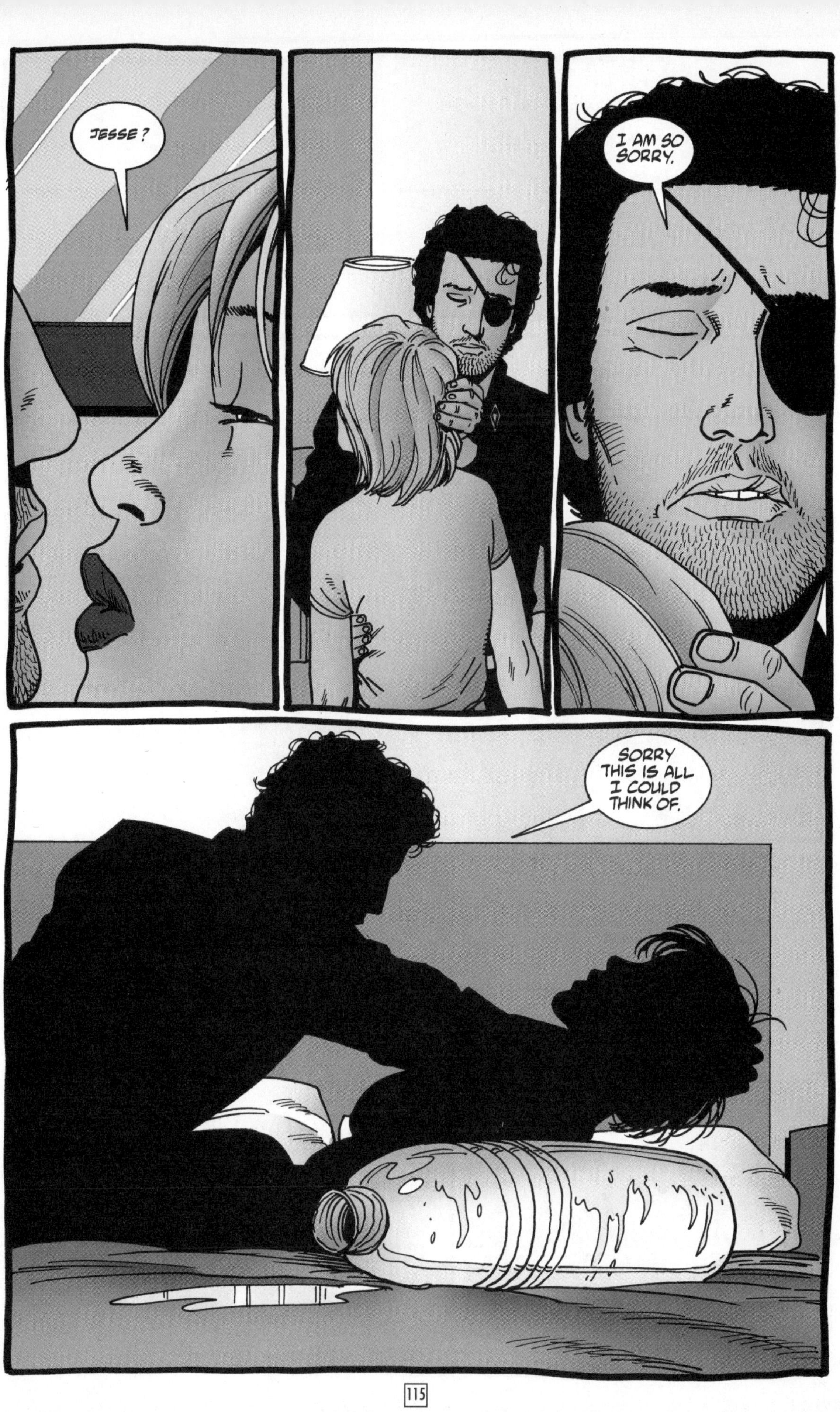
JESSE ?
I AM SO SORRY.
SORRY THIS IS ALL I COULD THINK OF.

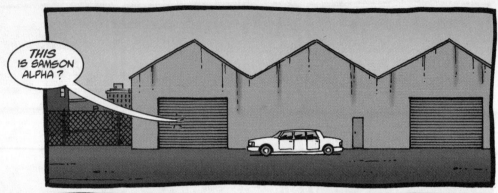

THIS IS SAMSON ALPHA?

THIS IS EVERYONE WE'VE GOT, IS THAT WHAT YOU'RE TRYING TO TELL ME? THE GRAIL'S ENTIRE MILITARY CAPABILITY CONSISTS OF TWO DOZEN MEN?

WE LOST NINETY PERCENT OF OUR SAMSON FORCE AT MASADA, MR. STARR. MONUMENT VALLEY TOOK CARE OF THE REST.

WHAT YOU HAVE HERE ARE CAPTAIN GANDER'S TEAM FROM LeSAINT MARIE, AND THE FEW DEEP COVER OPERATIVES WHO ACTUALLY BOTHERED TO SHOW UP.

WHAT?

WELL...MOST OF THEM DIDN'T EVEN ACKNOWLEDGE YOUR PRIORITY EDICT. THOSE WHO DID MENTIONED CONCERNS ABOUT GRAIL POLICY, LOSS OF FAITH IN THE CURRENT LEADERSHIP...

BUT READING BETWEEN THE LINES, I THINK THE PROBLEM IS THAT THEY ALL RATHER *LIKE* DEEP COVER.

I MEAN YOU'RE TALKING ABOUT PEOPLE WHO MOVE IN THE HIGHEST ECHELONS OF POLITICAL POWER AS THEY SHADOW THEIR TARGETS, PEOPLE WHO LIVE IN THE LAP OF LUXURY...YOU CAN SEE HOW THEY MIGHT NOT BE ALL THAT KEEN TO LEAVE IT...

THOSE *FUCKERS*--!

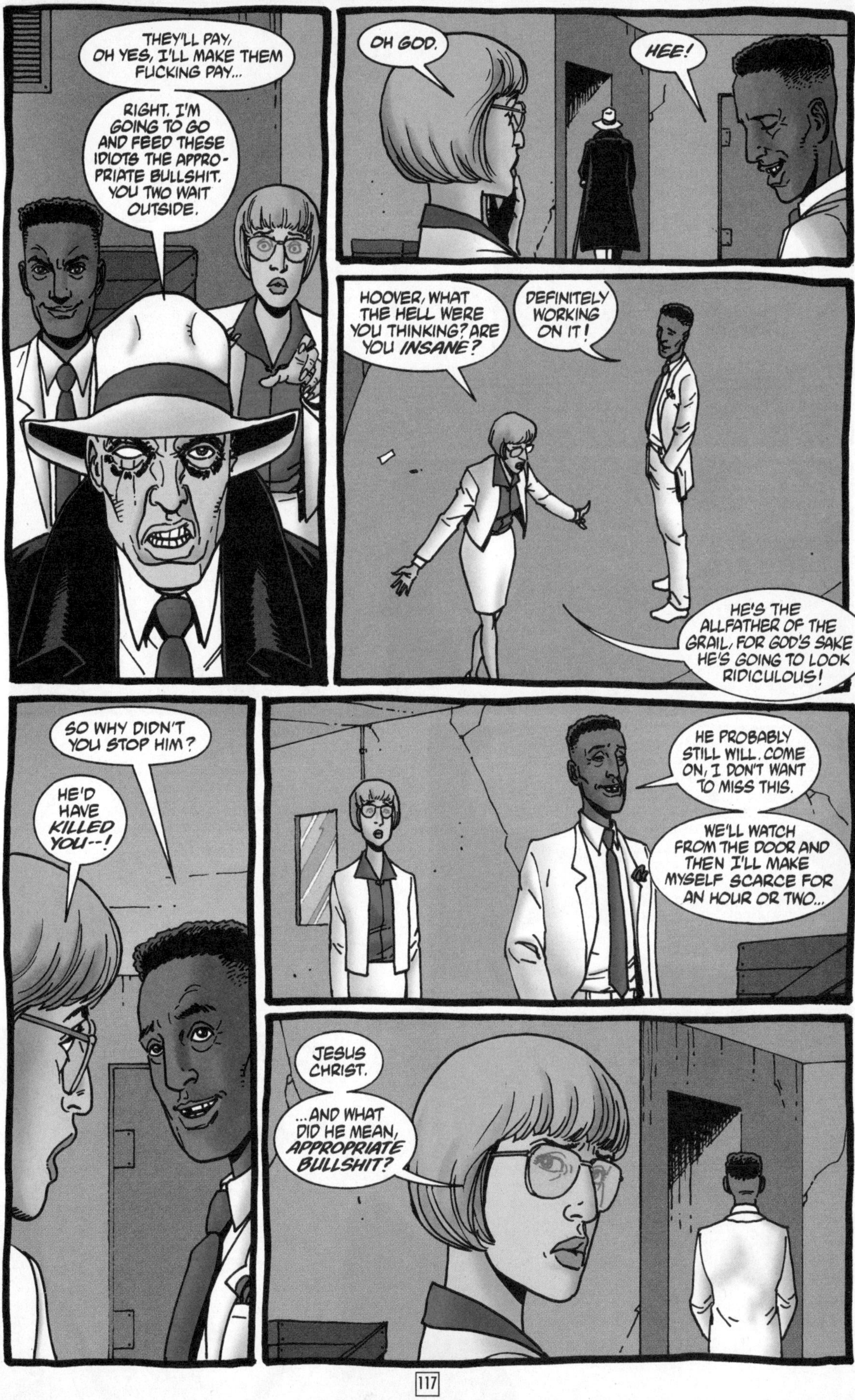
THEY'LL PAY, OH YES, I'LL MAKE THEM FUCKING PAY...
RIGHT. I'M GOING TO GO AND FEED THESE IDIOTS THE APPROPRIATE BULLSHIT. YOU TWO WAIT OUTSIDE.
OH GOD.
HEE!
HOOVER, WHAT THE HELL WERE YOU THINKING? ARE YOU *INSANE*?
DEFINITELY WORKING ON IT!
HE'S THE ALLFATHER OF THE GRAIL, FOR GOD'S SAKE! HE'S GOING TO LOOK RIDICULOUS!
SO WHY DIDN'T YOU STOP HIM?
HE'D HAVE *KILLED YOU--!*
HE PROBABLY STILL WILL. COME ON, I DON'T WANT TO MISS THIS.
WE'LL WATCH FROM THE DOOR AND THEN I'LL MAKE MYSELF SCARCE FOR AN HOUR OR TWO...
JESUS CHRIST.
...AND WHAT DID HE MEAN, *APPROPRIATE BULLSHIT?*

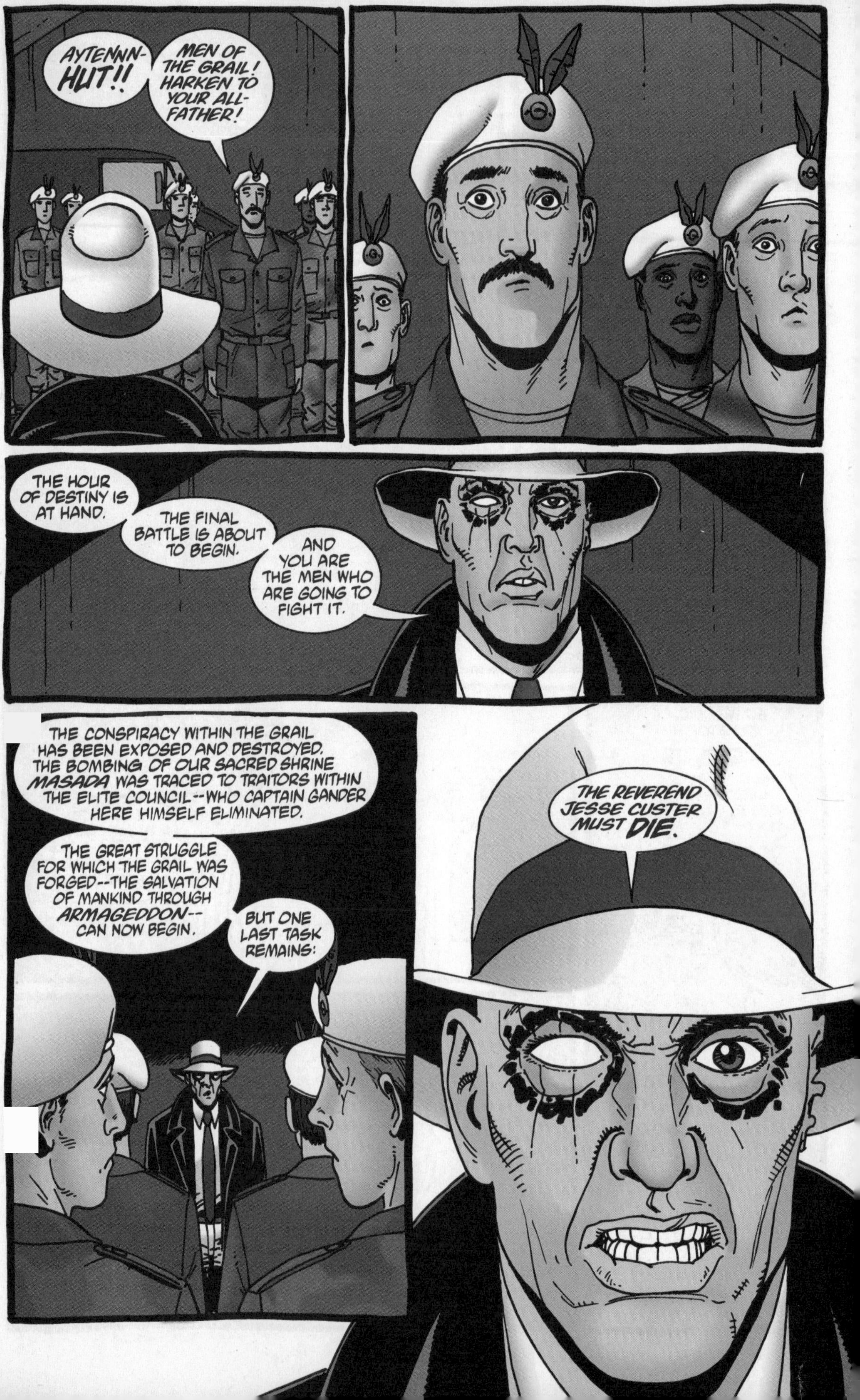
AYTENNN-HUT!!
MEN OF THE GRAIL! HARKEN TO YOUR ALL-FATHER!
THE HOUR OF DESTINY IS AT HAND.
THE FINAL BATTLE IS ABOUT TO BEGIN.
AND YOU ARE THE MEN WHO ARE GOING TO FIGHT IT.
THE CONSPIRACY WITHIN THE GRAIL HAS BEEN EXPOSED AND DESTROYED. THE BOMBING OF OUR SACRED SHRINE MASADA WAS TRACED TO TRAITORS WITHIN THE ELITE COUNCIL--WHO CAPTAIN GANDER HERE HIMSELF ELIMINATED.
THE GREAT STRUGGLE FOR WHICH THE GRAIL WAS FORGED--THE SALVATION OF MANKIND THROUGH ARMAGEDDON--CAN NOW BEGIN.
BUT ONE LAST TASK REMAINS:
THE REVEREND JESSE CUSTER MUST DIE.

THIS MAN IS OUR MOST *LETHAL* ENEMY. THE BLOOD HE HAS SPILLED--THE TOLL HE HAS TAKEN OF YOUR COMRADES-IN-ARMS -- CANNOT GO UNAVENGED.

FOR ARMAGEDDON TO COMMENCE, THIS *DEVIL* MUST BE EXORCISED. AND THAT IS WHY YOU HAVE BEEN BROUGHT HERE.

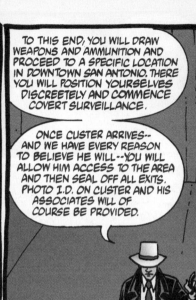

TO THIS END, YOU WILL DRAW WEAPONS AND AMMUNITION AND PROCEED TO A SPECIFIC LOCATION IN DOWNTOWN SAN ANTONIO. THERE YOU WILL POSITION YOURSELVES DISCREETELY AND COMMENCE COVERT SURVEILLANCE.

ONCE CUSTER ARRIVES-- AND WE HAVE EVERY REASON TO BELIEVE HE WILL--YOU WILL ALLOW HIM ACCESS TO THE AREA AND THEN SEAL OFF ALL EXITS. PHOTO I.D. ON CUSTER AND HIS ASSOCIATES WILL OF COURSE BE PROVIDED.

CAPTAIN GANDER AND I WILL HANDLE THE ACTUAL KILL. YOUR PRIORITY IS PERIMETER SECURITY.

THIS OPERATION IS CLASSIFIED *ULTRA-SECRET.* LOCAL LAW ENFORCEMENT HAS BEEN TAKEN CARE OF; IT IS VITAL THAT NO PUBLIC INTERFERENCE OR OBSERVATION BE PERMITTED.

USE OF LETHAL FORCE IS THEREFORE APPROVED.

FURTHERMORE, YOU MUST--

MUST...

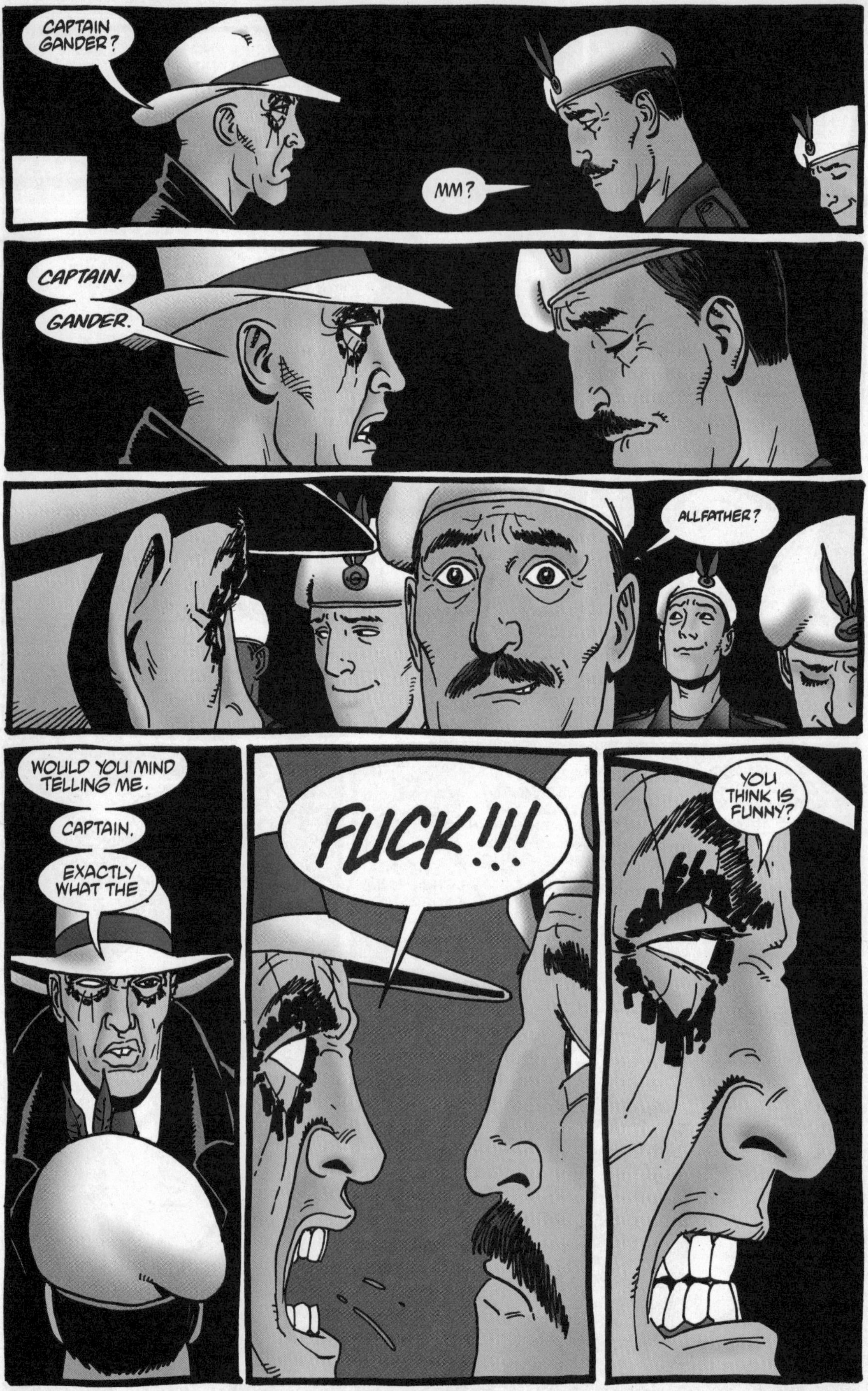
CAPTAIN GANDER?
MM?
CAPTAIN.
GANDER.
ALLFATHER?
WOULD YOU MIND TELLING ME.
CAPTAIN.
EXACTLY WHAT THE
FUCK!!!
YOU THINK IS FUNNY?

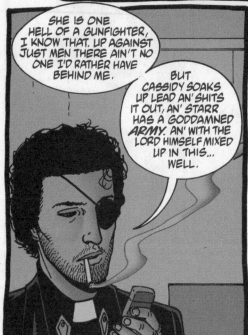

SHE IS ONE HELL OF A GUNFIGHTER, I KNOW THAT. UP AGAINST JUST MEN THERE AIN'T NO ONE I'D RATHER HAVE BEHIND ME.

BUT CASSIDY SOAKS UP LEAD AN' SHITS IT OUT, AN' STARR HAS A GODDAMNED *ARMY.* AN' WITH THE LORD HIMSELF MIXED UP IN THIS... WELL.

I SEEN HER DIE FOR REAL ONE TIME, AN' A HUNDRED MORE IN MY NIGHTMARES.

THERE IT IS.

DAMN, HOW COME DOIN' RIGHT AN' SHOOTIN' STRAIGHT'S SO EASY, EXCEPT WHEN IT COMES TO HOW YOU DEAL WITH WOMEN?

WELL, PILGRIM--

AIN'T A MAN ALIVE KIN GIVE YA THE ANSWER TO THAT'N.

HERR STARR--!

LOOK, I KNOW WHAT YOU MUST BE THINKING AND I REALLY *WAS* GOING TO STOP YOU, BUT YOU WERE IN SUCH A HURRY AND I JUST COULDN'T SEEM TO FIND THE OPPORTUNITY...

AND I MEAN, YOU KNOW, YOU HAVE TO ADMIT--

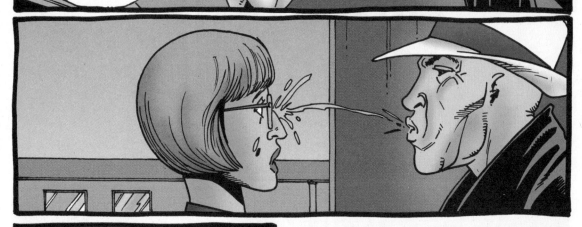

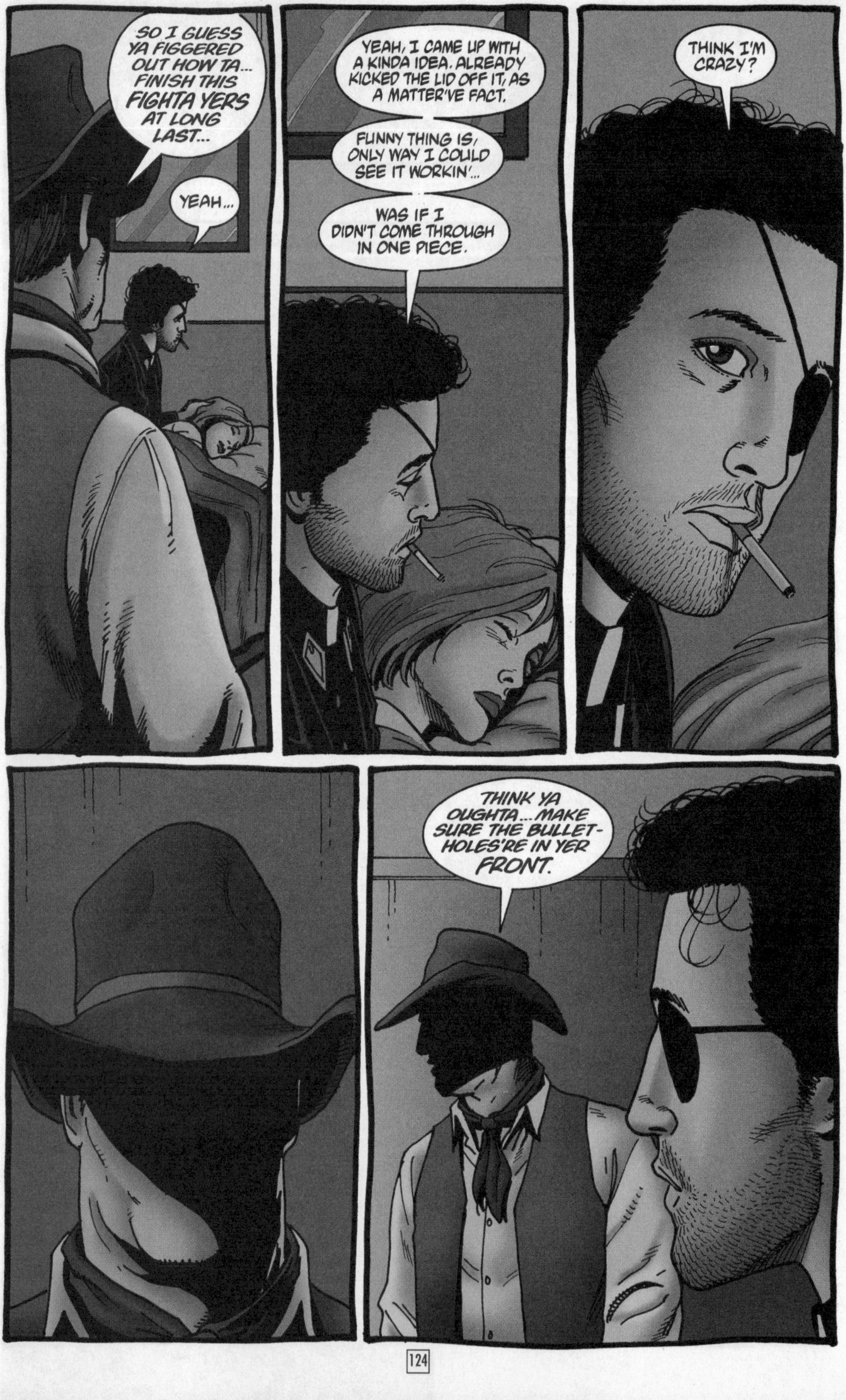
SO I GUESS YA FIGGERED OUT HOW TA... FINISH THIS FIGHTA YERS AT LONG LAST...
YEAH...
YEAH, I CAME UP WITH A KINDA IDEA. ALREADY KICKED THE LID OFF IT, AS A MATTER'VE FACT.
FUNNY THING IS, ONLY WAY I COULD SEE IT WORKIN'...
WAS IF I DIDN'T COME THROUGH IN ONE PIECE.
THINK I'M CRAZY?
THINK YA OUGHTA... MAKE SURE THE BULLET-HOLES'RE IN YER FRONT.

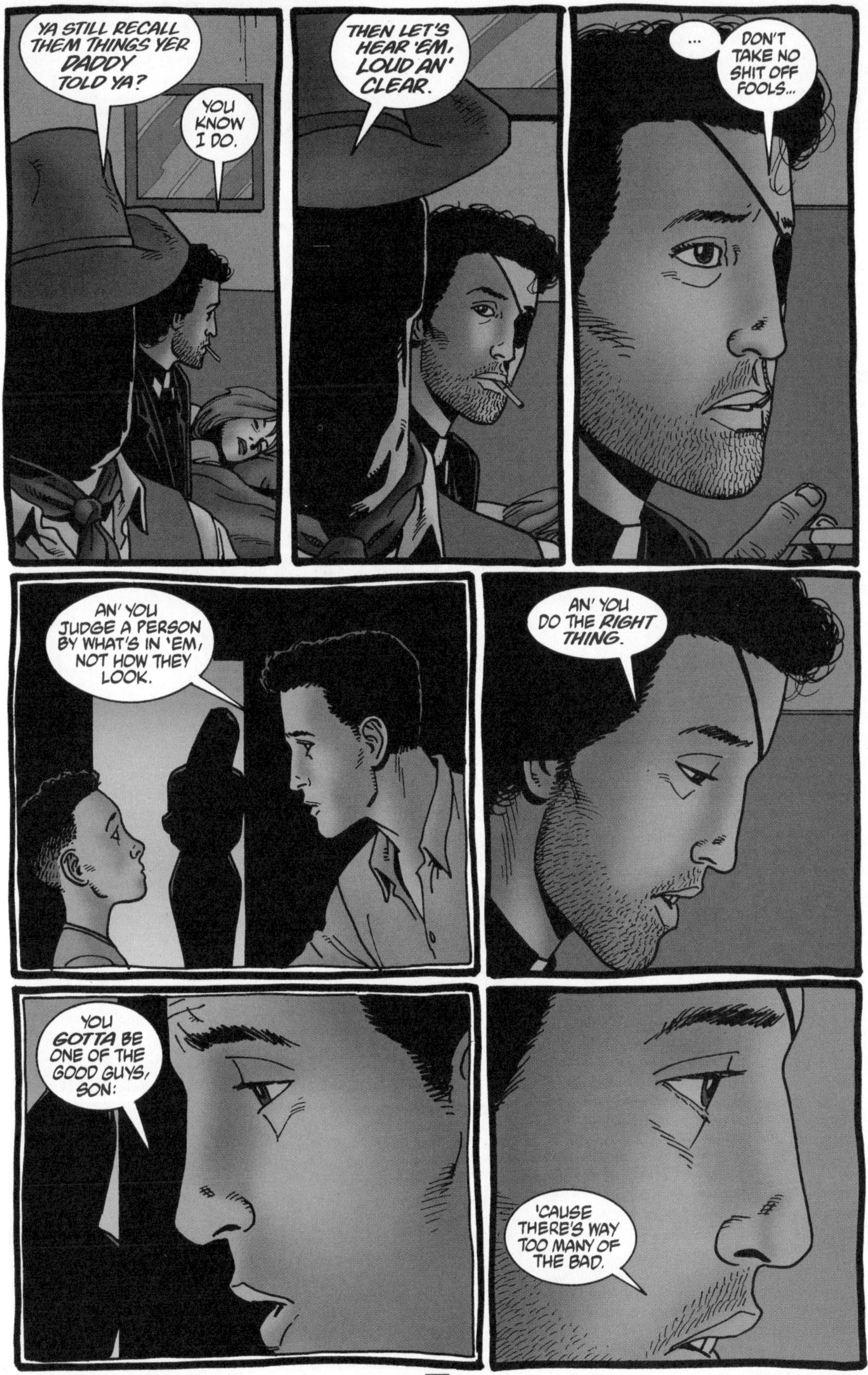

YA STILL RECALL THEM THINGS YER DADDY TOLD YA?
YOU KNOW I DO.
THEN LET'S HEAR 'EM, LOUD AN' CLEAR.
...
DON'T TAKE NO SHIT OFF FOOLS...
AN' YOU JUDGE A PERSON BY WHAT'S IN 'EM, NOT HOW THEY LOOK.
AN' YOU DO THE RIGHT THING.
YOU GOTTA BE ONE OF THE GOOD GUYS, SON:
'CAUSE THERE'S WAY TOO MANY OF THE BAD.

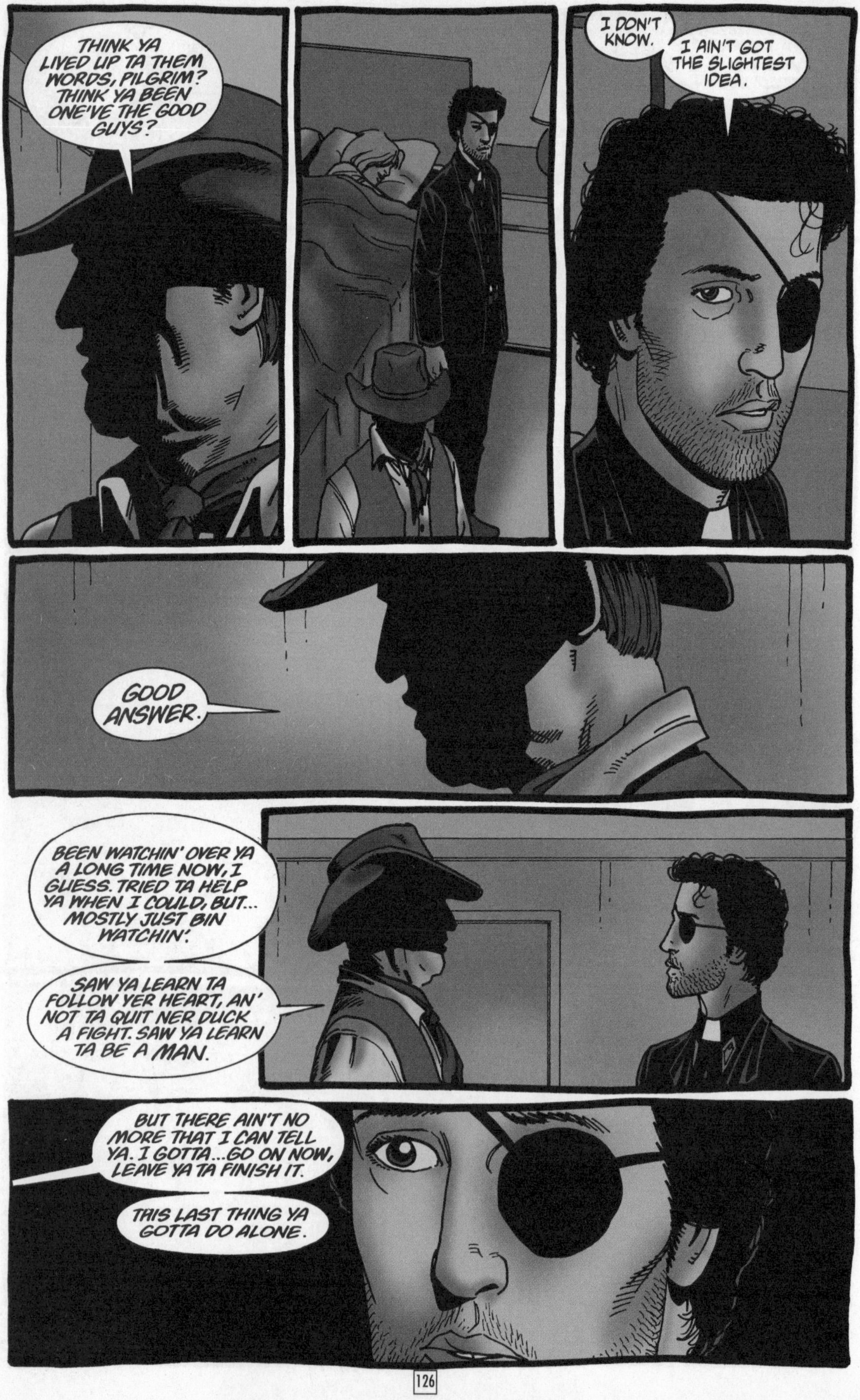
THINK YA LIVED UP TA THEM WORDS, PILGRIM? THINK YA BEEN ONE'VE THE GOOD GUYS?
I DON'T KNOW.
I AIN'T GOT THE SLIGHTEST IDEA.
GOOD ANSWER.
BEEN WATCHIN' OVER YA A LONG TIME NOW, I GUESS. TRIED TA HELP YA WHEN I COULD, BUT... MOSTLY JUST BIN WATCHIN'.
SAW YA LEARN TA FOLLOW YER HEART, AN' NOT TA QUIT NER DUCK A FIGHT. SAW YA LEARN TA BE A MAN.
BUT THERE AIN'T NO MORE THAT I CAN TELL YA. I GOTTA...GO ON NOW, LEAVE YA TA FINISH IT.
THIS LAST THING YA GOTTA DO ALONE.

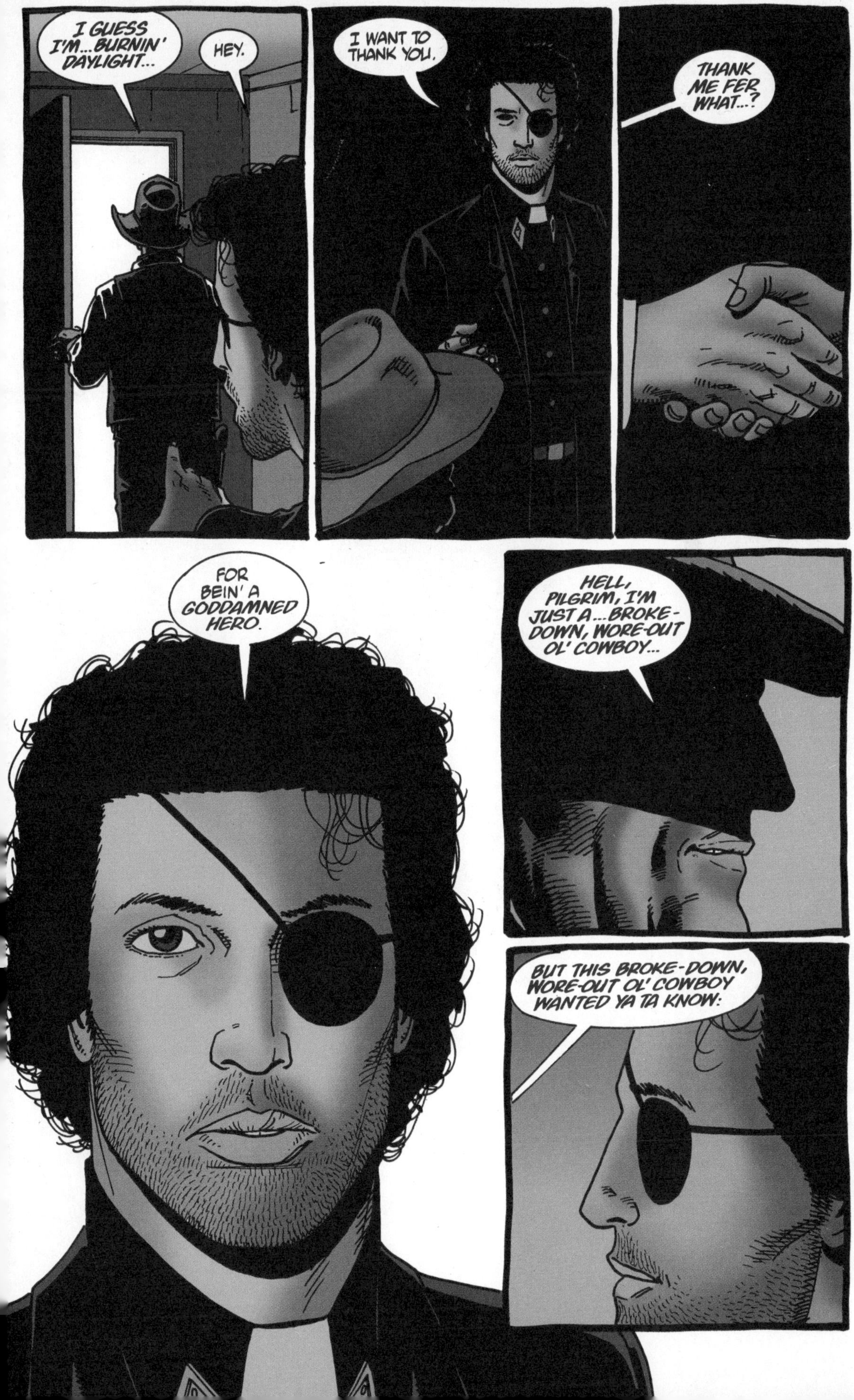
I GUESS I'M...BURNIN' DAYLIGHT...
HEY.
I WANT TO THANK YOU.
THANK ME FER WHAT...?
FOR BEIN' A GODDAMNED HERO.
HELL, PILGRIM, I'M JUST A...BROKE-DOWN, WORE-OUT OL' COWBOY...
BUT THIS BROKE-DOWN, WORE-OUT OL' COWBOY WANTED YA TA KNOW:

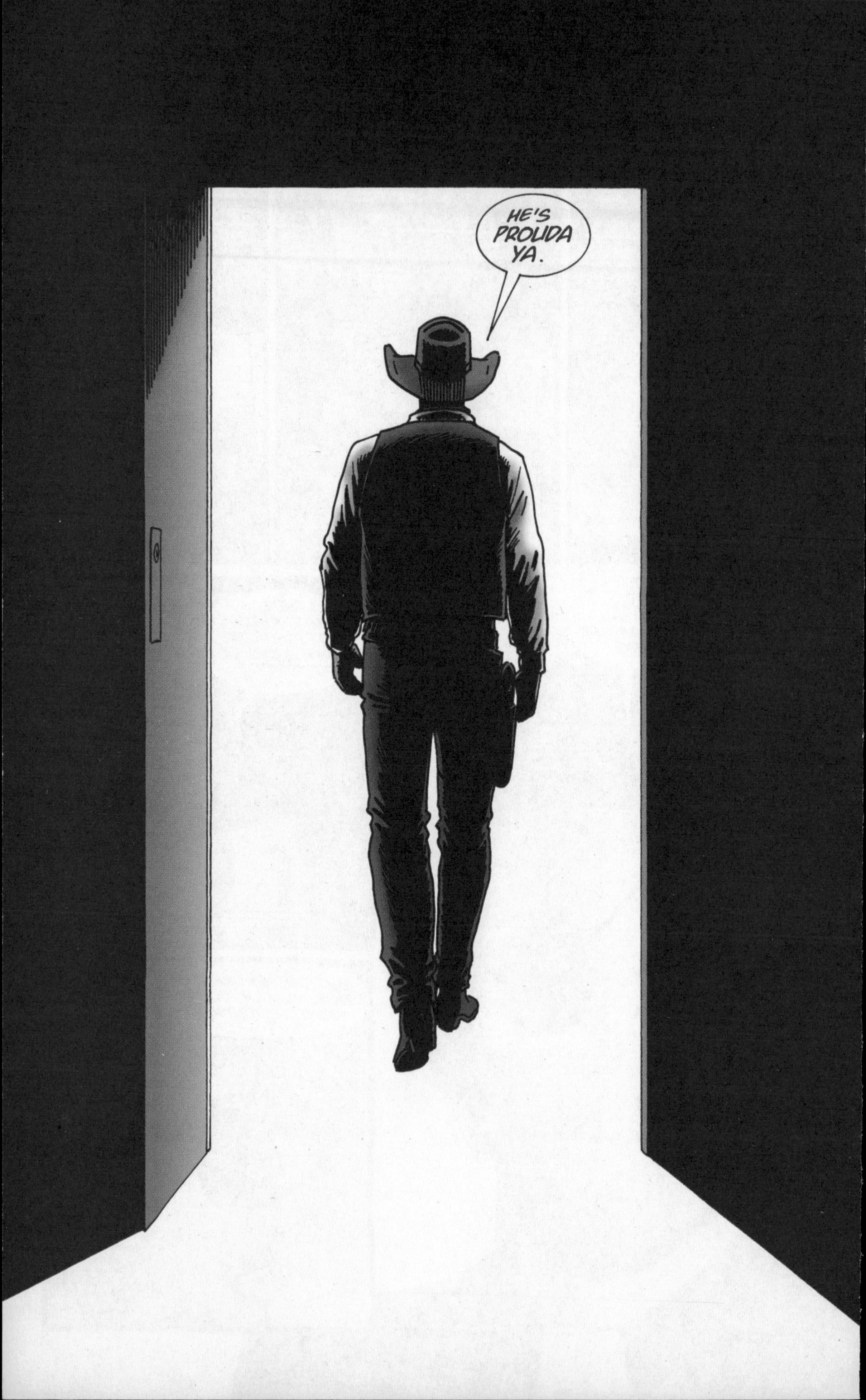
HE'S PROUDA YA.

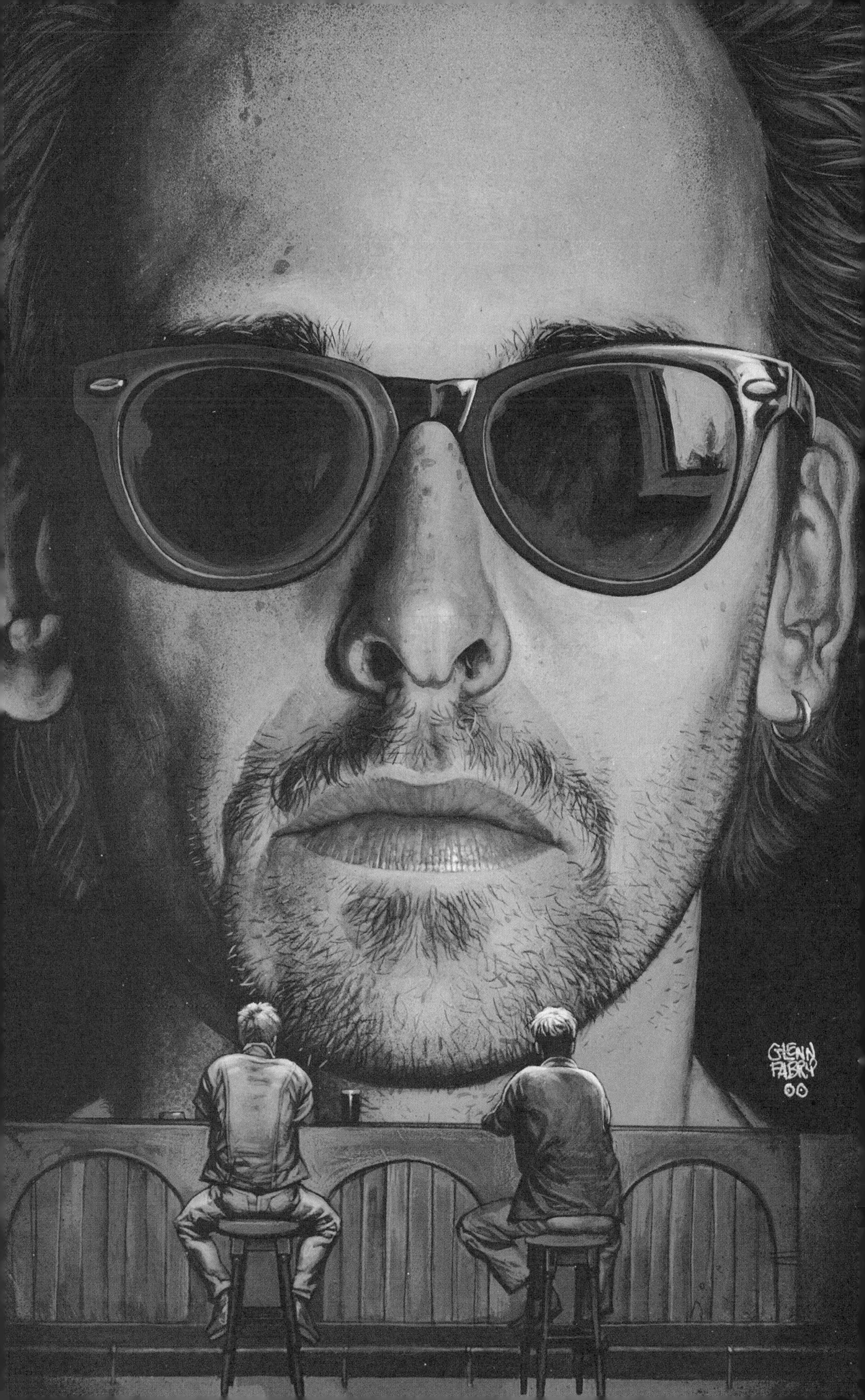
GLENN
FABRY
00

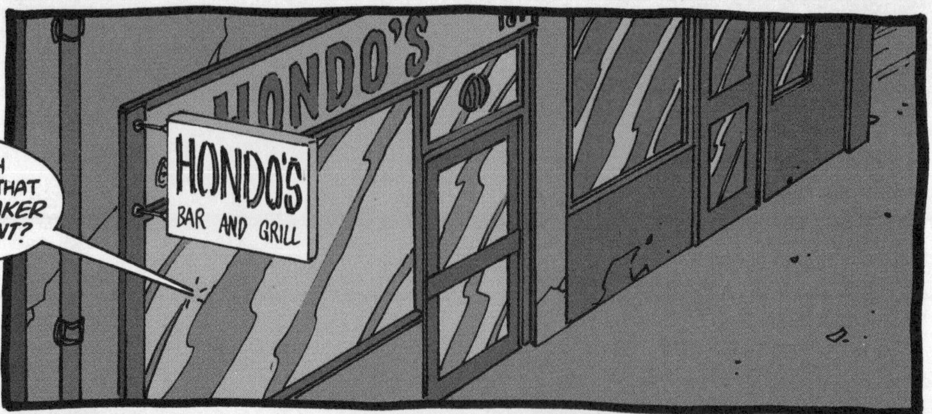
HONDO'S
HONDO'S BAR AND GRILL
DID YEH EVER SEE THAT FILM *BREAKER MORANT?*

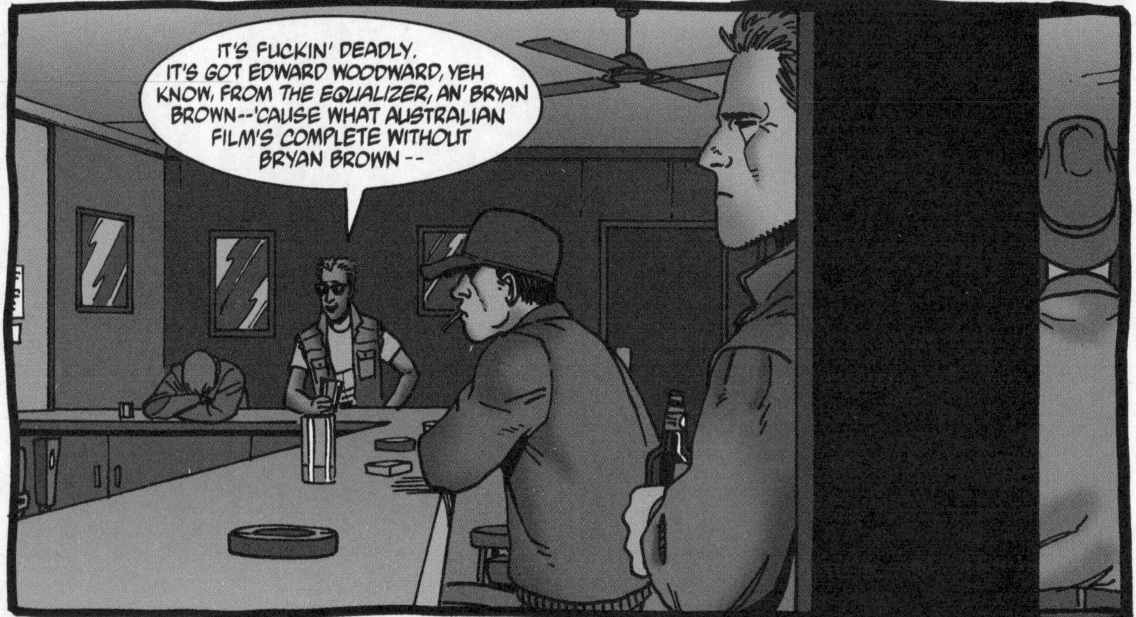
IT'S FUCKIN' DEADLY. IT'S GOT EDWARD WOODWARD, YEH KNOW, FROM *THE EQUALIZER*, AN' BRYAN BROWN--'CAUSE WHAT AUSTRALIAN FILM'S COMPLETE WITHOUT BRYAN BROWN --

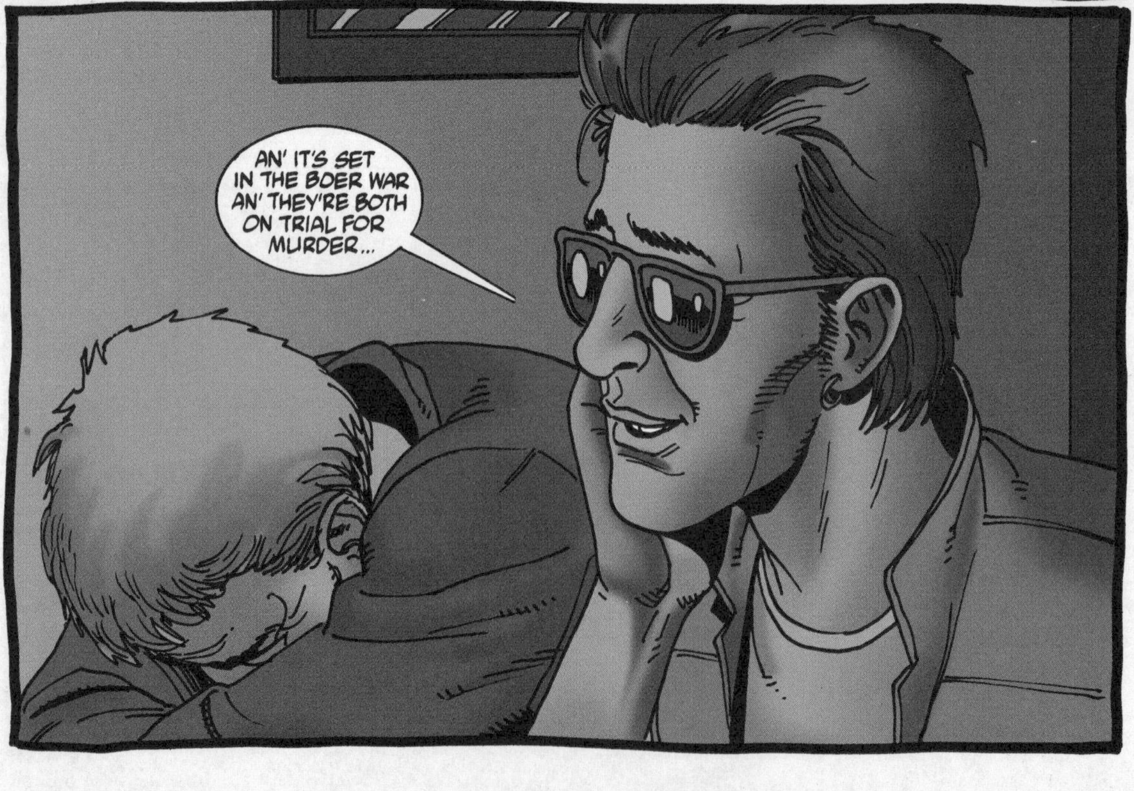
AN' IT'S SET IN THE BOER WAR AN' THEY'RE BOTH ON TRIAL FOR MURDER...

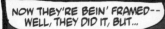

NOW THEY'RE BEIN' FRAMED-- WELL, THEY DID IT, BUT...

WELL IT'S SORT'VE COMPLICATED, YEH KNOW? YEH'LL HAVE TO WATCH THE MOVIE, I DON'T WANT TO RUIN IT FOR YEH.

BUT THEY'RE FOUND GUILTY AN' THEY'RE GONNA BE SHOT, AN' THE NIGHT BEFORE THE EXECUTION ONE'VE EDWARD WOODWARD'S MATES COMES ROUND TO BUST HIM OUT...

AND THIS IS ME FAVORITE BIT, I ALWAYS LOVE THIS--

'CAUSE, UH...

'CAUSE EDWARD WOODWARD DOESN'T WANNA GO.

SO HIS MATE'S SAYIN' COME ON, HE CAN GET A BOAT AN' GET OUT'VE THERE, HE CAN GO OFF AN' SEE THE WORLD...!

NAH, HE SAYS.

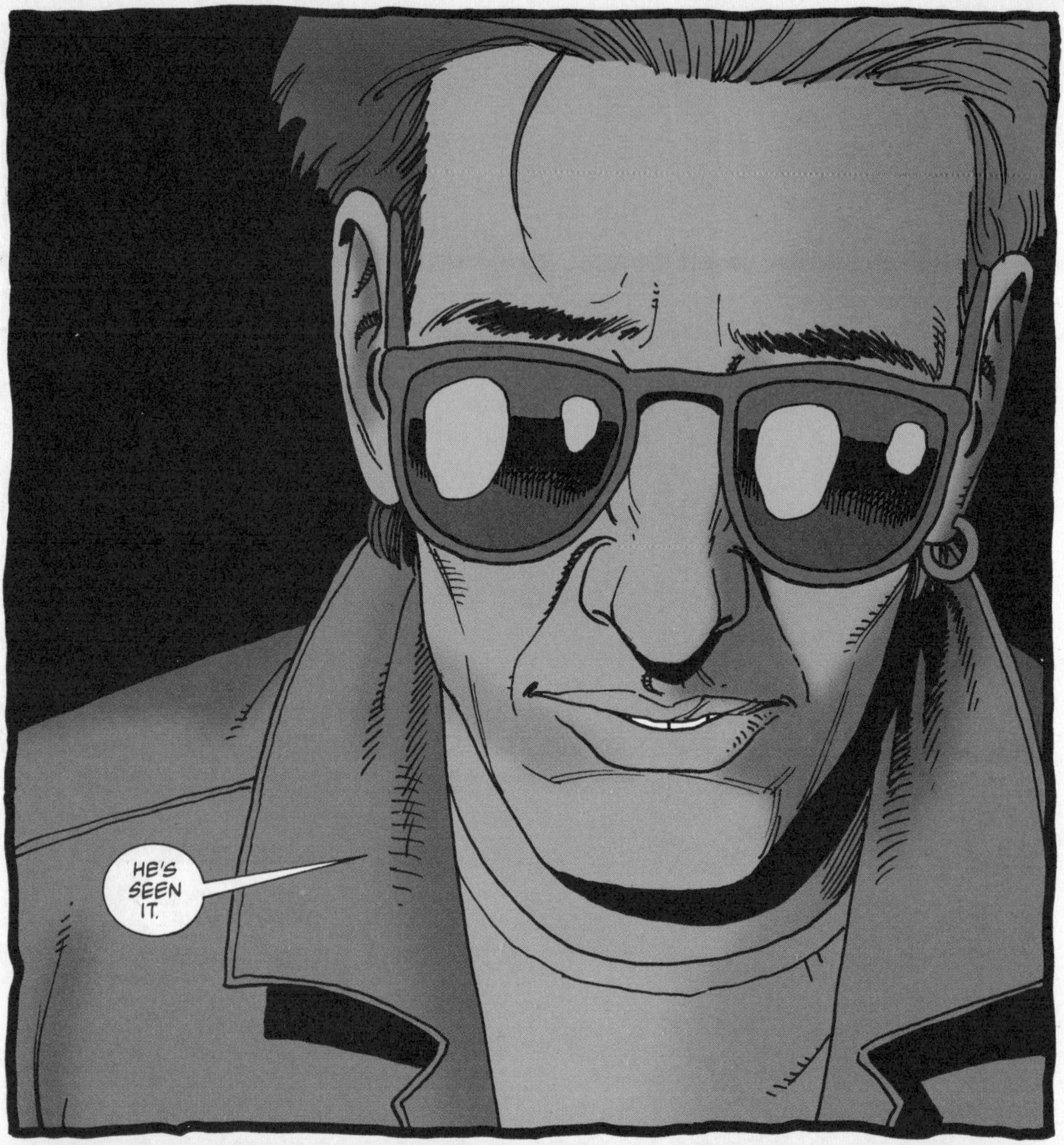
HE'S SEEN IT.

IF I KNEW THE WAY I'D GO BACK HOME

GARTH ENNIS - Writer STEVE DILLON - Artist
PAMELA RAMBO - Colorist CLEM ROBINS - Letterer AXEL ALONSO - Editor
PREACHER created by GARTH ENNIS and STEVE DILLON

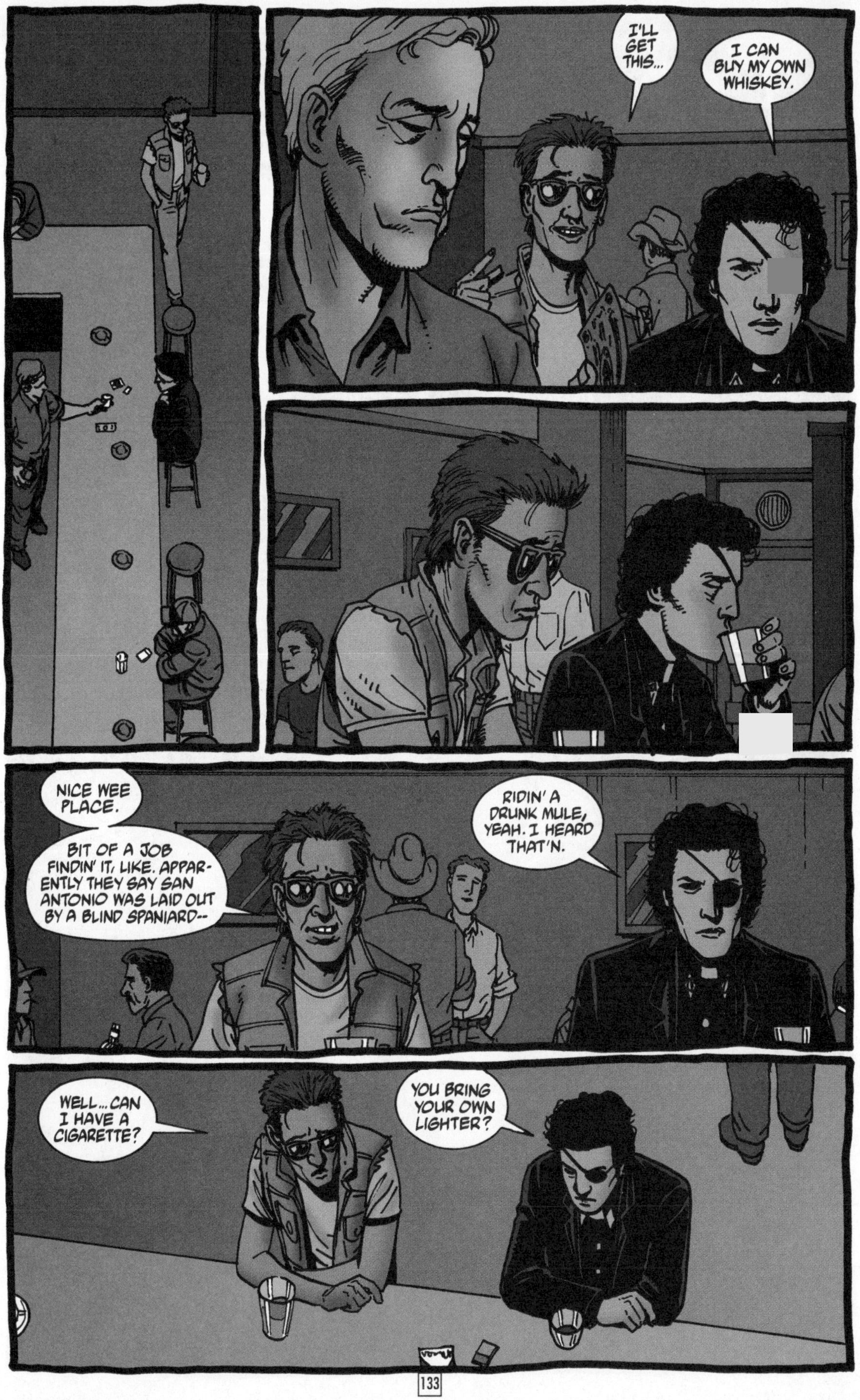
I'LL GET THIS...
I CAN BUY MY OWN WHISKEY.
NICE WEE PLACE.
BIT OF A JOB FINDIN' IT, LIKE. APPARENTLY THEY SAY SAN ANTONIO WAS LAID OUT BY A BLIND SPANIARD--
RIDIN' A DRUNK MULE, YEAH. I HEARD THAT'N.
WELL... CAN I HAVE A CIGARETTE?
YOU BRING YOUR OWN LIGHTER?

WHAT?

IT'S A JOKE.

OH...!

SO LOOK, I'VE GOT TO ASK: HOW THE FUCK DID YEH SURVIVE FALLIN' OUT'VE THAT PLANE?

THE GOOD LORD SAVED MY ASS. KINDA MY LAST CHANCE TO BACK OFF AN' LEAVE HIM BE.

JAYSIS. AN' NO DOUBT YEH'RE STILL HUNTIN' THE BASTARD, TOO.

D'YEH EVER WONDER IF YEH'RE WASTIN' YER TIME? YEH KNOW, RUNNIN' ROUND AFTER GOD ALMIGHTY HIM-FUCKIN'-SELF WHEN IT MAYBE WON'T MAKE A PICK'VE DIFFERENCE?

I MEAN YOU THINK ABOUT IT: GOD'S QUIT, THE WORLD'S MENTAL. BIG FUCKIN' SURPRISE...

WE HERE TO TALK ABOUT ME?

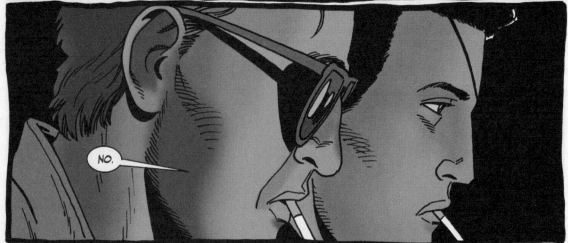

NO.

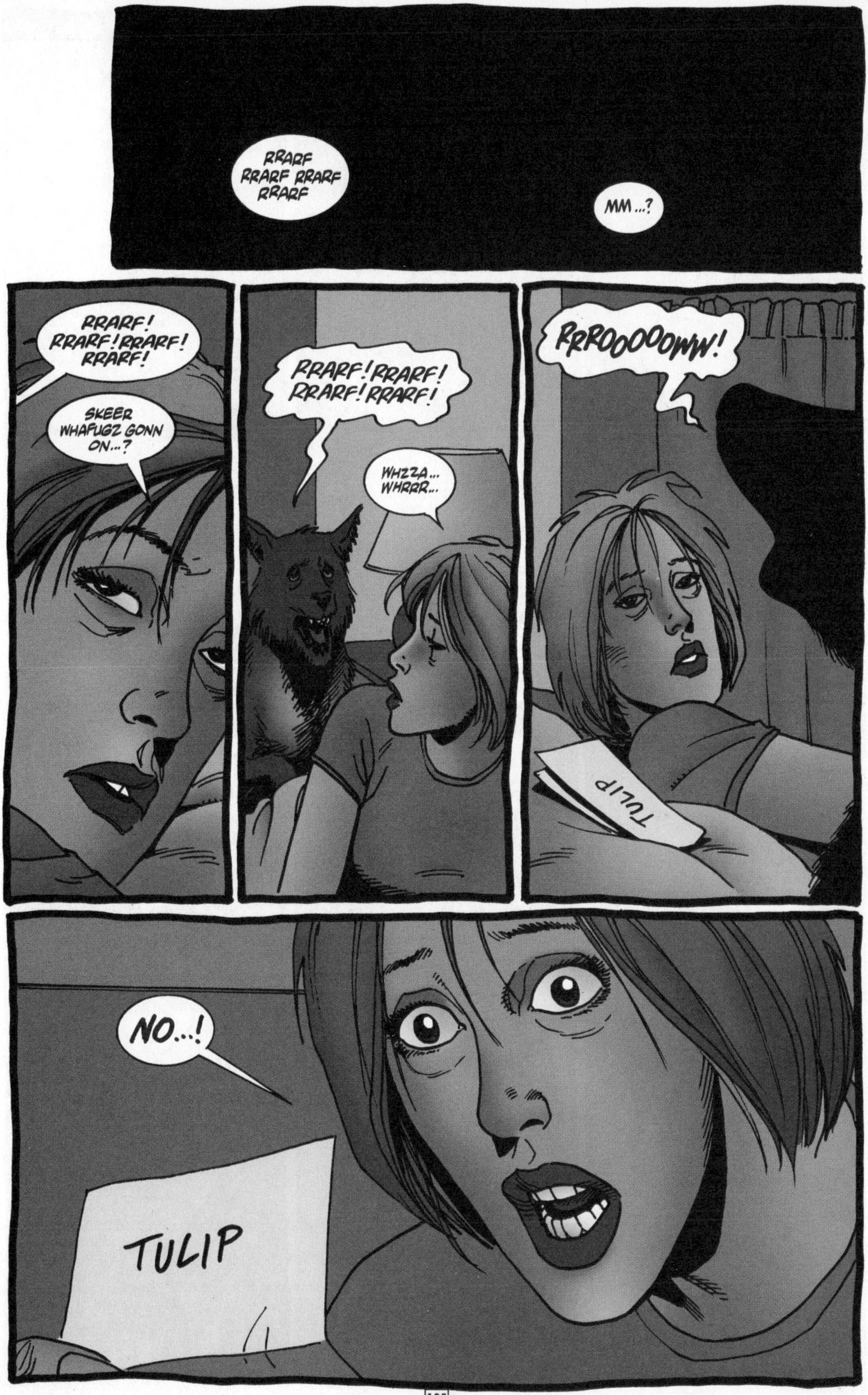
RRARF
RRARF RRARF
RRARF
MM...?
RRARF!
RRARF! RRARF!
RRARF!
SKEER
WHAFUGZ GONN
ON...?
RRARF! RRARF!
RRARF! RRARF!
WHZZA...
WHRRR...
RRROOOOOWW!
TULIP
NO...!
TULIP

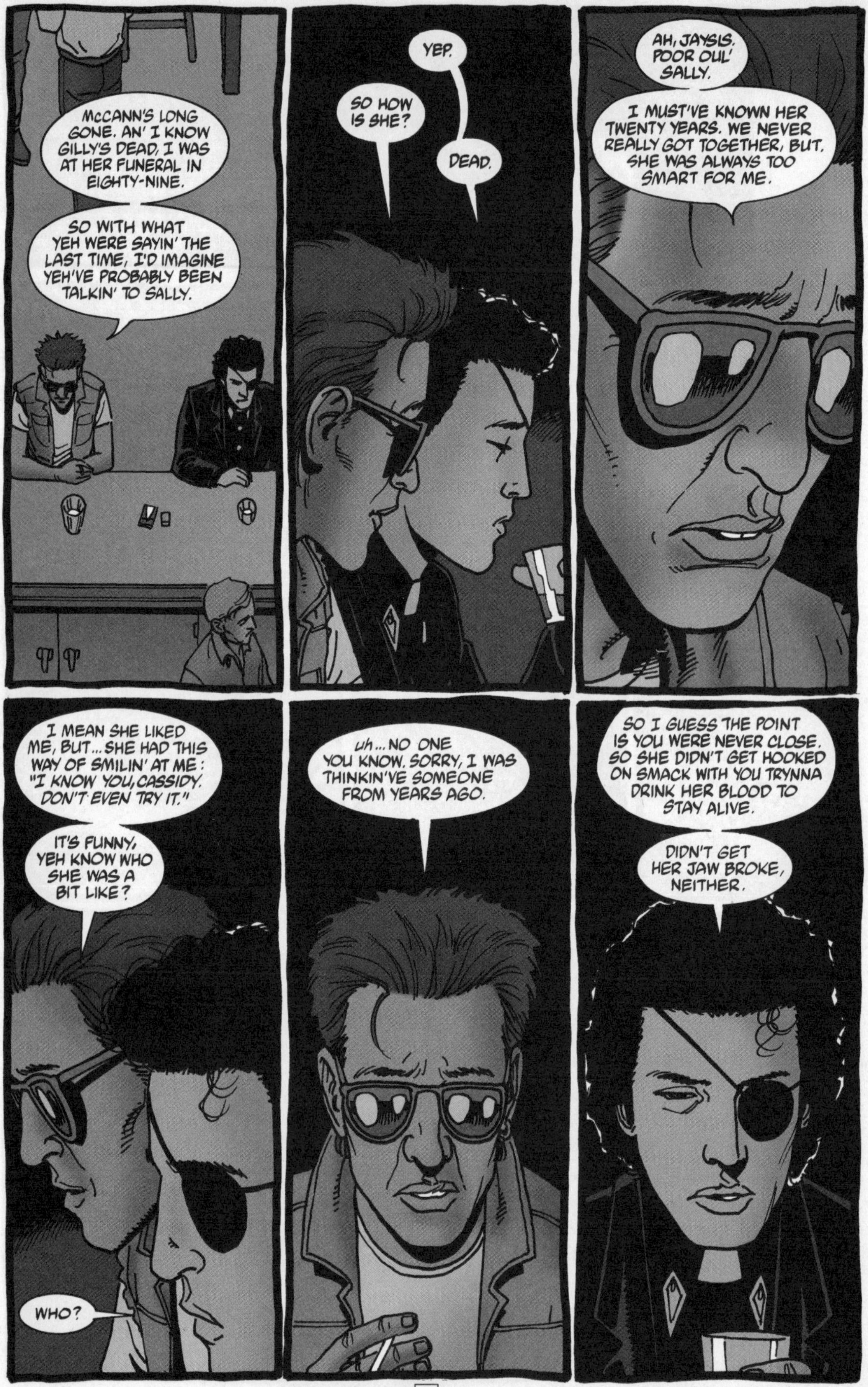
McCANN'S LONG GONE. AN' I KNOW GILLY'S DEAD, I WAS AT HER FUNERAL IN EIGHTY-NINE.
SO WITH WHAT YEH WERE SAYIN' THE LAST TIME, I'D IMAGINE YEH'VE PROBABLY BEEN TALKIN' TO SALLY.
SO HOW IS SHE?
YEP.
DEAD.
AH, JAYSIS. POOR OUL' SALLY.
I MUST'VE KNOWN HER TWENTY YEARS. WE NEVER REALLY GOT TOGETHER, BUT. SHE WAS ALWAYS TOO SMART FOR ME.
I MEAN SHE LIKED ME, BUT... SHE HAD THIS WAY OF SMILIN' AT ME: "I KNOW YOU, CASSIDY. DON'T EVEN TRY IT."
IT'S FUNNY, YEH KNOW WHO SHE WAS A BIT LIKE?
WHO?
uh... NO ONE YOU KNOW. SORRY, I WAS THINKIN'VE SOMEONE FROM YEARS AGO.
SO I GUESS THE POINT IS YOU WERE NEVER CLOSE. SO SHE DIDN'T GET HOOKED ON SMACK WITH YOU TRYNNA DRINK HER BLOOD TO STAY ALIVE.
DIDN'T GET HER JAW BROKE, NEITHER.

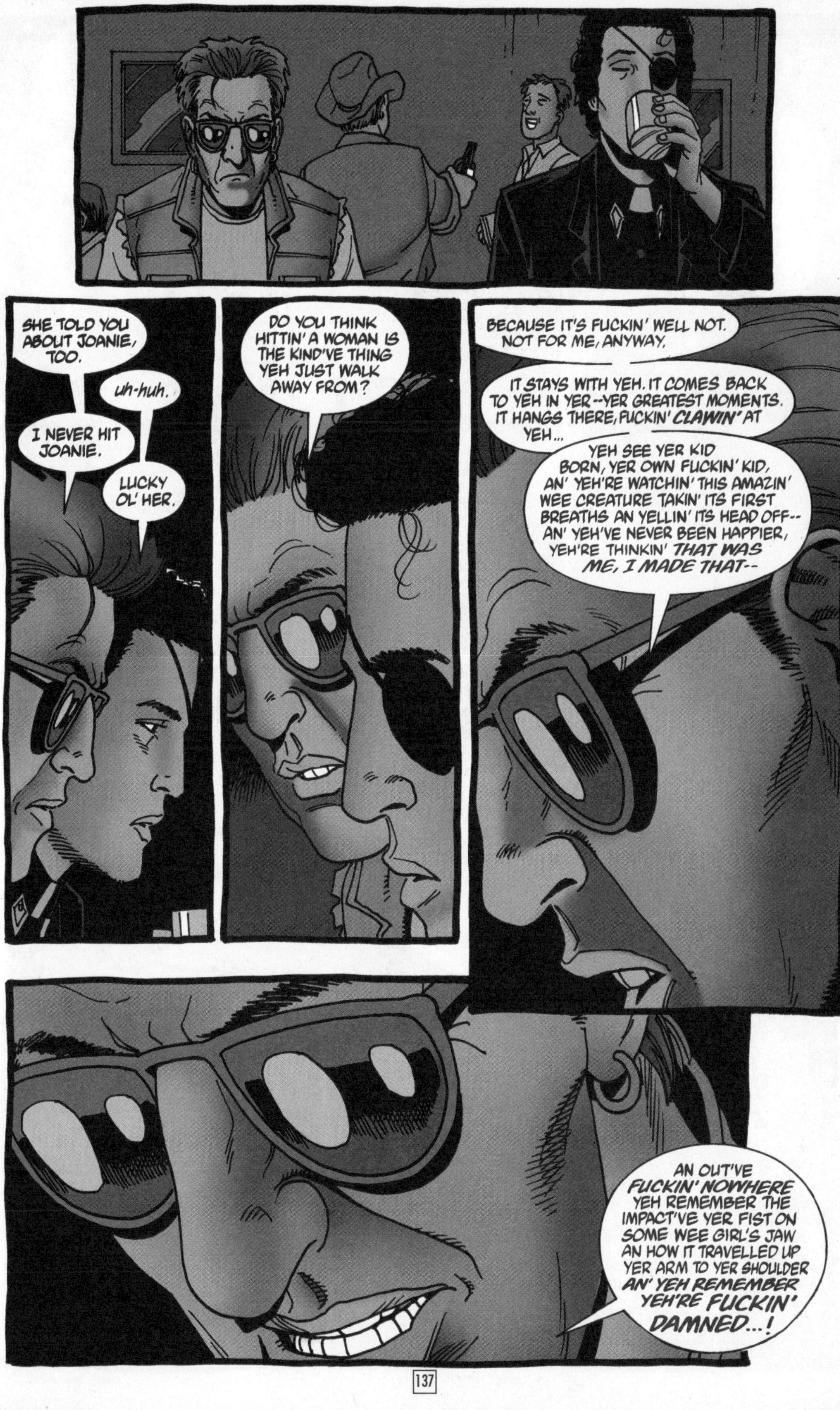
SHE TOLD YOU ABOUT JOANIE, TOO.
uh-huh.
I NEVER HIT JOANIE.
LUCKY OL' HER.
DO YOU THINK HITTIN' A WOMAN IS THE KIND'VE THING YEH JUST WALK AWAY FROM?
BECAUSE IT'S FUCKIN' WELL NOT. NOT FOR ME, ANYWAY.
IT STAYS WITH YEH. IT COMES BACK TO YEH IN YER--YER GREATEST MOMENTS. IT HANGS THERE, FUCKIN' CLAWIN' AT YEH...
YEH SEE YER KID BORN, YER OWN FUCKIN' KID, AN' YEH'RE WATCHIN' THIS AMAZIN' WEE CREATURE TAKIN' ITS FIRST BREATHS AN YELLIN' ITS HEAD OFF-- AN' YEH'VE NEVER BEEN HAPPIER, YEH'RE THINKIN' THAT WAS ME, I MADE THAT--
AN OUT'VE FUCKIN' NOWHERE YEH REMEMBER THE IMPACT'VE YER FIST ON SOME WEE GIRL'S JAW AN HOW IT TRAVELLED UP YER ARM TO YER SHOULDER AN' YEH REMEMBER YEH'RE FUCKIN' DAMNED...!

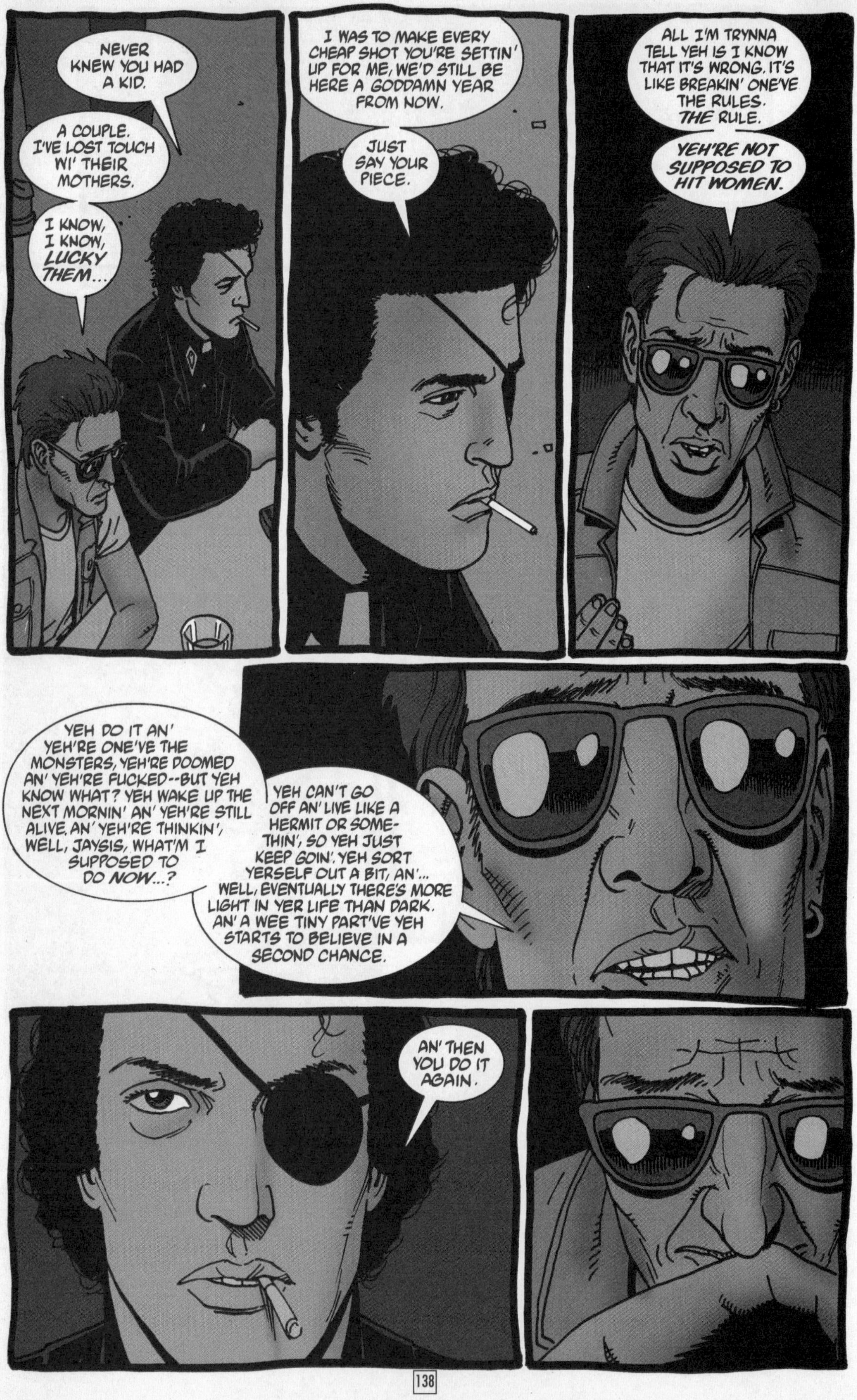
NEVER KNEW YOU HAD A KID.
A COUPLE. I'VE LOST TOUCH WI' THEIR MOTHERS.
I KNOW, I KNOW, LUCKY THEM...
I WAS TO MAKE EVERY CHEAP SHOT YOU'RE SETTIN' UP FOR ME, WE'D STILL BE HERE A GODDAMN YEAR FROM NOW.
JUST SAY YOUR PIECE.
ALL I'M TRYNNA TELL YEH IS I KNOW THAT IT'S WRONG. IT'S LIKE BREAKIN' ONE'VE THE RULES. THE RULE.
YEH'RE NOT SUPPOSED TO HIT WOMEN.
YEH DO IT AN' YEH'RE ONE'VE THE MONSTERS, YEH'RE DOOMED AN' YEH'RE FUCKED--BUT YEH KNOW WHAT? YEH WAKE UP THE NEXT MORNIN' AN' YEH'RE STILL ALIVE. AN' YEH'RE THINKIN', WELL, JAYSIS, WHAT'M I SUPPOSED TO DO NOW...?
YEH CAN'T GO OFF AN' LIVE LIKE A HERMIT OR SOME-THIN', SO YEH JUST KEEP GOIN'. YEH SORT YERSELF OUT A BIT, AN'... WELL, EVENTUALLY THERE'S MORE LIGHT IN YER LIFE THAN DARK. AN' A WEE TINY PART'VE YEH STARTS TO BELIEVE IN A SECOND CHANCE.
AN' THEN YOU DO IT AGAIN.

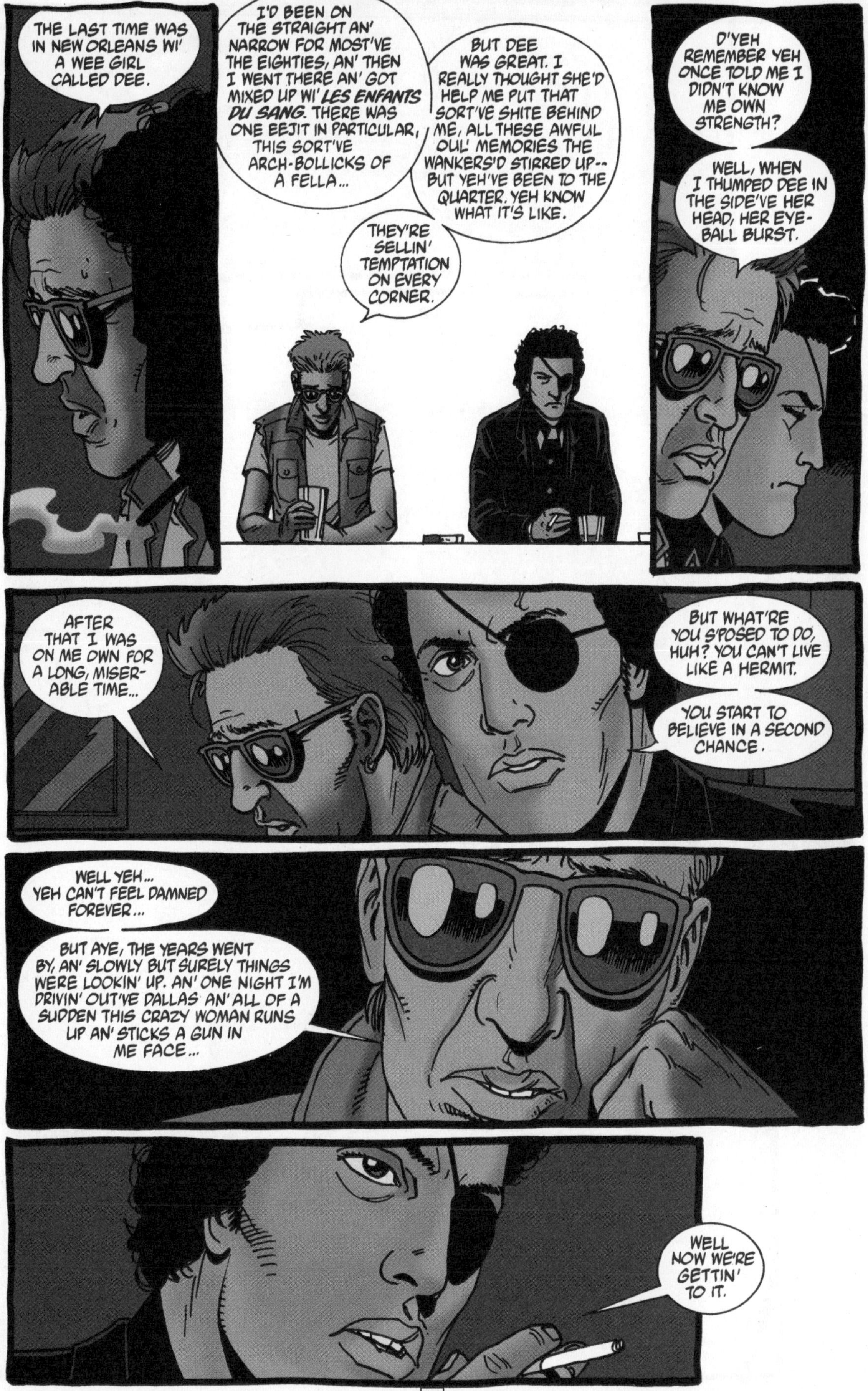
THE LAST TIME WAS IN NEW ORLEANS WI' A WEE GIRL CALLED DEE.
I'D BEEN ON THE STRAIGHT AN' NARROW FOR MOST'VE THE EIGHTIES, AN' THEN I WENT THERE AN' GOT MIXED UP WI' LES ENFANTS DU SANG. THERE WAS ONE BEJIT IN PARTICULAR, THIS SORT'VE ARCH-BOLLICKS OF A FELLA...
BUT DEE WAS GREAT. I REALLY THOUGHT SHE'D HELP ME PUT THAT SORT'VE SHITE BEHIND ME, ALL THESE AWFUL OUL' MEMORIES THE WANKERS'D STIRRED UP-- BUT YEH'VE BEEN TO THE QUARTER. YEH KNOW WHAT IT'S LIKE.
THEY'RE SELLIN' TEMPTATION ON EVERY CORNER.
D'YEH REMEMBER YEH ONCE TOLD ME I DIDN'T KNOW ME OWN STRENGTH?
WELL, WHEN I THUMPED DEE IN THE SIDE'VE HER HEAD, HER EYE-BALL BURST.
AFTER THAT I WAS ON ME OWN FOR A LONG, MISER-ABLE TIME...
BUT WHAT'RE YOU S'POSED TO DO, HUH? YOU CAN'T LIVE LIKE A HERMIT.
YOU START TO BELIEVE IN A SECOND CHANCE.
WELL YEH... YEH CAN'T FEEL DAMNED FOREVER...
BUT AYE, THE YEARS WENT BY, AN' SLOWLY BUT SURELY THINGS WERE LOOKIN' UP. AN' ONE NIGHT I'M DRIVIN' OUT'VE DALLAS AN' ALL OF A SUDDEN THIS CRAZY WOMAN RUNS UP AN' STICKS A GUN IN ME FACE...
WELL NOW WE'RE GETTIN' TO IT.

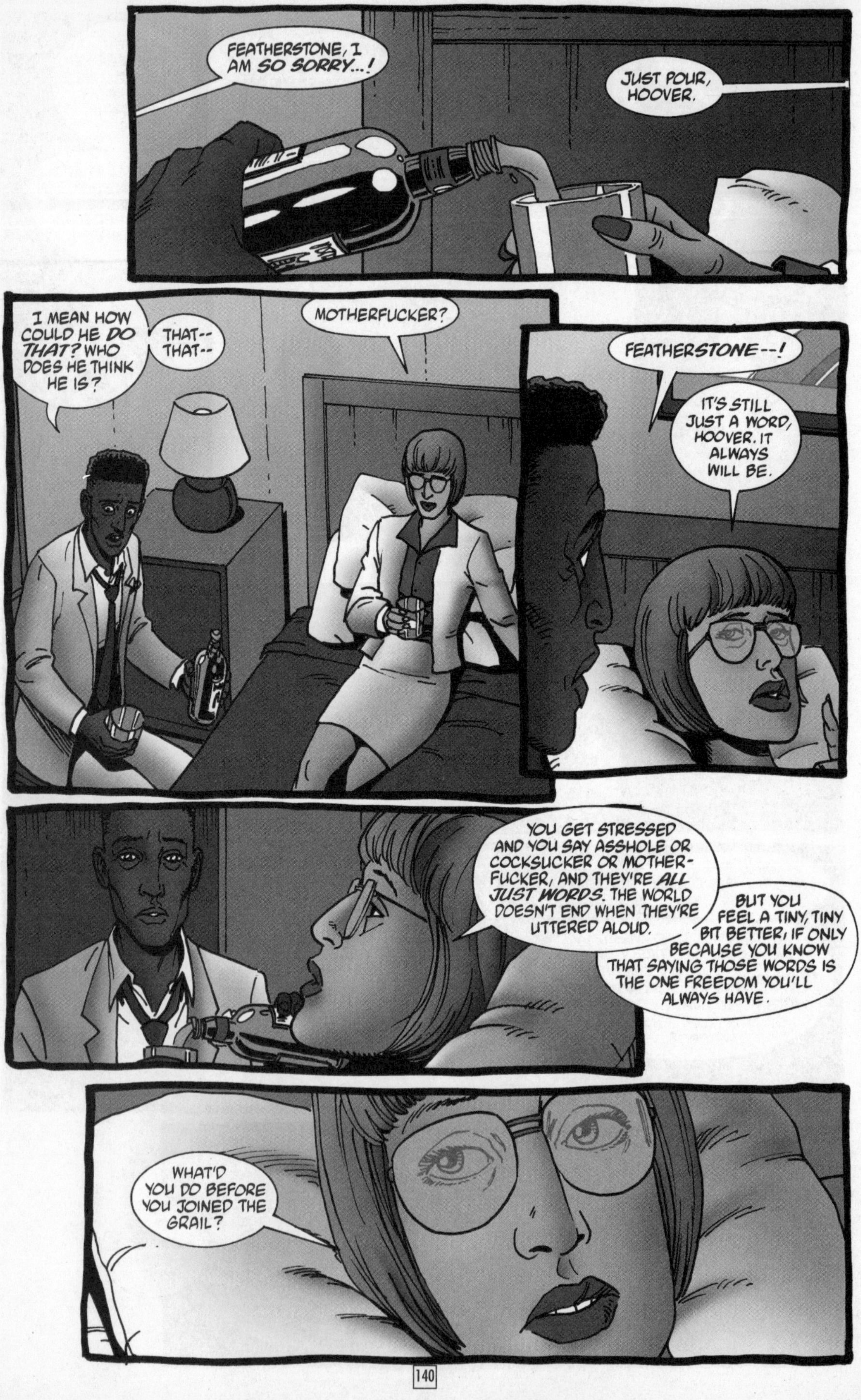

FEATHERSTONE, I AM SO SORRY...!
JUST POUR, HOOVER.
I MEAN HOW COULD HE DO THAT? WHO DOES HE THINK HE IS?
THAT-- THAT--
MOTHERFUCKER?
FEATHERSTONE--!
IT'S STILL JUST A WORD, HOOVER. IT ALWAYS WILL BE.
YOU GET STRESSED AND YOU SAY ASSHOLE OR COCKSUCKER OR MOTHER-FUCKER, AND THEY'RE ALL JUST WORDS. THE WORLD DOESN'T END WHEN THEY'RE UTTERED ALOUD.
BUT YOU FEEL A TINY, TINY BIT BETTER, IF ONLY BECAUSE YOU KNOW THAT SAYING THOSE WORDS IS THE ONE FREEDOM YOU'LL ALWAYS HAVE.
WHAT'D YOU DO BEFORE YOU JOINED THE GRAIL?

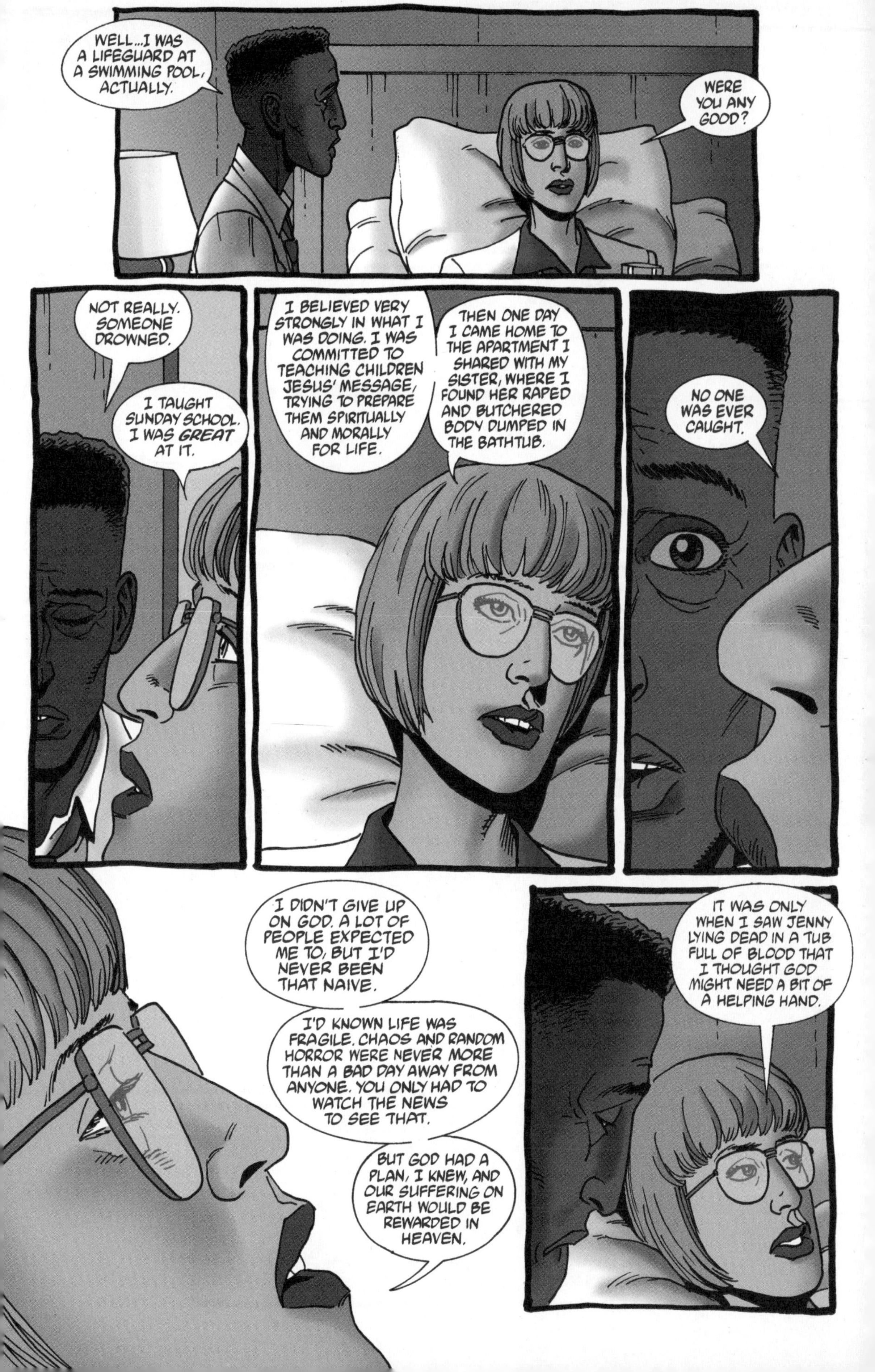
WELL...I WAS A LIFEGUARD AT A SWIMMING POOL, ACTUALLY.
WERE YOU ANY GOOD?
NOT REALLY. SOMEONE DROWNED.
I TAUGHT SUNDAY SCHOOL. I WAS GREAT AT IT.
I BELIEVED VERY STRONGLY IN WHAT I WAS DOING. I WAS COMMITTED TO TEACHING CHILDREN JESUS' MESSAGE, TRYING TO PREPARE THEM SPIRITUALLY AND MORALLY FOR LIFE.
THEN ONE DAY I CAME HOME TO THE APARTMENT I SHARED WITH MY SISTER, WHERE I FOUND HER RAPED AND BUTCHERED BODY DUMPED IN THE BATHTUB.
NO ONE WAS EVER CAUGHT.
I DIDN'T GIVE UP ON GOD. A LOT OF PEOPLE EXPECTED ME TO, BUT I'D NEVER BEEN THAT NAIVE.
I'D KNOWN LIFE WAS FRAGILE. CHAOS AND RANDOM HORROR WERE NEVER MORE THAN A BAD DAY AWAY FROM ANYONE. YOU ONLY HAD TO WATCH THE NEWS TO SEE THAT.
BUT GOD HAD A PLAN, I KNEW, AND OUR SUFFERING ON EARTH WOULD BE REWARDED IN HEAVEN.
IT WAS ONLY WHEN I SAW JENNY LYING DEAD IN A TUB FULL OF BLOOD THAT I THOUGHT GOD MIGHT NEED A BIT OF A HELPING HAND.

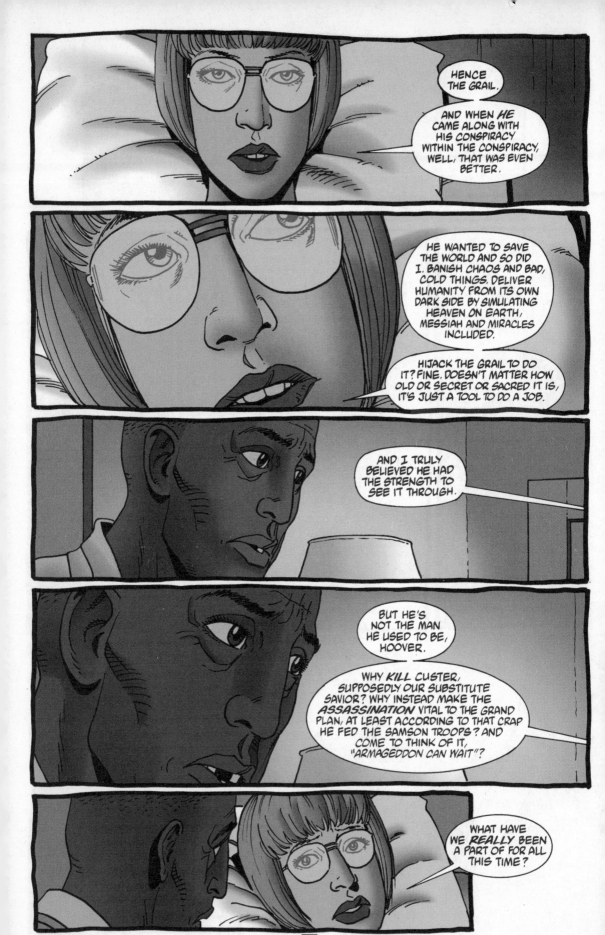

HENCE THE GRAIL.

AND WHEN *HE* CAME ALONG WITH HIS CONSPIRACY WITHIN THE CONSPIRACY, WELL, THAT WAS EVEN BETTER.

HE WANTED TO SAVE THE WORLD AND SO DID I. BANISH CHAOS AND BAD, COLD THINGS. DELIVER HUMANITY FROM ITS OWN DARK SIDE BY SIMULATING HEAVEN ON EARTH, MESSIAH AND MIRACLES INCLUDED.

HIJACK THE GRAIL TO DO IT? FINE. DOESN'T MATTER HOW OLD OR SECRET OR SACRED IT IS, IT'S JUST A TOOL TO DO A JOB.

AND I TRULY BELIEVED HE HAD THE STRENGTH TO SEE IT THROUGH.

BUT HE'S NOT THE MAN HE USED TO BE, HOOVER.

WHY *KILL* CUSTER, SUPPOSEDLY OUR SUBSTITUTE SAVIOR? WHY INSTEAD MAKE THE *ASSASSINATION* VITAL TO THE GRAND PLAN, AT LEAST ACCORDING TO THAT CRAP HE FED THE SAMSON TROOPS? AND COME TO THINK OF IT, "ARMAGEDDON CAN WAIT"?

WHAT HAVE WE *REALLY* BEEN A PART OF FOR ALL THIS TIME?

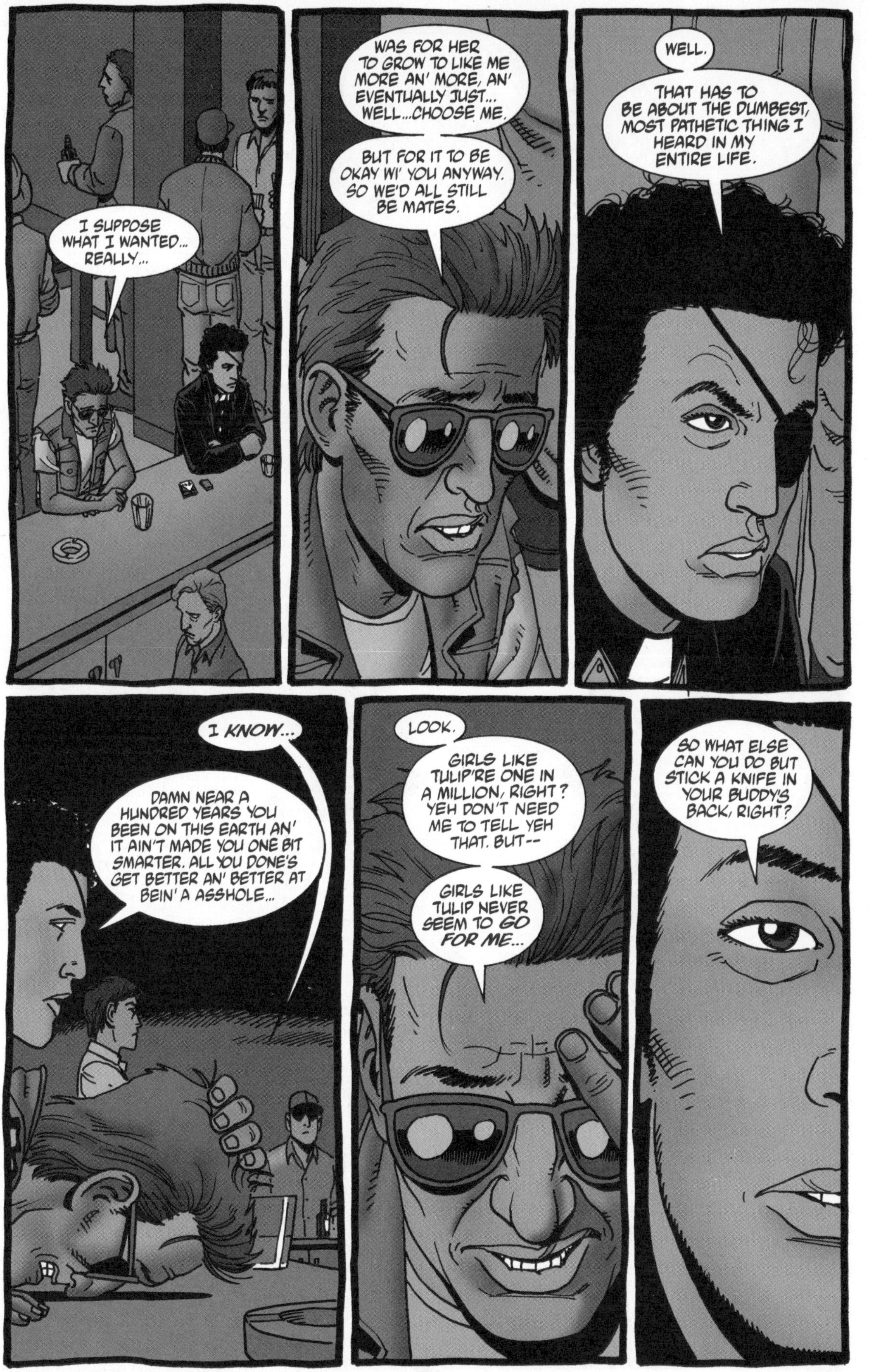

I SUPPOSE WHAT I WANTED... REALLY...
WAS FOR HER TO GROW TO LIKE ME MORE AN' MORE, AN' EVENTUALLY JUST... WELL...CHOOSE ME.
BUT FOR IT TO BE OKAY WI' YOU ANYWAY. SO WE'D ALL STILL BE MATES.
WELL.
THAT HAS TO BE ABOUT THE DUMBEST, MOST PATHETIC THING I HEARD IN MY ENTIRE LIFE.
I KNOW...
DAMN NEAR A HUNDRED YEARS YOU BEEN ON THIS EARTH AN' IT AIN'T MADE YOU ONE BIT SMARTER. ALL YOU DONE'S GET BETTER AN' BETTER AT BEIN' A ASSHOLE...
LOOK.
GIRLS LIKE TULIP'RE ONE IN A MILLION, RIGHT? YEH DON'T NEED ME TO TELL YEH THAT. BUT--
GIRLS LIKE TULIP NEVER SEEM TO GO FOR ME...
SO WHAT ELSE CAN YOU DO BUT STICK A KNIFE IN YOUR BUDDY'S BACK, RIGHT?

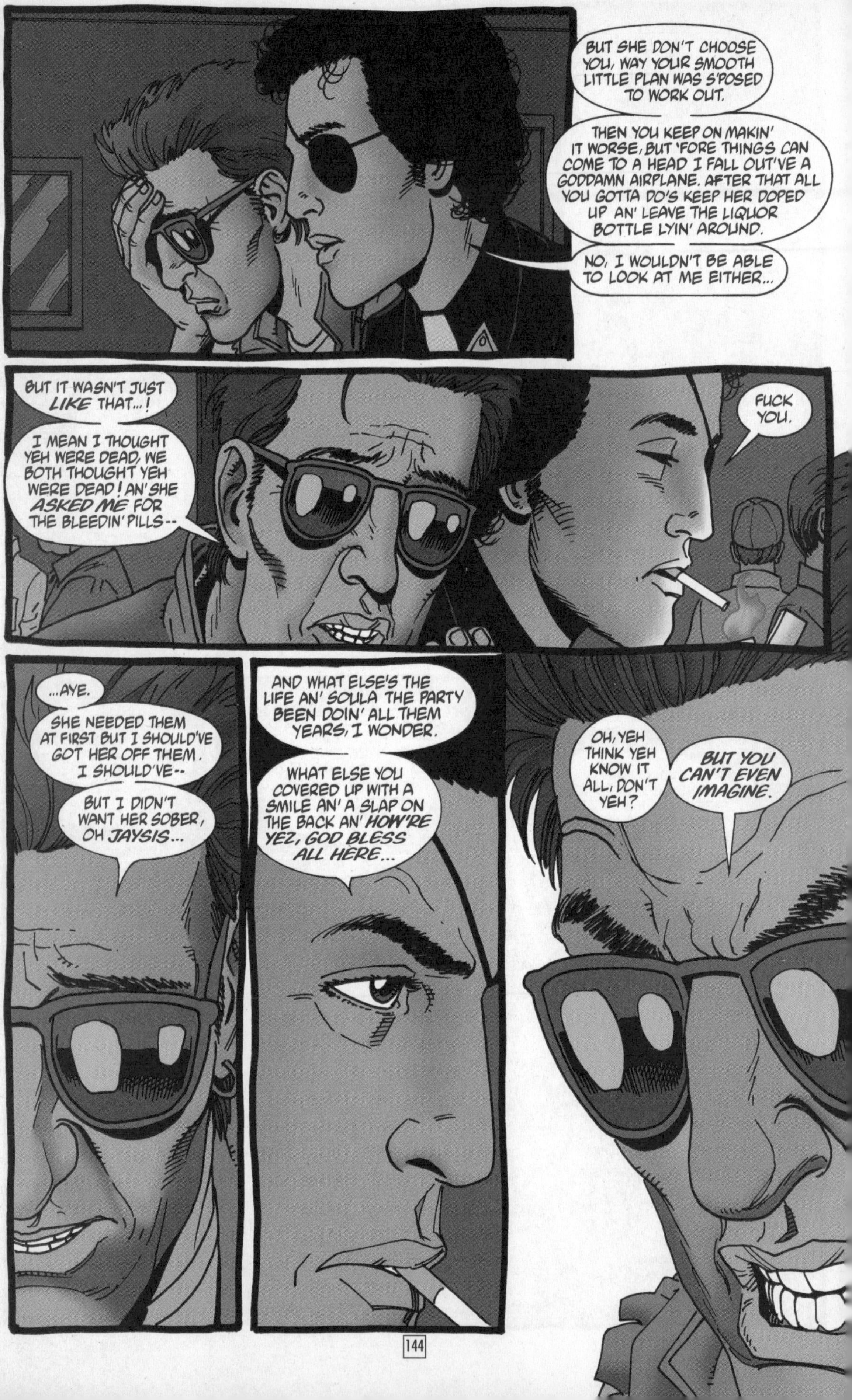
BUT SHE DON'T CHOOSE YOU, WAY YOUR SMOOTH LITTLE PLAN WAS S'POSED TO WORK OUT.
THEN YOU KEEP ON MAKIN' IT WORSE, BUT 'FORE THINGS CAN COME TO A HEAD I FALL OUT'VE A GODDAMN AIRPLANE. AFTER THAT ALL YOU GOTTA DO'S KEEP HER DOPED UP AN' LEAVE THE LIQUOR BOTTLE LYIN' AROUND.
NO, I WOULDN'T BE ABLE TO LOOK AT ME EITHER...
BUT IT WASN'T JUST *LIKE* THAT...!
I MEAN I THOUGHT YEH WERE DEAD, WE BOTH THOUGHT YEH WERE DEAD! AN' SHE *ASKED ME* FOR THE BLEEDIN' PILLS--
FUCK YOU.
...AYE.
SHE NEEDED THEM AT FIRST BUT I SHOULD'VE GOT HER OFF THEM. I SHOULD'VE--
BUT I DIDN'T WANT HER SOBER, OH *JAYSIS*...
AND WHAT ELSE'S THE LIFE AN' SOULA THE PARTY BEEN DOIN' ALL THEM YEARS, I WONDER.
WHAT ELSE YOU COVERED UP WITH A SMILE AN' A SLAP ON THE BACK AN' *HOW'RE YEZ, GOD BLESS ALL HERE*...
OH, YEH THINK YEH KNOW IT ALL, DON'T YEH?
BUT YOU CAN'T EVEN IMAGINE.

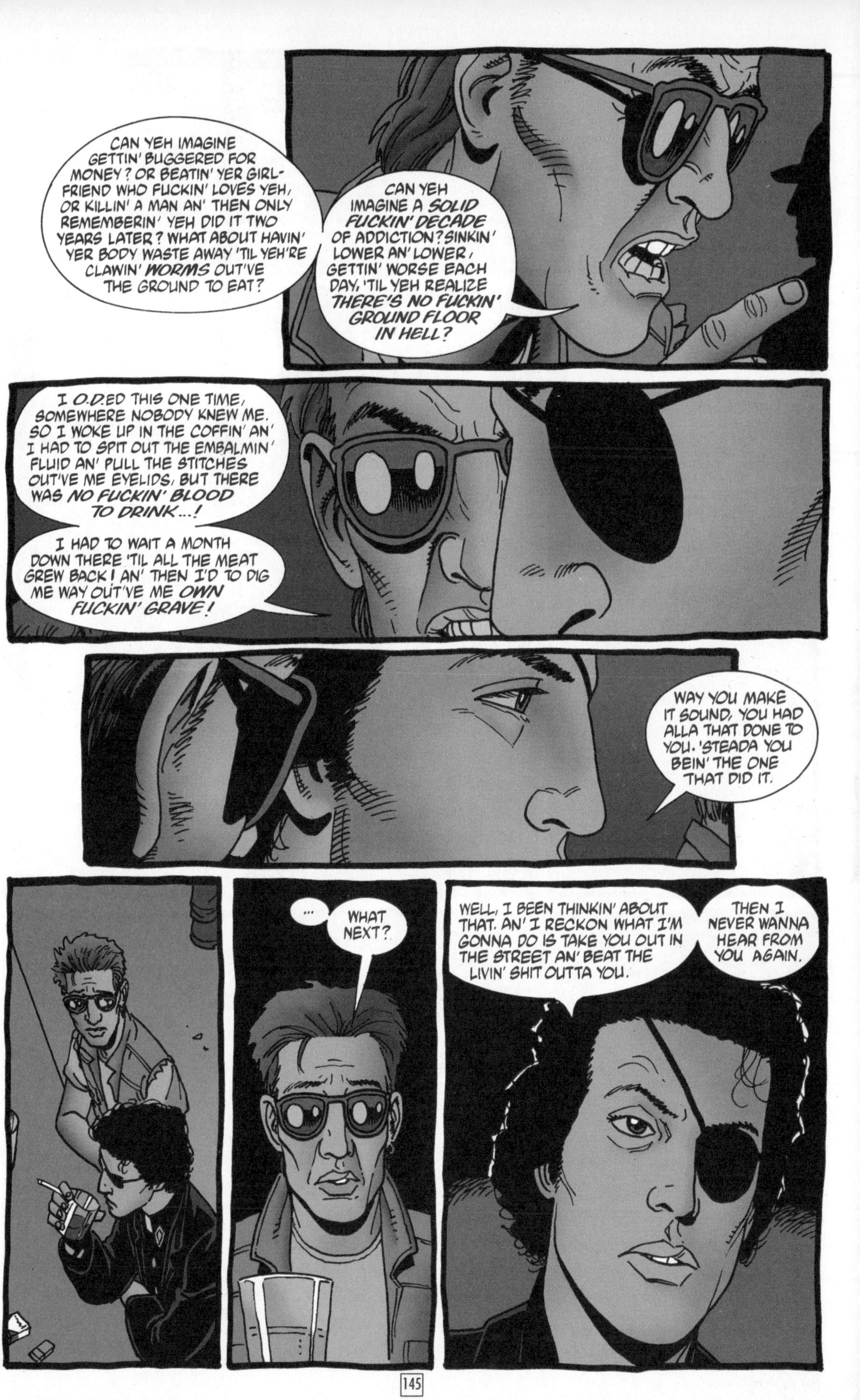
CAN YEH IMAGINE GETTIN' BUGGERED FOR MONEY? OR BEATIN' YER GIRL-FRIEND WHO FUCKIN' LOVES YEH, OR KILLIN' A MAN AN' THEN ONLY REMEMBERIN' YEH DID IT TWO YEARS LATER? WHAT ABOUT HAVIN' YER BODY WASTE AWAY 'TIL YEH'RE CLAWIN' WORMS OUT'VE THE GROUND TO EAT?
CAN YEH IMAGINE A SOLID FUCKIN' DECADE OF ADDICTION? SINKIN' LOWER AN' LOWER, GETTIN' WORSE EACH DAY, 'TIL YEH REALIZE THERE'S NO FUCKIN' GROUND FLOOR IN HELL?
I O.D.ED THIS ONE TIME, SOMEWHERE NOBODY KNEW ME. SO I WOKE UP IN THE COFFIN' AN' I HAD TO SPIT OUT THE EMBALMIN' FLUID AN' PULL THE STITCHES OUT'VE ME EYELIDS, BUT THERE WAS NO FUCKIN' BLOOD TO DRINK...!
I HAD TO WAIT A MONTH DOWN THERE 'TIL ALL THE MEAT GREW BACK! AN' THEN I'D TO DIG ME WAY OUT'VE ME OWN FUCKIN' GRAVE!
WAY YOU MAKE IT SOUND, YOU HAD ALLA THAT DONE TO YOU. 'STEADA YOU BEIN' THE ONE THAT DID IT.
...
WHAT NEXT?
WELL, I BEEN THINKIN' ABOUT THAT. AN' I RECKON WHAT I'M GONNA DO IS TAKE YOU OUT IN THE STREET AN' BEAT THE LIVIN' SHIT OUTTA YOU.
THEN I NEVER WANNA HEAR FROM YOU AGAIN.

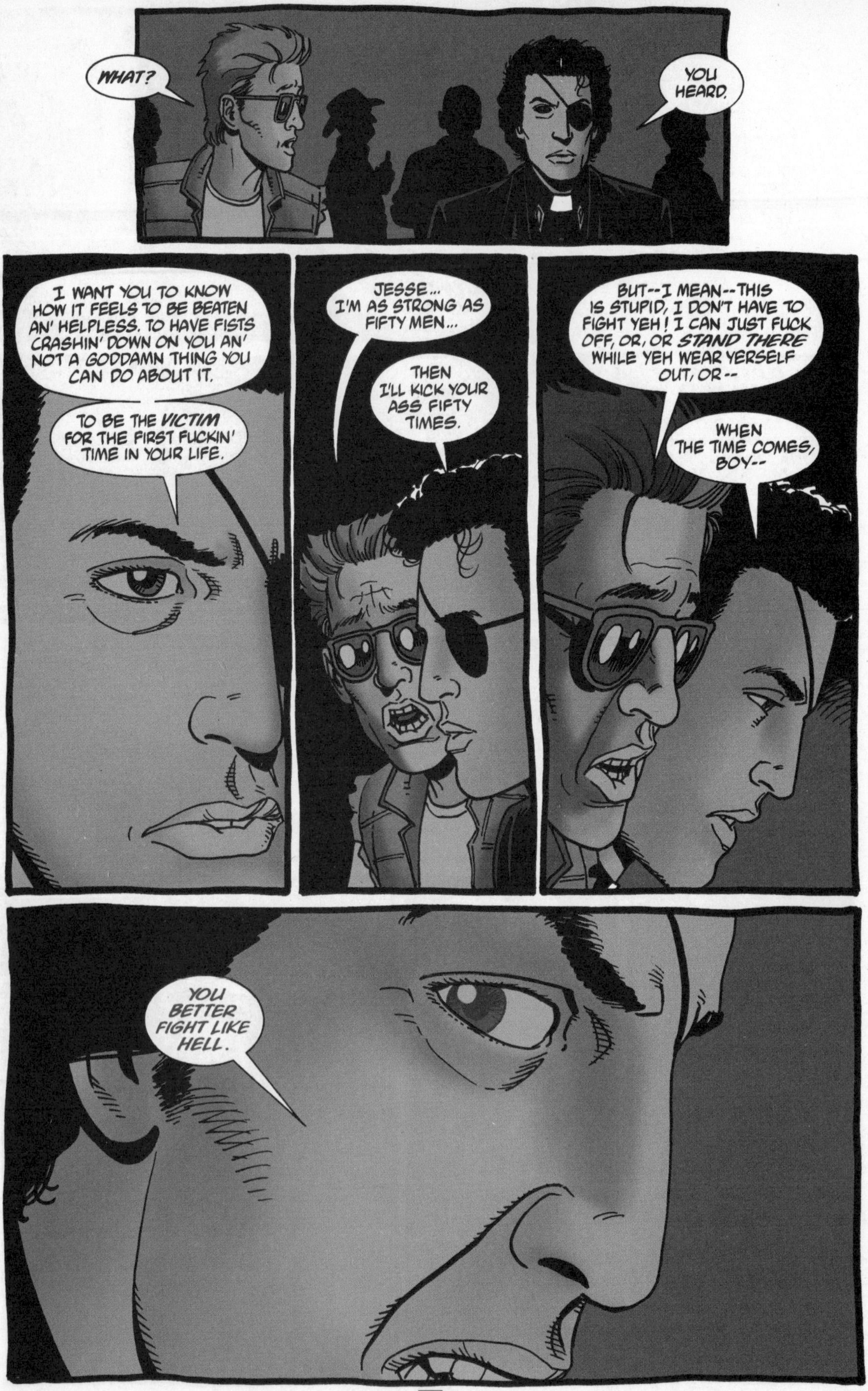

WHAT?
YOU HEARD.
I WANT YOU TO KNOW HOW IT FEELS TO BE BEATEN AN' HELPLESS. TO HAVE FISTS CRASHIN' DOWN ON YOU AN' NOT A GODDAMN THING YOU CAN DO ABOUT IT.
TO BE THE *VICTIM* FOR THE FIRST FUCKIN' TIME IN YOUR LIFE.
JESSE... I'M AS STRONG AS FIFTY MEN...
THEN I'LL KICK YOUR ASS FIFTY TIMES.
BUT--I MEAN--THIS IS STUPID, I DON'T HAVE TO FIGHT YEH! I CAN JUST FUCK OFF, OR, OR *STAND THERE* WHILE YEH WEAR YERSELF OUT, OR--
WHEN THE TIME COMES, BOY--
YOU BETTER FIGHT LIKE HELL.

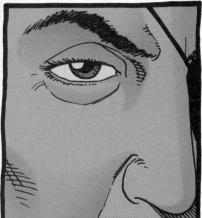

SAY! I BET MAH BUDDY BIG JOHN *FIVE DOLLARS* YOU TWO FAGGOTS GOT LOST AN' COME IN HERE BY ACCIDENT--AN' I WAS TO EVEN *TALK* TO YA, YA'D HIGHTAIL IT OUT THE DOOR AN' NOT DARE SAY A GODDAMN WORD!

SO WHAT'S IT GONNA BE, *LADIES?!*

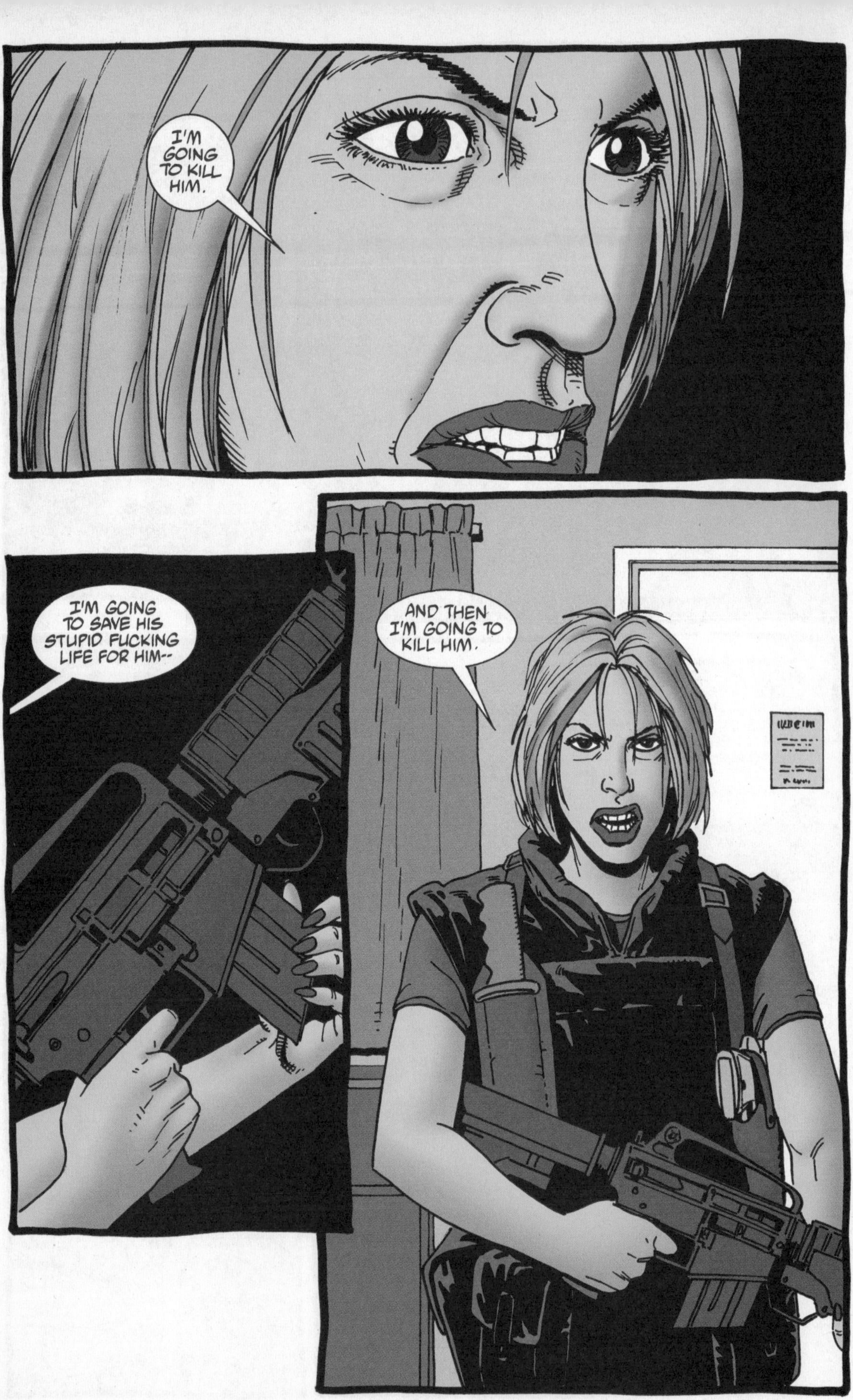
I'M GOING TO KILL HIM.
I'M GOING TO SAVE HIS STUPID FUCKING LIFE FOR HIM--
AND THEN I'M GOING TO KILL HIM.

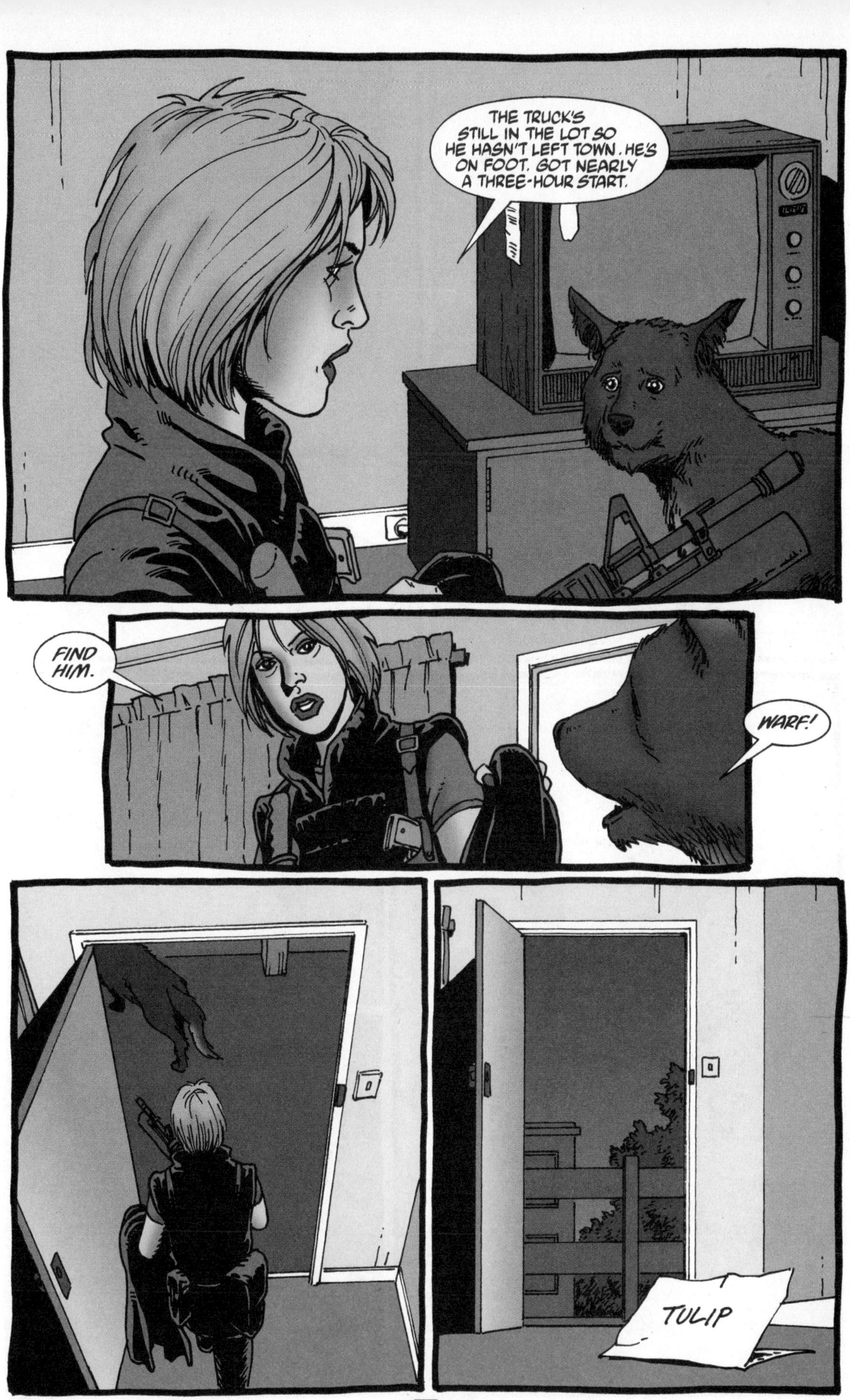

THE TRUCK'S STILL IN THE LOT SO HE HASN'T LEFT TOWN. HE'S ON FOOT. GOT NEARLY A THREE-HOUR START.
FIND HIM.
WARF!
TULIP

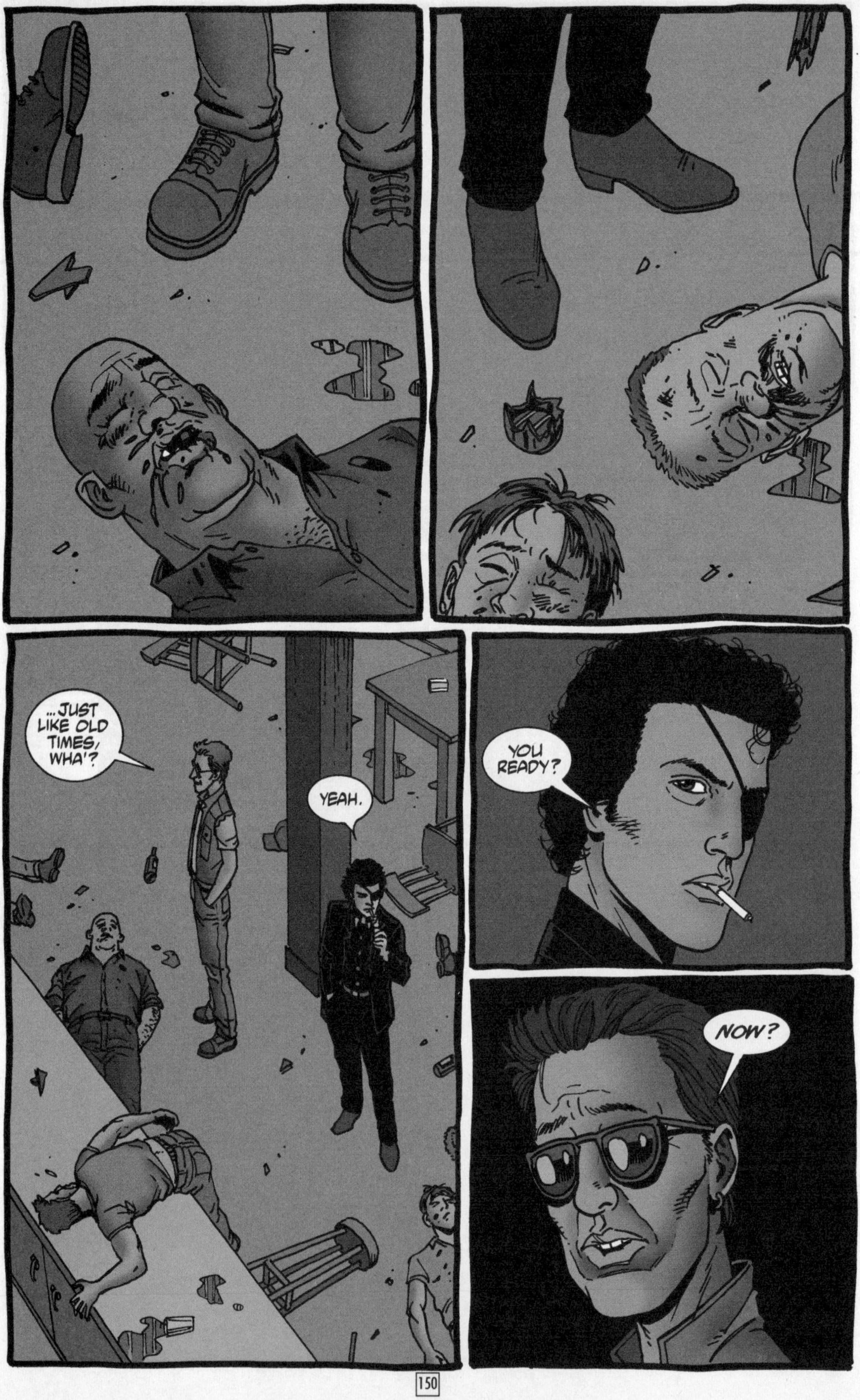
...JUST LIKE OLD TIMES, WHA'?
YEAH.
YOU READY?
NOW?

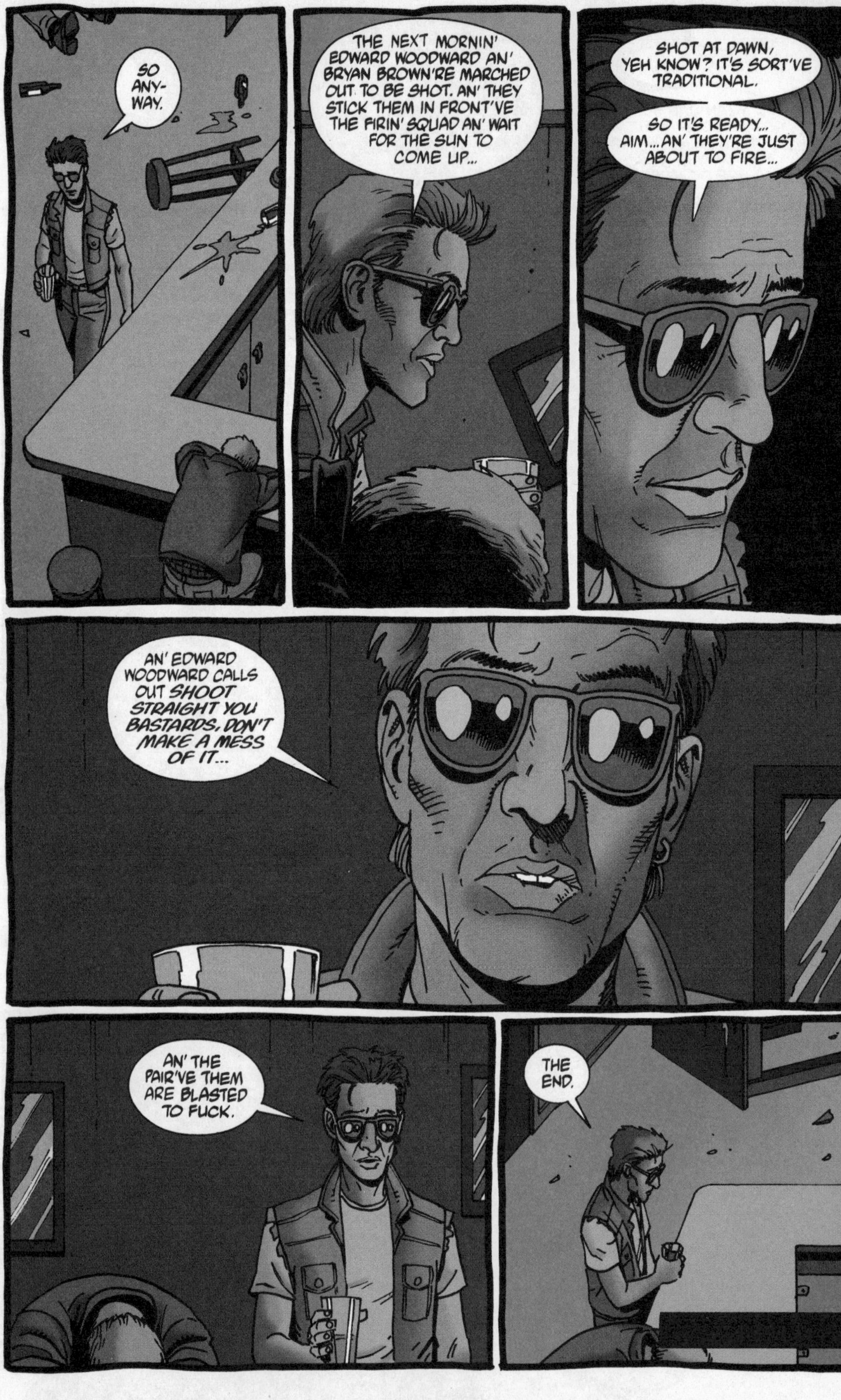
SO ANY-WAY.
THE NEXT MORNIN' EDWARD WOODWARD AN' BRYAN BROWN'RE MARCHED OUT TO BE SHOT. AN' THEY STICK THEM IN FRONT'VE THE FIRIN' SQUAD AN' WAIT FOR THE SUN TO COME UP...
SHOT AT DAWN, YEH KNOW? IT'S SORT'VE TRADITIONAL.
SO IT'S READY... AIM...AN' THEY'RE JUST ABOUT TO FIRE...
AN' EDWARD WOODWARD CALLS OUT *SHOOT STRAIGHT YOU BASTARDS, DON'T MAKE A MESS OF IT...*
AN' THE PAIR'VE THEM ARE BLASTED TO FUCK.
THE END.

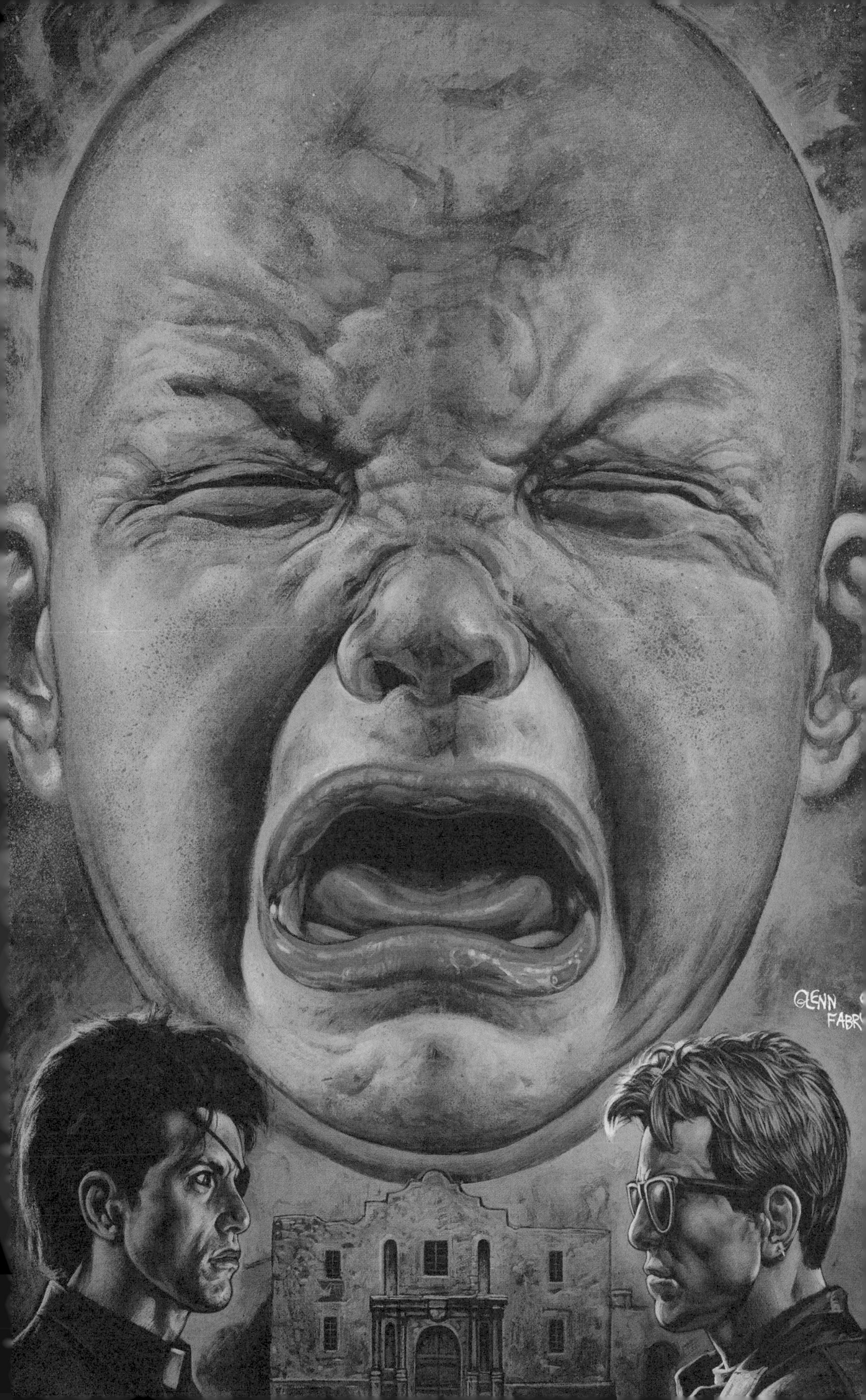

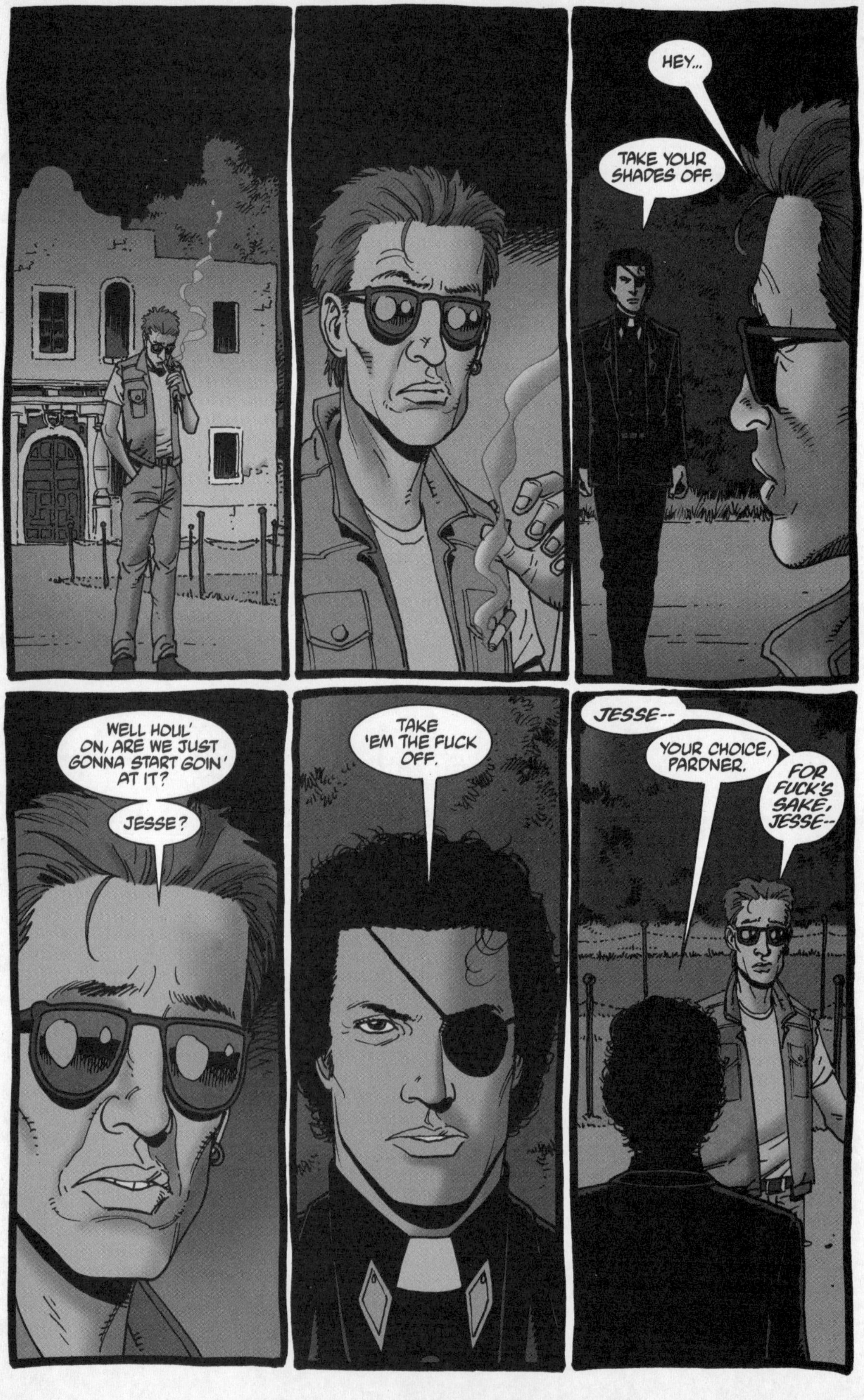

HEY...
TAKE YOUR SHADES OFF.
WELL HOUL' ON, ARE WE JUST GONNA START GOIN' AT IT?
JESSE?
TAKE 'EM THE FUCK OFF.
JESSE--
YOUR CHOICE, PARDNER.
FOR FUCK'S SAKE, JESSE--

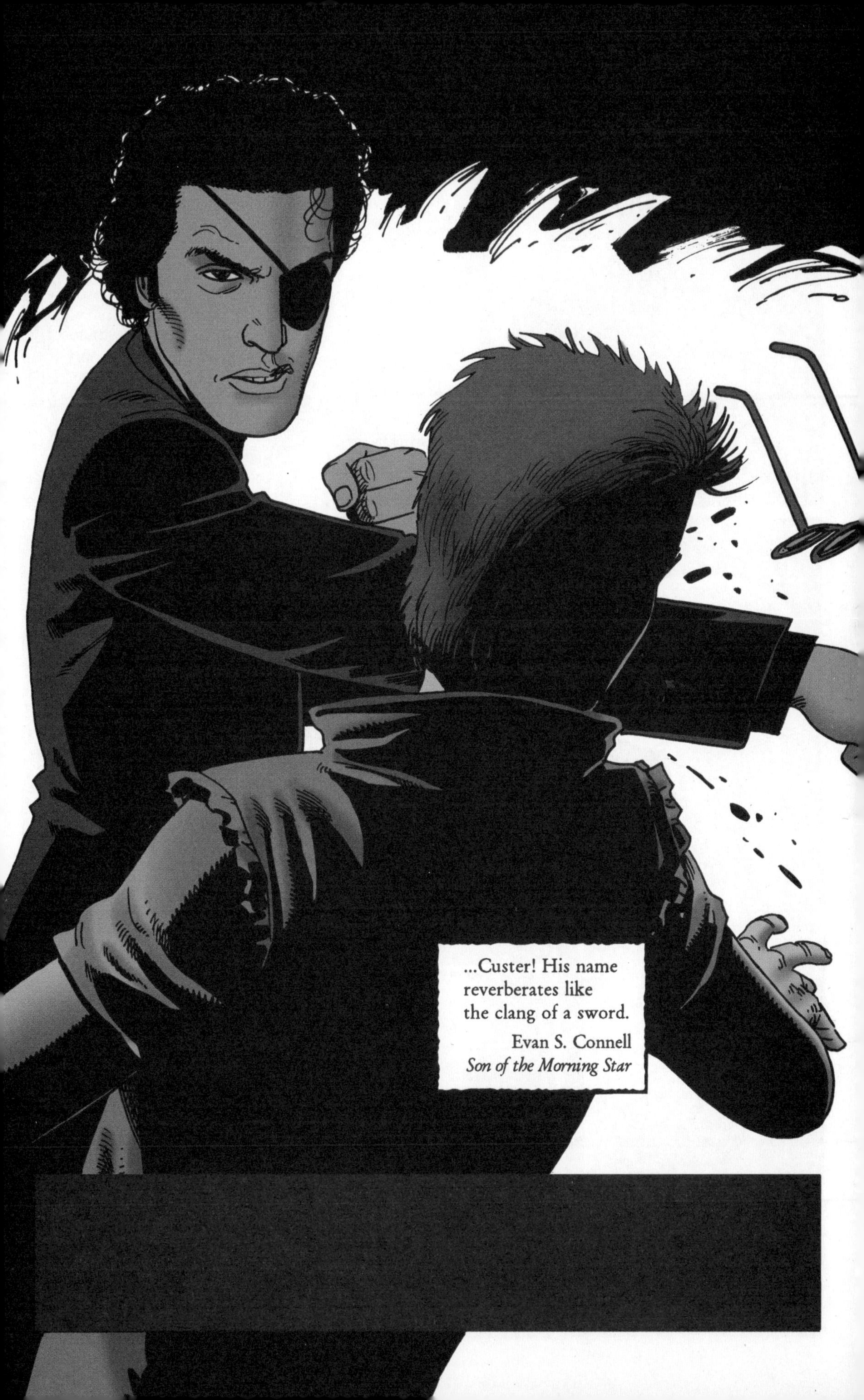
...Custer! His name reverberates like the clang of a sword.
Evan S. Connell
Son of the Morning Star

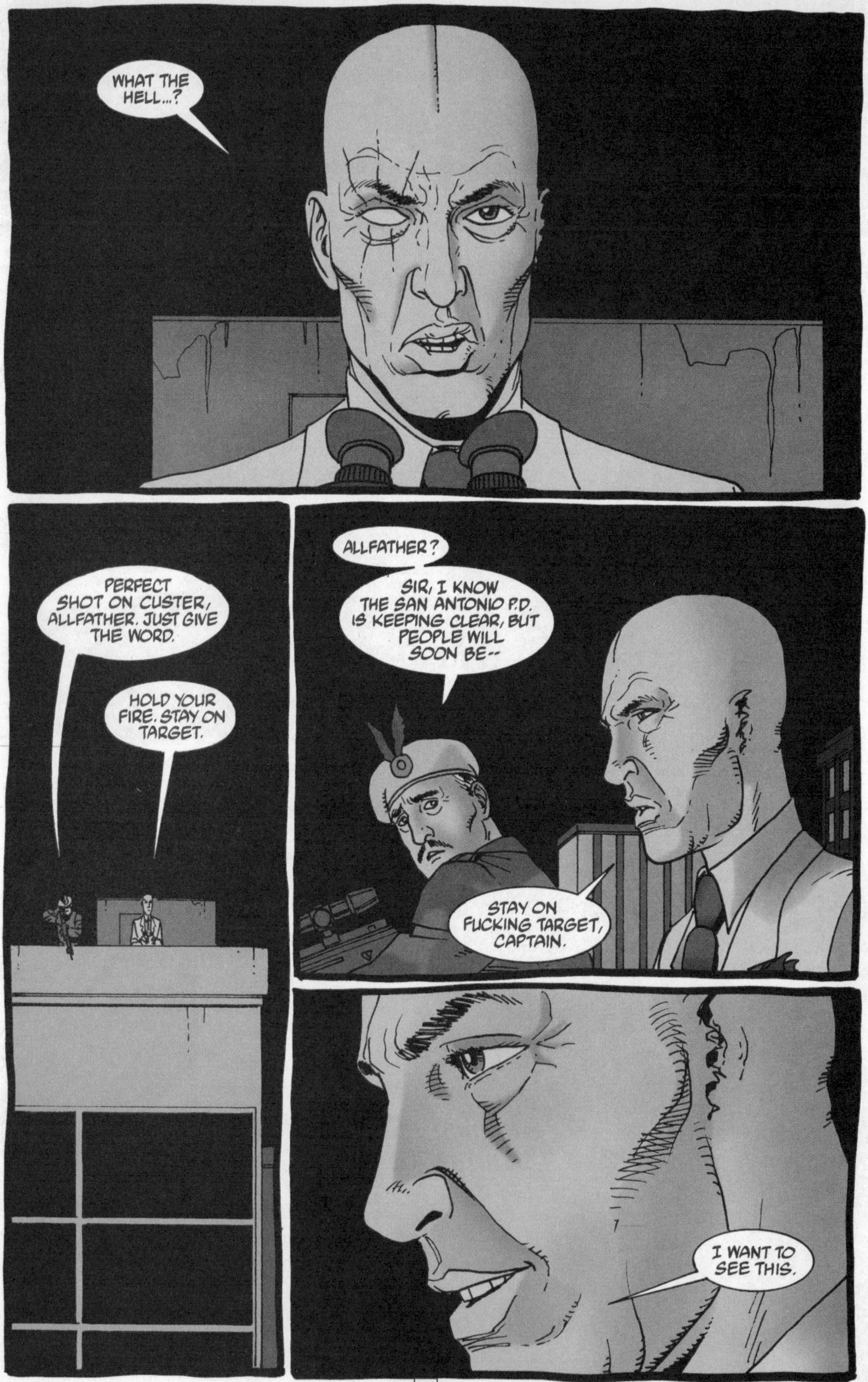
WHAT THE HELL...?
PERFECT SHOT ON CUSTER, ALLFATHER. JUST GIVE THE WORD.
HOLD YOUR FIRE. STAY ON TARGET.
ALLFATHER?
SIR, I KNOW THE SAN ANTONIO P.D. IS KEEPING CLEAR, BUT PEOPLE WILL SOON BE--
STAY ON FUCKING TARGET, CAPTAIN.
I WANT TO SEE THIS.

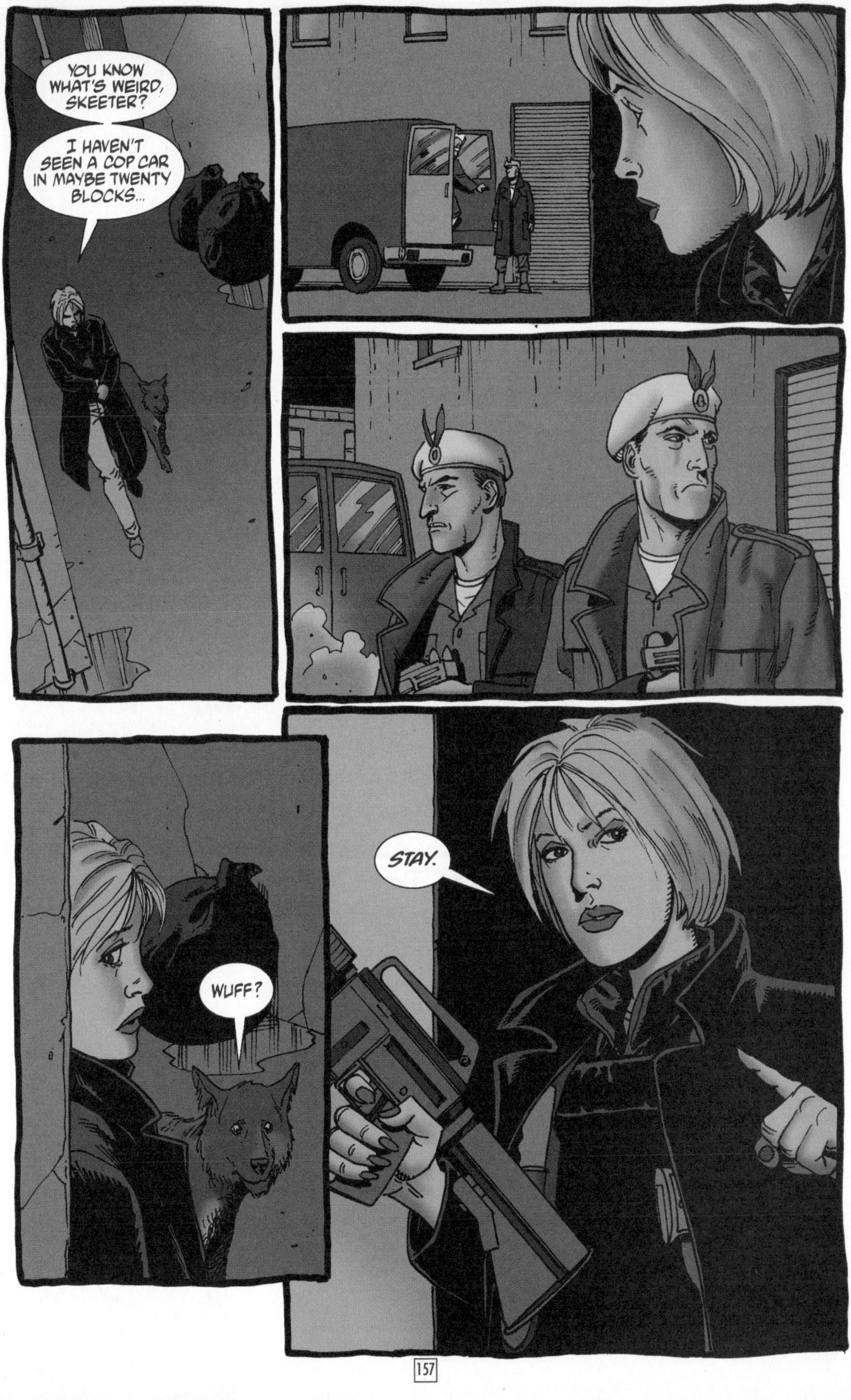
YOU KNOW WHAT'S WEIRD, SKEETER?
I HAVEN'T SEEN A COP CAR IN MAYBE TWENTY BLOCKS...
WUFF?
STAY.

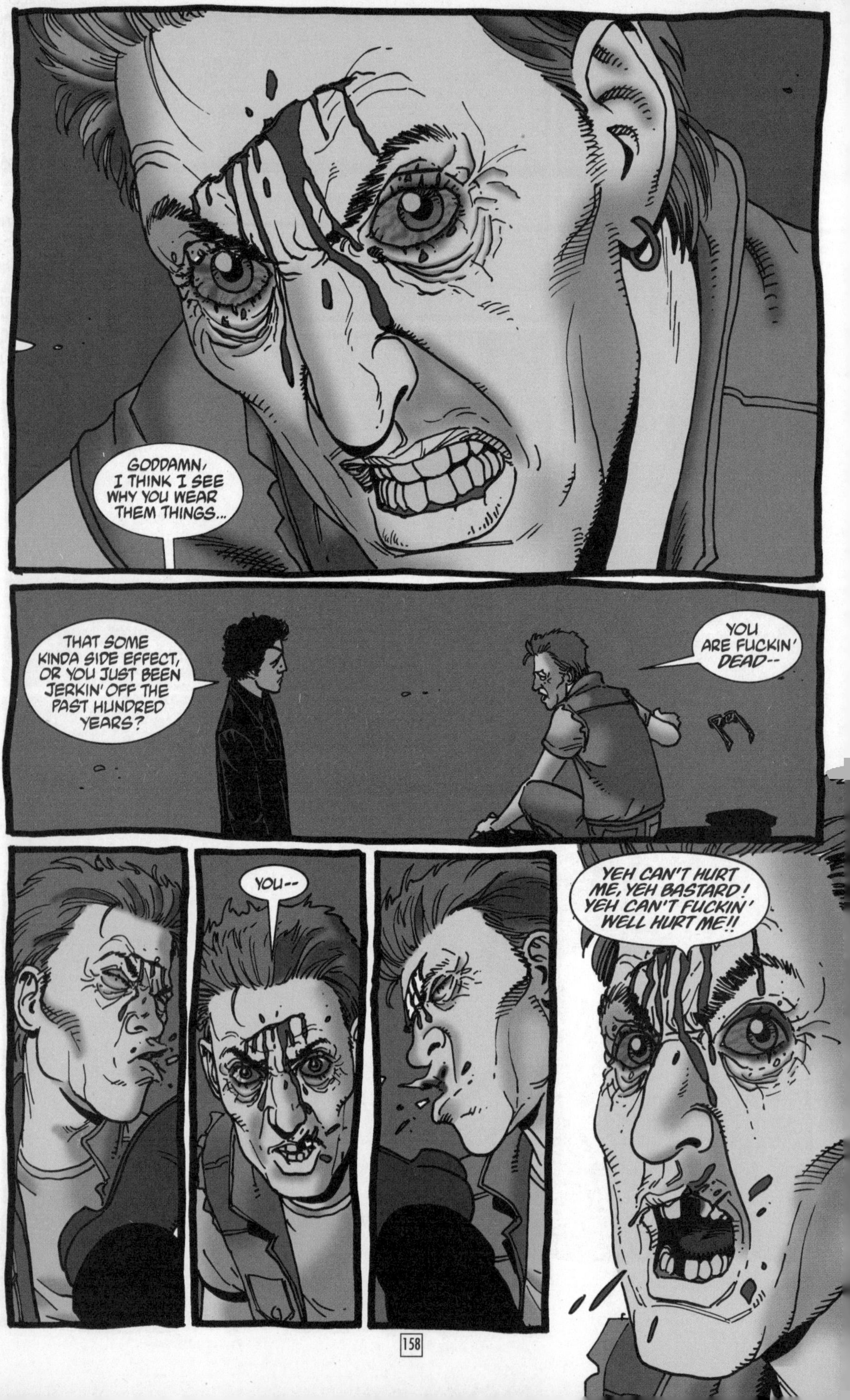
GODDAMN, I THINK I SEE WHY YOU WEAR THEM THINGS...
THAT SOME KINDA SIDE EFFECT, OR YOU JUST BEEN JERKIN' OFF THE PAST HUNDRED YEARS?
YOU ARE FUCKIN' DEAD--
YOU--
YEH CAN'T HURT ME, YEH BASTARD! YEH CAN'T FUCKIN' WELL HURT ME!!

THAT A FACT?

THAT CUT IN YOUR FOREHEAD-- THAT STINGS SOME, DON'T IT? MUST REALLY BE PISSIN' YOU OFF...

EYES FILLIN' UP WITH BLOOD... GETTIN' HARDER AN' HARDER TO SEE...

I CAN STILL FUCKIN' SMELL YEH--

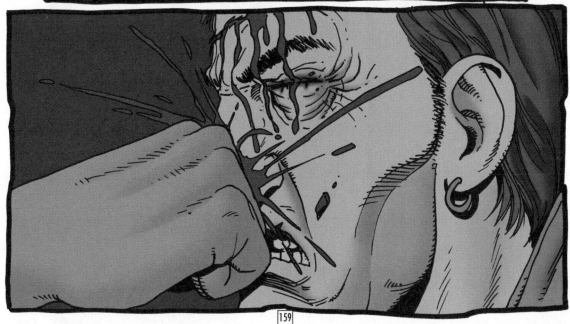

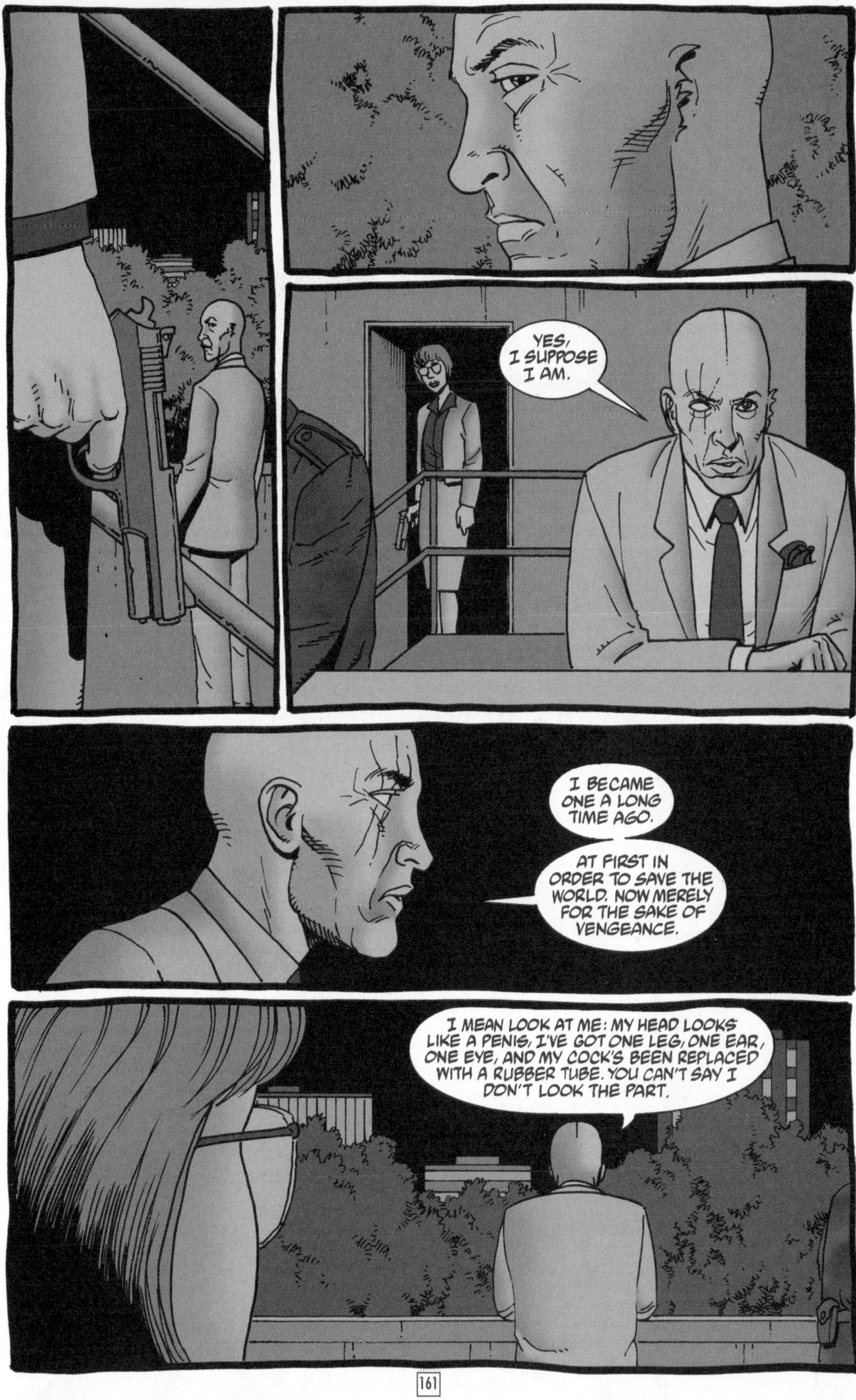
YES, I SUPPOSE I AM.
I BECAME ONE A LONG TIME AGO.
AT FIRST IN ORDER TO SAVE THE WORLD. NOW MERELY FOR THE SAKE OF VENGEANCE.
I MEAN LOOK AT ME: MY HEAD LOOKS LIKE A PENIS, I'VE GOT ONE LEG, ONE EAR, ONE EYE, AND MY COCK'S BEEN REPLACED WITH A RUBBER TUBE. YOU CAN'T SAY I DON'T LOOK THE PART.

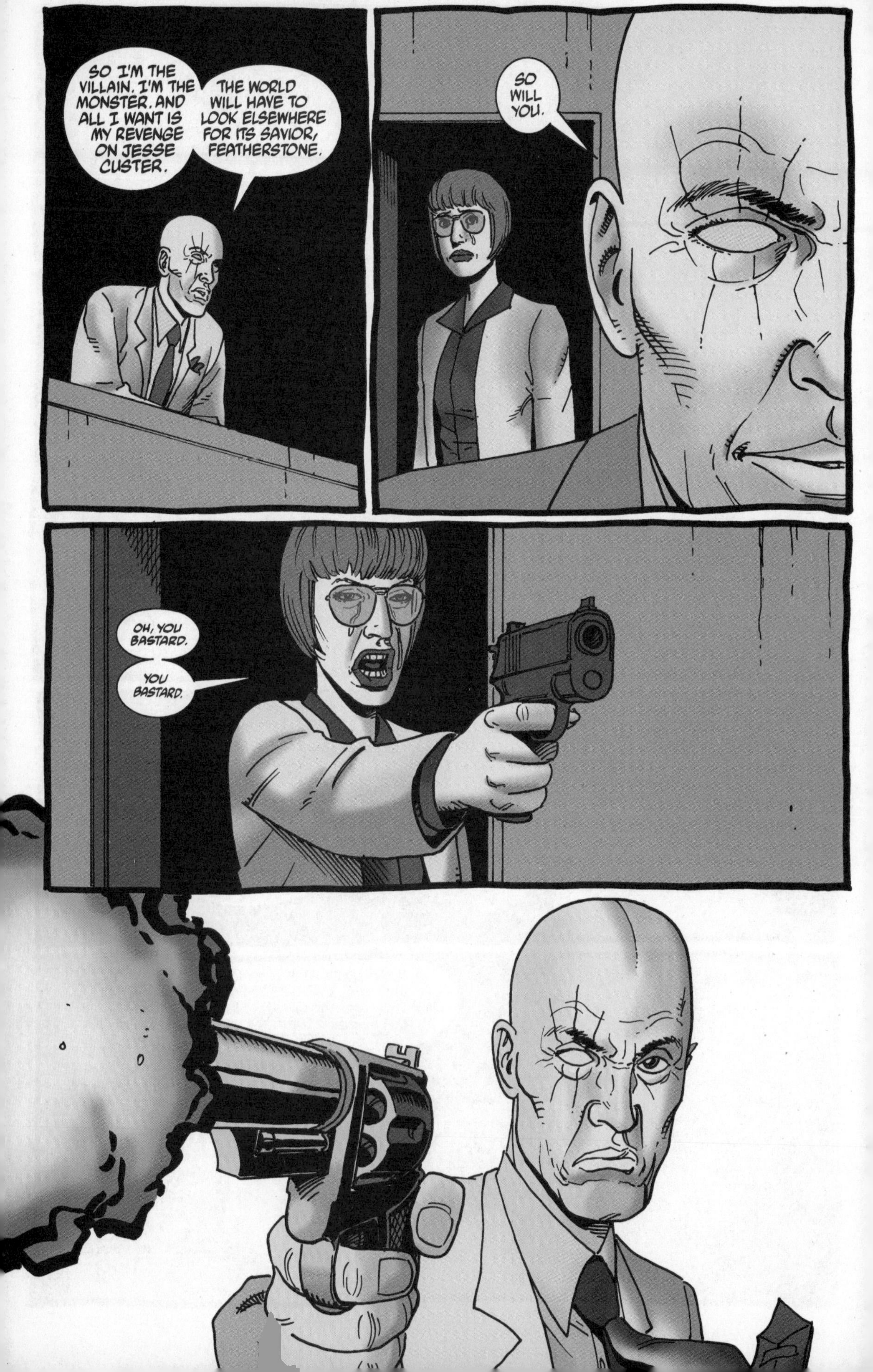
SO I'M THE VILLAIN. I'M THE MONSTER. AND ALL I WANT IS MY REVENGE ON JESSE CUSTER.
THE WORLD WILL HAVE TO LOOK ELSEWHERE FOR ITS SAVIOR, FEATHERSTONE.
SO WILL YOU.
OH, YOU BASTARD.
YOU BASTARD.

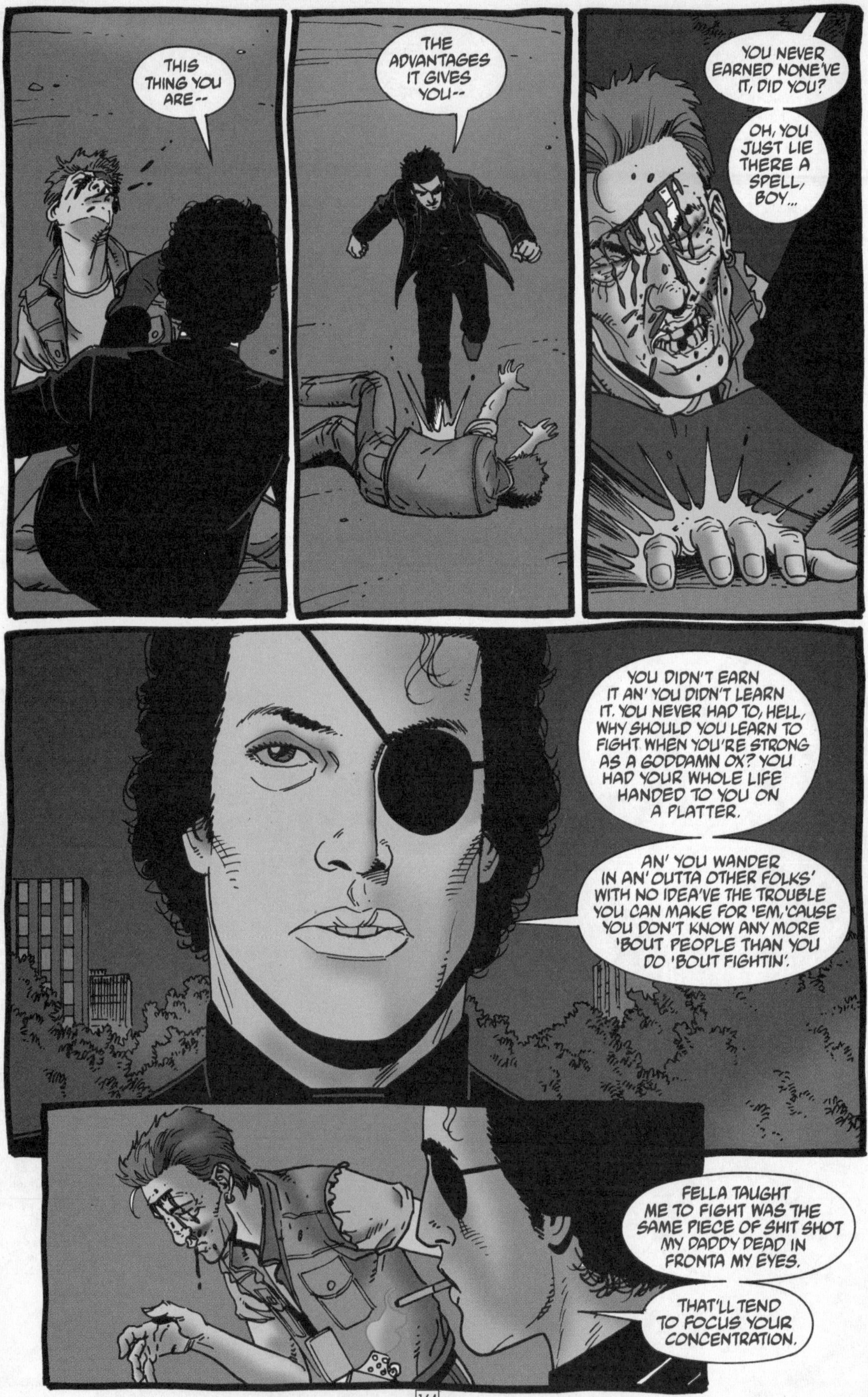
THIS THING YOU ARE--
THE ADVANTAGES IT GIVES YOU--
YOU NEVER EARNED NONE'VE IT, DID YOU?
OH, YOU JUST LIE THERE A SPELL, BOY...
YOU DIDN'T EARN IT AN' YOU DIDN'T LEARN IT. YOU NEVER HAD TO, HELL, WHY SHOULD YOU LEARN TO FIGHT WHEN YOU'RE STRONG AS A GODDAMN OX? YOU HAD YOUR WHOLE LIFE HANDED TO YOU ON A PLATTER.
AN' YOU WANDER IN AN' OUTTA OTHER FOLKS' WITH NO IDEA'VE THE TROUBLE YOU CAN MAKE FOR 'EM, 'CAUSE YOU DON'T KNOW ANY MORE 'BOUT PEOPLE THAN YOU DO 'BOUT FIGHTIN'.
FELLA TAUGHT ME TO FIGHT WAS THE SAME PIECE OF SHIT SHOT MY DADDY DEAD IN FRONTA MY EYES.
THAT'LL TEND TO FOCUS YOUR CONCENTRATION.

HA!!

AAAWWWHHHH...!

THAT HURT, HUH?

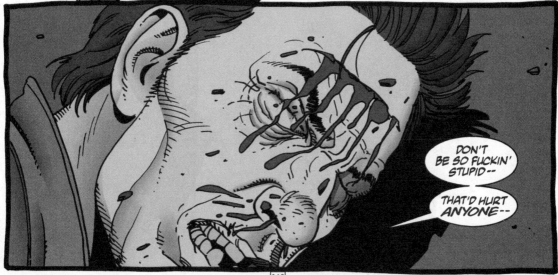

DON'T BE SO FUCKIN' STUPID--

THAT'D HURT ANYONE--

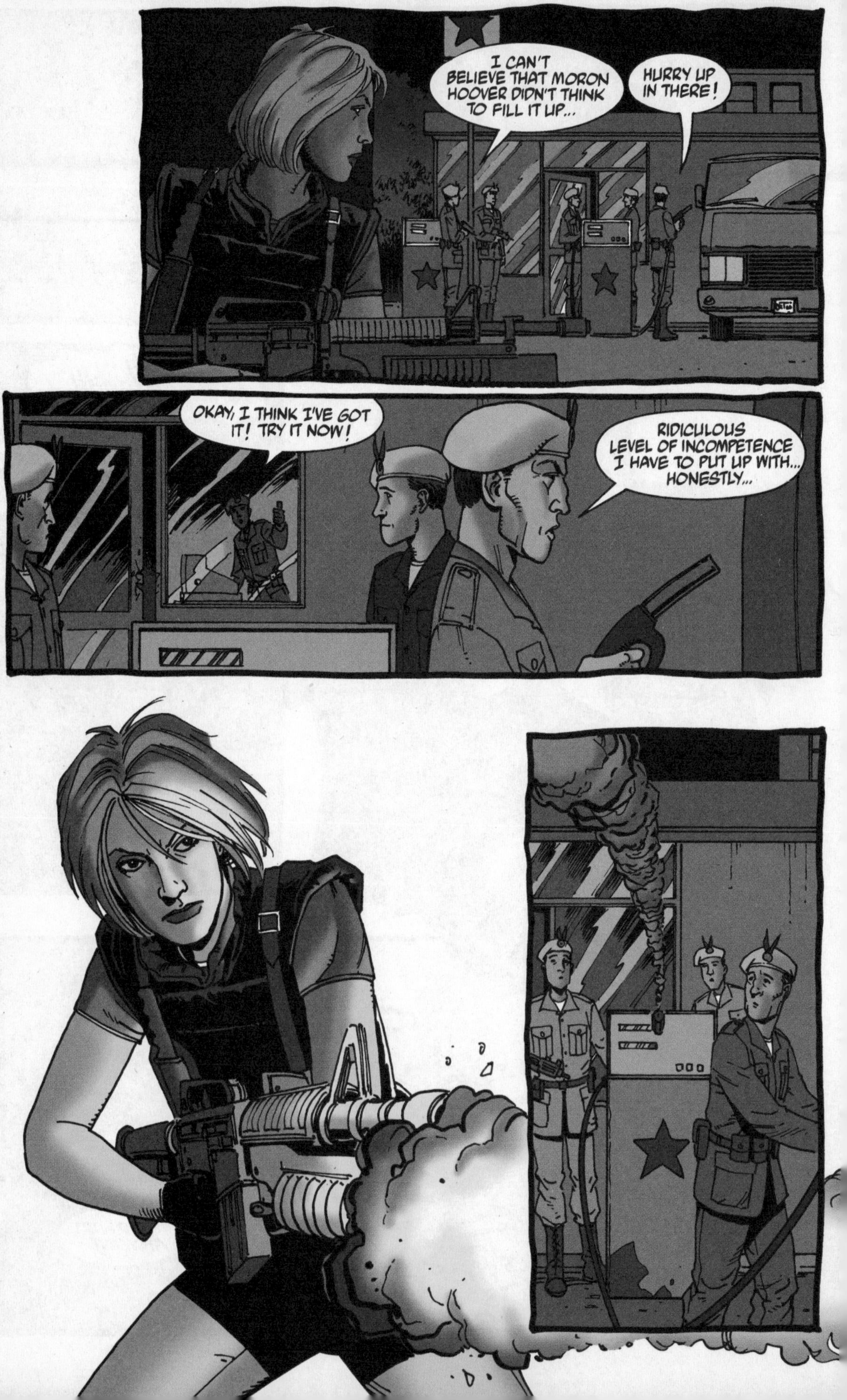
I CAN'T BELIEVE THAT MORON HOOVER DIDN'T THINK TO FILL IT UP...
HURRY UP IN THERE!
OKAY, I THINK I'VE GOT IT! TRY IT NOW!
RIDICULOUS LEVEL OF INCOMPETENCE I HAVE TO PUT UP WITH... HONESTLY...

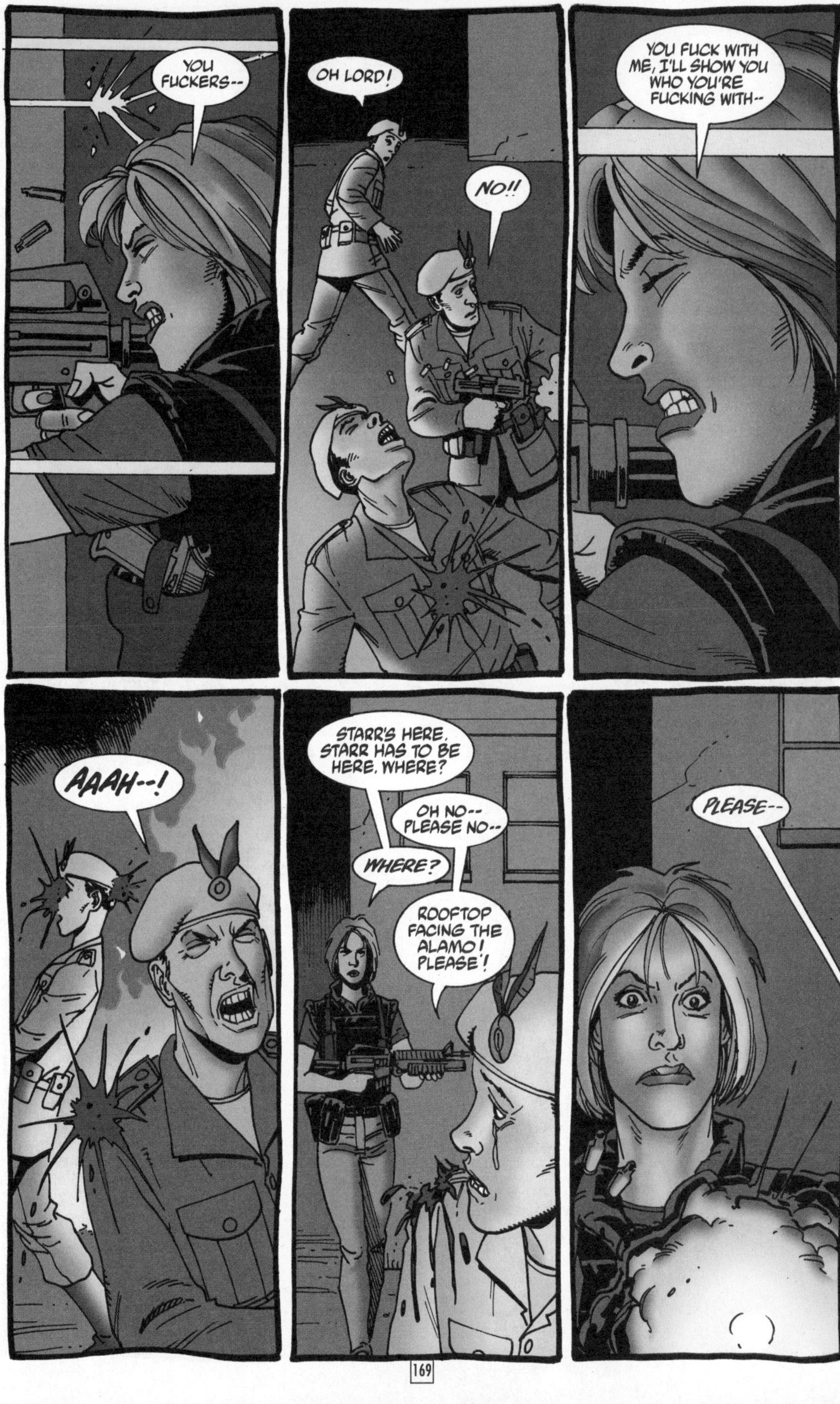
YOU FUCKERS--
OH LORD!
NO!!
YOU FUCK WITH ME, I'LL SHOW YOU WHO YOU'RE FUCKING WITH--
AAAH--!
STARR'S HERE. STARR HAS TO BE HERE. WHERE?
OH NO-- PLEASE NO--
WHERE?
ROOFTOP FACING THE ALAMO! PLEASE!
PLEASE--

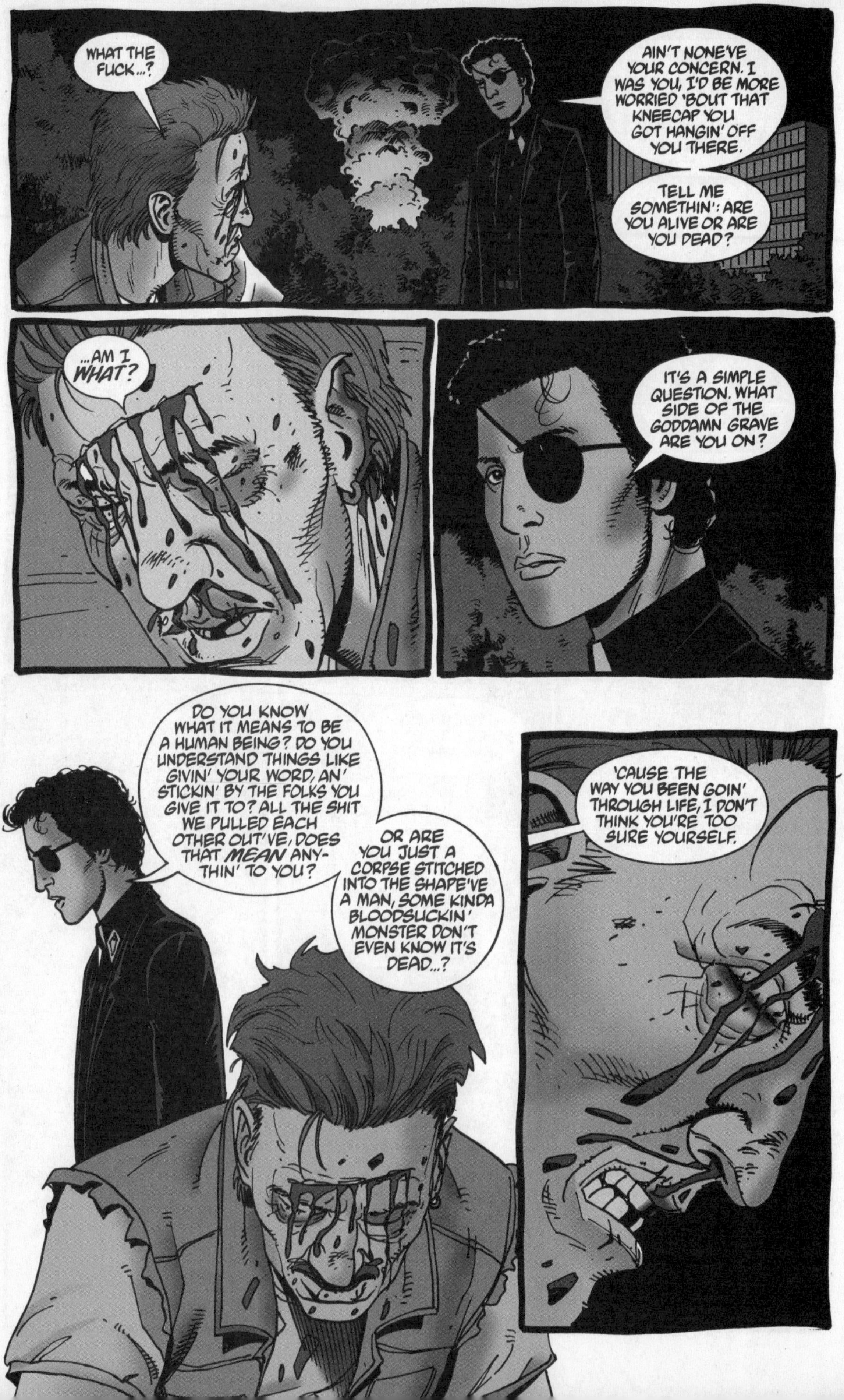
WHAT THE FUCK...?
AIN'T NONE'VE YOUR CONCERN. I WAS YOU, I'D BE MORE WORRIED 'BOUT THAT KNEECAP YOU GOT HANGIN' OFF YOU THERE.
TELL ME SOMETHIN': ARE YOU ALIVE OR ARE YOU DEAD?
...AM I *WHAT?*
IT'S A SIMPLE QUESTION. WHAT SIDE OF THE GODDAMN GRAVE ARE YOU ON?
DO YOU KNOW WHAT IT MEANS TO BE A HUMAN BEING? DO YOU UNDERSTAND THINGS LIKE GIVIN' YOUR WORD, AN' STICKIN' BY THE FOLKS YOU GIVE IT TO? ALL THE SHIT WE PULLED EACH OTHER OUT'VE, DOES THAT *MEAN* ANY-THIN' TO YOU?
OR ARE YOU JUST A CORPSE STITCHED INTO THE SHAPE'VE A MAN, SOME KINDA BLOODSUCKIN' MONSTER DON'T EVEN KNOW IT'S DEAD...?
'CAUSE THE WAY YOU BEEN GOIN' THROUGH LIFE, I DON'T THINK YOU'RE TOO SURE YOURSELF.

C'MON THEN! C'MON!

I'LL FUCKIN' SHOW YEH--

BEHIND YOU, YOU DUMB SHIT.

RRAAAAHH!

REMEMBER SI?

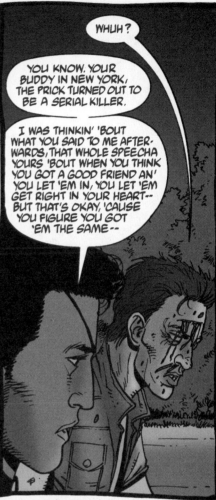

WHUH?

YOU KNOW. YOUR BUDDY IN NEW YORK, THE PRICK TURNED OUT TO BE A SERIAL KILLER.

I WAS THINKIN' 'BOUT WHAT YOU SAID TO ME AFTERWARDS, THAT WHOLE SPEECHA YOURS 'BOUT WHEN YOU THINK YOU GOT A GOOD FRIEND AN' YOU LET 'EM IN, YOU LET 'EM GET RIGHT IN YOUR HEART-- BUT THAT'S OKAY, 'CAUSE YOU FIGURE YOU GOT 'EM THE SAME--

AN' IT TURNS OUT THEY'RE JUST ANOTHER FUCKER?

DID YOU MEAN SI? OR WERE YOU, SOME PARTA YOU, TRYNNA WARN ME?

WAS THAT REALLY YOU YOU WERE TALKIN' ABOUT?

IT WAS NOT! IT FUCKIN' WELL WAS NOT! THAT'S NOT ME!

WHO THE FUCK DO YOU THINK YOU ARE, SAYIN' THESE FUCKIN' THINGS! WHO THE FUCK ARE YOU TO JUDGE ME?!

ALLFATHER, I'M GETTING MORE AND MORE UNEASY ABOUT THIS...

STAY ON TARGET.

BUT WHAT'S GOING ON, EXACTLY? WHAT WAS THAT YOU SAID TO YOUR ADJUTANT, THAT BUSINESS ABOUT--

STAY ON TARGET.

MOTHERFUCKER.

YOU EVIL, TWISTED MOTHER-FUCKER.

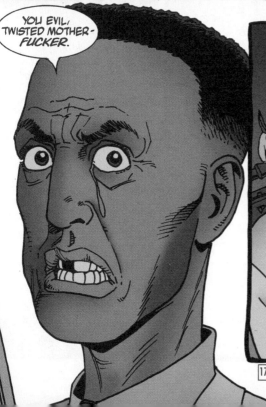

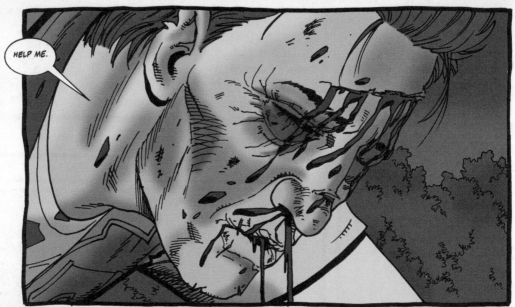

HELP ME.

WHAT?

HELP ME, I SAID.

YEH'RE THE ONLY ONE THAT CAN.

WHAT THE FUCK'RE YOU--

NO. NO, LISTEN TO ME NOW. MY TURN TO SPEAK.

BE TOTALLY FUCKIN' HONEST NOW.

THE FIRST TIME WE MET, BY THAT ROADSIDE, WHEN THE COPS WERE AFTER YOU AN' TULIP.

YEH LOOKED ME IN THE EYES LIKE YEH WERE WEIGHIN' UP WHAT SORT'VE A FELLA I WAS, AN' YEH ASKED IF YEZ COULD HAVE A RIDE WHEN YEH COULD'VE JUST TAKEN ME TRUCK, AN' THEN YEH LET ME STICK AROUND LATER, TOO...

TOTALLY... FUCKIN'... HONEST.

WHY?

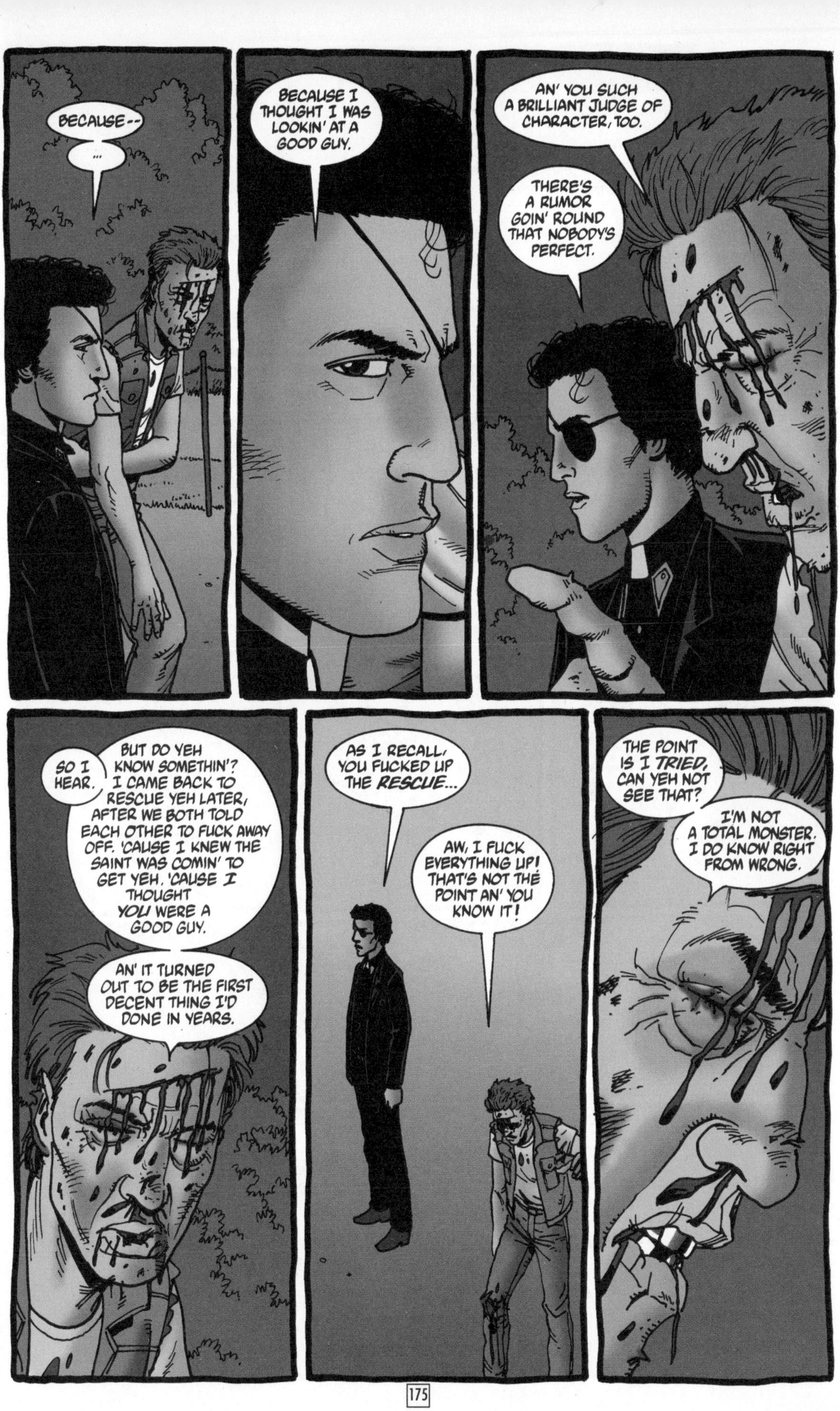
BECAUSE--
...
BECAUSE I THOUGHT I WAS LOOKIN' AT A GOOD GUY.
AN' YOU SUCH A BRILLIANT JUDGE OF CHARACTER, TOO.
THERE'S A RUMOR GOIN' ROUND THAT NOBODY'S PERFECT.
SO I HEAR.
BUT DO YEH KNOW SOMETHIN'? I CAME BACK TO RESCUE YEH LATER, AFTER WE BOTH TOLD EACH OTHER TO FUCK AWAY OFF. 'CAUSE I KNEW THE SAINT WAS COMIN' TO GET YEH. 'CAUSE I THOUGHT YOU WERE A GOOD GUY.
AN' IT TURNED OUT TO BE THE FIRST DECENT THING I'D DONE IN YEARS.
AS I RECALL, YOU FUCKED UP THE RESCUE...
AW, I FUCK EVERYTHING UP! THAT'S NOT THE POINT AN' YOU KNOW IT!
THE POINT IS I TRIED, CAN YEH NOT SEE THAT?
I'M NOT A TOTAL MONSTER. I DO KNOW RIGHT FROM WRONG.

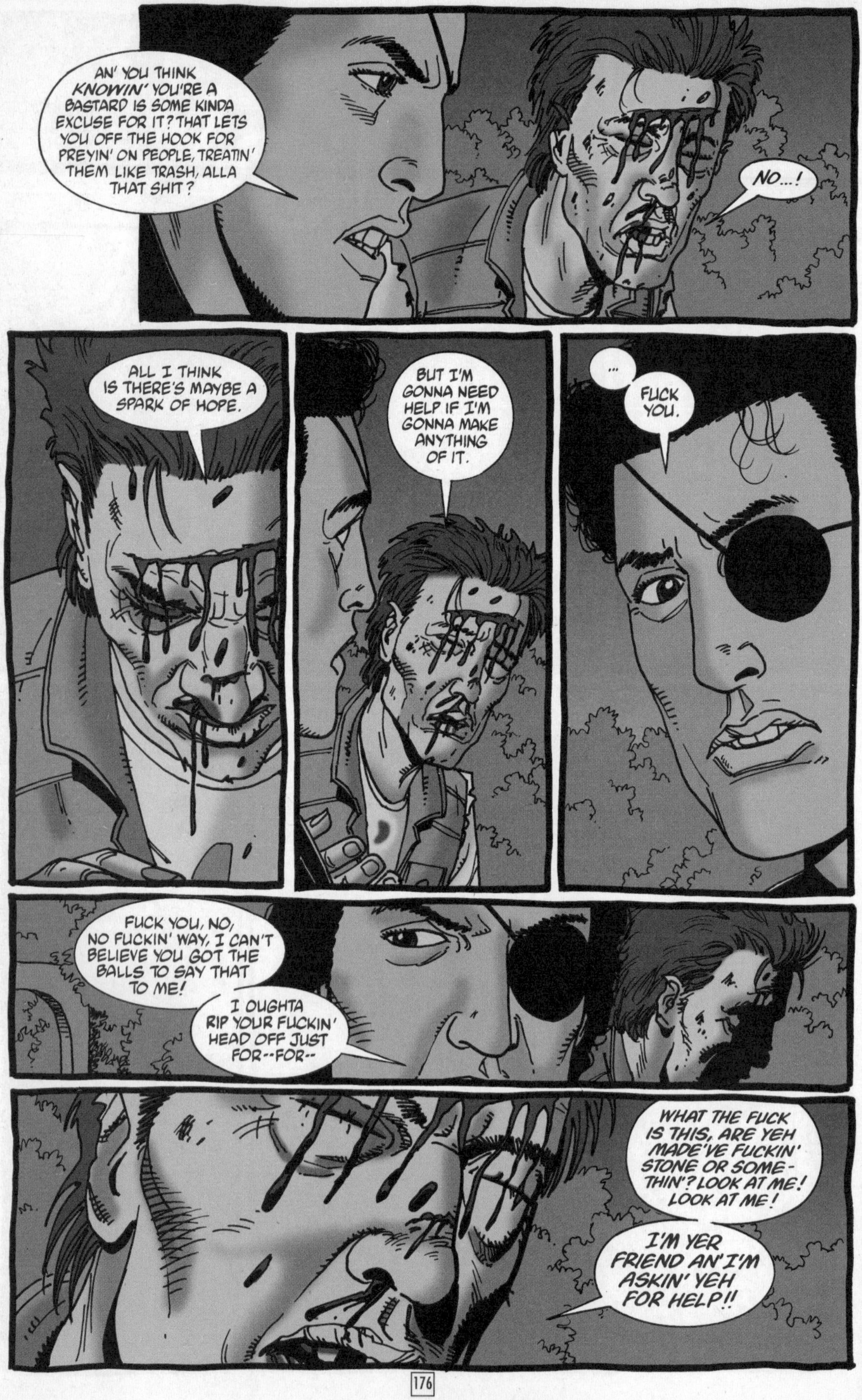

AN' YOU THINK KNOWIN' YOU'RE A BASTARD IS SOME KINDA EXCUSE FOR IT? THAT LETS YOU OFF THE HOOK FOR PREYIN' ON PEOPLE, TREATIN' THEM LIKE TRASH, ALLA THAT SHIT?
NO...!
ALL I THINK IS THERE'S MAYBE A SPARK OF HOPE.
BUT I'M GONNA NEED HELP IF I'M GONNA MAKE ANYTHING OF IT.
...
FUCK YOU.
FUCK YOU, NO, NO FUCKIN' WAY, I CAN'T BELIEVE YOU GOT THE BALLS TO SAY THAT TO ME!
I OUGHTA RIP YOUR FUCKIN' HEAD OFF JUST FOR--FOR--
WHAT THE FUCK IS THIS, ARE YEH MADE'VE FUCKIN' STONE OR SOME-THIN'? LOOK AT ME! LOOK AT ME!
I'M YER FRIEND AN' I'M ASKIN' YEH FOR HELP!!

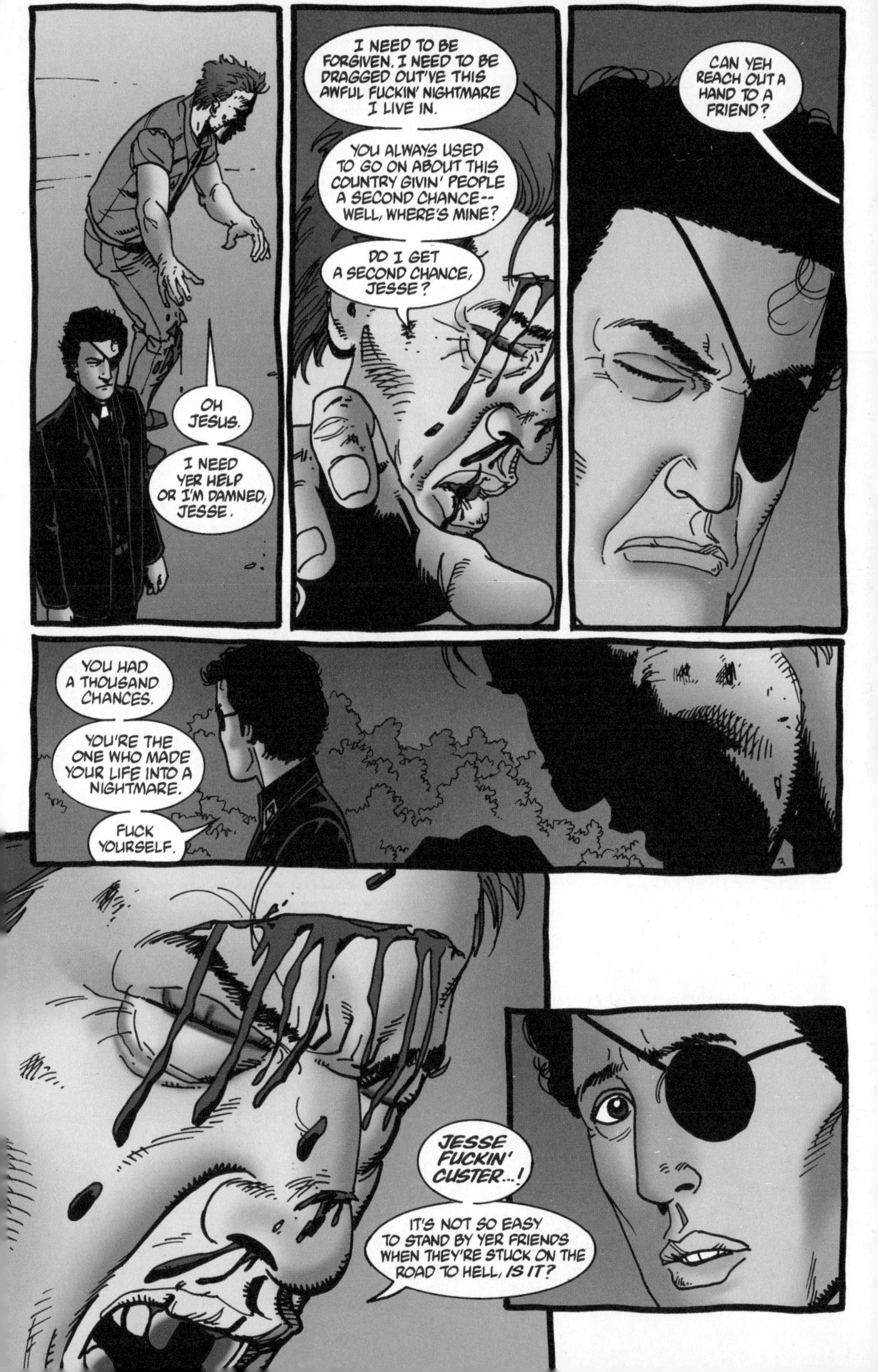

OH JESUS.
I NEED YER HELP OR I'M DAMNED, JESSE.
I NEED TO BE FORGIVEN. I NEED TO BE DRAGGED OUT'VE THIS AWFUL FUCKIN' NIGHTMARE I LIVE IN.
YOU ALWAYS USED TO GO ON ABOUT THIS COUNTRY GIVIN' PEOPLE A SECOND CHANCE-- WELL, WHERE'S MINE?
DO I GET A SECOND CHANCE, JESSE?
CAN YEH REACH OUT A HAND TO A FRIEND?
YOU HAD A THOUSAND CHANCES.
YOU'RE THE ONE WHO MADE YOUR LIFE INTO A NIGHTMARE.
FUCK YOURSELF.
JESSE FUCKIN' CUSTER...!
IT'S NOT SO EASY TO STAND BY YER FRIENDS WHEN THEY'RE STUCK ON THE ROAD TO HELL, IS IT?

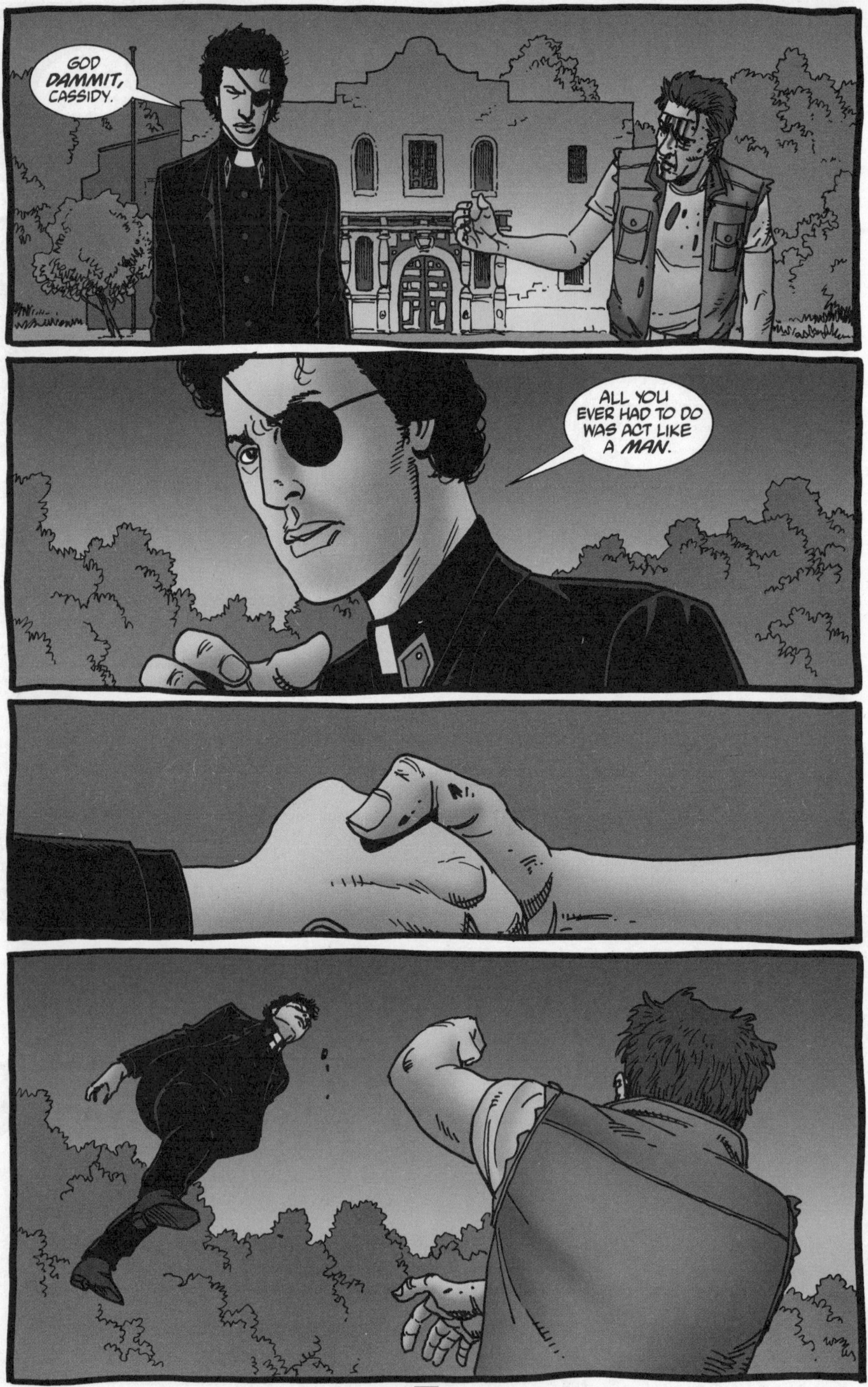
GOD *DAMMIT,* CASSIDY.
ALL YOU EVER HAD TO DO WAS ACT LIKE A *MAN*.

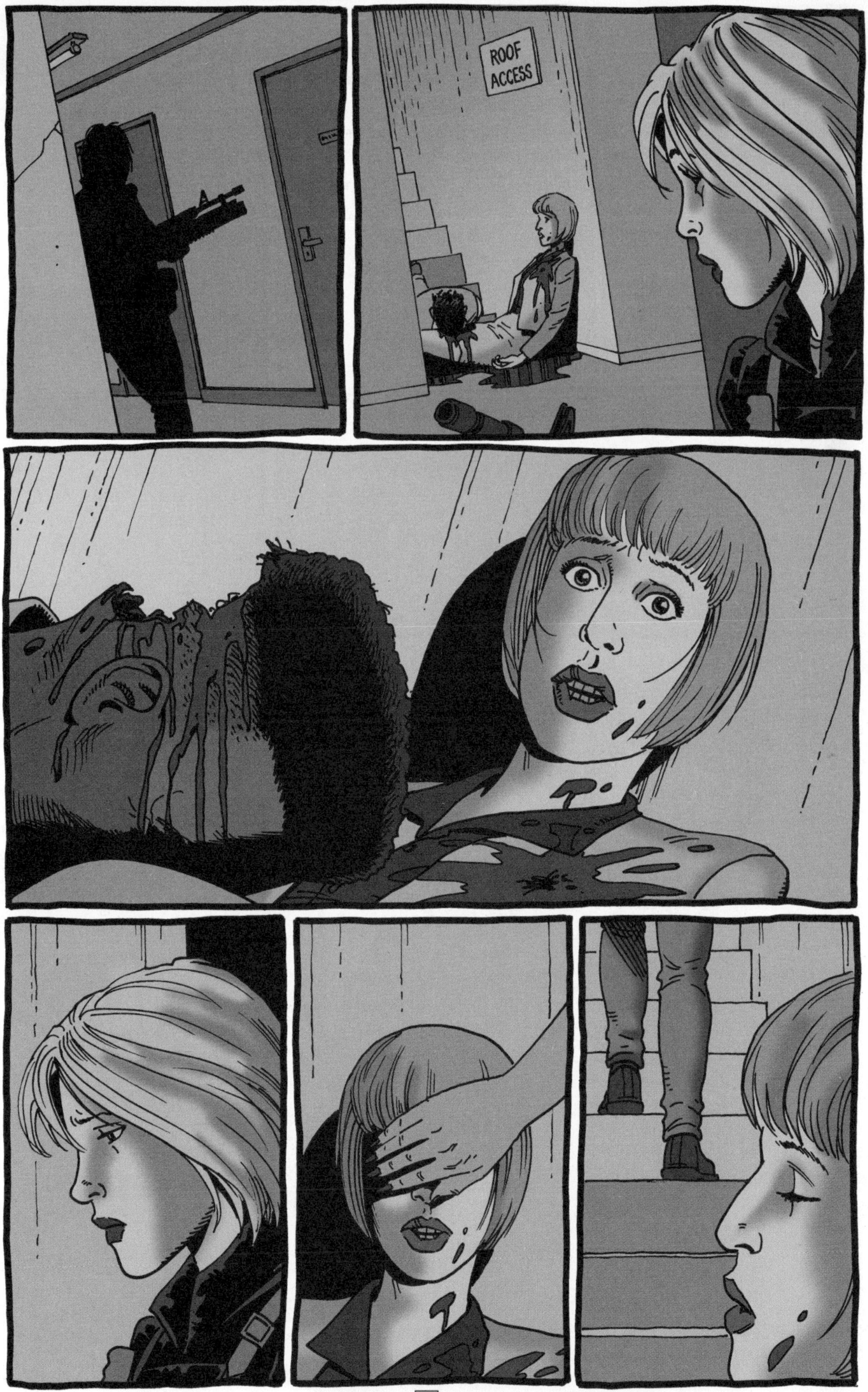
ROOF
ACCESS

DON'T GET UP, JESSE.

I MEAN IT. SERIOUSLY.

YER BREASTBONE'S BROKEN. I HEARD IT GO. IF YEH TRY AN' STAND IT'LL MAYBE STICK IN YER HEART.

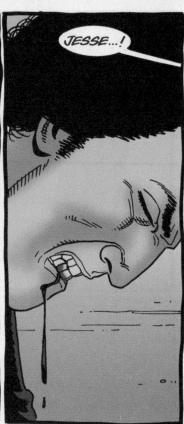

JESSE...!

O...

LET'S GO.

JAYSIS...

WHAT THE FUCK DO THEY MAKE LADS LIKE YOU FROM?

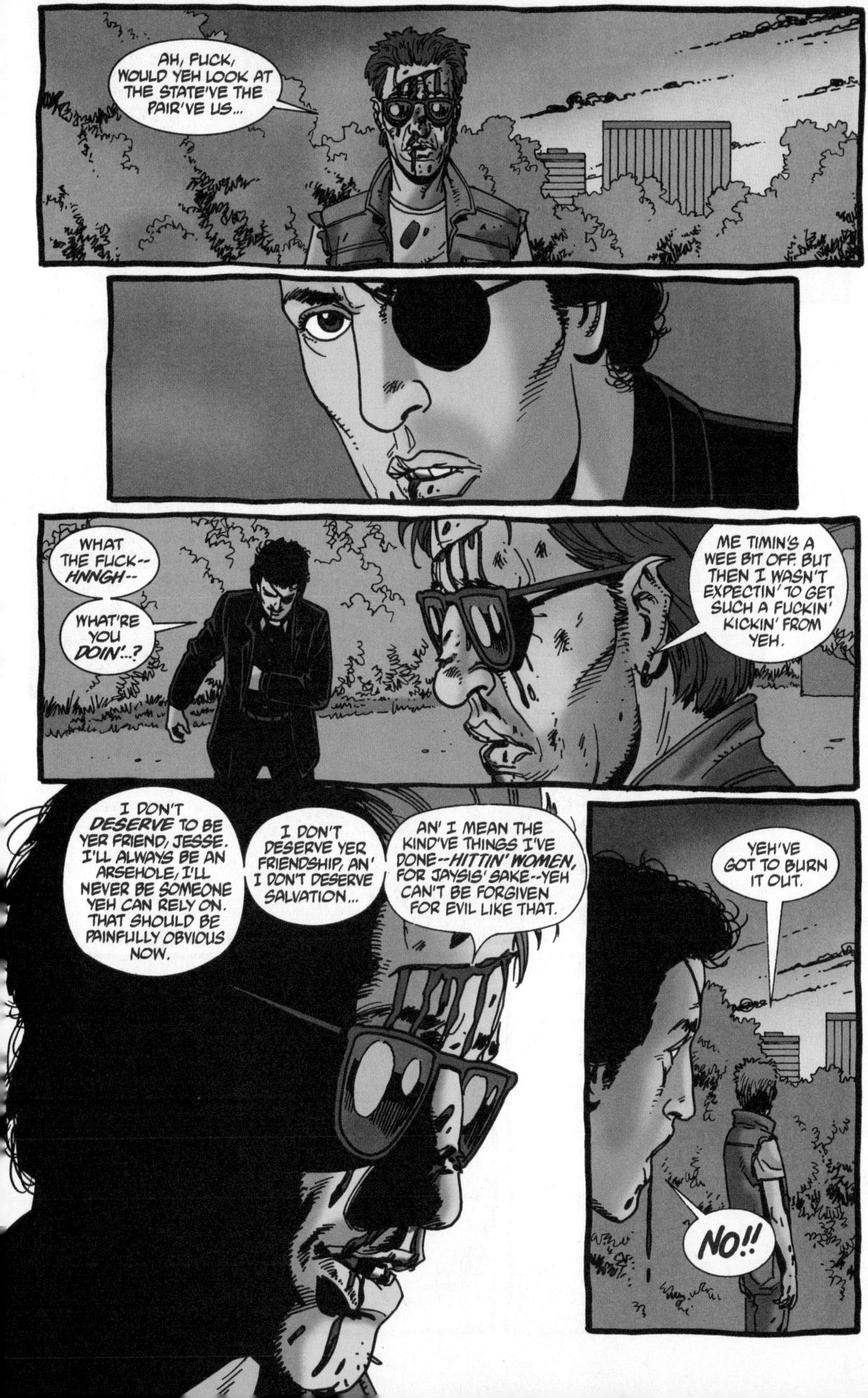
AH, FUCK, WOULD YEH LOOK AT THE STATE'VE THE PAIR'VE US...
WHAT THE FUCK-- HNNGH--
WHAT'RE YOU DOIN'..?
ME TIMIN'S A WEE BIT OFF. BUT THEN I WASN'T EXPECTIN' TO GET SUCH A FUCKIN' KICKIN' FROM YEH.
I DON'T DESERVE TO BE YER FRIEND, JESSE. I'LL ALWAYS BE AN ARSEHOLE, I'LL NEVER BE SOMEONE YEH CAN RELY ON. THAT SHOULD BE PAINFULLY OBVIOUS NOW.
I DON'T DESERVE YER FRIENDSHIP, AN' I DON'T DESERVE SALVATION...
AN' I MEAN THE KIND'VE THINGS I'VE DONE--HITTIN' WOMEN, FOR JAYSIS' SAKE--YEH CAN'T BE FORGIVEN FOR EVIL LIKE THAT.
YEH'VE GOT TO BURN IT OUT.
NO!!

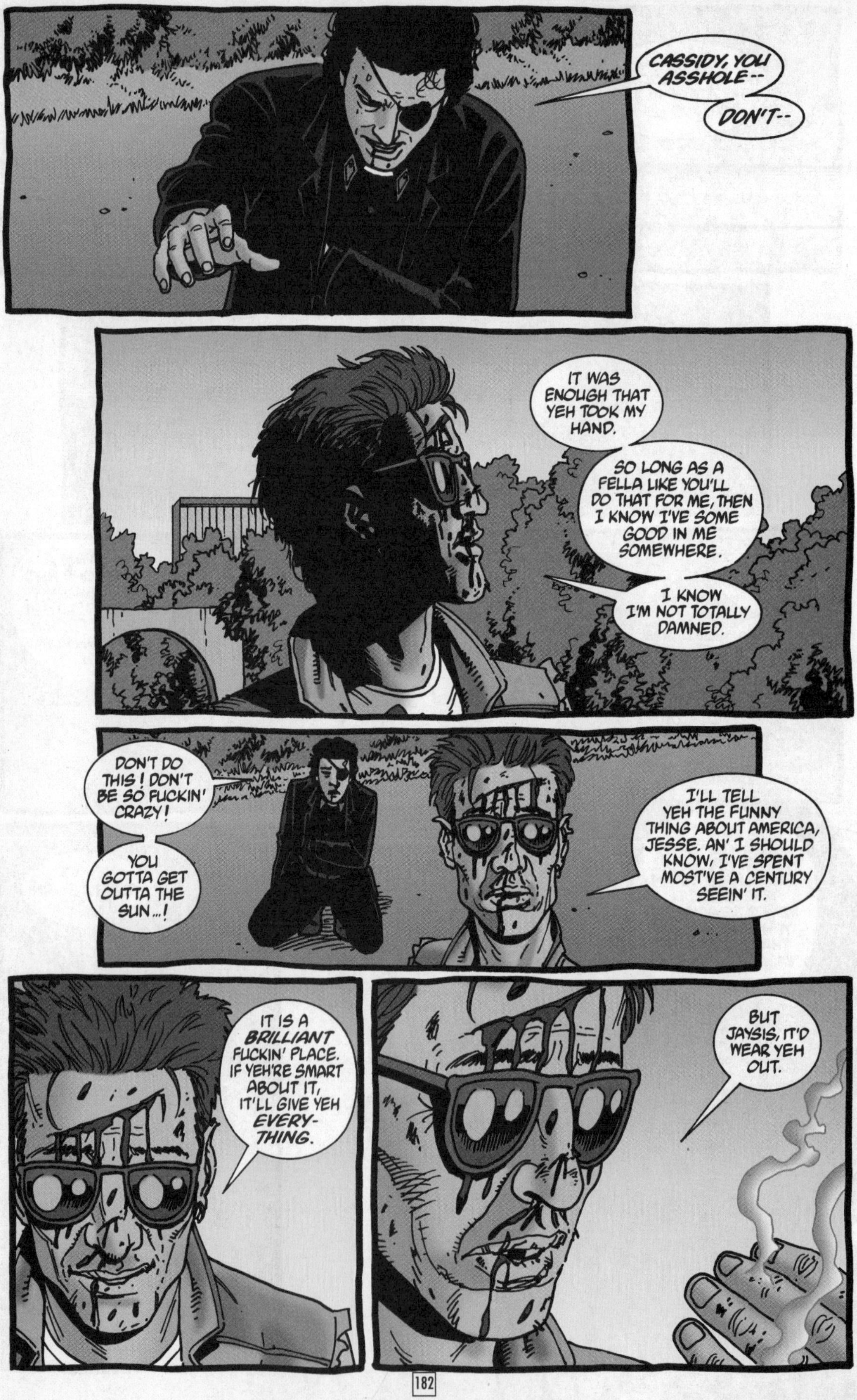
CASSIDY, YOU ASSHOLE--
DON'T--
IT WAS ENOUGH THAT YEH TOOK MY HAND.
SO LONG AS A FELLA LIKE YOU'LL DO THAT FOR ME, THEN I KNOW I'VE SOME GOOD IN ME SOMEWHERE.
I KNOW I'M NOT TOTALLY DAMNED.
DON'T DO THIS! DON'T BE SO FUCKIN' CRAZY!
YOU GOTTA GET OUTTA THE SUN...!
I'LL TELL YEH THE FUNNY THING ABOUT AMERICA, JESSE. AN' I SHOULD KNOW, I'VE SPENT MOST'VE A CENTURY SEEIN' IT.
IT IS A BRILLIANT FUCKIN' PLACE. IF YEH'RE SMART ABOUT IT, IT'LL GIVE YEH EVERYTHING.
BUT JAYSIS, IT'D WEAR YEH OUT.

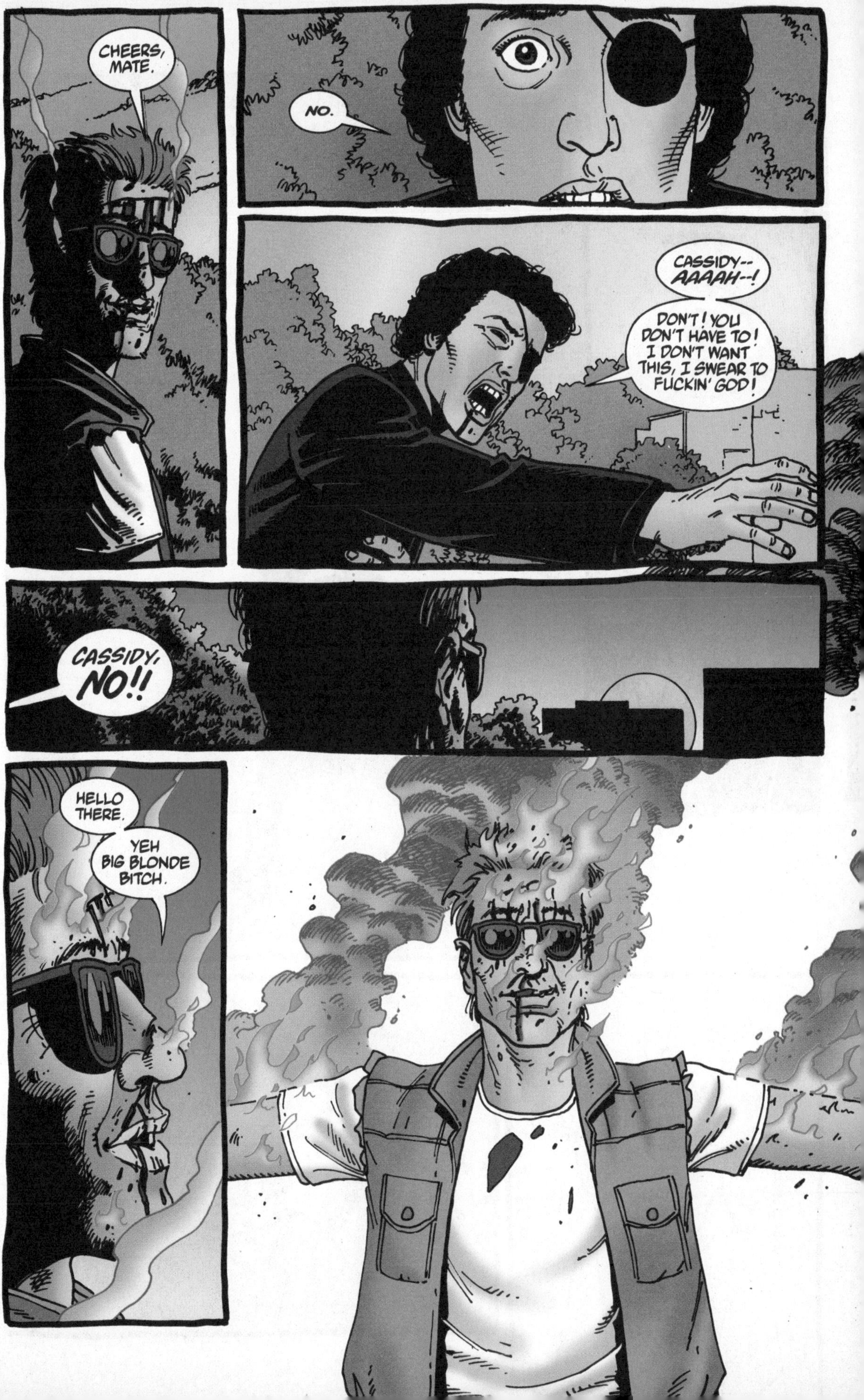
CHEERS, MATE.
NO.
CASSIDY-- AAAAH--!
DON'T! YOU DON'T HAVE TO! I DON'T WANT THIS, I SWEAR TO FUCKIN' GOD!
CASSIDY, NO!!
HELLO THERE.
YEH BIG BLONDE BITCH.

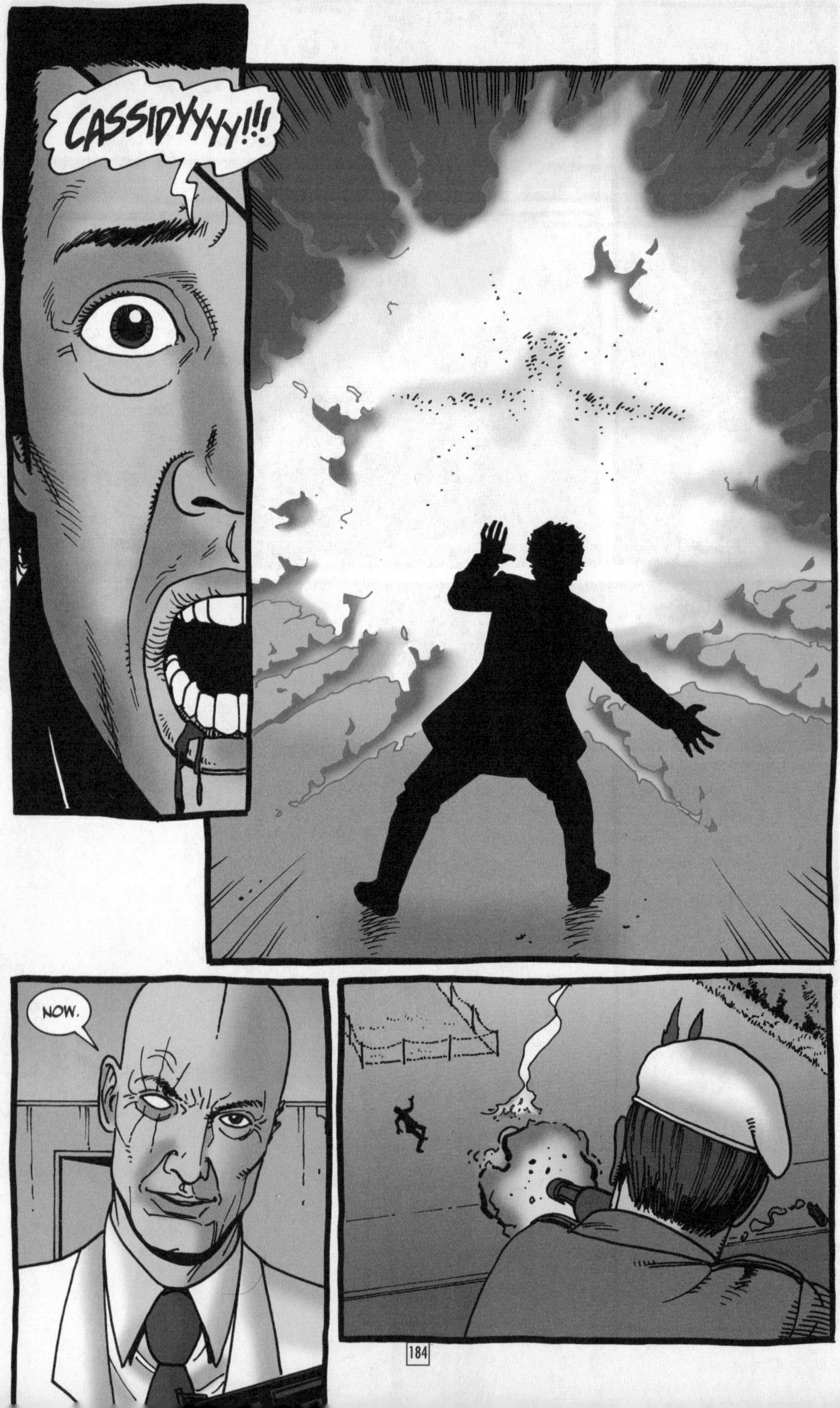
CASSIDYYYY!!!
NOW.

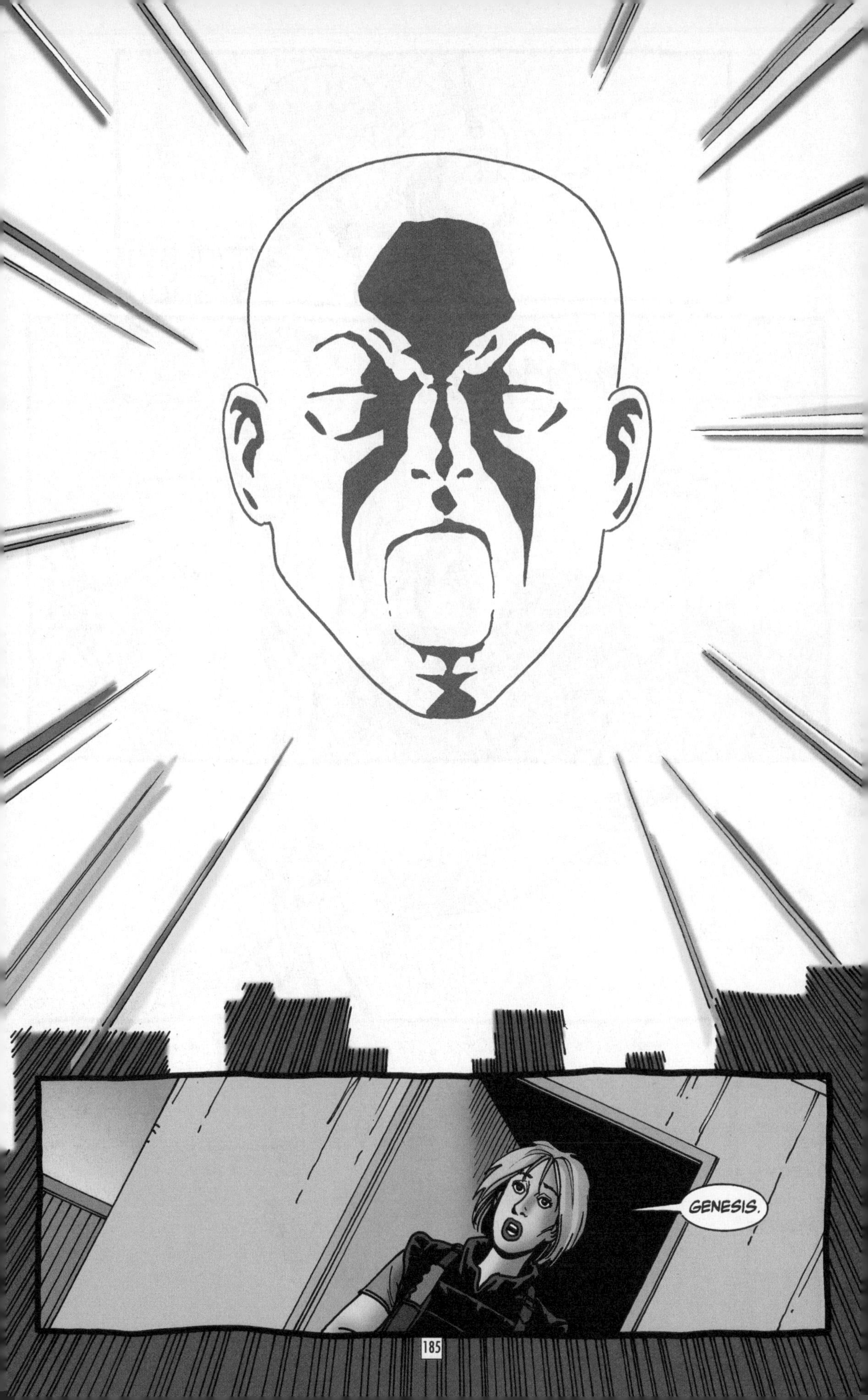
GENESIS.

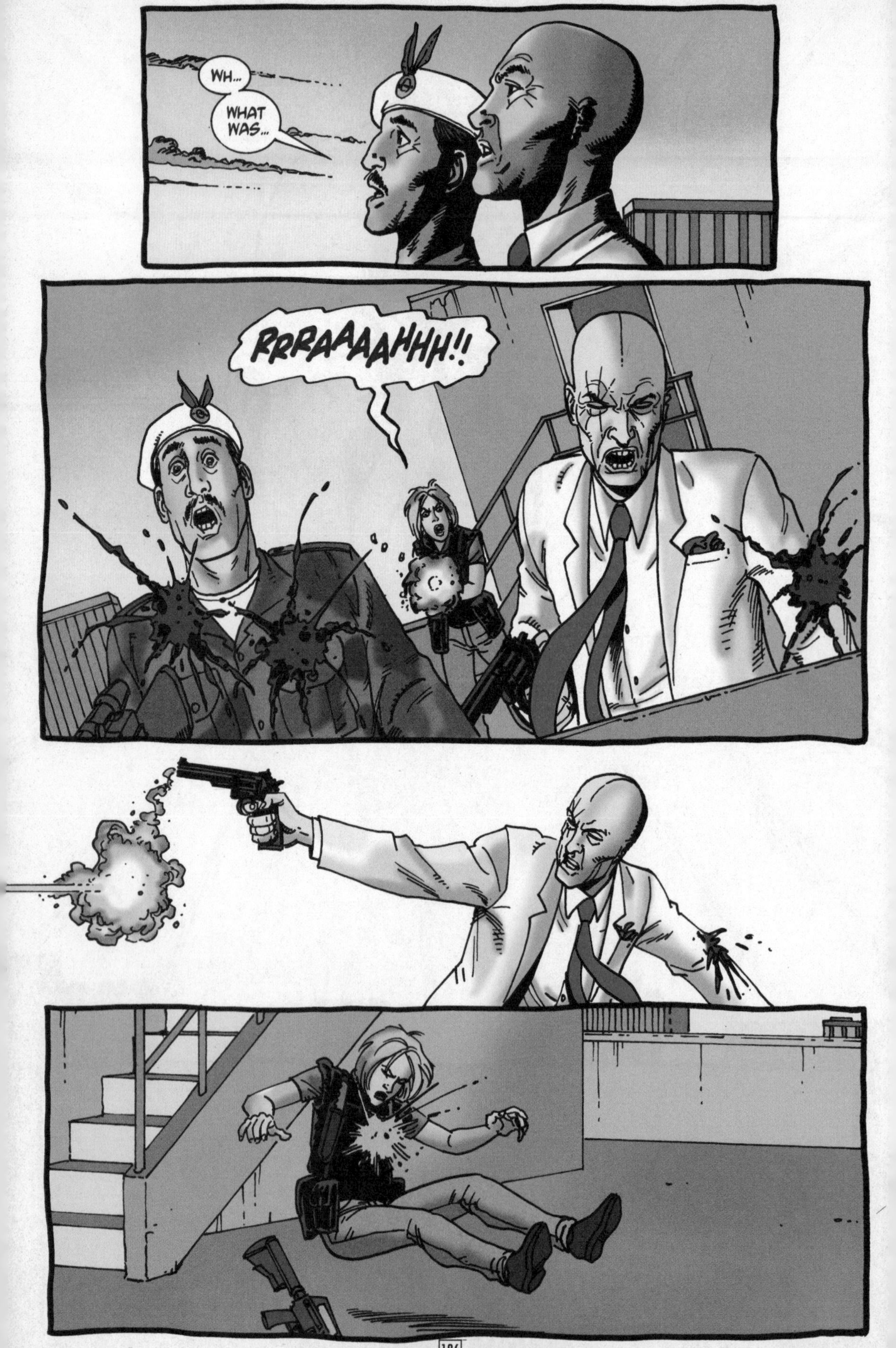
WH...
WHAT WAS...
RRRAAAAHHH!!

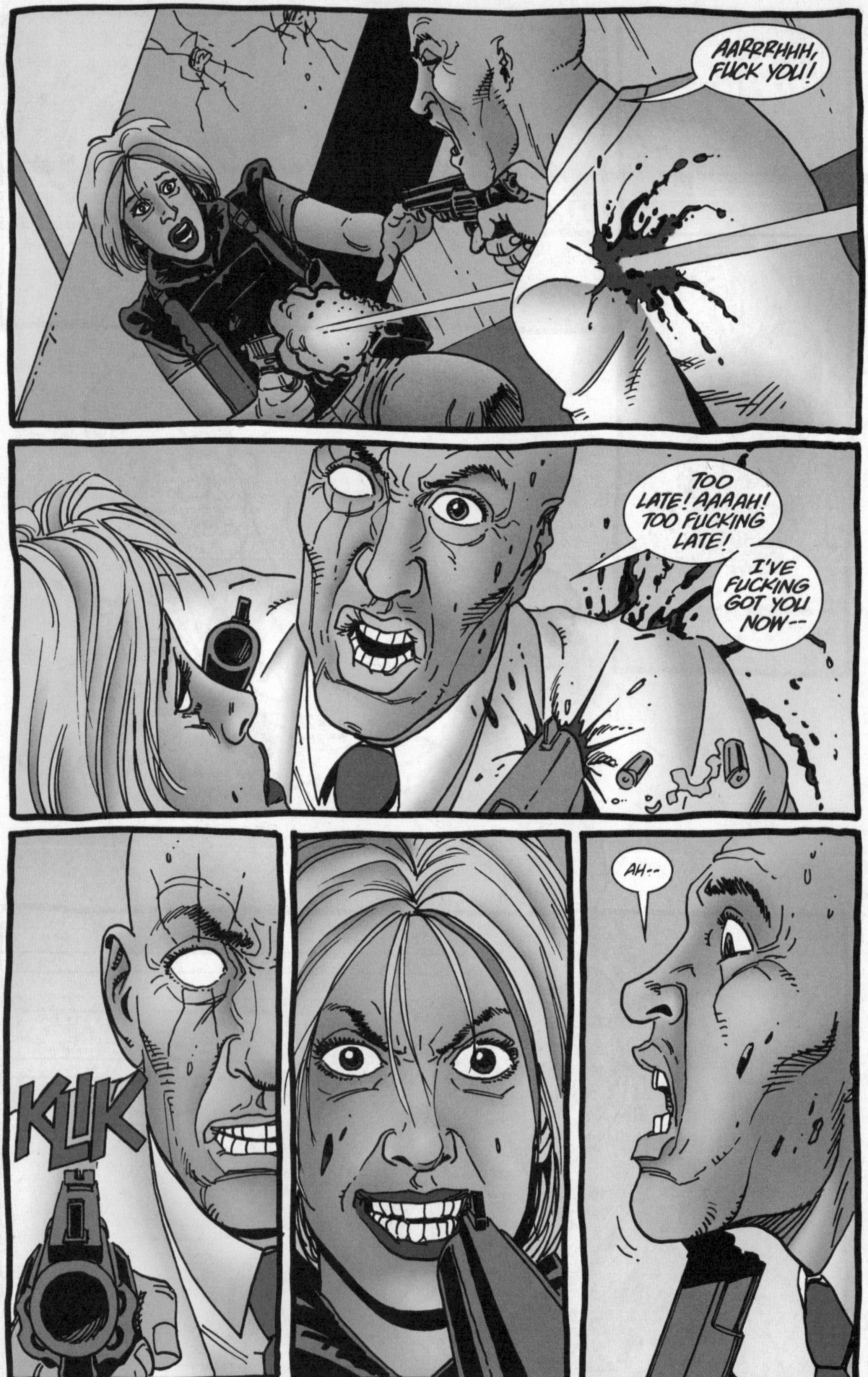
AARRRHHH, FUCK YOU!
TOO LATE! AAAAH! TOO FUCKING LATE!
I'VE FUCKING GOT YOU NOW--
KLIK
AH--

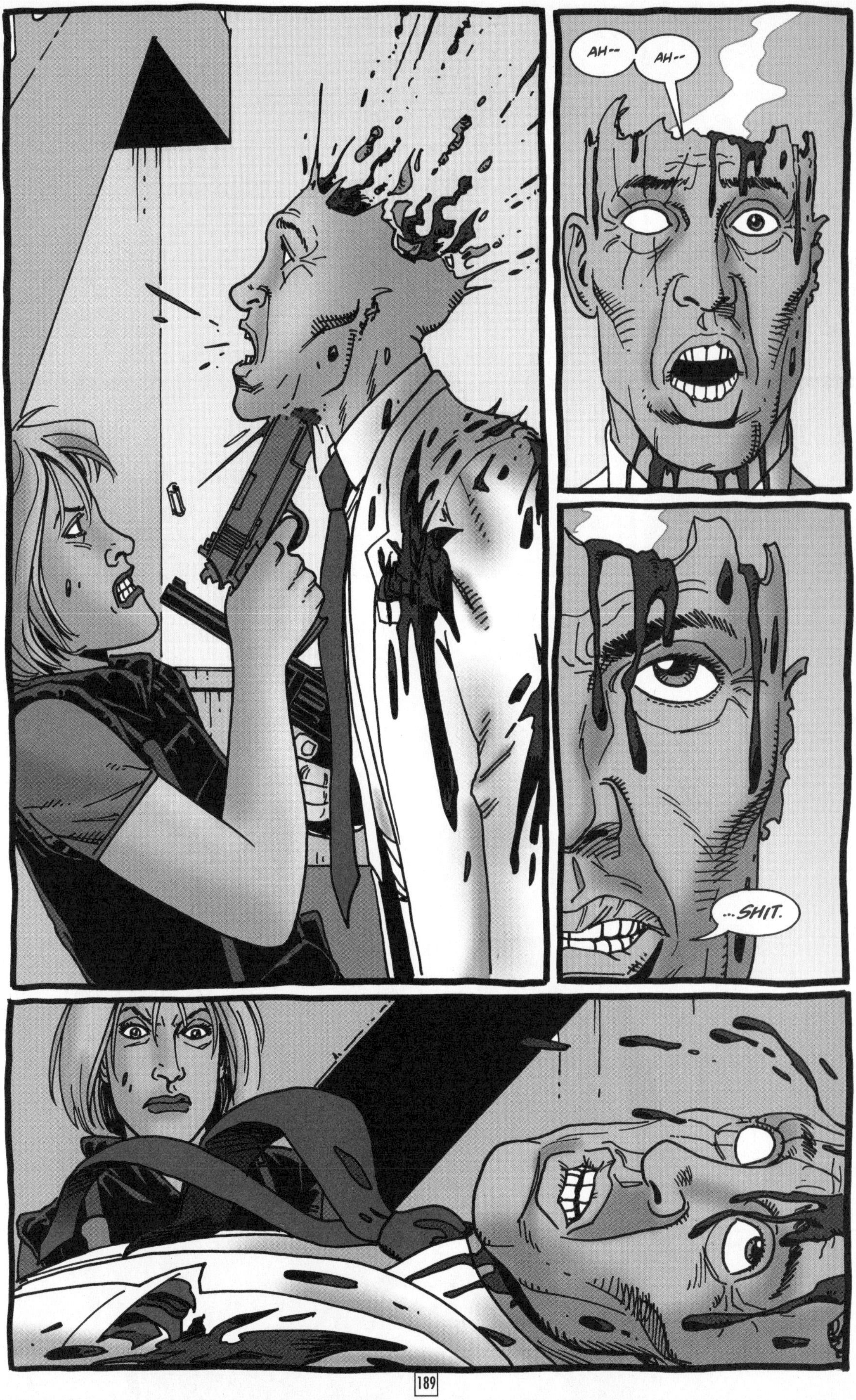
AH--
AH--
...SHIT.

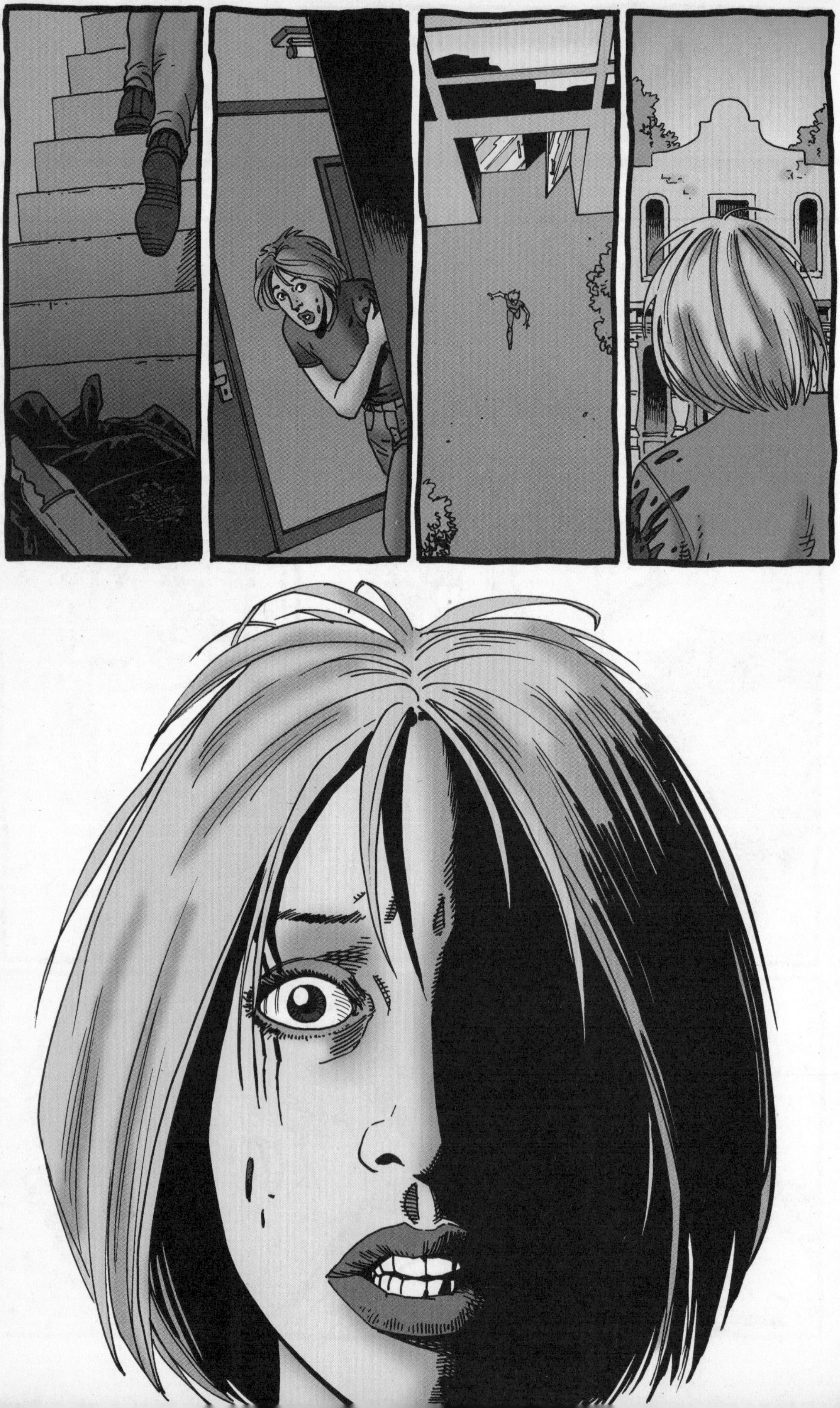

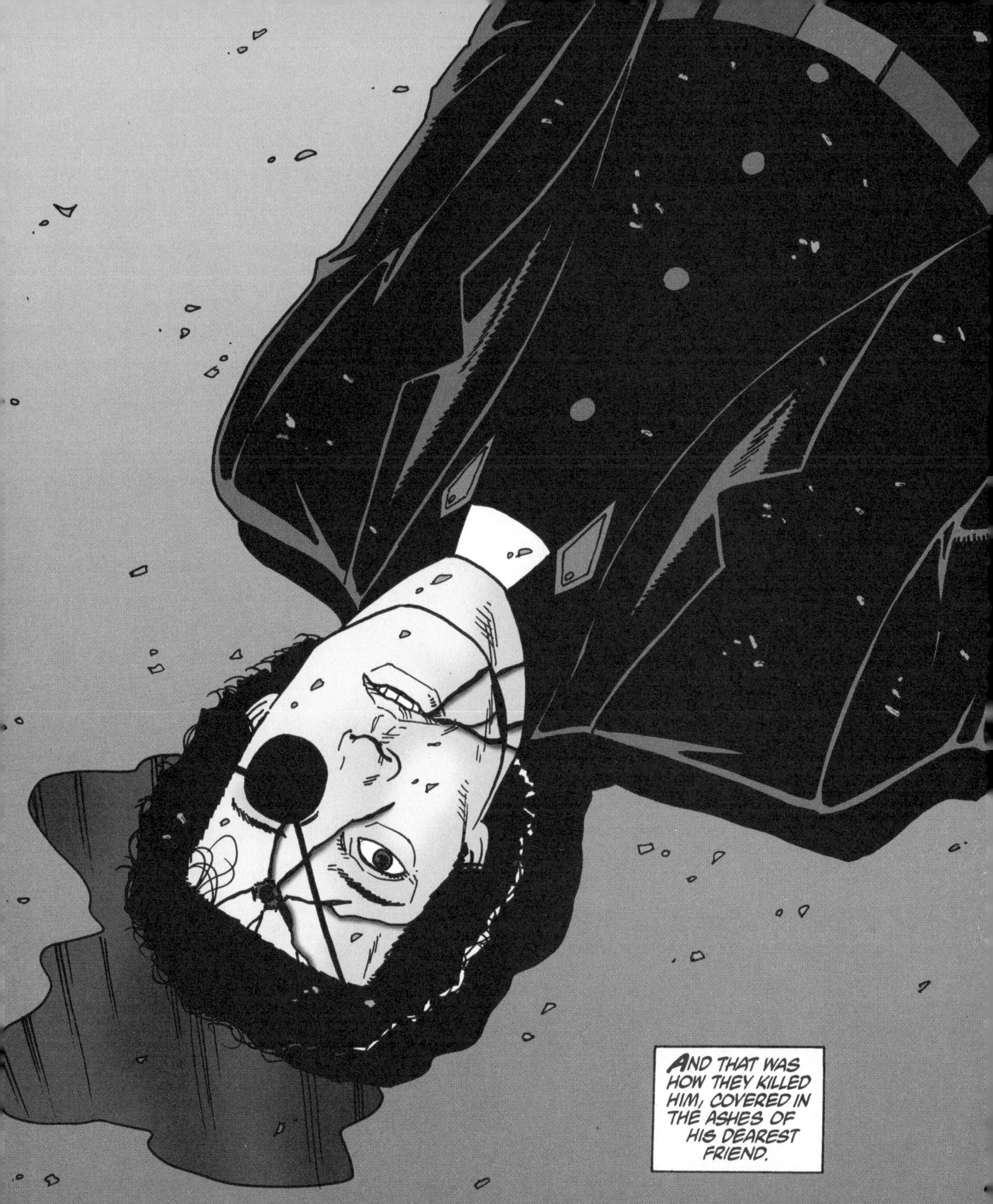
AND THAT WAS HOW THEY KILLED HIM, COVERED IN THE ASHES OF HIS DEAREST FRIEND.

SHOOT STRAIGHT YOU BASTARDS

GARTH ENNIS - Writer STEVE DILLON - Artist

PAMELA RAMBO - Colorist CLEM ROBINS - Letterer AXEL ALONSO - Editor

PREACHER created by GARTH ENNIS and STEVE DILLON

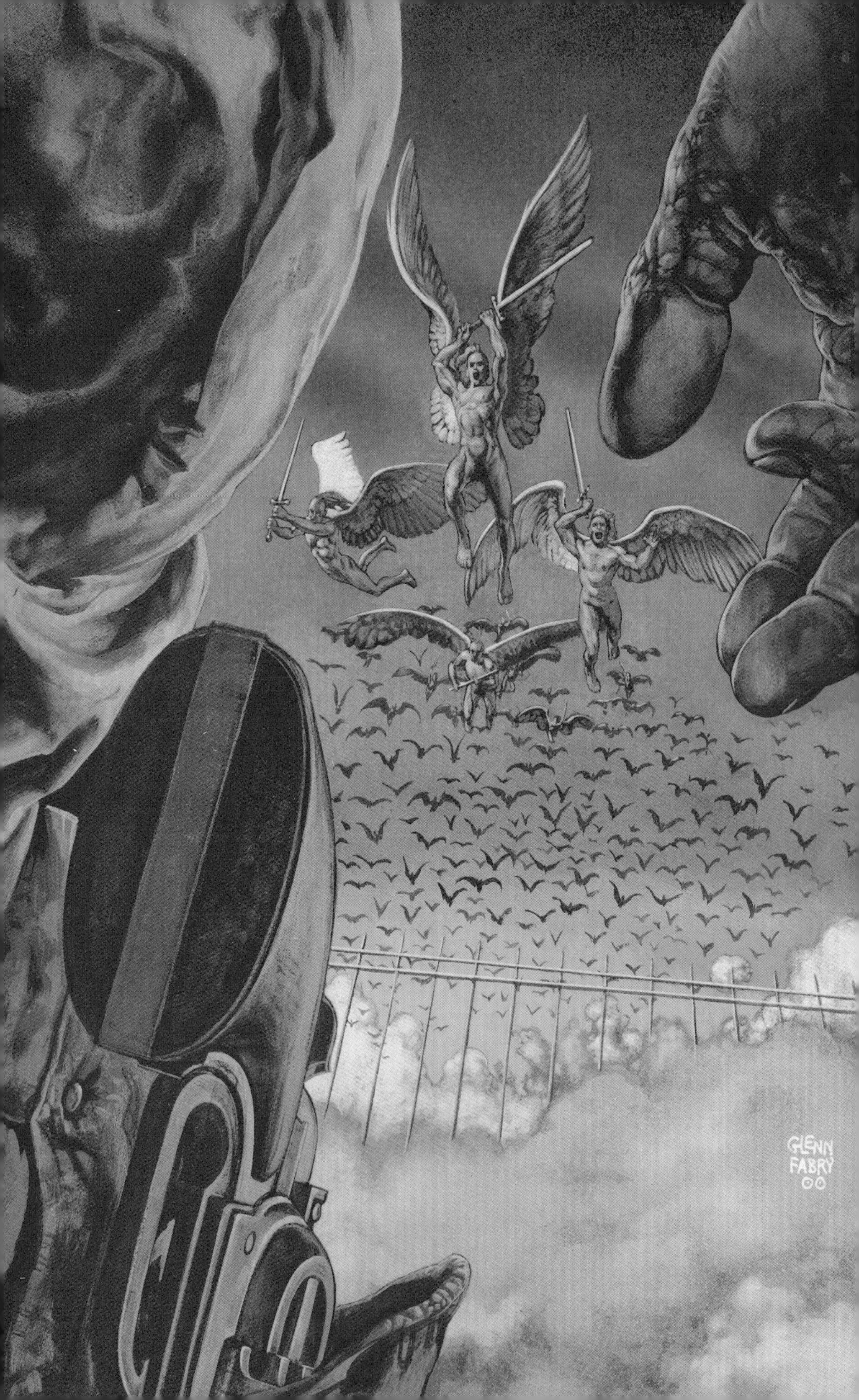
GLENN
FABRY
00

But Captain," the boy said, "They say you were the most famous Ranger. They say you've carried Captain McCrae three thousand miles just to bury him. They say you started the first ranch in Montana. My boss will fire me if I don't talk to you. They say you're a man of vision."

"Yes, a hell of a vision," Call said. He was forced to put spurs to the dun to get away from the boy, who stood scribbling on a pad.

—Larry McMurtry, *Lonesome Dove*

So we banged the drum slowly and we played the fife lowly
And silently wept as we bore him along
For we all loved our comrade, so brave and handsome
We all loved our comrade, although he'd done wrong.

— *The Cowboy's Lament*

I was told when I grew up I could be anything I wanted: a fireman, a policeman, a doctor — even President, it seemed. And for the first time in the history of mankind, something new, called an astronaut. But like so many kids brought up on a steady diet of Westerns, I always wanted to be the avenging cowboy hero — that lone voice in the wilderness, fighting corruption and evil wherever I found it, and standing for freedom, truth and justice. And in my heart of hearts I still track the remnants of that dream wherever I go, in my endless ride into the setting sun.

— Bill Hicks, *Revelations*

MY DARLING,

I GUESS THE FIRST THING YOU'LL THINK IS, WELL, THIS OUGHT TO BE PRETTY GODDAMN GOOD. BUT THIS ISN'T ANY KIND OF EXCUSE LIKE THE LAST TIME. IT'S JUST THE DUMB SON OF A BITCH YOU FELL IN LOVE WITH TELLING YOU THE EVEN DUMBER THING HE'S DONE.

I KNOW YOU'LL TAKE THIS HARD, BUT WHEN IT CAME TO IT I COULDN'T FACE WHAT I HAD TO WITH YOU BY MY SIDE. I WAS SCARED YOU'D GET HURT OR KILLED, AND THE THOUGHT OF YOU DYING WAS MORE THAN I COULD STAND. SO YES, I'VE RUN OUT ON YOU AGAIN. WORSE, I'VE DRUGGED YOU SO YOU'LL SLEEP THROUGH WHAT'S ABOUT TO HAPPEN. HERE IS WHY.

WHEN ALL THIS CRAZINESS BEGAN I TOOK ON A TASK THAT I COULD NOT IGNORE. I SWORE TO FIND THE LORD GOD AND FORCE HIM TO CONFESS TO HIS PEOPLE THE SIN HE COMMITTED AGAINST THEM: TO HIS BETRAYAL OF MANKIND BY ABANDONING HIS PLACE IN HEAVEN. IF I DID NOT TRY TO SET THIS TERRIBLE THING TO RIGHTS, THEN I WOULD BE NO KIND OF MAN AT ALL.

BUT WHAT SEEMED SO EASY TO FIGURE BACK THEN HAS BECOME A HELL OF A LOT MORE COMPLICATED. YOU AND I HAVE BOTH SEEN GOD FACE TO FACE, AND WHAT HE SAID THOSE TIMES SET ME TO THINKING. WHEN I LEARNED WHAT GENESIS ITSELF KNEW — AND HALF THE SECRETS OF HEAVEN ARE LOCKED INSIDE THIS DAMN SPOOK OF MINE — I KNEW I HAD AN EVEN HARDER JOB TO DO.

THE LORD IS NOT THE LOVING GOD HE SWORE TO US HE WAS. INSTEAD HE'S JUST A GOD WHO FEEDS ON LOVE. THE CREATION OF MANKIND WAS THE ACT OF AN EGOMANIAC, PLAIN AND SIMPLE — TO CHOOSE TO FOLLOW GOD WOULD BE A CONSCIOUS ACT, AND THEREFORE ALL THE MORE PLEASING TO HIM. THE RESULT WAS A WORLD THAT CAN NEVER KNOW PEACE, BUT I GUESS THAT NEVER BOTHERED HIM.

CAUSING A WAR BETWEEN HIS ANGELS WAS NOTHING BUT A CHEAP, STUPID TEST OF WHO WOULD CHOOSE HIM OR REJECT HIM, AND ENGINEERING THE RISE OF A POWER BEYOND HIS OWN IN GENESIS — WELL, THAT'S WHERE HE WENT LOOKING FOR LOVE SOMEWHERE VERY, VERY BAD, AND WHAT IT GOT HIM WAS HAVING TO RUN FOR HIS LIFE. WHAT IT GOT THE WORLD WAS A NIGHTMARE.

THESE ARE NOT THE ACTIONS OF A LOVING GOD. THEY ARE THE FUCKED-UP, TWISTED MACHINATIONS OF A BEING DANGEROUSLY SET ON BEING ADORED, AND I BELIEVE HUMANITY MUST BE FREE OF HIM, IF WE'RE TO HAVE ANY CHANCE OF MAKING IT AT ALL.

NOW MAYBE I COULD HAVE HUNTED DOWN THE LORD, BUT I DOUBT IT VERY MUCH, NOT EVEN IN A HUNDRED LIFETIMES. AND MAYBE I COULD HAVE FORCED HIM TO CONFESS WHAT HE'D DONE — I GUESS I HAVE THE POWER, AFTER ALL. BUT THE REAL TROUBLE RUNS A LOT DEEPER THAN THAT. AND HERE'S WHERE I SKIN THIS THING DOWN TO THE BONE.

WOULD FOLKS BUY IT? WOULD THEY BELIEVE THEY'D SEEN GOD? WOULD THEY ACKNOWLEDGE THAT THEY'D HEARD HIS VOICE? OR WOULD THEY SAY IT WAS ONE BIG SPECIAL EFFECT, AND GO ON BELIEVING EXACTLY WHAT SUITED THEM?

BECAUSE IF THERE WAS ONE THING I LEARNED IN THOSE FIVE GODAWFUL YEARS AS PREACHER TO THAT SHITHOLE TOWN OF ANNVILLE, IT'S THAT FOLKS NEVER BELIEVE MORE THAN WHAT'S CONVENIENT. WHAT THEY CALL THEIR FAITH IS JUST A HOOK: THEY HANG THEIR HOPES ON IT AT THE BEST OF TIMES, THEY HANG THE BAD STUFF

THEY DO TO OTHER FOLKS ON IT AT THE WORST. AND WHILE THEY WORSHIP A GOD THAT SUITS THEIR NEEDS, THE REAL GOD THRIVES ON THEIR STUPID, MISDIRECTED LOVE, AND DOES BAD, BAD THINGS TO THIS WORLD WITH THE POWER IT GRANTS HIM.

SO GOD HAS GOT TO GO, TULIP. HE DESERVES IT FOR THE THINGS HE'S DONE, BUT MORE THAN THAT THE WORLD JUST PLAIN NEEDS TO BE RID OF HIM. WHICH IS WHY I MADE A DEAL WITH THE SAINT OF KILLERS.

THE SAINT IS GOING TO KILL THE LORD ALMIGHTY.

NOW HE CAN ONLY DO IT IF HE'S GOT GOD IN HIS SIGHTS, AND THE ONE PLACE HE CAN BE SURE OF FINDING GOD IS IN HEAVEN. BUT GOD WON'T GO BACK THERE UNTIL HE KNOWS THAT GENESIS IS GONE, BECAUSE HE KNOWS THAT I COULD USE ITS POWER TO HUNT HIM EVEN THERE. AND HE CAN'T BE SURE THAT GENESIS IS GONE UNLESS HE KNOWS THAT I AM DEAD.

I SENT WORD TO OUR OLD FRIEND STARR THAT I'LL BE IN SAN ANTONIO TONIGHT, SO HE'LL COME RUNNING WITH THAT BUNCH OF ASSHOLES HE CALLS AN ARMY. I HAVE BUSINESS OF MY OWN WITH CASSIDY, WHICH BY GOD IS ONE THING I INTEND TO TAKE CARE OF WITH MY OWN TWO HANDS. AND THEN I GUESS STARR'S BOYS WILL TAKE CARE OF ME, AND THE SAINT WILL TAKE CARE OF THEM, AND THEN HE'LL GO ON TO HEAVEN AND SETTLE THINGS WITH GOD.

BUT YOU, MY PRECIOUS ANGEL, WILL SLEEP THROUGH THE WHOLE GODDAMN AFFAIR.

I WISH LIKE HELL I COULD HAVE COME UP WITH SOMETHING BETTER, SOMETHING SMARTER, BUT THIS WAS THE ONLY WAY I COULD THINK OF TO DISCHARGE THE RESPONSIBILITY I TOOK ON. NOT JUST THE TASK I SET MYSELF, BUT IN A STRANGE KIND OF WAY THE OBLIGATION OF A PREACHER TO SERVE THE LORD AS BEST HE CAN. I WILL TRADE MY LIFE FOR HIS, AND IN DOING SO I WILL PUT AN END TO HIM.

MY GREATEST REGRET—MY ONLY TRUE REGRET, BECAUSE I HAVE LIVED ONE HELL OF A LIFE BY ANY MAN'S RECKONING—IS THAT I WILL NEVER SEE YOU AGAIN. YOU WERE THE ONE CONSTANT IN THE TIME I SPENT ON THIS EARTH. IN A WORLD THAT SOMETIMES SEEMED LIKE HELL AND SOMETIMES LIKE A FREAK SHOW, THAT BROKE MY HEART A HUNDRED TIMES, YOU WERE THE ONE WHO NEVER LET ME DOWN. I ONLY WISH I COULD SAY I DID THE SAME FOR YOU.

OH, I SWEAR. I'M WRITING THIS AS EVENING DRAWS ON AND I'M WATCHING YOU SLEEP IN THE TWILIGHT, AND YOU ARE SO BEAUTIFUL IT CUTS ME LIKE A KNIFE. IF I COULD CRY, IF THE TRASH WHO KILLED MY DADDY HADN'T TAKEN THAT FROM ME, I WOULD.

I LOVE YOU, TULIP.

ALWAYS, ALWAYS, ALWAYS. JESSE

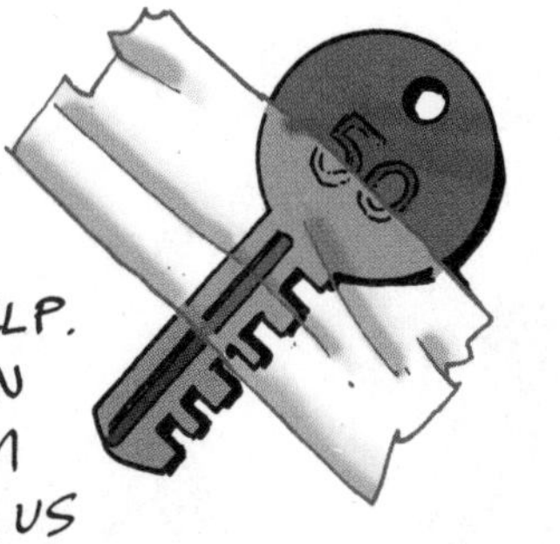

50

P.S.: THIS IS A SMALL THING, BUT I HOPE IT WILL BE OF HELP. THIS KEY FITS A LOCKER IN THE BUS STATION IN DALLAS. IN THERE IS ALL THE MONEY LEFT FROM THE OLD DAYS, FROM OUR MISSPENT YOUTH WITH AMY, THAT I WAS SAVING FOR US WHEN WE COULDN'T DO WITHOUT IT. IT'S NO GREAT FORTUNE, BUT MAYBE YOU CAN FIND A USE FOR IT.

AND SO OF COURSE HE CAME BACK TO LIFE, JUST AS SHE HAD--AND JUST AS SHE HAD, HE FELT

LESS.

KINDA... DIMINISHED, EVEN.

LIKE I'M ALIVE BUT I KNOW I WAS DEAD, AN'IT'S SOMETHIN' I CAN'T PUT BEHIND ME.

THAT'S PRETTY MUCH HOW I FELT, TOO.

I WASN'T SURE IF I'D CATCH YOU...

YOU DIDN'T. I'M OUT OF HERE. YOU'RE NEVER GOING TO SEE ME AGAIN.

DO NOT TRY TO PERSUADE ME OTHERWISE.

I WOULDN'T DARE.

I NO LONGER HAVE THE RIGHT.

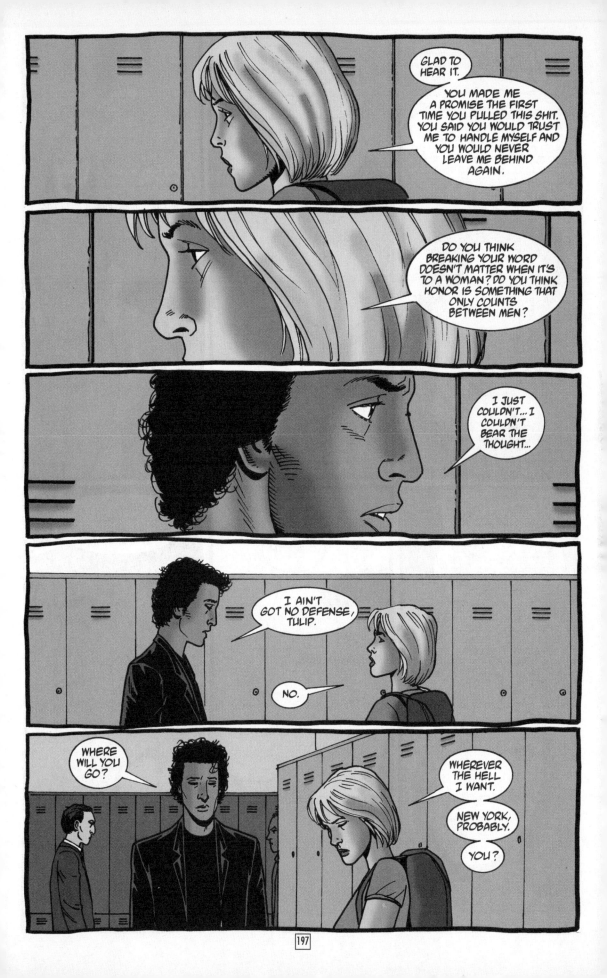

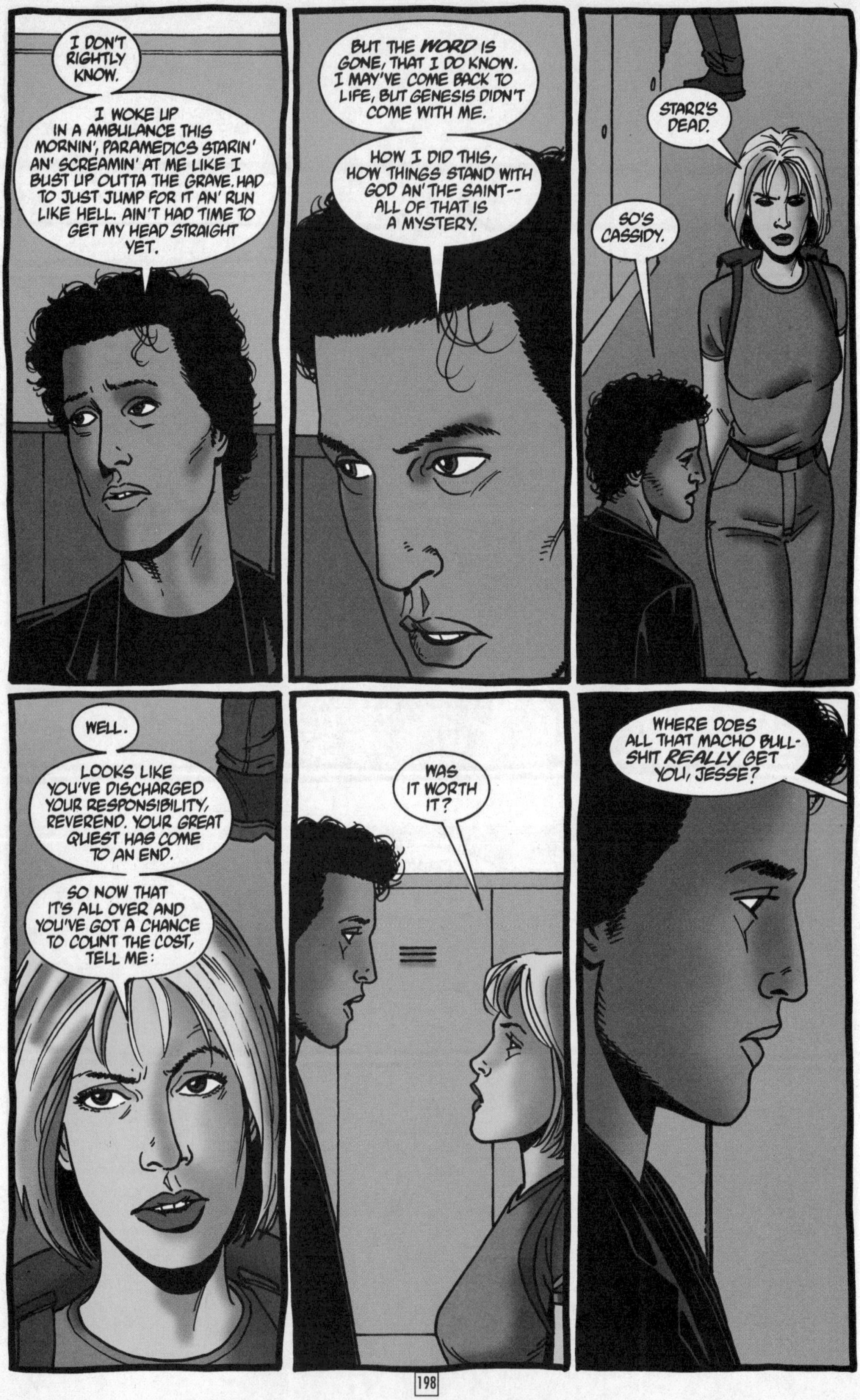

I DON'T RIGHTLY KNOW.
I WOKE UP IN A AMBULANCE THIS MORNIN', PARAMEDICS STARIN' AN' SCREAMIN' AT ME LIKE I BUST UP OUTTA THE GRAVE. HAD TO JUST JUMP FOR IT AN' RUN LIKE HELL. AIN'T HAD TIME TO GET MY HEAD STRAIGHT YET.
BUT THE *WORD* IS GONE, THAT I DO KNOW. I MAY'VE COME BACK TO LIFE, BUT GENESIS DIDN'T COME WITH ME.
HOW I DID THIS, HOW THINGS STAND WITH GOD AN' THE SAINT-- ALL OF THAT IS A MYSTERY.
STARR'S DEAD.
SO'S CASSIDY.
WELL.
LOOKS LIKE YOU'VE DISCHARGED YOUR RESPONSIBILITY, REVEREND. YOUR GREAT QUEST HAS COME TO AN END.
SO NOW THAT IT'S ALL OVER AND YOU'VE GOT A CHANCE TO COUNT THE COST, TELL ME:
WAS IT WORTH IT?
WHERE DOES ALL THAT MACHO BULL-SHIT *REALLY* GET YOU, JESSE?

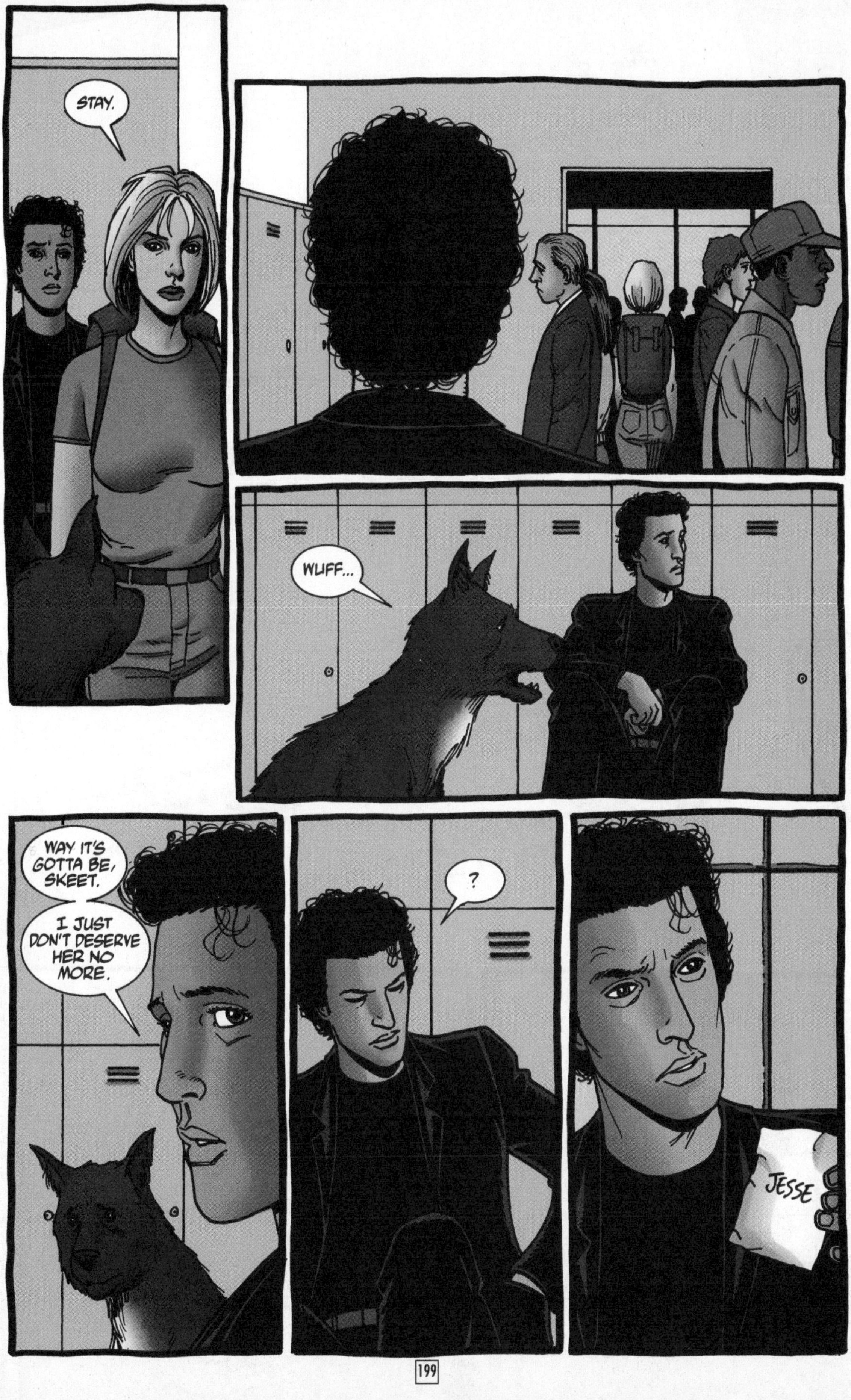
STAY.
WUFF...
WAY IT'S GOTTA BE, SKEET.
I JUST DON'T DESERVE HER NO MORE.
?
JESSE

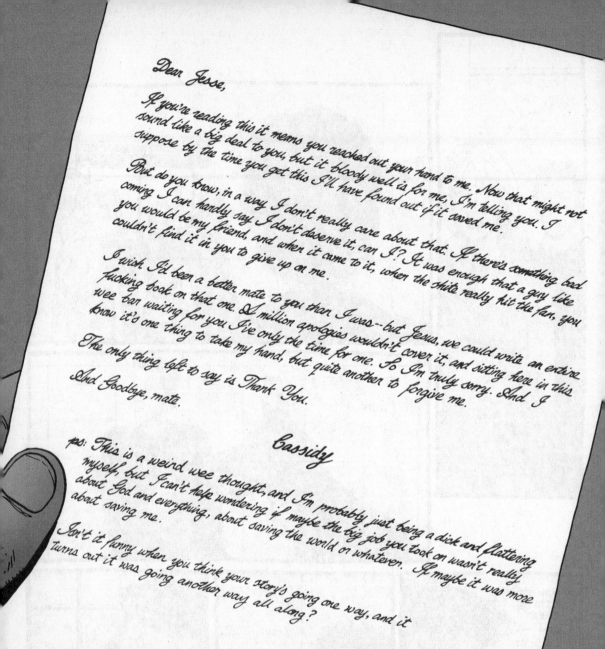

Dear Jesse,

If you're reading this it means you reached out your hand to me. Now that might not sound like a big deal to you, but it bloody well is for me, I'm telling you. I suppose by the time you get this I'll have found out if it saved me.

But do you know, in a way I don't really care about that. If there's something bad coming I can hardly say I don't deserve it, can I? It was enough that a guy like you would be my friend, and when it came to it, when the shite really hit the fan, you couldn't find it in you to give up on me.

I wish I'd been a better mate to you than I was--but Jesus, we could write an entire fucking book on that one. A million apologies wouldn't cover it, and sitting here in this wee bar waiting for you I've only the time for one. So I'm truly sorry. And I know it's one thing to take my hand, but quite another to forgive me.

The only thing left to say is Thank You.

And Goodbye, mate.

Cassidy

ps: This is a weird wee thought, and I'm probably just being a dick and flattering myself, but I can't help wondering if maybe the big job you took on wasn't really about God and everything, about saving the world or whatever. If maybe it was more about saving me.

Isn't it funny when you think your story's going one way, and it turns out it was going another way all along?

WELL GOODBYE TO YOU, MY GOOD FRIEND.

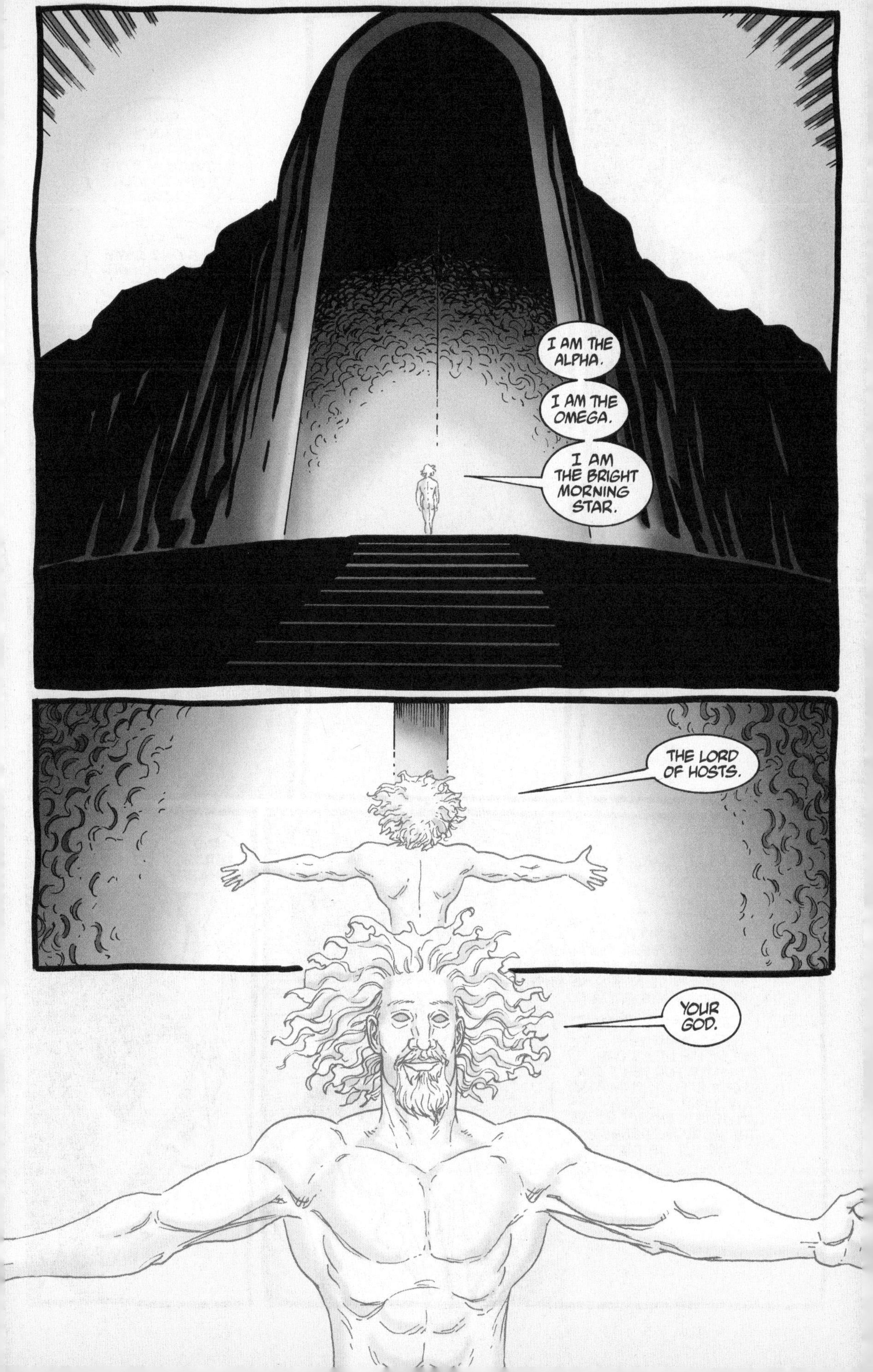
I AM THE ALPHA.
I AM THE OMEGA.
I AM THE BRIGHT MORNING STAR.
THE LORD OF HOSTS.
YOUR GOD.

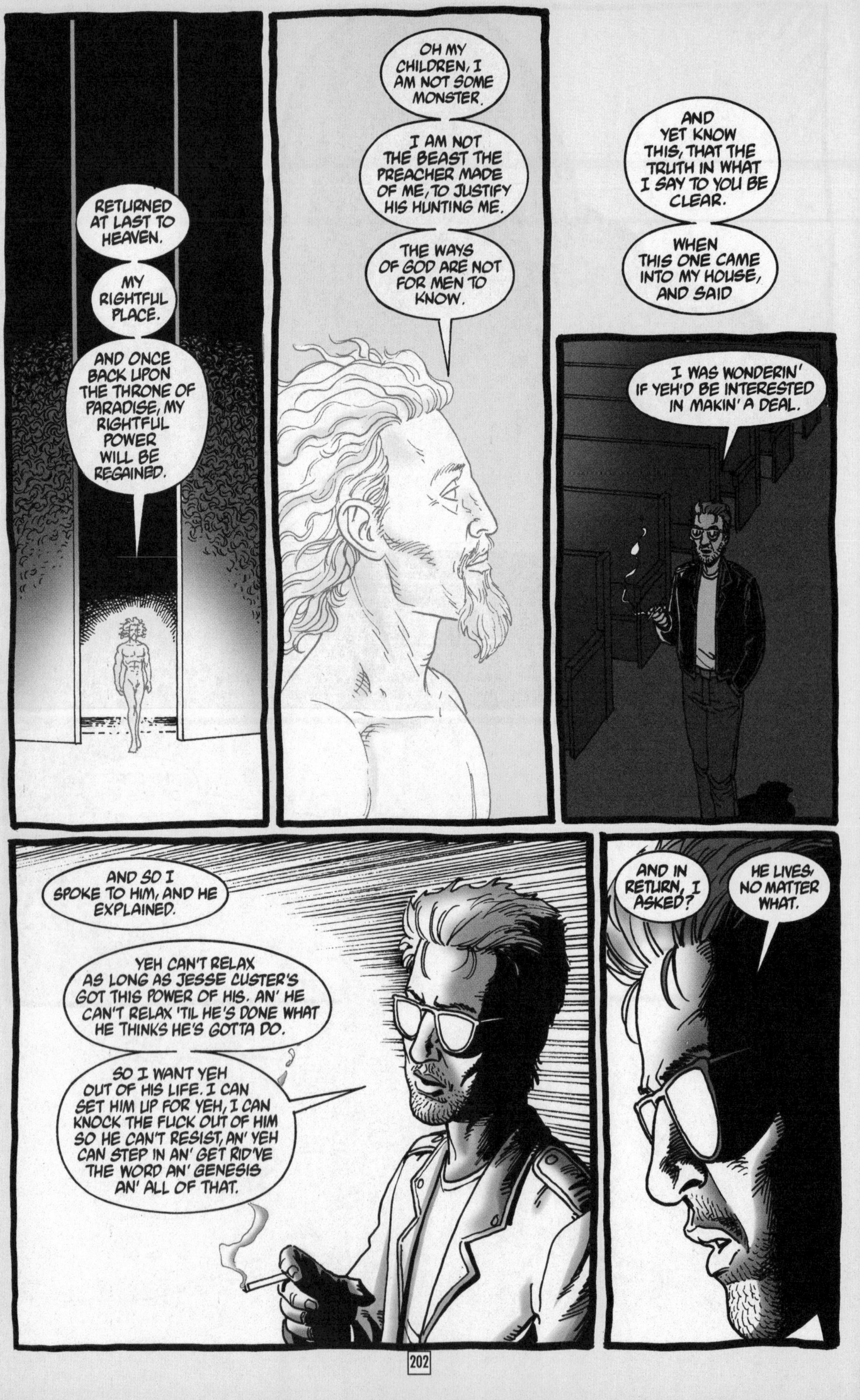
RETURNED AT LAST TO HEAVEN.
MY RIGHTFUL PLACE.
AND ONCE BACK UPON THE THRONE OF PARADISE, MY RIGHTFUL POWER WILL BE REGAINED.
OH MY CHILDREN, I AM NOT SOME MONSTER.
I AM NOT THE BEAST THE PREACHER MADE OF ME, TO JUSTIFY HIS HUNTING ME.
THE WAYS OF GOD ARE NOT FOR MEN TO KNOW.
AND YET KNOW THIS, THAT THE TRUTH IN WHAT I SAY TO YOU BE CLEAR.
WHEN THIS ONE CAME INTO MY HOUSE, AND SAID
I WAS WONDERIN' IF YEH'D BE INTERESTED IN MAKIN' A DEAL.
AND SO I SPOKE TO HIM, AND HE EXPLAINED.
YEH CAN'T RELAX AS LONG AS JESSE CUSTER'S GOT THIS POWER OF HIS. AN' HE CAN'T RELAX 'TIL HE'S DONE WHAT HE THINKS HE'S GOTTA DO.
SO I WANT YEH OUT OF HIS LIFE. I CAN SET HIM UP FOR YEH, I CAN KNOCK THE FUCK OUT OF HIM SO HE CAN'T RESIST, AN' YEH CAN STEP IN AN' GET RID'VE THE WORD AN' GENESIS AN' ALL OF THAT.
AND IN RETURN, I ASKED?
HE LIVES, NO MATTER WHAT.

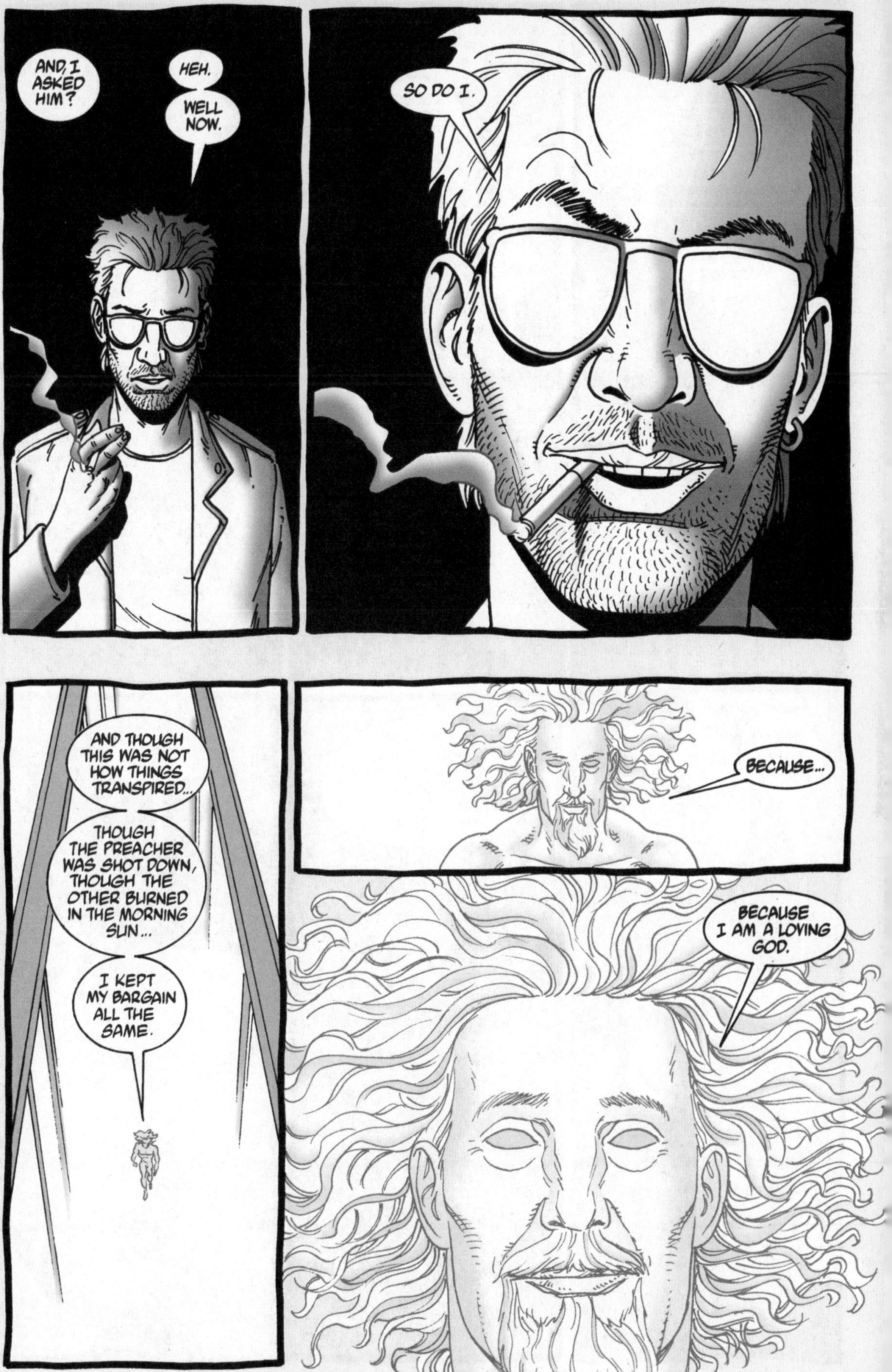
AND, I ASKED HIM?
HEH.
WELL NOW.
SO DO I.
AND THOUGH THIS WAS NOT HOW THINGS TRANSPIRED...
THOUGH THE PREACHER WAS SHOT DOWN, THOUGH THE OTHER BURNED IN THE MORNING SUN...
I KEPT MY BARGAIN ALL THE SAME.
BECAUSE...
BECAUSE I AM A LOVING GOD.

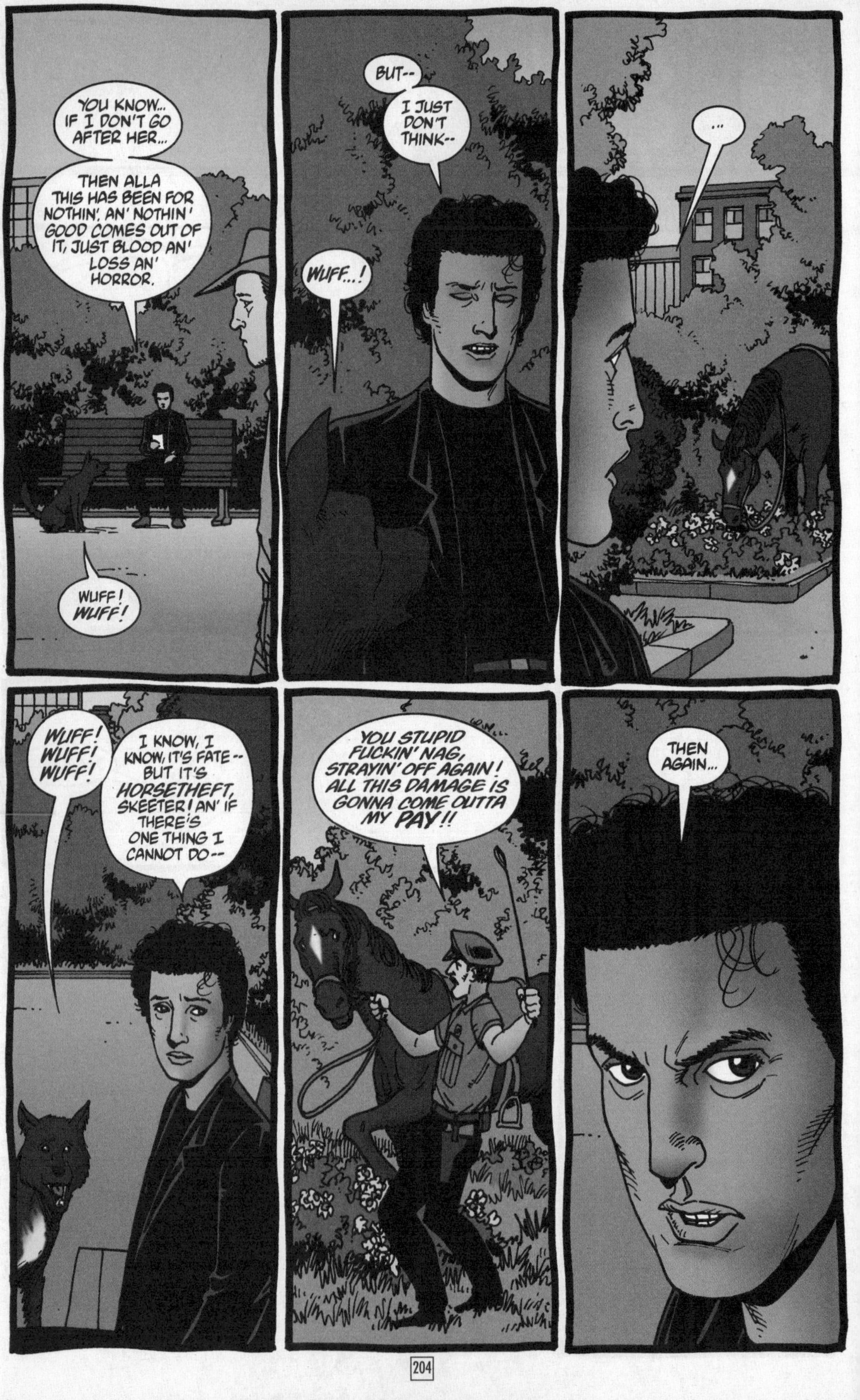
YOU KNOW... IF I DON'T GO AFTER HER...
THEN ALLA THIS HAS BEEN FOR NOTHIN', AN' NOTHIN' GOOD COMES OUT OF IT, JUST BLOOD AN' LOSS AN' HORROR.
WUFF! WUFF!
BUT--
I JUST DON'T THINK--
WUFF...!
...
WUFF! WUFF! WUFF!
I KNOW, I KNOW, IT'S FATE-- BUT IT'S HORSETHEFT, SKEETER! AN' IF THERE'S ONE THING I CANNOT DO--
YOU STUPID FUCKIN' NAG, STRAYIN' OFF AGAIN! ALL THIS DAMAGE IS GONNA COME OUTTA MY PAY!!
THEN AGAIN...

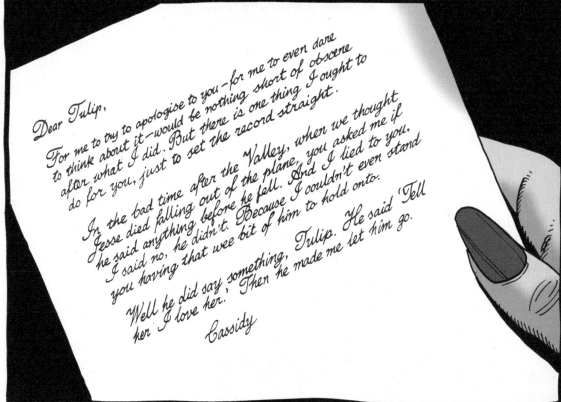

Dear Tulip,

For me to try to apologise to you—for me to even dare to think about it—would be nothing short of obscene after what I did. But there is one thing I ought to do for you, just to set the record straight.

In the bad time after the Valley, when we thought Jesse died falling out of the plane, you asked me if he said anything before he fell. And I lied to you. I said no, he didn't. Because I couldn't even stand you having that wee bit of him to hold onto.

Well he did say something, Tulip. He said 'Tell her I love her.' Then he made me let him go.

Cassidy

HEY.

TULIP

YOU CAME AFTER ME.

I HAD TO.

PEOPLE LIKE YOU AN' ME DON'T FIND EACH OTHER TOO OFTEN IN THIS DAMN WORLD.

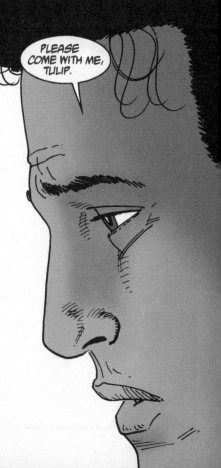

PLEASE COME WITH ME, TULIP.

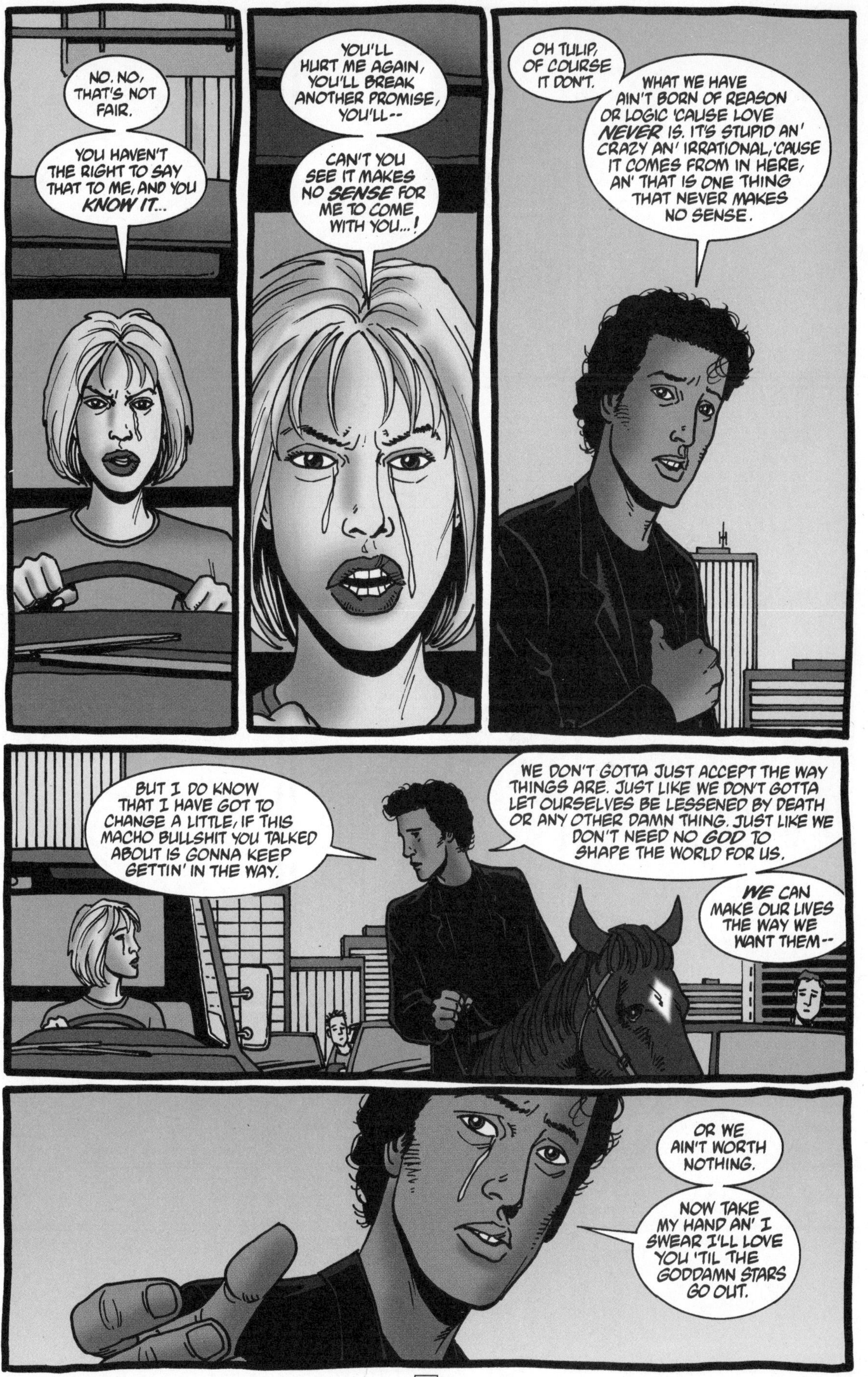
NO. NO, THAT'S NOT FAIR.
YOU HAVEN'T THE RIGHT TO SAY THAT TO ME, AND YOU *KNOW IT*...
YOU'LL HURT ME AGAIN, YOU'LL BREAK ANOTHER PROMISE, YOU'LL--
CAN'T YOU SEE IT MAKES NO *SENSE* FOR ME TO COME WITH YOU...!
OH TULIP, OF COURSE IT DON'T.
WHAT WE HAVE AIN'T BORN OF REASON OR LOGIC 'CAUSE LOVE *NEVER* IS. IT'S STUPID AN' CRAZY AN' IRRATIONAL, 'CAUSE IT COMES FROM IN HERE, AN' THAT IS ONE THING THAT NEVER MAKES NO SENSE.
BUT I DO KNOW THAT I HAVE GOT TO CHANGE A LITTLE, IF THIS MACHO BULLSHIT YOU TALKED ABOUT IS GONNA KEEP GETTIN' IN THE WAY.
WE DON'T GOTTA JUST ACCEPT THE WAY THINGS ARE. JUST LIKE WE DON'T GOTTA LET OURSELVES BE LESSENED BY DEATH OR ANY OTHER DAMN THING. JUST LIKE WE DON'T NEED NO *GOD* TO SHAPE THE WORLD FOR US.
WE CAN MAKE OUR LIVES THE WAY WE WANT THEM--
OR WE AIN'T WORTH NOTHING.
NOW TAKE MY HAND AN' I SWEAR I'LL LOVE YOU 'TIL THE GODDAMN STARS GO OUT.

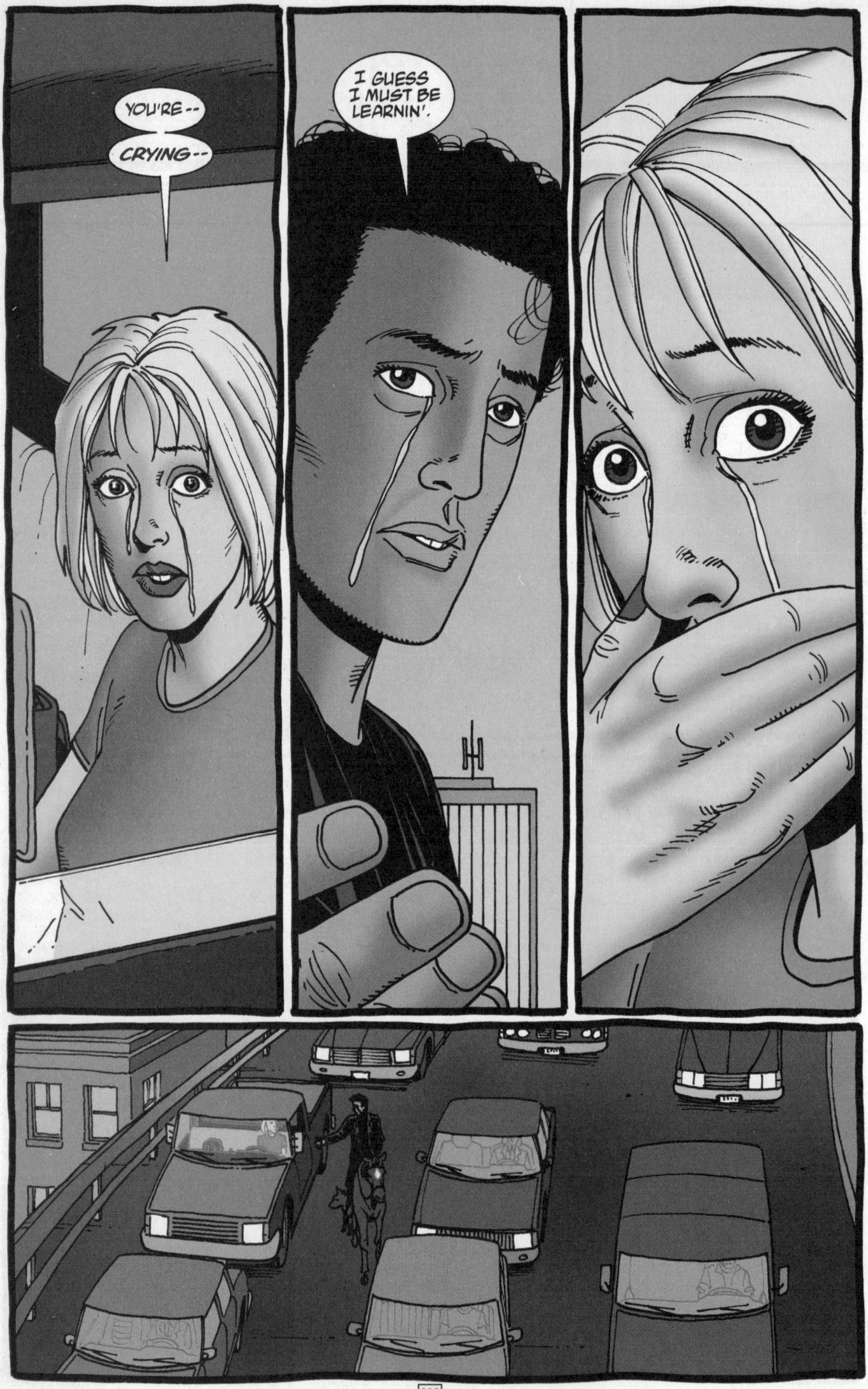
YOU'RE--
CRYING--
I GUESS I MUST BE LEARNIN'.

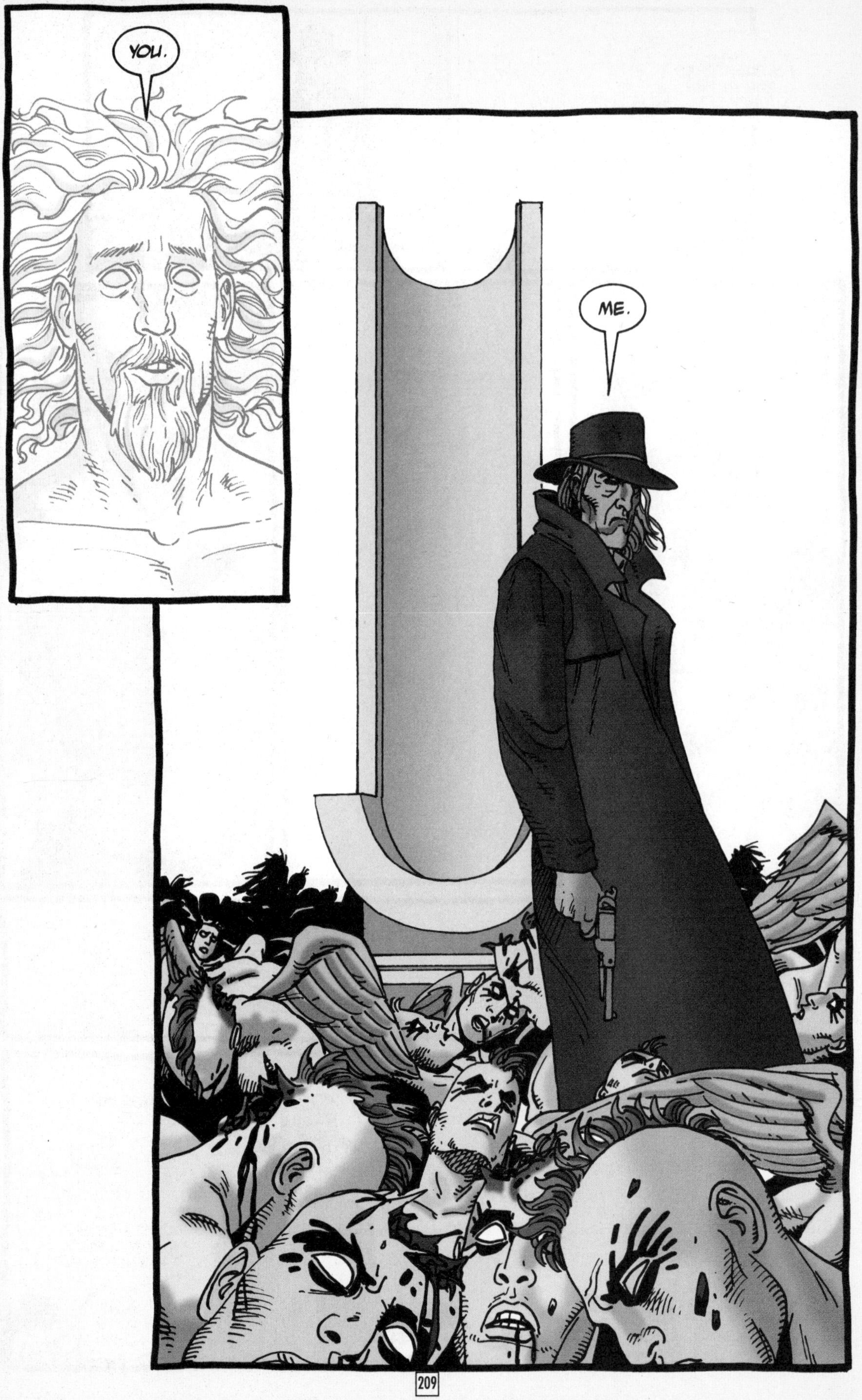
YOU.
ME.

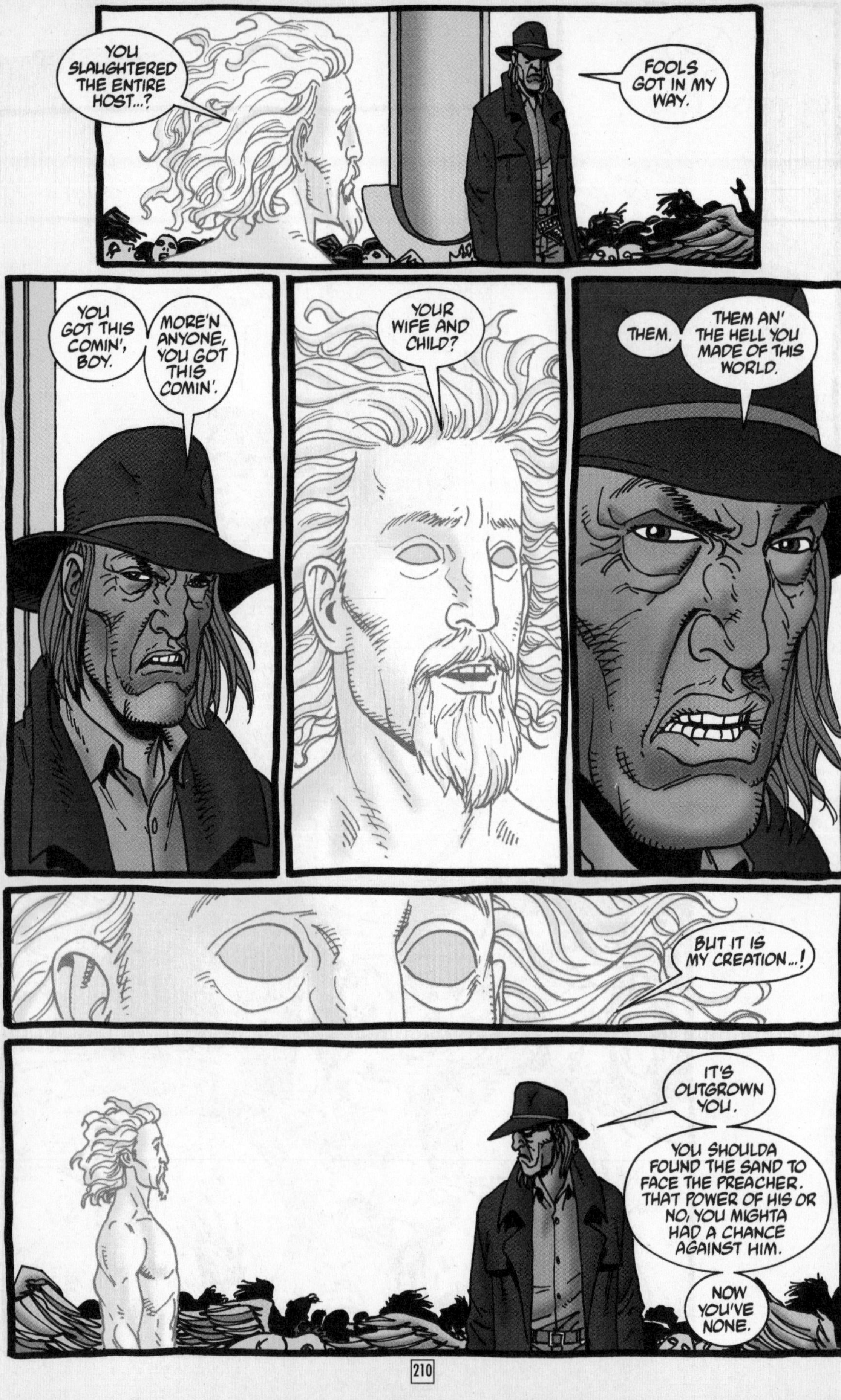
YOU SLAUGHTERED THE ENTIRE HOST...?
FOOLS GOT IN MY WAY.
YOU GOT THIS COMIN', BOY.
MORE'N ANYONE, YOU GOT THIS COMIN'.
YOUR WIFE AND CHILD?
THEM.
THEM AN' THE HELL YOU MADE OF THIS WORLD.
BUT IT IS MY CREATION...!
IT'S OUTGROWN YOU.
YOU SHOULDA FOUND THE SAND TO FACE THE PREACHER. THAT POWER OF HIS OR NO, YOU MIGHTA HAD A CHANCE AGAINST HIM.
NOW YOU'VE NONE.

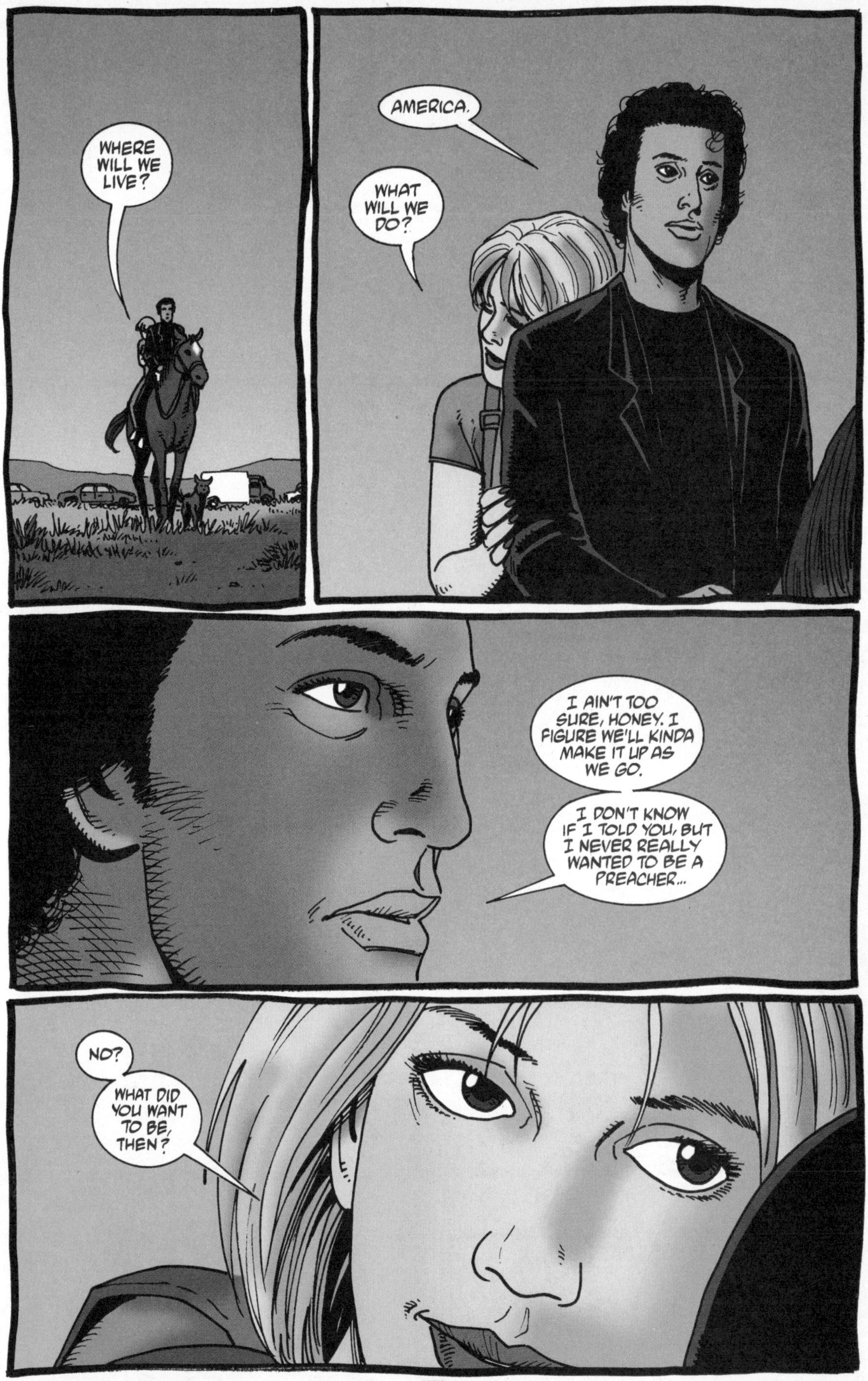
WHERE WILL WE LIVE?
AMERICA.
WHAT WILL WE DO?
I AIN'T TOO SURE, HONEY. I FIGURE WE'LL KINDA MAKE IT UP AS WE GO.
I DON'T KNOW IF I TOLD YOU, BUT I NEVER REALLY WANTED TO BE A PREACHER...
NO?
WHAT DID YOU WANT TO BE, THEN?

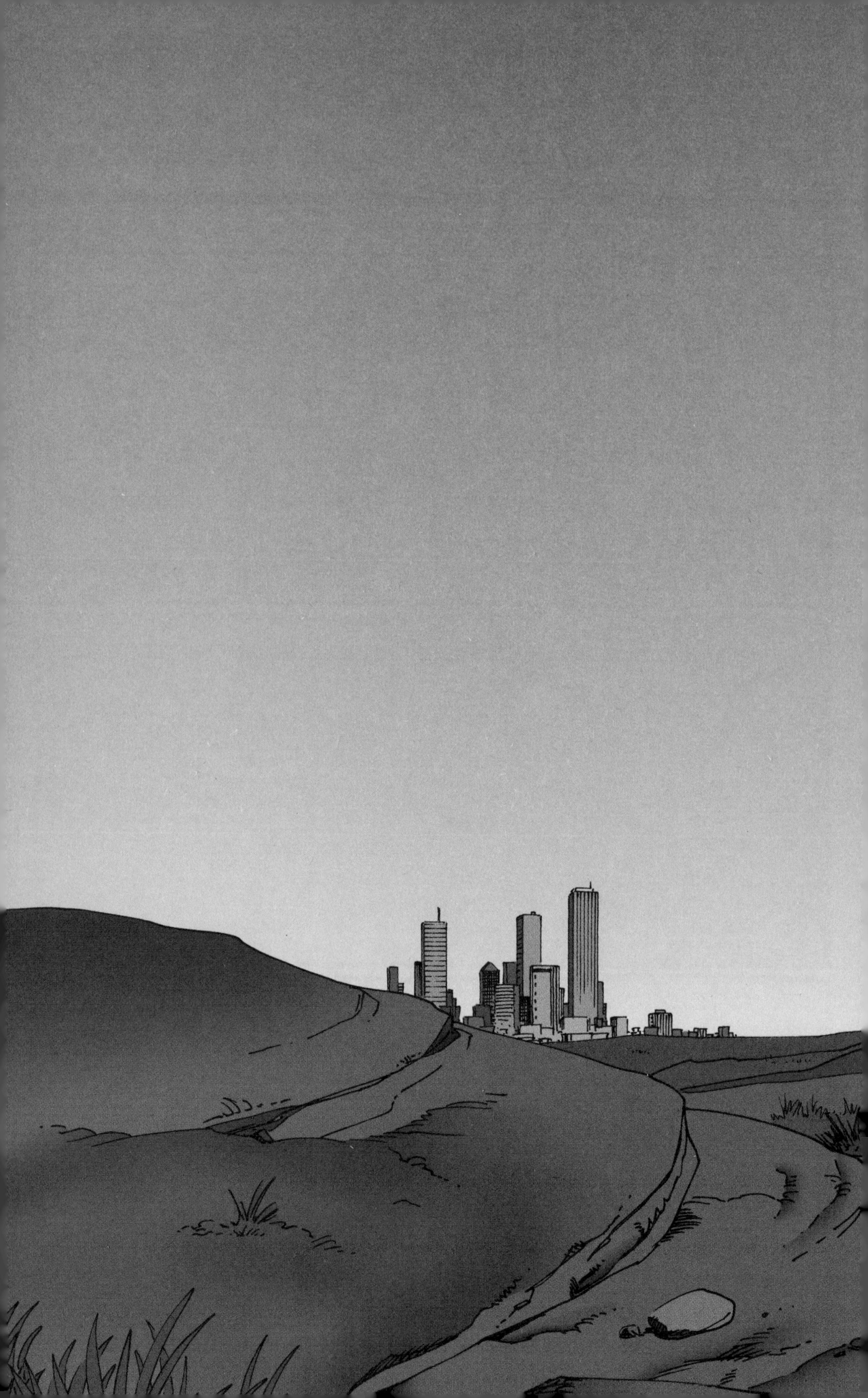

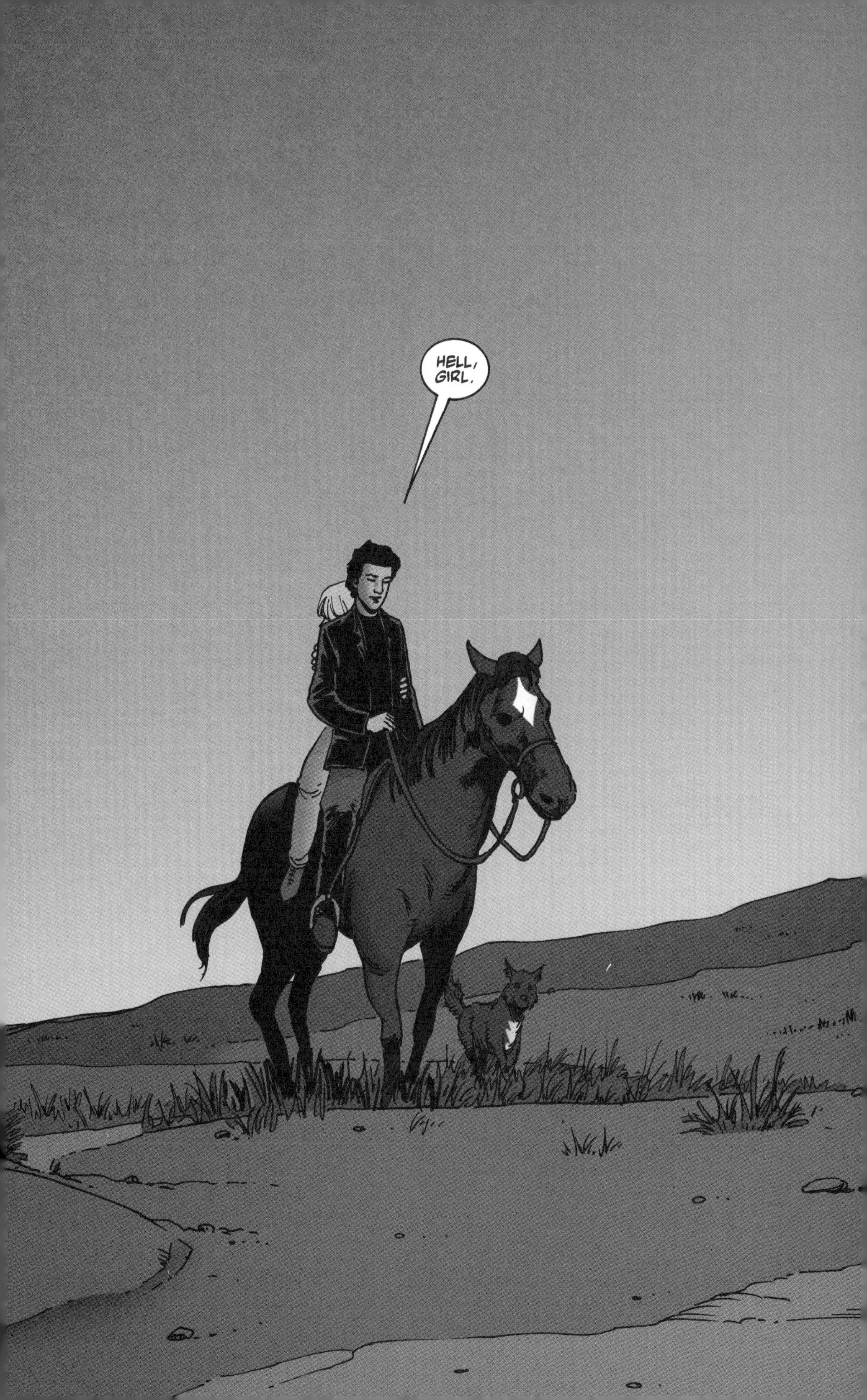
HELL, GIRL.

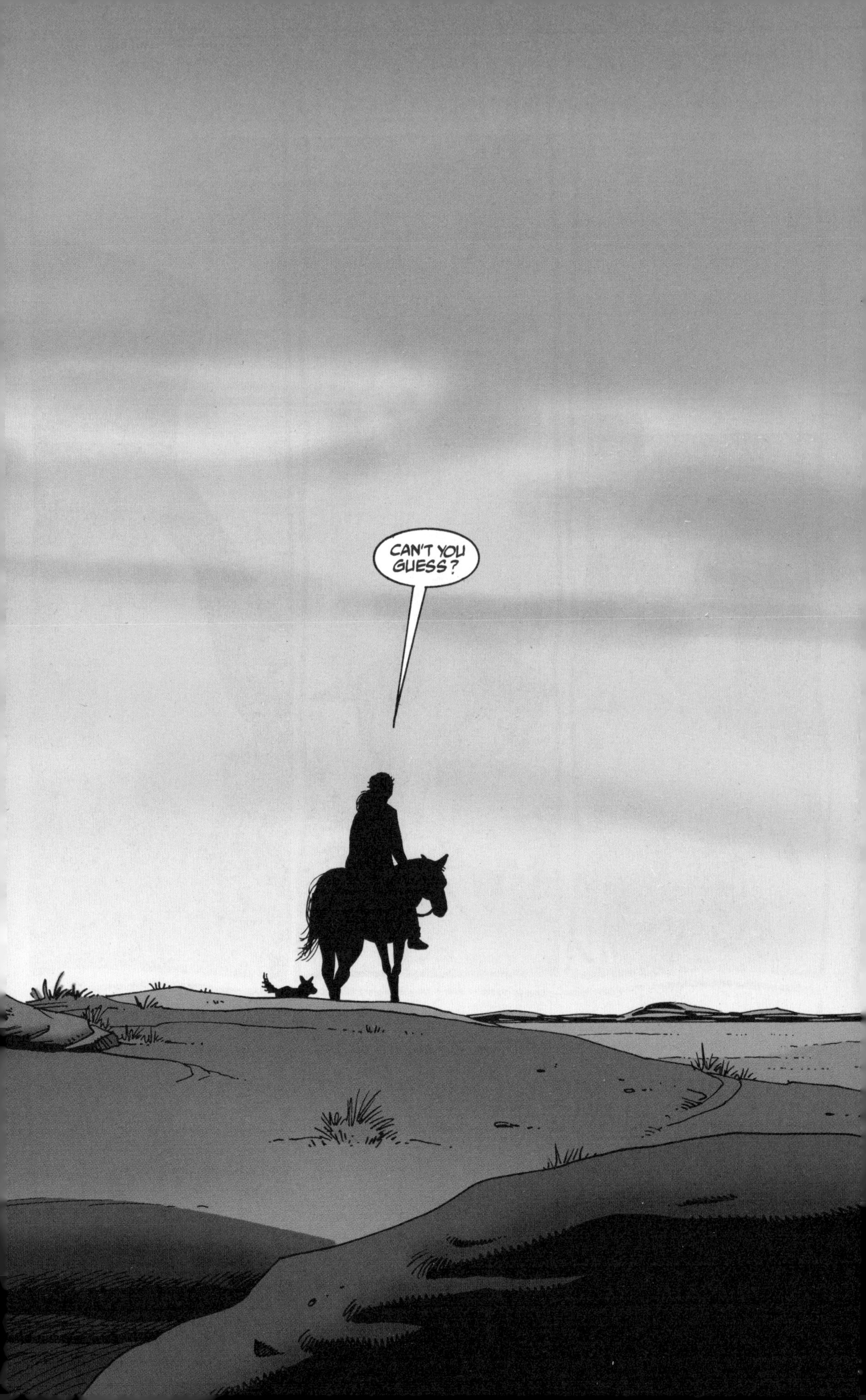
CAN'T YOU GUESS?

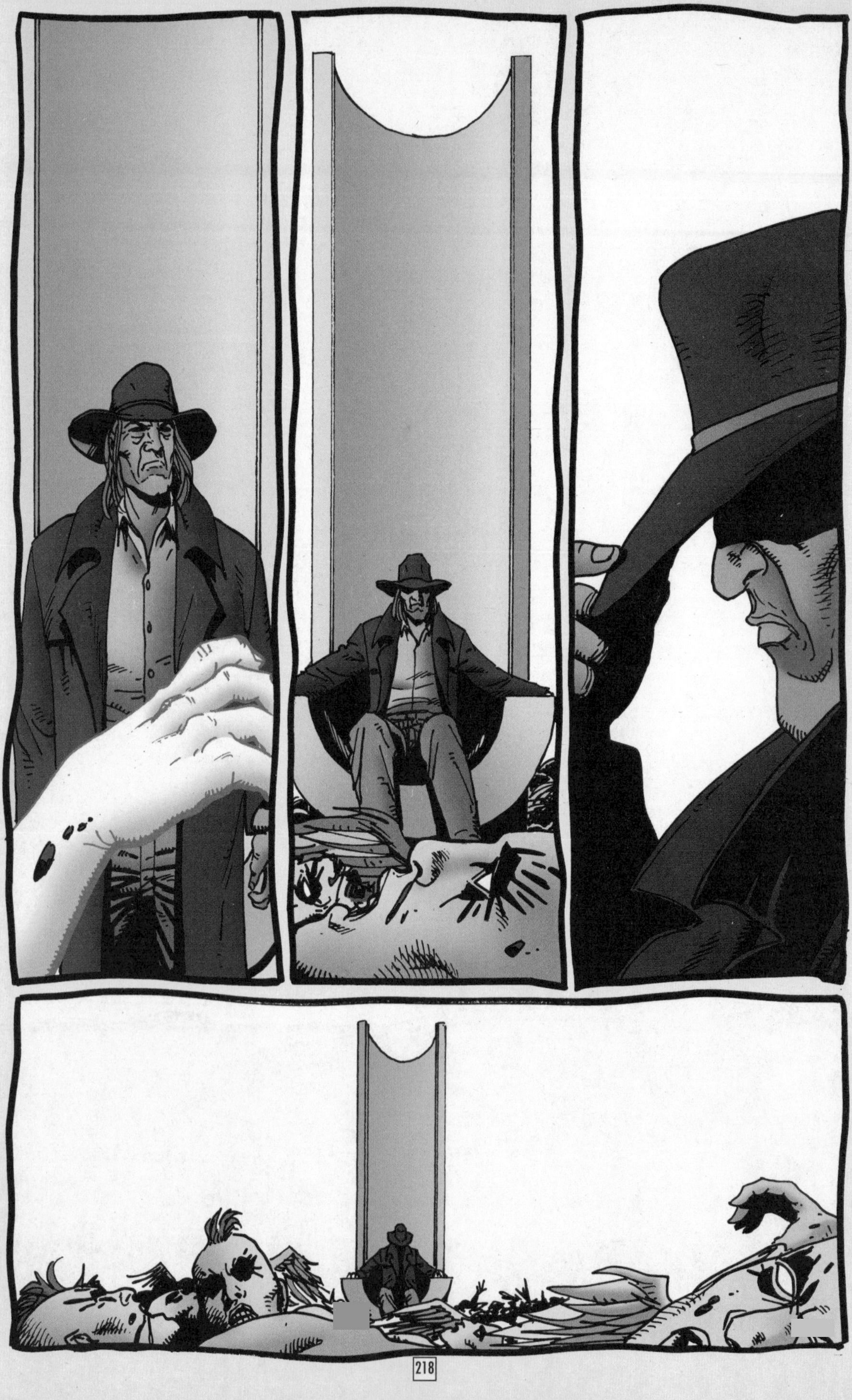

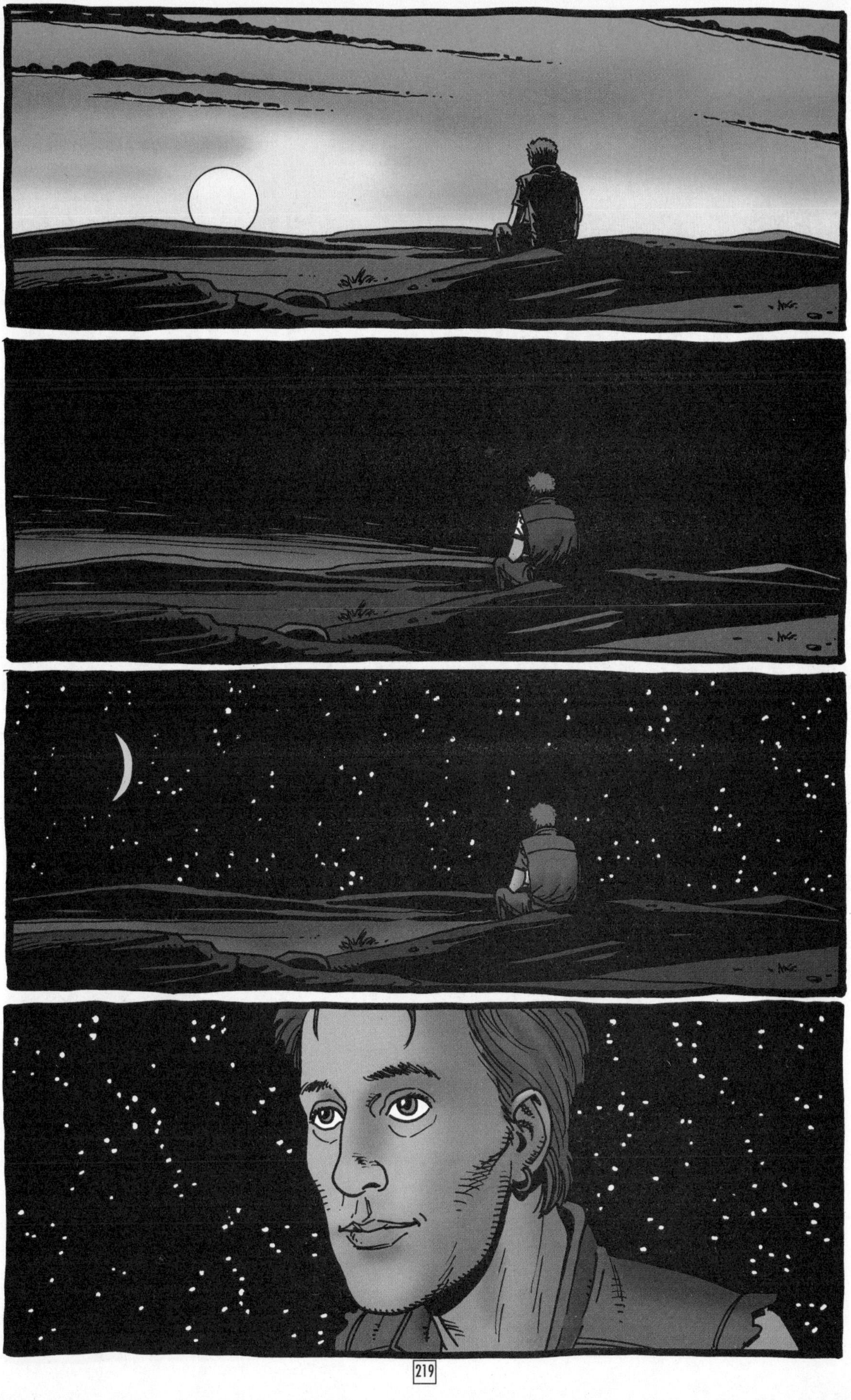

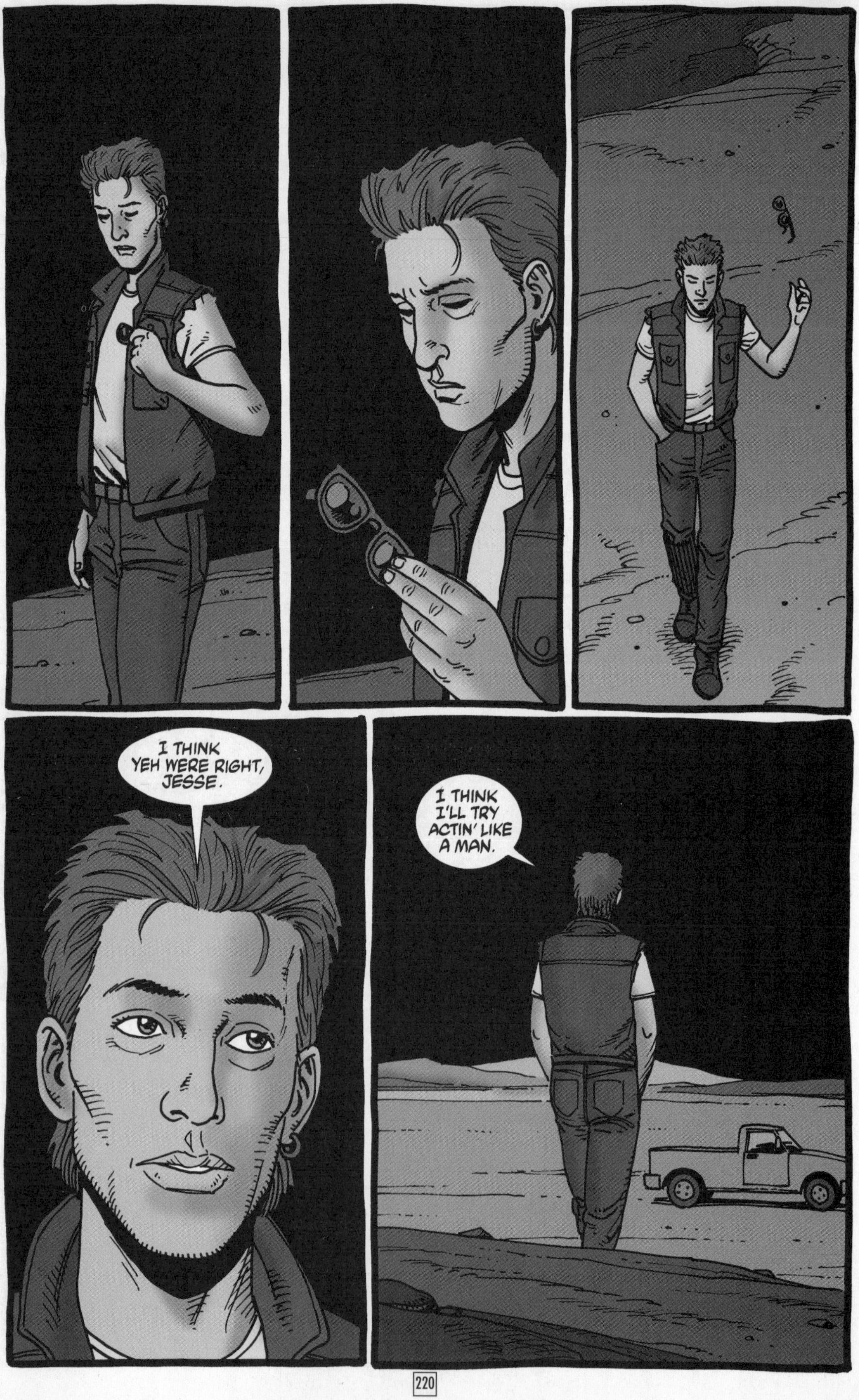
I THINK YEH WERE RIGHT, JESSE.
I THINK I'LL TRY ACTIN' LIKE A MAN.

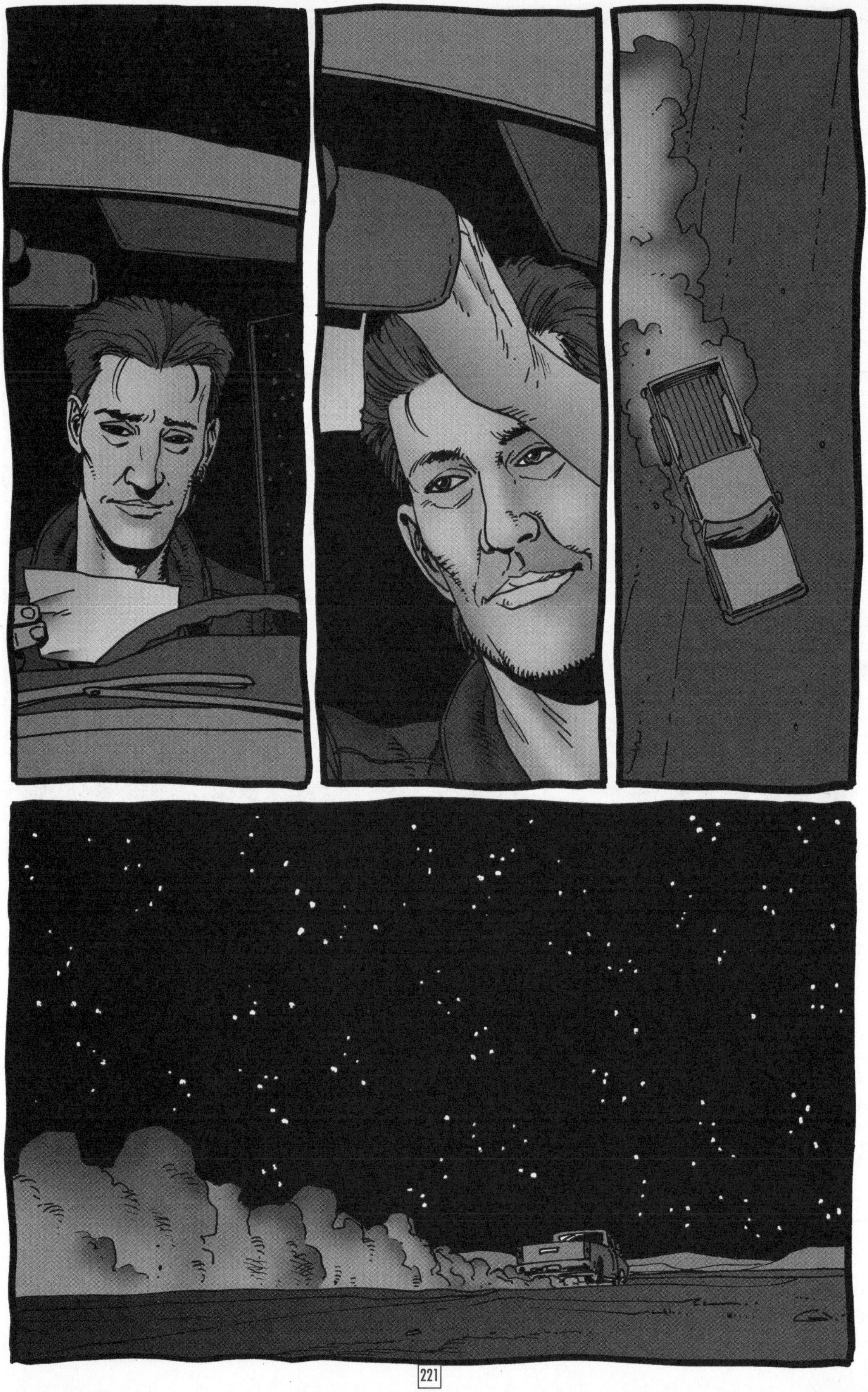

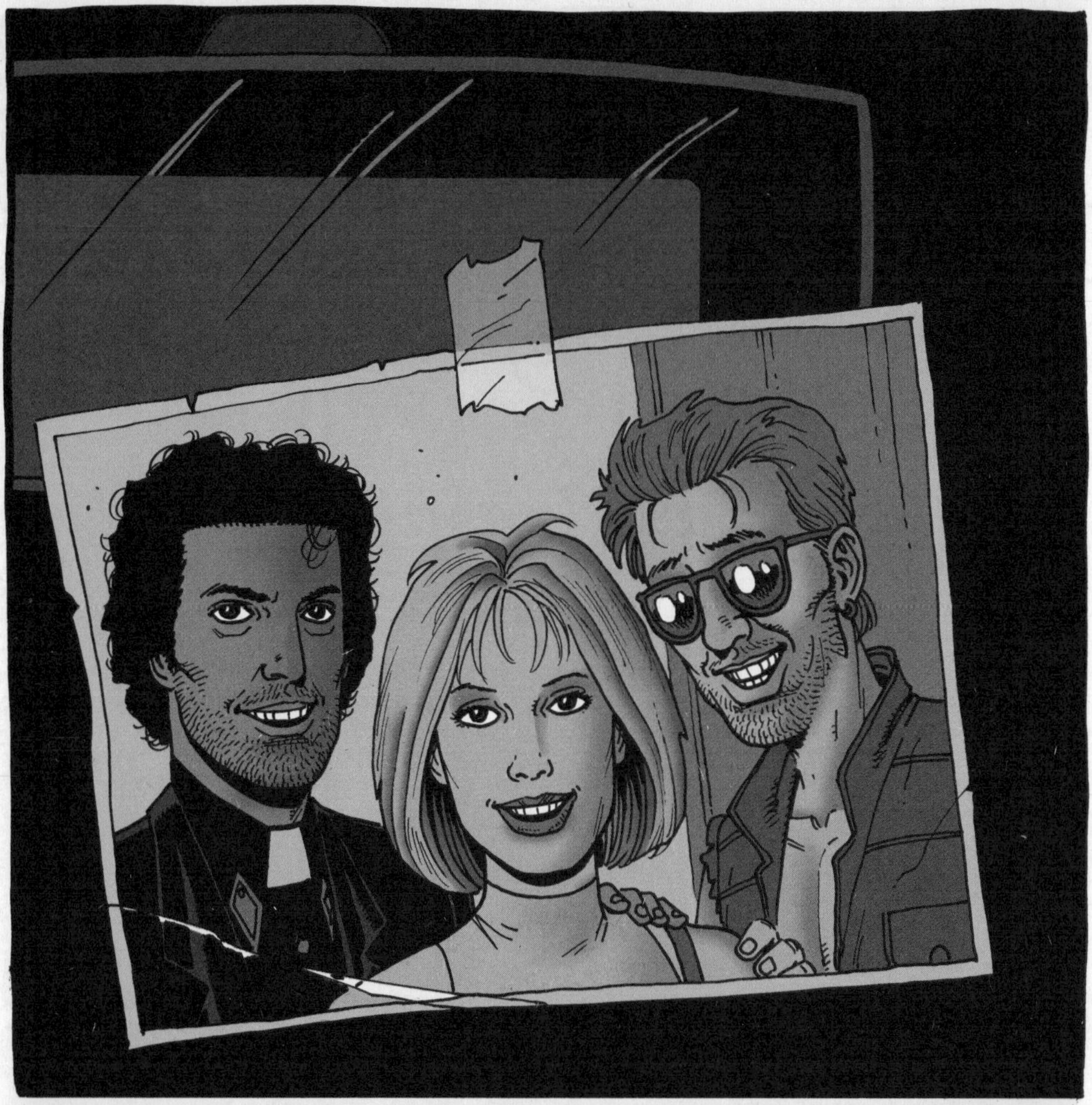

A HELL OF A VISION

GARTH ENNIS - Writer STEVE DILLON - Artist

PAMELA RAMBO - Colorist CLEM ROBINS - Letterer AXEL ALONSO - Editor

PREACHER created by GARTH ENNIS and STEVE DILLON

PREACHER

PINUP GALLERY

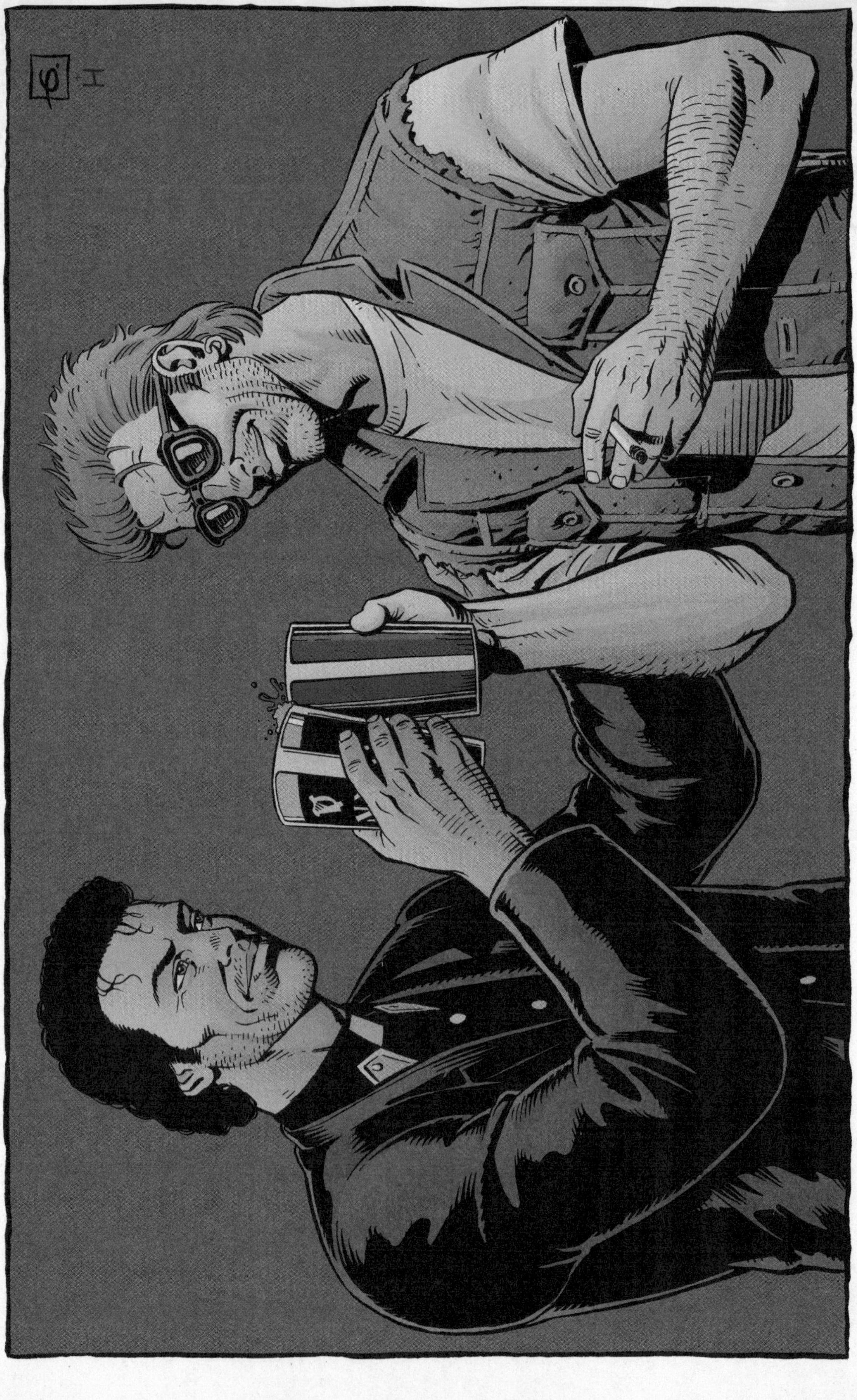

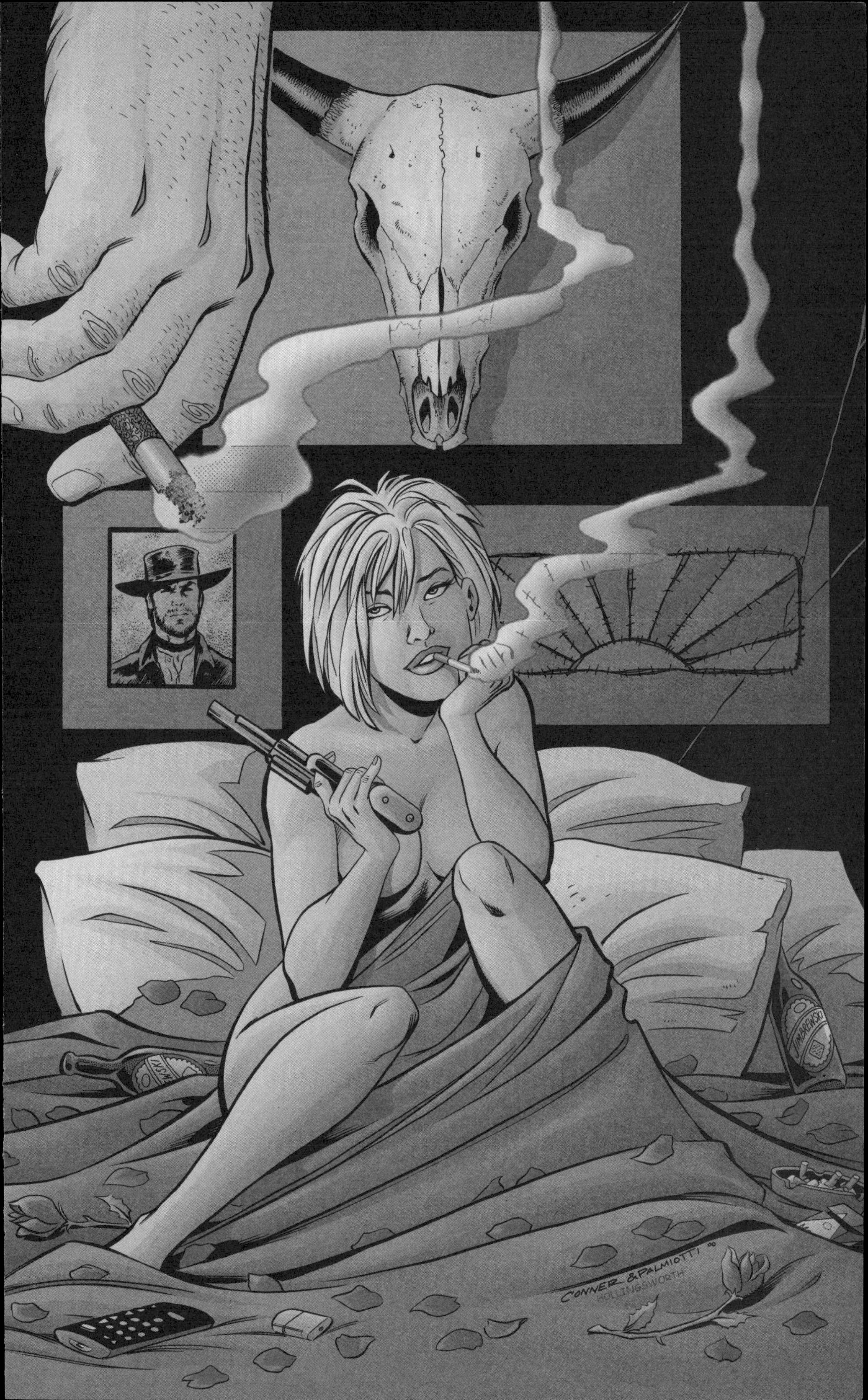
JIMBREWSKI
CONNER & PALMIOTTI
HOLLINGSWORTH

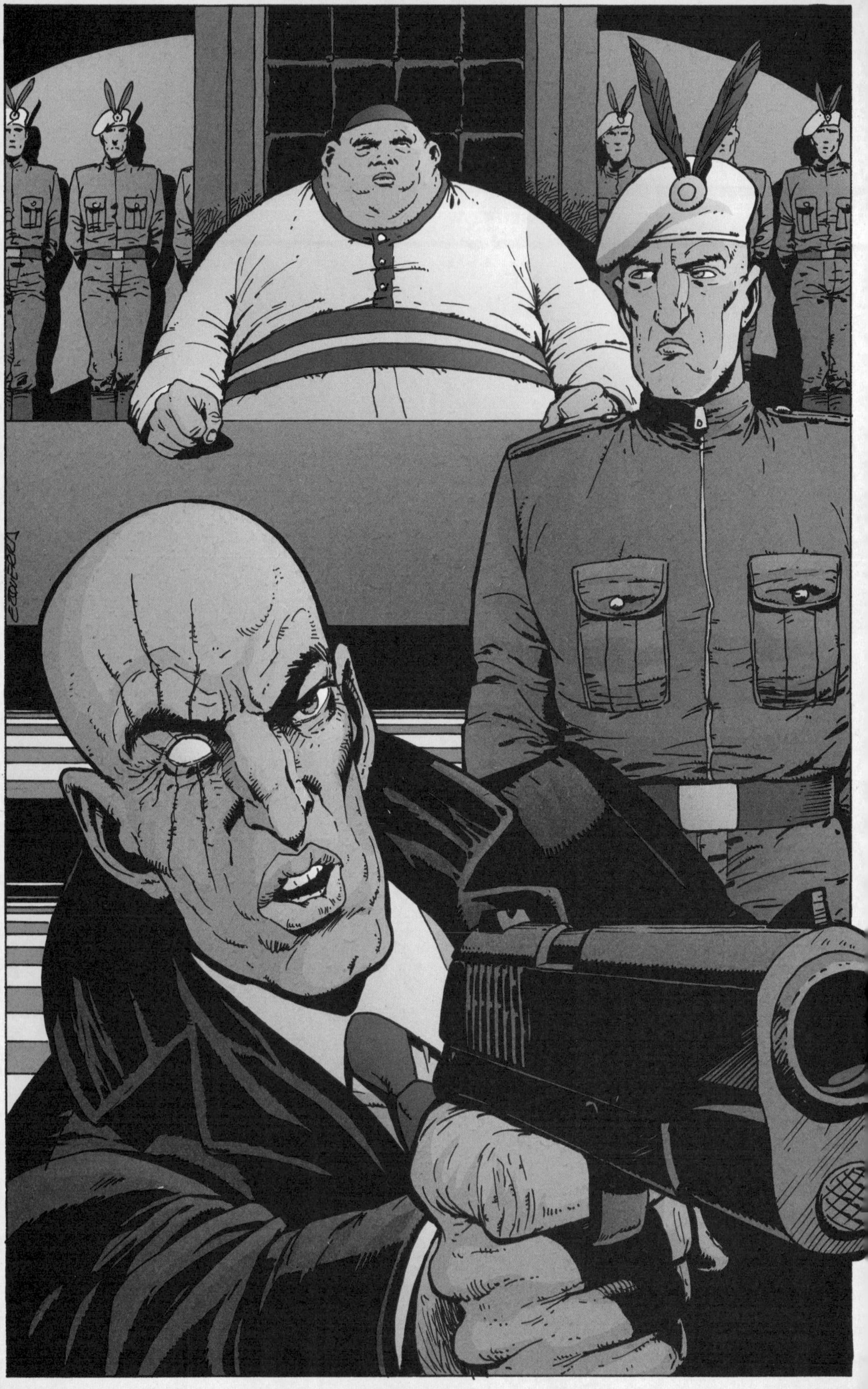

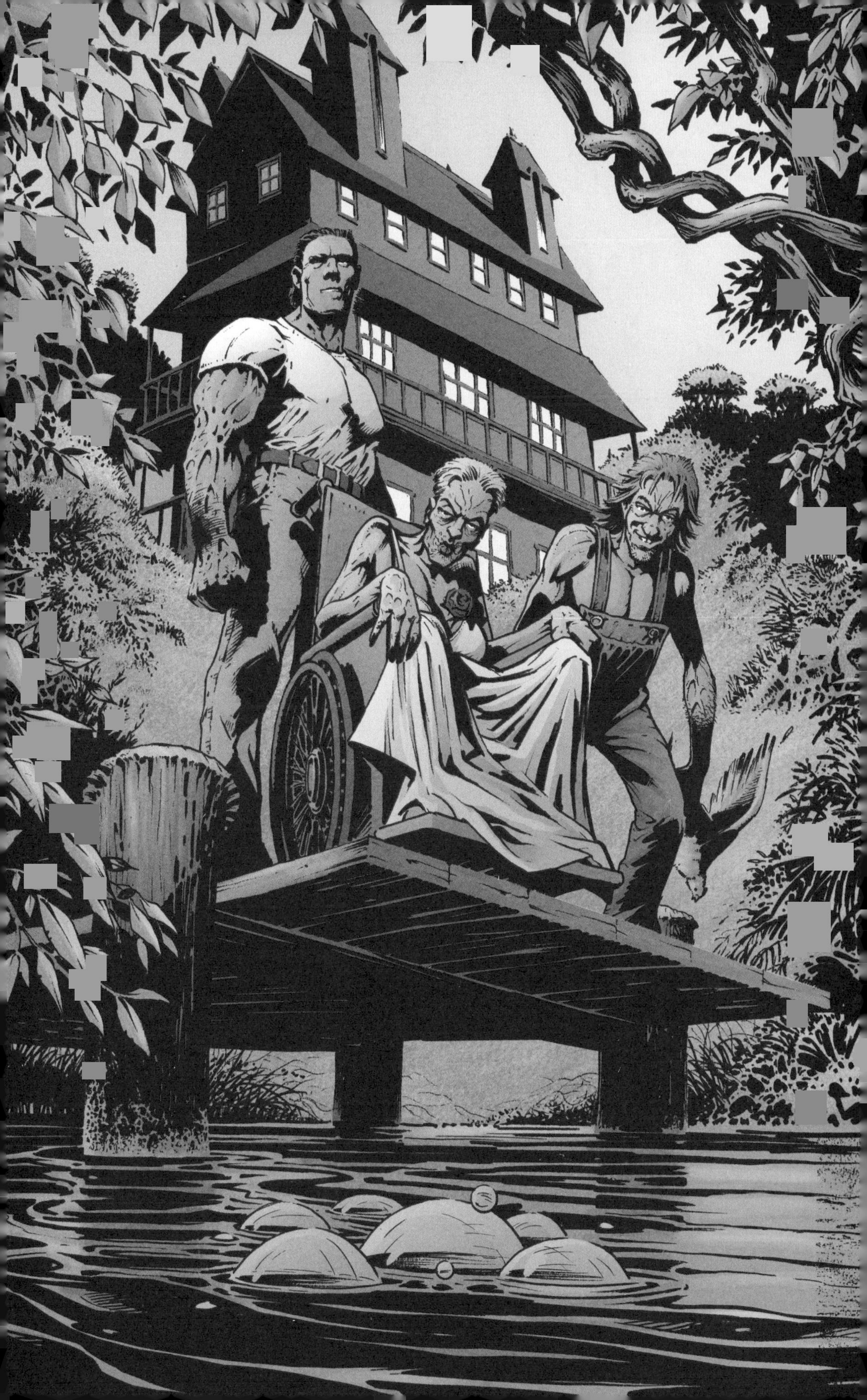

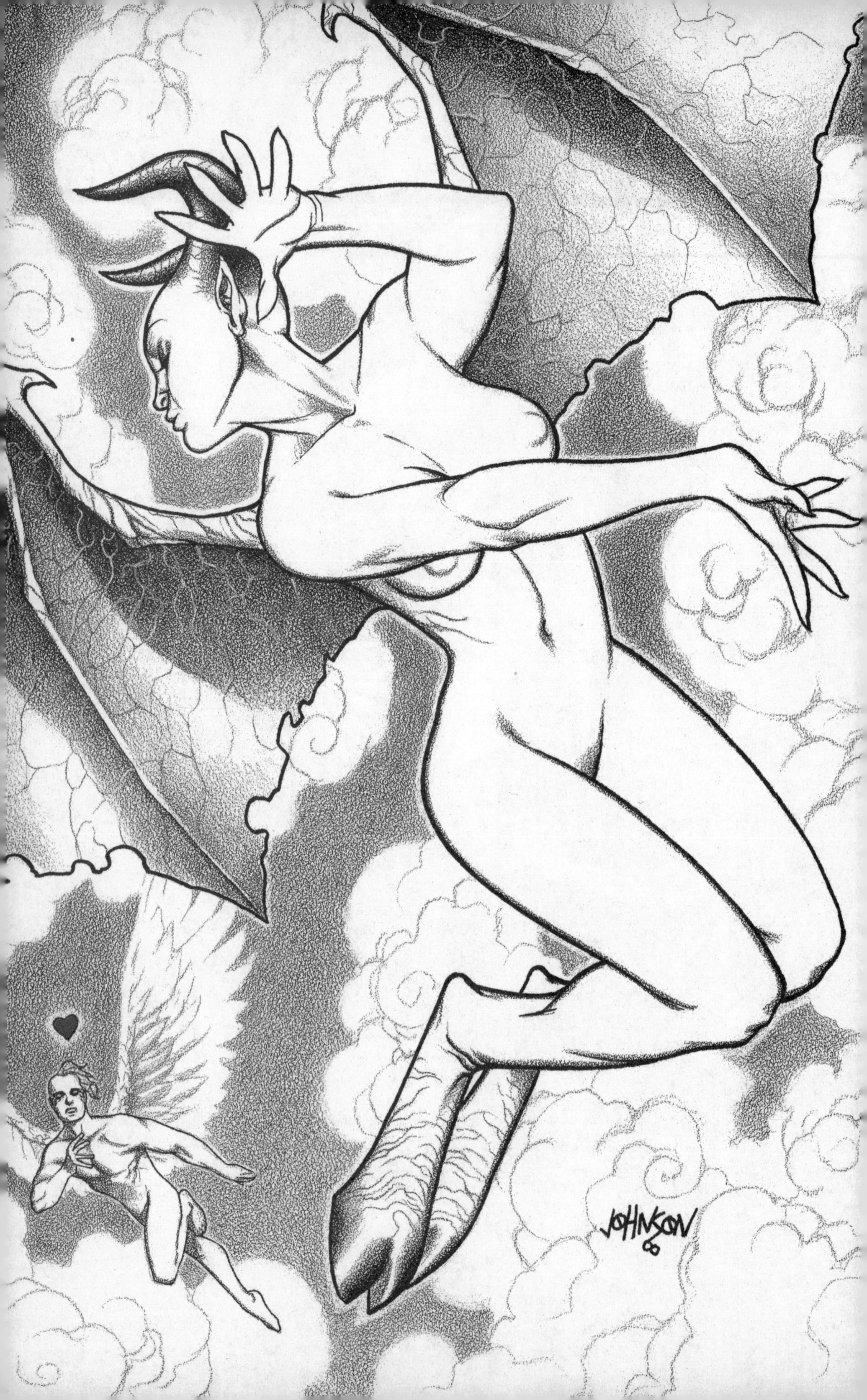
JOHNSON
06

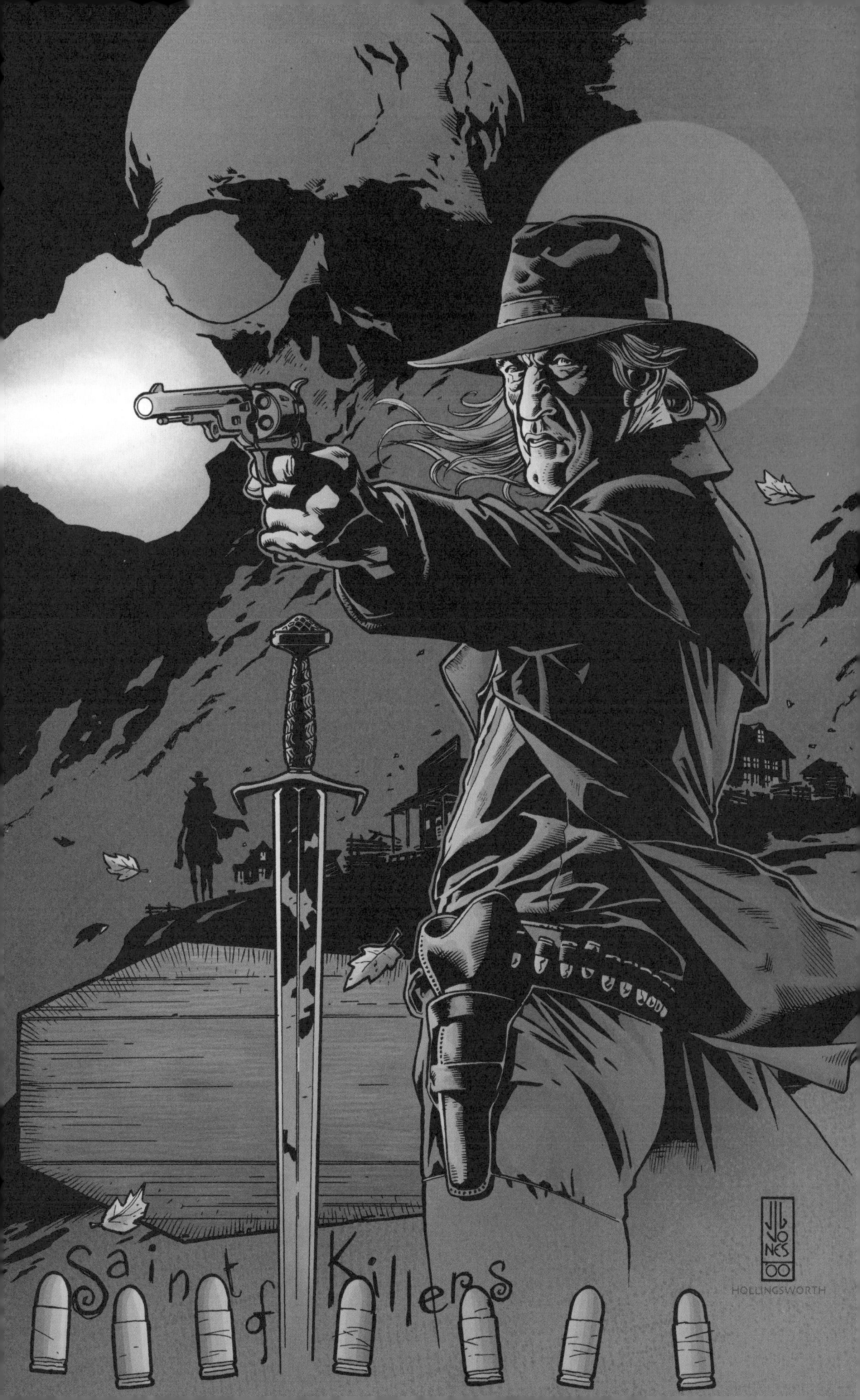
Saint of Killers
JG JONES 00
HOLLINGSWORTH

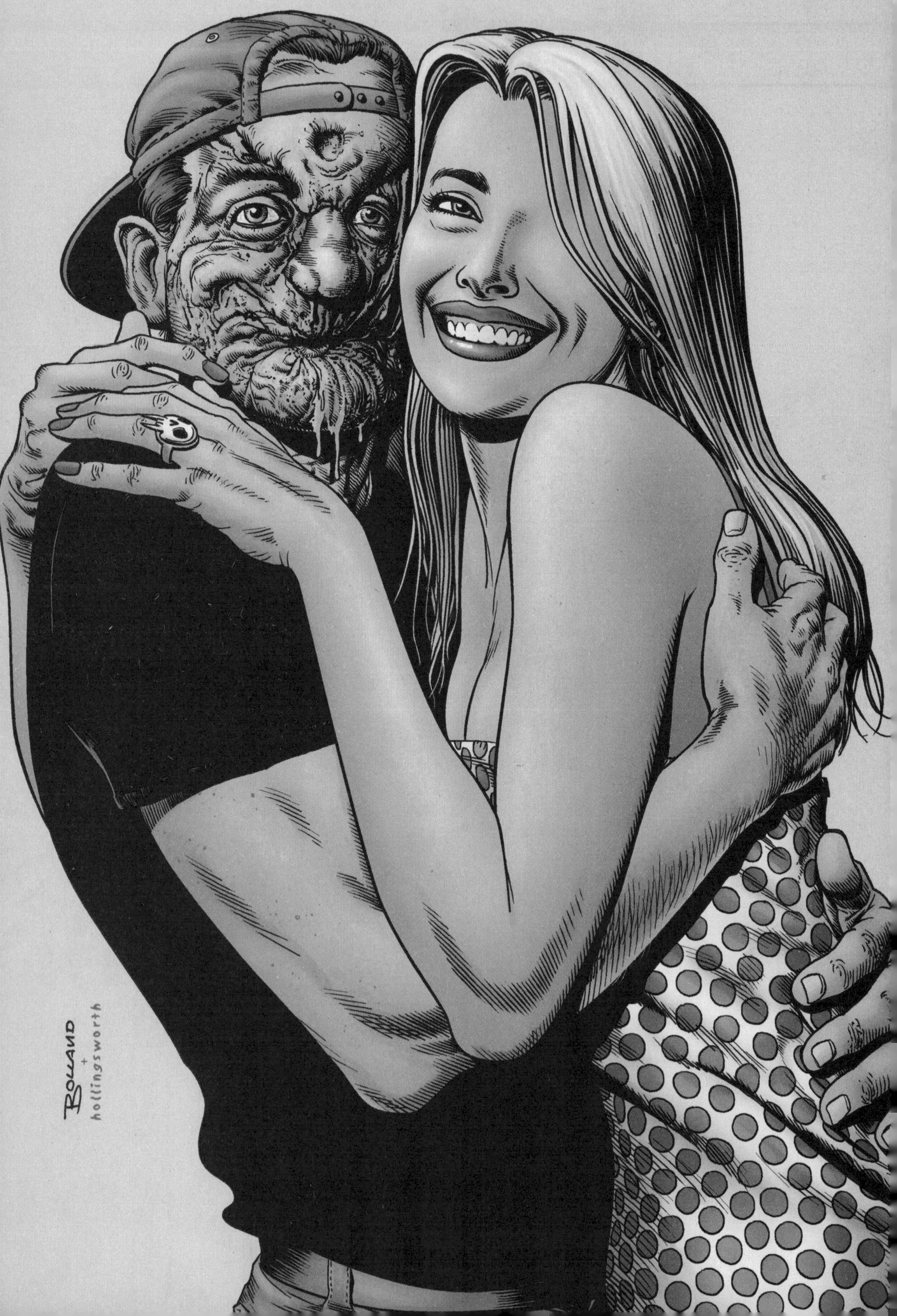
BOLLAND
+
hollingsworth

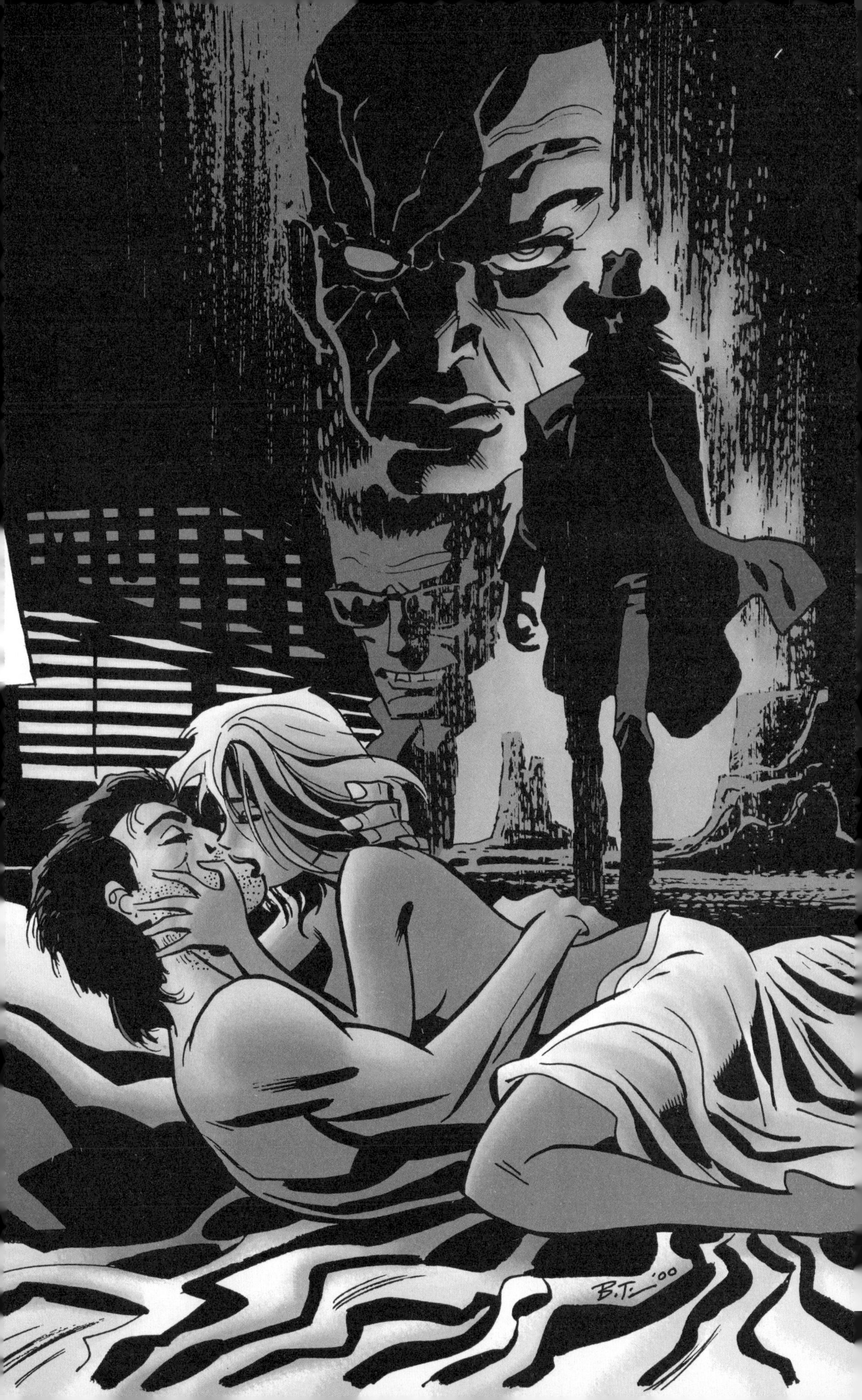
B.T. '00

Look for these other VERTIGO books:

All Vertigo titles are Suggested for Mature Readers

100 BULLETS
Brian Azzarello/Eduardo Risso
With one special briefcase, Agent Graves gives you the chance to kill without retribution. But what is the real price for this chance — and who is setting it?

Vol 1: FIRST SHOT, LAST CALL
Vol 2: SPLIT SECOND CHANCE
Vol 3: HANG UP ON THE HANG LOW
Vol 4: A FOREGONE TOMORROW
Vol 5: THE COUNTERFIFTH DETECTIVE
Vol 6: SIX FEET UNDER THE GUN

ANIMAL MAN
Grant Morrison/Chas Truog/
Doug Hazlewood/various
A minor super-hero's consciousness is raised higher and higher until he becomes aware of his own fictitious nature in this revolutionary and existential series.

Vol 1: ANIMAL MAN
Vol 2: ORIGIN OF THE SPECIES
Vol 3: DEUS EX MACHINA

THE BOOKS OF MAGIC
Neil Gaiman/various
A quartet of fallen mystics introduce the world of magic to young Tim Hunter, who is destined to become the world's most powerful magician.

THE BOOKS OF MAGIC
John Ney Rieber/Peter Gross/various
The continuing trials and adventures of Tim Hunter, whose magical talents bring extra trouble and confusion to his adolescence.

Vol 1: BINDINGS
Vol 2: SUMMONINGS
Vol 3: RECKONINGS
Vol 4: TRANSFORMATIONS
Vol 5: GIRL IN THE BOX
Vol 6: THE BURNING GIRL
Vol 7: DEATH AFTER DEATH

DEATH: AT DEATH'S DOOR
Jill Thompson
Part fanciful *manga* retelling of the acclaimed THE SANDMAN: SEASON OF MISTS and part original story of the party from Hell.

DEATH: THE HIGH COST OF LIVING
Neil Gaiman/Chris Bachalo/
Mark Buckingham
One day every century, Death assumes mortal form to learn more about the lives she must take.

DEATH: THE TIME OF YOUR LIFE
Neil Gaiman/Chris Bachalo/
Mark Buckingham/Mark Pennington
A young lesbian mother strikes a deal with Death for the life of her son in a story about fame, relationships, and rock and roll.

FABLES
Bill Willingham/Lan Medina/
Mark Buckingham/Steve Leialoha
The immortal characters of popular fairy tales have been driven from their homelands and now live hidden among us, trying to cope with life in 21st-century Manhattan.

Vol 1: LEGENDS IN EXILE
Vol 2: ANIMAL FARM
Vol 3: STORYBOOK LOVE

HELLBLAZER
Jamie Delano/Garth Ennis/Warren Ellis/
Brian Azzarello/Steve Dillon/
Marcelo Frusin/various
Where horror, dark magic, and bad luck meet, John Constantine is never far away.

ORIGINAL SINS
DANGEROUS HABITS
FEAR AND LOATHING
TAINTED LOVE
DAMNATION'S FLAME
RAKE AT THE GATES OF HELL
SON OF MAN
HAUNTED
HARD TIME
GOOD INTENTIONS
FREEZES OVER
HIGHWATER

THE INVISIBLES
Grant Morrison/various
The saga of a terrifying conspiracy and the resistance movement combating it — a secret underground of ultra-cool guerrilla cells trained in ontological and physical anarchy.

Vol 1: SAY YOU WANT A REVOLUTION

Vol 2: APOCALIPSTICK
Vol 3: ENTROPY IN THE U.K.
Vol 4: BLOODY HELL IN AMERICA
Vol 5: COUNTING TO NONE
Vol 6: KISSING MR. QUIMPER
Vol 7: THE INVISIBLE KINGDOM

LUCIFER
Mike Carey/Peter Gross/
Scott Hampton/Chris Weston/
Dean Ormston/various
Walking out of Hell (and out of the pages of THE SANDMAN), an ambitious Lucifer Morningstar creates a new cosmos modeled after his own image.

Vol 1: DEVIL IN THE GATEWAY
Vol 2: CHILDREN AND MONSTERS
Vol 3: A DALLIANCE WITH THE DAMNED
Vol 4: THE DIVINE COMEDY
Vol 5: INFERNO

PREACHER
Garth Ennis/Steve Dillon/various
A modern American epic of life, death, God, love, and redemption — filled with sex, booze, and blood.

Vol 1: GONE TO TEXAS
Vol 2: UNTIL THE END OF THE WORLD
Vol 3: PROUD AMERICANS
Vol 4: ANCIENT HISTORY
Vol 5: DIXIE FRIED
Vol 6: WAR IN THE SUN
Vol 7: SALVATION
Vol 8: ALL HELL'S A-COMING
Vol 9: ALAMO

THE SANDMAN
Neil Gaiman/various
One of the most acclaimed and celebrated comics titles ever published.

Vol 1: PRELUDES & NOCTURNES
Vol 2: THE DOLL'S HOUSE
Vol 3: DREAM COUNTRY
Vol 4: SEASON OF MISTS
Vol 5: A GAME OF YOU
Vol 6: FABLES & REFLECTIONS
Vol 7: BRIEF LIVES
Vol 8: WORLDS' END

Vol 9: THE KINDLY ONES
Vol 10: THE WAKE
Vol 11: ENDLESS NIGHTS

SWAMP THING: DARK GENESIS
Len Wein/Berni Wrightson
A gothic nightmare is brought to life with this horrifying yet poignant story of a man transformed into a monster.

SWAMP THING
Alan Moore/Stephen Bissette/
John Totleben/Rick Veitch/various
The writer and the series that revolutionized comics — a masterpiece of lyrical fantasy.

Vol 1: SAGA OF THE SWAMP THING
Vol 2: LOVE & DEATH
Vol 3: THE CURSE
Vol 4: A MURDER OF CROWS
Vol 5: EARTH TO EARTH
Vol 6: REUNION

TRANSMETROPOLITAN
Warren Ellis/Darick Robertson/various
An exuberant trip into a frenetic future, where outlaw journalist Spider Jerusalem battles hypocrisy, corruption, and sobriety.

Vol 1: BACK ON THE STREET
Vol 2: LUST FOR LIFE
Vol 3: YEAR OF THE BASTARD
Vol 4: THE NEW SCUM
Vol 5: LONELY CITY
Vol 6: GOUGE AWAY
Vol 7: SPIDER'S THRASH
Vol 8: DIRGE
Vol 9: THE CURE
Vol 10: ONE MORE TIME

Y: THE LAST MAN
Brian K. Vaughan/Pia Guerra/
José Marzán, Jr.
An unexplained plague kills every male mammal on Earth — all except Yorick Brown and his pet monkey. Will he survive this new, emasculated world to discover what killed his fellow men?

Vol 1: UNMANNED
Vol 2: CYCLES
Vol 3: ONE SMALL STEP

BARNUM!
Howard Chaykin/David Tischman/
Niko Henrichon

BLACK ORCHID
Neil Gaiman/Dave McKean

HEAVY LIQUID
Paul Pope

HUMAN TARGET
Peter Milligan/Edvin Biukovic

HUMAN TARGET: FINAL CUT
Peter Milligan/Javier Pulido

I DIE AT MIDNIGHT
Kyle Baker

IN THE SHADOW OF EDGAR ALLAN POE
Jonathon Scott Fuqua/
Stephen John Phillips/Steven Parke

JONNY DOUBLE
Brian Azzarello/Eduardo Risso

KING DAVID
Kyle Baker

THE LOSERS: ANTE UP
Andy Diggle/Jock

MR. PUNCH
Neil Gaiman/Dave McKean

THE MYSTERY PLAY
Grant Morrison/Jon J Muth

THE NAMES OF MAGIC
Dylan Horrocks/Richard Case

**NEIL GAIMAN & CHARLES VESS'
STARDUST**
Neil Gaiman/Charles Vess

NEIL GAIMAN'S MIDNIGHT DAYS
Neil Gaiman/Matt Wagner/various

ORBITER
Warren Ellis/Colleen Doran

**PREACHER: DEAD OR ALIVE
(THE COLLECTED COVERS)**
Glenn Fabry

PROPOSITION PLAYER
Bill Willingham/Paul Guinan/Ron Randall

**THE SANDMAN:
THE DREAM HUNTERS**
Neil Gaiman/Yoshitaka Amano

**THE SANDMAN: DUST COVERS — THE
COLLECTED SANDMAN COVERS 1989-1997**
Dave McKean/Neil Gaiman

THE SANDMAN PRESENTS: THE FURIES
Mike Carey/John Bolton

**THE SANDMAN PRESENTS:
TALLER TALES**
Bill Willingham/various

**SHADE, THE CHANGING MAN:
THE AMERICAN SCREAM**
Peter Milligan/Chris Bachalo

UNCLE SAM
Steve Darnall/Alex Ross

UNDERCOVER GENIE
Kyle Baker

UNKNOWN SOLDIER
Garth Ennis/Kilian Plunkett

V FOR VENDETTA
Alan Moore/David Lloyd

VEILS
Pat McGreal/Stephen John Phillips/
José Villarrubia/Rebecca Guay

WHY I HATE SATURN
Kyle Baker

THE WITCHING HOUR
Jeph Loeb/Chris Bachalo/Art Thibert

YOU ARE HERE
Kyle Baker

Visit us at www.vertigocomics.com for more information on these and many other titles from VERTIGO and DC Comics
or call 1-888-COMIC BOOK for the comics shop nearest you, or go to your local book store.

VER0014